www.Explorer-Publishing.com

Passionately Publishing...

Introduction

Abu Dhabi Explorer 4th Edition

First Published 2001
Second Edition 2002
Third Edition 2003
Fourth Edition 2004 ISBN 976-8182-58-X

Front Cover Photograph — Paul Thuysbaert

Printed and bound by Emirates Printing Press, Dubai, United Arab Emirates.

Explorer Publishing & Distribution LLC
PO Box 34275, Dubai
United Arab Emirates
Phone (+971 4) 335 3520
Fax (+971 4) 335 3529
Email Info@Explorer-Publishing.com
Web www.Explorer-Publishing.com

Printing Authorisation Number: 971, August 4th 2004

www.Explorer-Publishing.com

Authors

Ayne-Marie Leitch
Barbara Daw
Elizabeth Fonseca
Emma Davey
Jane Daley
Lucy Samuels

Publishing

Publisher — Alistair MacKenzie, Alistair@Explorer-Publishing.com

Publishing Manager — Peter D'Onghia, Peter@Explorer-Publishing.com

Editorial/Content

Senior Editor — Lena Moosa, Lena@Explorer-Publishing.com

Contributing Editors — Anju Govil, Jane Roberts, Tracey Pitts

Content Manager — Louise Mellodew, Louise@Explorer-Publishing.com

Researcher — Yolanda Rodrigues, Yolanda@Explorer-Publishing.com

Design

Graphic Designers — Jayde Fernandes, Jayde@Explorer-Publishing.com; Zainudheen Madathil, Zain@Explorer-Publishing.com

Photography

Photographers — Pamela Grist, Pamela@Explorer-Publishing.com; Derrick Pereira

Sales & Advertising

Sales & Marketing Manager — Amanda Harkin, Amanda@Explorer-Publishing.com

Media Sales Executives — Alena Hykes, Alena@Explorer-Publishing.com; Heidi Green

Sales/PR Administrator — Janice Menezes, Janice@Explorer-Publishing.com

Distribution

Distribution Manager — Ivan Rodrigues, Ivan@Explorer-Publishing.com

Distribution Executives — Abdul Gafoor, Gafoor@Explorer-Publishing.com; Mannie Lugtu, Mannie@Explorer-Publishing.com; Stephen Drilon, Stephen@Explorer-Publishing.com; Rafi Jamal, Rafi@Explorer-Publishing.com

Administration

Accounts Manager — Kamal Basha, Kamal@Explorer-Publishing.com

Account Administrator — Geraldine Fernandes, Geraldin@Explorer-Publishing.com

Administration Manager — Nadia D'Souza, Nadia@Explorer-Publishing.com

Dear Adoring Abu Dhabi Fans,

Like the joy that accompanies the birth of a bouncing baby, we at Explorer Publishing are proud and honoured to announce the long awaited arrival of the 4th edition of the **Abu Dhabi Explorer**.

Conception as you can imagine involved a lot of date planning, checking of temperatures, and endless fun! At the point of no return we worried that we had done the right thing. When it took longer than we anticipated, we worried that our approach was correct. We analysed endlessly whether it was a good time to do it but at the same time knew that this was going to be the best thing that we had ever done. The following nine months were full of anxiety, and growing pains. But the waiting paid off and in the final stages there was much huffing and puffing, heaving and pushing and even quite a bit of bad language towards the end, but when it finally arrived it brought a tear to all our eyes. We couldn't believe how perfect it was.

We wanted to wrap it up lovingly and bring it around personally for you to coo over but we decided instead to send it out to stand on its own two feet. We were confident that as it was so unbelievably full of knowledge and experience already that it would be able to flourish in its own right out there in the big wide world.

Of course now it's here it will take over your life, it will demand your undivided attention and you won't have time to do anything but refer to it constantly. Its **Activities** will take up so much of your time you'll wonder when you'll ever be able to cut your toe nails again. **Going Out** for meals will be an altogether different experience, **Shopping** will never be the same again and you'll need a **Map** to know whether you're coming or going.

But treat it well and it will support you unconditionally into your old age, it will provide you with endless hours of fun and entertainment, and you will talk about it proudly to all of your friends... then we can start planning the next one.

Look after it - it's precious!

The Explorer Team

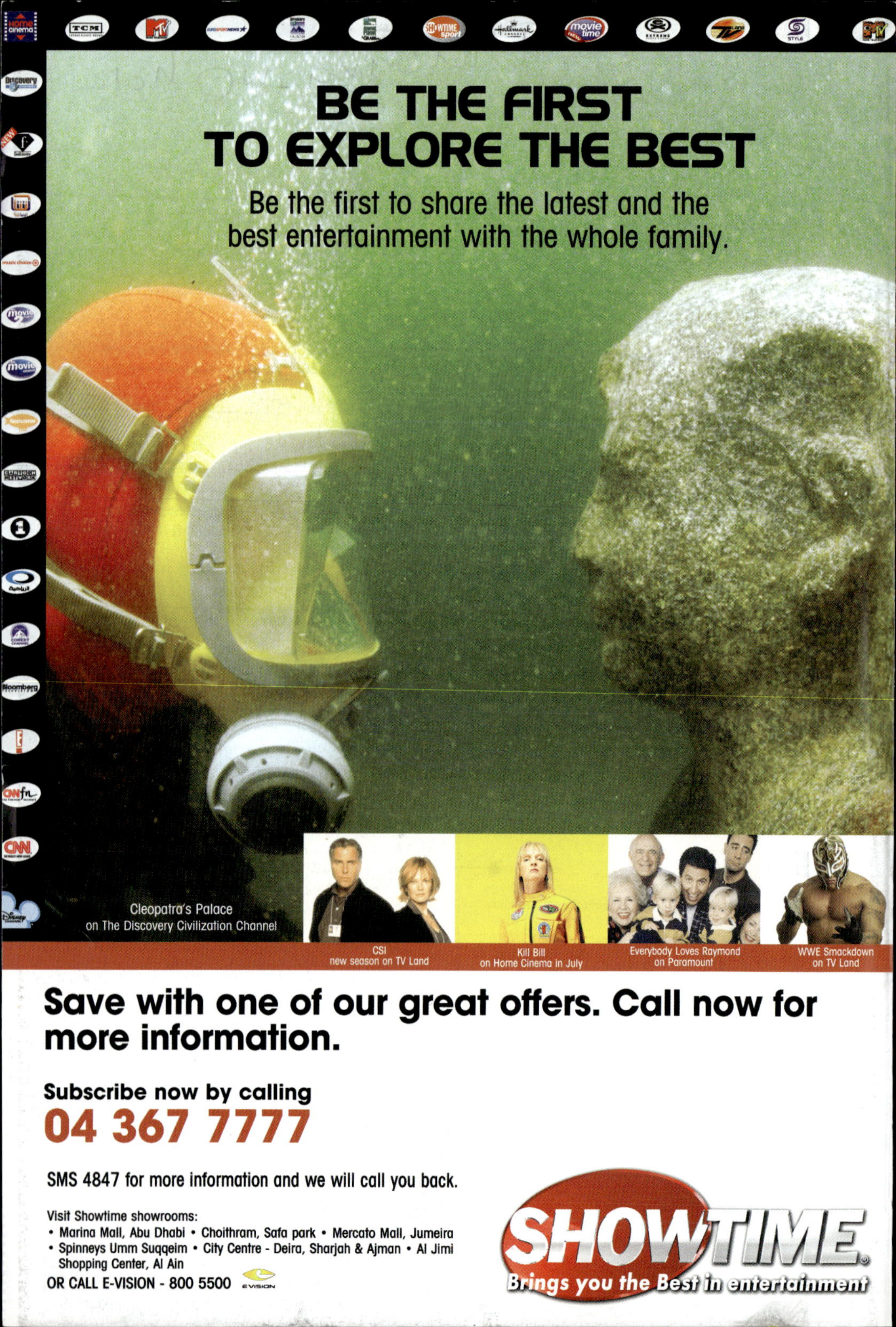
BE THE FIRST
TO EXPLORE THE BEST
Be the first to share the latest and the best entertainment with the whole family.
Cleopatra's Palace
on The Discovery Civilization Channel
CSI
new season on TV Land
Kill Bill
on Home Cinema in July
Everybody Loves Raymond
on Paramount
WWE Smackdown
on TV Land
Save with one of our great offers. Call now for more information.
Subscribe now by calling
04 367 7777
SMS 4847 for more information and we will call you back.
Visit Showtime showrooms:
• Marina Mall, Abu Dhabi • Choithram, Safa park • Mercato Mall, Jumeira
• Spinneys Umm Suqqeim • City Centre - Deira, Sharjah & Ajman • Al Jimi Shopping Center, Al Ain
OR CALL E-VISION - 800 5500
E-VISION
SHOWTIME®
Brings you the Best in entertainment

Online Explorer

Visit us online! Our Website is better than ever, keeping you abreast of the flux with the latest updated information and a full range of our titles. Check it all out on **www.Explorer-Publishing.com**.

Web Updates

A tremendous amount of research, effort and passion goes into making our guidebooks. However, in this dynamic and fast paced environment, decisions are swiftly taken and quickly implemented. We will try to provide you with the most current updates on those things which have changed DRAMATICALLY.

To view any changes, visit our Website: **www.Explorer-Publishing.com**

1. Click on **Insiders' City Guides -> Dubai Explorer -> Updates** to check on any updates that may interest you.
2. All updates are in Adobe PDF format*. You may print in colour or black & white and update your guide immediately.
3. If you are aware of any mistakes, or have any comments concerning any aspect of this publication, please fill in our online reader response form. We certainly appreciate your time and feedback.

**If you do not have Adobe Reader, download it from (www.adobe.com) or use the link from our Website.*

Alistair MacKenzie

Media Mogul

Alistair's dream would be to run Explorer Publishing from a remote wadi somewhere in the Hajar mountains; to have a completely functional office setup in the port-a-loo, powered by solar energy reflected from his shaving mirror. As a dedicated and paid up member of the 'You Can't Just Stay In & Watch TV This Weekend Again!' brigade, Alistair is a true inspiration to the non outdoorsy types.

Peter D'Onghia

The Godfather

Poor Peter struggles with a constant identity crisis. Is he an Aussie with a penchant for questionably loud beach shirts? Or an Italian stallion who knows more about olive oil than Popeye? Either way, Peter mate, cooking pasta on the 'barbie' is not one of your better ideas!

Louise M

Louise is a
deadlines.
desk twice
else's In tr
desking' w
mysterious
samples co
office have
plans are a
photocopi
follows he

Pete Maloney

Pencil Pusher

As mentioned in last year's edition, Poor Pete moved from Manchester for there wasn't a single girl left in the region that he hadn't dated. Well, history has a way of repeating itself and alas, Dubai is also proving too small a town. He's currently working huge amounts of overtime to fund his purchase of a camel and thus, do away with colossal taxi fares to the outer reaches of Al Ain.

Zainudheen Madathil

Doodle Maestro

We believe that Zainudheen's real name is John, and that he kept changing it to more and more obscure alternatives in a bid to escape Alistair's phone calls. When he ran out of letters and landed at 'Z', he surrendered. What he's left with is a name no one can pronounce and a life of doodling and designing his way back into the real world.

Derric

Followir
his sup
and 4 y
Fronts f
underw
Derrick
being ju
rather t
We have
time rol
office c
he fits i
working
privileg
animals

And a great big thanks to all the following people who, with only a few small bribes of fizzy pop and chocolate, have us cre
Alan P, APB, Chris, Clare, David, DPJP, Ed, EDMM, Fiona, Graeme W, Grahame L, Heidi, Jennifer, Justin Scholes, KWM, Kathy, M

ellodew

Meat Packer

pro at routinely avoiding How? She never sits at the same and hides her stuff in everyone ys. Her theory is that 'hot h wild abandon will leave her and undetected. However, DNA lected from post its all over the confirmed her existence, and oot to trap her by the before the rest of the crew example.

Amanda Harkin

Publicity Junky

When Amanda marched into our office wearing pin stripes and heels, we thought she'd come to audit our books – so we held her hostage! But since no one will pay her ransom, she now spends her time chewing through her shackles and sending out subliminal help messages embedded in Explorer press releases.

Jayde Fernandes

Master Craftsman

Jayde is working with us only until his record deal with a boy band is finalised. He is often spotted practising his MTV Award speech in front of the men's room mirror, whilst considering if he would be better blonde. He's a born performer – the performance he puts up to get out of work each day is amazing!

Janice Menezes

Admin Queen

As a former circus lion tamer, Janice's prowess with a whip and a chair, were excellent skills for taming the sales team and ensuring a good performance. She misses the bright lights of the Big Top but says that the clowns are pretty much the same.

Geneva EXPLORER

k Pereira

Techno Guru

g his split from rmodel girlfriend, ars modelling Y r a leading ar manufacturer, was frustrated at dged on his looks an his IT abilities. given him a part tinkering with mputers, which between with under d children and

Lena Moosa

Big Ed

our own little tinkerbell, Lena buzzes around the office waving her magic wand over our badly written text. She can spot a typo from Sharjah and can make a silk purse out of the dodgiest of sow's ears. In fact, she makes everything look so good that, had she created the world, all the men would resemble George Clooney and chocolate would have the calorific value of a carrot!

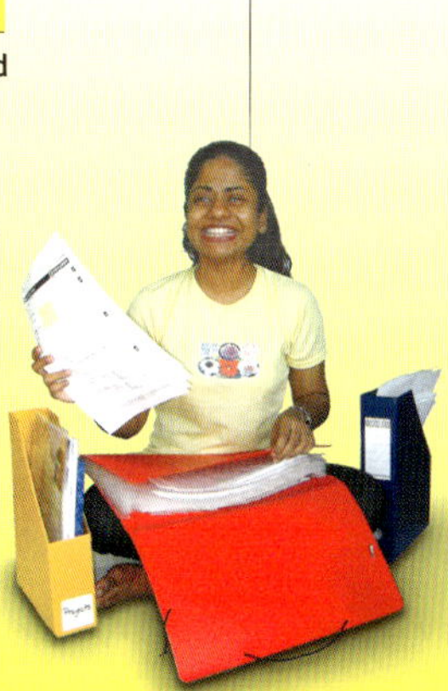

Geraldine Fernandes

The Enigma

Geraldine is so young she was being born when most of us were getting married and starting pension plans. Her youth is reflected in her super energy and she whizzes around the office at the speed of sound, doing things it takes us crumblies hours just to think about. However, working for Explorer, she will also age at the speed of light, so we expect her to be slowing down any time soon.

te this guide with their invaluable contributions:
ark & Fiona W, Mandevu, Melodie, MMI, MM Halabi, Peter St, Troy & Allison Priest & Wendy M

Sneak a Peek...

Online Explorer

Who Are You?

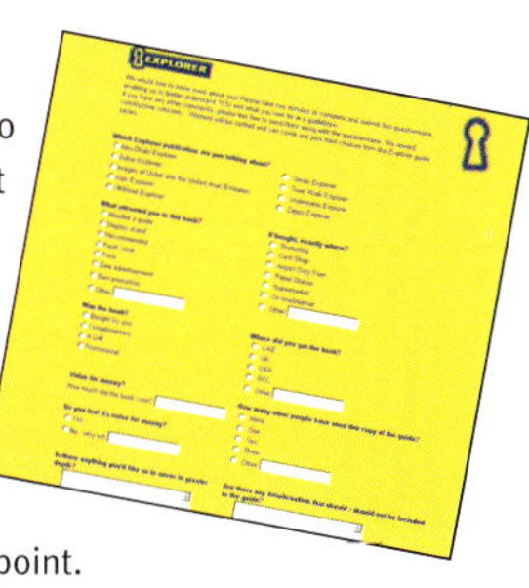

We would love to know more about you. We would equally love to know what we have done right or wrong, or if we have accidentally misled you at some point.

Please take a minute to fill out the Reader Response Form on our Website. To do so:

1. Visit **www.Explorer-Publishing.com**
2. At the top right, click on Response Form
3. Fill it out and enlighten us

Free Fabulous Food – aka 'the FFF'

Gluttons and connoisseurs interested in bona fide, calorified membership to the FFF Fest, know that you can now realise your fantasy of becoming a food reporter. We do have certain prerequisites*.

You should:

1. Frequently dine out
2. Know which hands hold the knife and fork
3. Love the challenge of doing restaurant reviews incognito

(*Good looks, charm, wit and humour are a bonus)

Whether it's your grandma, maid, boyfriend, colleague, slave (or even favourite Martian!), reporting knows no boundaries and they can all qualify. Log on to www.EatOutSpeakOut.com for details.

Explorer Community

Whether it's an idea, a correction, an opinion or simply a recommendation, we want to hear from you. Log on and be part of the Explorer Community – let your opinions be heard, viewed, compiled and printed.

THE EXPLORER 'B' TEAM

In media & publishing, our team is like no other. Companies will sell you images of dedication and hard work – humourless professionalism drowning in a sea of serious business acumen and policies. We just work hard... then play hard! Hand picked for our abilities and our personalities, we enjoy our clients as they enjoy us, building a unique business relationship full of creativity and respect with our customers. The end result is quality! quality! quality... and a smile...

gues

Head Honcho

to answer
.e 'What time is it?'
ely conjuring up
ional spreadsheets
him the position of
Manager in
don't think he
ibutes anything,
announcements
midday marker...
hs and pie charts
g anyway.

Abdul Gafoor

Ace Circulator

Gafoor is on the run from the police for tippex-ing digits out of number plates and selling them to rich wannabes. There are currently 3,498,236 cars cruising Sheikh Zayed Road (including 3 Explorer Caddy vans) all bearing the number plate 'DUBAI 1'. He is bound to Explorer for the next 5 years till he pays off the office supply overspend.

Stephen Drilen

Wheeler Dealer

After spending many years in the perfume industry, Stephen made a breakthrough by combining his work with his love of singing and off-roading. The result had camels all over the northern emirates smelling like summer meadow and singing the sound of music to each passing 4x4. He didn't make his fortune, but the camels are off to Las Vegas.

Rafi Jamal

Speed Freak

Recently responsible for ensuring that all of the World Bank dignitaries got to the conference on time, Rafi could not have foretold the consequences of stopping off for a quick doughnut. Now, world debt is at an all time high and interest rates have gone through the roof, and all for the sake of a Crispy Crème. At Explorer, the doughnuts are ALWAYS the priority – so he fits in just fine.

Yolanda Rodrigues

Sexy Seeker

Knick named 'Sniffer', Yoyo was voted the noisiest parker in the office and therefore perfect as Explorer's researcher. To test her skills for this post, we wrote a secret on a post it and hid it in the smallest drawer in the furthest room of the tallest tower in the vastest land... and gave her five minutes to find it. She found it in three minutes and spent the last two embellishing it beyond recognition.

Alena Hykes

Sales Supergirl

Alena should be working as a linguist for the United Nations since she speaks most languages known to man. We, however, offered her better career prospects and way better pay. A former Greek spy, she has escaped the Greek & Czech mafia and is residing with us under an assumed name until the United Nations improves their offer!

Nadia DSouza

Nosey Parker

Nadia's ability to calm even the most frenzied of situations came from her vast experience with the LAPD in talking crazies down from high ledges. It's a skill that has come in handy when nearing print deadlines, as she somehow manages to retrieve our editor off the 5th floor window ledge.

Mannie Lugtu

Distribution Demon

Mannie was a 70's disco champion who made quite a name for himself on the New York club scene. Alas, his LA shirt and disco trousers eventually got a bit tight on him, and he retired to Dubai to manage a sequin emporium. He can be found sparkling the length and breadth of Al Wasl Road in our Caddy, tapping his steering wheel to Boney M remixes.

Ivan Rodr

Ivan's abilit
questions li
by immedia
multidimen
in Excel wo
Distributior
Explorer. W
actually dis
but his lunc
are a timely
and the gra
look stunni

Pamela Grist

Happy Snapper

Ever since she was asked to write a feature on whether blondes have more fun, most of Pam's spare time is consumed under a shower cap waiting for the latest hair colour to develop. When she's not indulging her passion for photography, she's auditioning for shampoo ads, which makes sense as she's 'Head & Shoulders' above the competition.

Kamal Basha

Chief Bean Counter

Kamal fights a losing battle to set a formal dress code in the office by unfailingly wearing rather smart shirts and neckties. However, the reason behind his well turned out image may have something to do with the fact that he holds the office record for coming in to work just before lunchtime! The beauty routine's taking too long, buddy...

Explorer Insiders' City Guides

These are no ordinary guidebooks. They are your lifestyle support system, medicine for the bored, ointment for the aimless, available over the counter and prescribed by those in the know. An essential resource for residents, tourists and business people, they cover everything worth knowing about the city and where to do it.

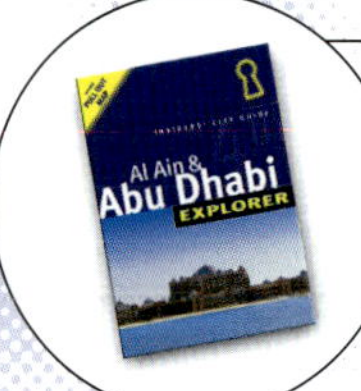

Abu Dhabi Explorer

Just when you thought it couldn't get any better! The 4th edition of the **Abu Dhabi Explorer** has been radically revised and revamped, making it the ultimate insiders' guidebook. A lifetime of information is sorted into easy reference sections with recommendations, advice and guidance on every aspect of residing in Abu Dhabi & Al Ain. Written by residents with a zest for life, this book is an essential resource for anyone exploring this beautiful emirate.

ISBN 976-8182-58-X **Retail Price** Dhs.65, €18

Dubai Explorer

The 8th stunning edition of Dubai Explorer has broken the mould in insiders' city guides. A prodigy amongst its peers, and still the best selling in its class, the **Dubai Explorer** has done it again with its newest annual addition.

Full of all of the favourite sections, we bring you even more places to eat, sleep shop and socialise, as well as an enormous amount of must have information on everything you need to know to survive and enjoy the city of Dubai.

ISBN 976-8182-47-4 **Retail Price** Dhs.65 €18

Geneva Explorer

Following the hugely popular style of the **Explorer** city guides, the **Geneva Explorer** too, has raised the bar for quality guidebooks in the region. A resident team of writers, photographers and lovers of life have sold their souls to exhaustive research, bringing you a guidebook packed with insider recommendations, practical information and the most accurate coverage around. Written by residents thoroughly familiar with the inside track, this is THE essential must-have for anyone wanting to explore this multicultural haven. **(Due out 4th quarter 2004)**

ISBN 976-8182-44-x **Retail Price** Dhs.65 €18

Oman Explorer

As the list of fascinating insights grew beyond the city limits of Muscat, the **Oman Explorer** was born. Now covering the whole of this largely unspoilt country, this guidebook has become an in-depth catalogue of the region's life, leisure and entertainment. Based on the legendary formula of the **Dubai Explorer**, every aspect of existence in Oman is covered, with no stone left unturned. This is essential reading for anyone exploring this gorgeous country – be it residents, visitors or business trippers. **(Due out 4th quarter 2004)**

ISBN 976-8182-07-5 **Retail Price** Dhs.65 €18

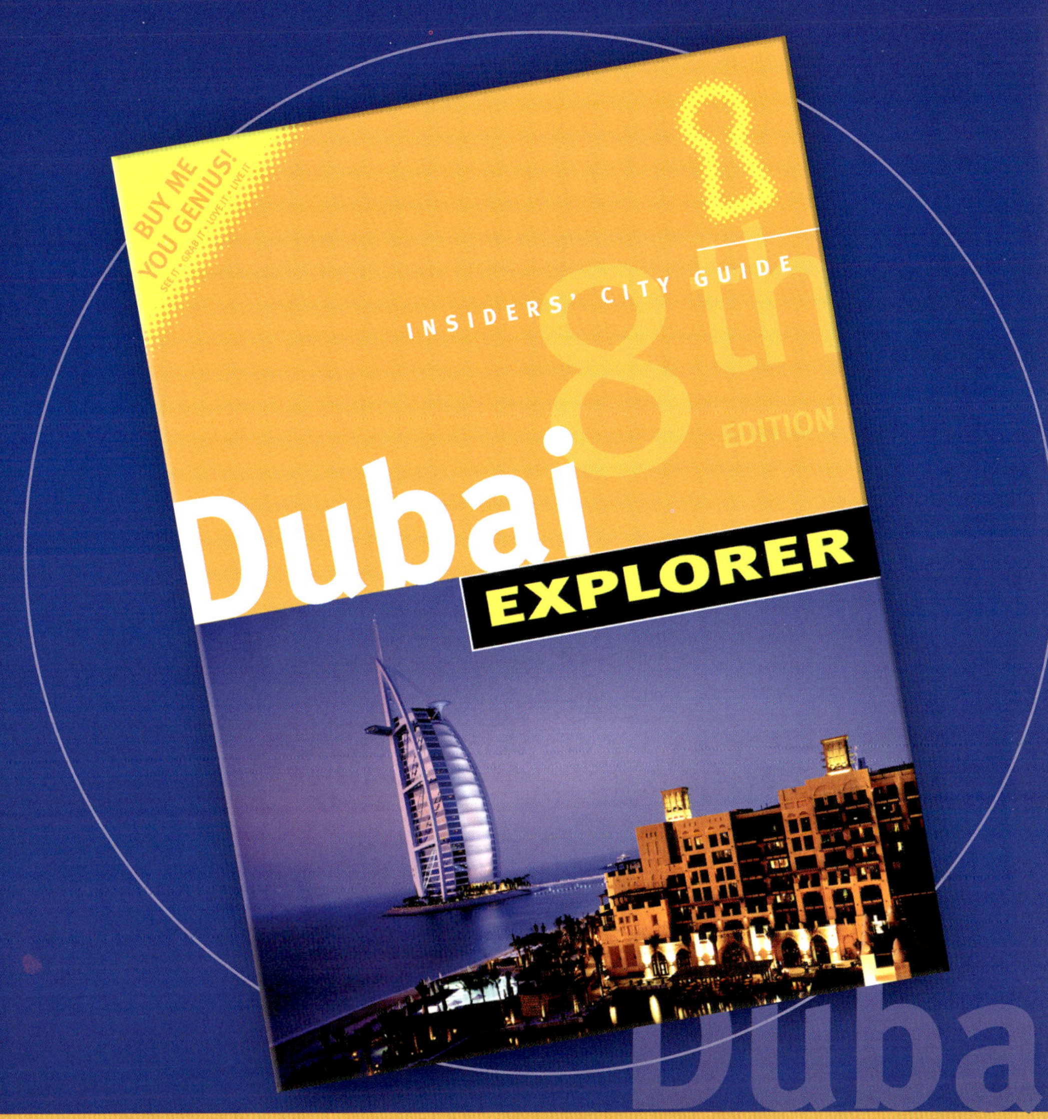
BUY ME YOU GENIUS!
SEE IT • GRAB IT • LOVE IT • LIVE IT
8
INSIDERS' CITY GUIDE
8th
EDITION
Dubai
EXPLORER
Duba

Going Out

Maps

Index

Shopping

Activities

Exploring

General Information

New Residents

Other Products

Apart from our wondrous array of city guides, activity guides and photography books, we offer other titles so innovative, they cannot be categorised. From the Hand-Held Explorer (our revolutionary digital guidebook) to the Street Map Explorer (your guide to getting around), these popular products have been bought, used, loved and lived.

Hand-Held Explorer (Dubai)

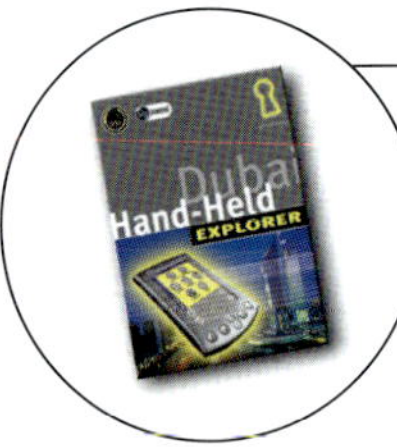

The **Dubai Explorer** goes digital. Interactive, informative and innovative, this easy to install software for your PDA offers you all the info from your favourite guidebook at your fingertips. Browse through restaurant reviews at the push of a button, scroll through and peruse a multitude of activities, and dive into a mountain of must know data at a glance. Your PDA will be undernourished without it!

ISBN 976-8182-40-7 **Retail Price** Dhs.65 €18

Street Map Explorer (Dubai)

The most accurate and up to date map on Dubai has arrived! The **Street Map Explorer (Dubai)** is a concise and comprehensive compendium of street names, cross referenced with an A to Z index of businesses and tourist attractions. In this fast developing city, this expansive and handy guidebook will soon become your favourite travel mate and a standard tool for navigating this ever-growing metropolis.

ISBN 976-8182-10-5 **Retail Price** Dhs.45 €18

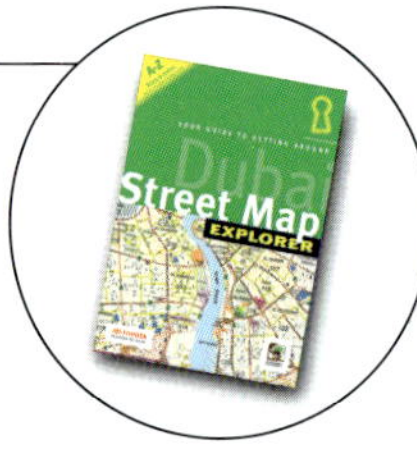

Dubai Tourist Map

This much awaited second edition of the **Dubai Tourist Map**, compiled and published by Dubai Muncipality, offers visitors and residents the best chance of getting from A to B. Key places of interest are highlighted and brief descriptions of the main tourist attractions are enhanced by colour photographs. An index of the community street and building numbering system ensures that the city can be easily navigated. This map is a must for anyone in Dubai.

ISBN 976-8182-16-4 **Retail Price** Dhs.35 €14.95

Zappy Explorer (Dubai)

Aptly dubbed the 'ultimate culture shock antidote', this guide is **Explorer's** solution to the complexities and perplexities of Dubai's administrative maze. A clear, straightforward set of procedures assists residents through the basics of life in this city, from opening a bank account and connecting your phone to buying a car and marrying your true love. Including detailed information on ministry and government department requirements, what to bring lists, reference maps and much more, the **Zappy Explorer** is your best chance of getting things done next to bribery or force!

ISBN 976-8182-25-3 **Retail Price** Dhs.65 €18

Explorer Photography Books

Where words fail, a picture speaks volumes. Look at the world though new eyes as the lens captures places you never knew existed. These award winning books are valuable additions to bookshelves everywhere.

Dubai: Tomorrow's City Today

Stunning photographs shed light on the beauty and functionality of contemporary Dubai, a city that is a model of diversity, development and progress. Explore its historical highlights, municipal successes, innovative plans and civic triumphs, as you wonder at the grandeur in store for the future.

ISBN 976-8182-35-0 **Retail Price** Dhs.165 €45

Images of Abu Dhabi & the UAE

This visual showcase shares the aesthetic and lush wonders of the emirate of Abu Dhabi as spectacular images disclose the marvels of the capital and the diversity of astounding locations throughout the seven emirates.

ISBN 976-8182-28-8 **Retail Price** Dhs.165 €45

Images of Dubai & the UAE

Images of Dubai shares the secrets of this remarkable land and introduces newcomers to the wonders of Dubai and the United Arab Emirates. Journey along golden beaches under a pastel sunset, or deep into the mesmerising sands of the desert. View the architectural details of one of the most visually thrilling urban environments in the world, and dive undersea to encounter the reef creatures that live there. This book is for all those who love this country as well as those who think they might like to.

ISBN 976-8182-28-8 **Retail Price** Dhs.165 €45

Sharjah's Architectural Splendour

Take a guided tour of some of the highlights of Sharjah's architecture. Through the lens, this book captures small, aesthetic details and grand public compounds, the mosques and souks of this remarkable city. Striking photographs are linked together with text that is both analytical and informative. Whether you are a long term resident or a brief visitor, this volume of images will undoubtedly surprise and delight.

ISBN 976-8182-29-6 **Retail Price** Dhs.165 €45

Explorer Activity Guides

Why not visit stunning marine life and mysterious wrecks, or stand poised on the edge of a natural wadi or pool in the mountains? Get a tan and a life with our activity guidebooks.

Family Explorer (Dubai & Abu Dhabi)

The one and only handbook for families in Dubai and Abu Dhabi has finally arrived. Jam packed with hundreds of innovative ideas, you can now enjoy a multitude of both indoor and outdoor activity options with your little ones, or follow the guidance and tips provided on practical topics such as education and medical care. Written by experienced parents residing in the Emirates, the **Family Explorer** is, without a doubt, the essential resource for families and kids aged up to 14 years. **(Due out 3rd quarter 2004)**

ISBN 976-8182-34-2 **Retail Price** Dhs.65 €18

Off-Road Explorer (UAE)

You haven't truly been to the Emirates until you've experienced its delights off the beaten track. Dear to the hearts of the indigenous and the insane, this pastime involves hours of zooming 4x4s up sand dunes and hours of digging them out again! The **Off-Road Explorer (UAE)** is a brilliant array of outback route maps designed for the adventurous and the anxious alike. Satellite images superimposed with step-by-step route directions, safety information and stunning photography, make this a perfect addition to your four wheeler.

ISBN 976-8182-37-7 **Retail Price** Dhs.95 €29

Underwater Explorer (UAE)

Opening the doors to liquid heaven in the UAE, this handy book details the top 58 dive sites that avid divers would not want to miss. Informative illustrations, shipwreck data & stunning marine life photographs combined with suggested dive plans cater to divers of all abilities. Whether you're a passionate diver or just pottering, you will not want to be without this crucial resource.

ISBN 976-8182-36-9 **Retail Price** Dhs.65 €18

Off-Road Explorer (Oman)

Coming Soon!

General Information

EXPLORER

General Info

Table of Contents

General Information

Aerial view of Abu Dhabi

Country Overview

Geography

Situated on the northeastern part of the Arabian Peninsula, the United Arab Emirates (UAE) is bordered by the Kingdom of Saudi Arabia to the south and west, and the Sultanate of Oman to the east and north. The UAE shares 457 kilometres of its border with Saudi Arabia and 410 kilometres with Oman. It has a coastline on both the Gulf of Oman and the Arabian Gulf, and is south of the strategically important Strait of Hormuz. The geographic co-ordinates for the UAE are 24 00 N, 54 00 E.

The country is made up of seven different emirates (Abu Dhabi, Ajman, Dubai, Fujairah, Ras Al Khaimah, Sharjah and Umm Al Quwain), which were formerly all independent sheikhdoms. The total area of the country is about 83,600 square kilometres, most of which lies in the Abu Dhabi emirate.

The country's 1,318 kilometres of coastline is dotted with golden beaches, 100 kilometres of which lie on the Gulf of Oman. The coast on the Arabian Gulf is littered with coral reefs and over 200 mostly uninhabited islands. Sabkha (salt flats), stretches of gravel plain and vast spans of desert terrain characterise much of the inland region. Lying close to the Gulf of Oman are the majestic Hajar mountains that rise from the Musandam Peninsula in the north, via eastern UAE, and flow into Oman, forming a backbone that runs through the country.

Much of the emirate of Abu Dhabi is made up of the infamous Rub Al Khali or Empty Quarter desert, which is common to the Kingdom of Saudi Arabia and the Sultanate of Oman. This arid, stark desert is famous for its spectacular sand dunes that are broken by the occasional lush oasis.

Visitors to Abu Dhabi will find a land of startling contrasts – occasional irrigated farmlands appear as a green paradise amidst endless stretches of desert terrain and vast tracts of sabkha. The city of Abu Dhabi, located on a low lying, 'scorpion shaped' island, is a modern and lush metropolis, graced with tree lined streets, futuristic skyscrapers, rich shopping malls, international luxury hotels and cultural centres, and surrounded by the sparkling turquoise waters of the Arabian Gulf. The famous 'Manhattan' skyline reflected in the azure waters along the Corniche offers a striking contrast to the large gardens and green boulevards that are spread across the island.

Al Ain, the second city, lies to the east on the border with Oman. Primarily an oasis town that is surrounded by a hostile desert, this 'Garden City' (as it is also known) portrays a vision of cool tranquillity. The other main region of the emirate is the Liwa oasis, which is at the centre of the Al Dhafra area. Set amidst towering red dunes, Liwa is the last main inhabited outpost before the great western desert of the Rub Al Khali.

Maps

To find your way around, pick up the Arab World Map Library's fold out map of Abu Dhabi. It includes the main areas of Abu Dhabi and a more detailed street guide to the city centre, and is available from any good bookstore.

Together with its rich desert heritage and bygone days as a fishing village, Abu Dhabi has become a truly unique and diverse destination – a symbiosis of modernity and traditional Arabian customs.

History

Less than 50 years ago, the emirate of Abu Dhabi was little more than an empty desert inhabited by nomadic Bedouin tribes, with just a sprinkling of villages in the more fertile areas. The capital city, Abu Dhabi, located on the northern side of the island, consisted of two or three hundred palm ('barasti') huts, a few coral buildings and the large, white Ruler's Fort. Looking at today's modern city and emirate of Abu Dhabi, it is hard to reconcile with the extent of changes that have occurred in the intervening years.

In 1761, the leader of the Bani Yas Bedouin tribe moved his people to this island. The abundant wildlife won the island its name (Abu Dhabi translated means 'Father of the Gazelle'). However, not much altered till the discovery of oil in 1950, and despite the chances for fishing and grazing, it was not until the discovery of a freshwater well in 1793 that the ruling Al Nahyan family, based in the south of the country at the Liwa Oasis, moved to the island. In Liwa, on the edge of the stark Empty Quarter desert, the Al Nahyan family lived a traditional Bedouin life with their main source of livelihood being animal husbandry and small scale agriculture. Descendants of the Al Nahyan family, in alliance with other important Bedouin tribes in the region, have ruled the emirate of Abu Dhabi ever since.

By the 1800s, the town had considerably developed and prospered mainly from pearling, which brought in important trade and revenue. From 1855 to 1909, under the reign of Sheikh Zayed bin Mohammed (also known as 'Zayed the Great'), Abu Dhabi rose in prominence to become the most powerful emirate along the western coast of the Arabian Peninsula. His influence was profound and it was during his rule that Abu Dhabi and the other emirates to the north accepted the protection of Britain in 1892. The British regarded the Gulf region as an important communication link with their empire in India, and wished to ensure that other world powers, in particular France and Russia, did not extend their influence in the region. The area became known as the Trucial States (or Trucial Coast), a name that stayed until the departure of the British in 1971.

Emirs or Sheikhs?

While the term 'emirate' comes from the ruling title of 'emir', the rulers of the UAE are referred to as sheikhs.

The death of Zayed the Great lead to a conflict amongst his descendants for leadership, and the emirate fell into decline. In the 1930s, due to the world recession as well as the creation of the cultured pearl industry in Japan, pearl trade in the Gulf collapsed. No longer able to rely on this valuable commodity for income, Abu Dhabi slid from a position of relative wealth to the poorest of all the emirates.

The ascension of Sheikh Shakhbut bin Sultan brought a reasonable degree of stability along with the realisation that oil might be the answer to their economic problems. In 1939, he granted concessions to a British company to search for oil, but it was not until 1958 that huge reserves were discovered offshore by an Anglo-French consortium. Four years later, exports began and Abu Dhabi was on its way to becoming an incredibly wealthy state. Sheikh Shakhbut's rule, however, was considered rather idiosyncratic and, in 1966, the British, who still had a certain degree of influence in the country, helped to replace him with his brother Sheikh Zayed bin Sultan Al Nahyan, the governor of the oasis town of Al Ain.

Two years later, the British announced their withdrawal from the region and encouraged the separate states to consider uniting under one flag. The ruling sheikhs, in particular Sheikh Zayed and the ruler of Dubai, realised that by joining forces, they would have a stronger voice in the wider Middle East region. Hence, negotiations began to try and form a single state consisting of Bahrain, Qatar and the Trucial States, but the process collapsed when Bahrain and Qatar chose to become independent states. Still, the Trucial States remained committed to forming an alliance and, in 1971, the federation of the United Arab Emirates was created (excluding the emirate of Ras Al Khaimah, which joined in 1972). Under the agreement, each emirate retained a certain degree of autonomy with Abu Dhabi (and to a lesser extent, Dubai) giving the most input into the federation. The leaders of the new federation elected Sheikh Zayed bin Sultan Al Nahyan as their first president – a position he has held ever since.

The creation of the United Arab Emirates hasn't been without its problems, the main ones arising from disputes over boundaries between the different emirates. At the end of Sheikh Zayed's first term in 1976 as president, he threatened to resign if the other rulers didn't settle the demarcation of their borders. The threat was an effective way of ensuring co-operation but, although more focus is now given to the importance of the federation as a whole, the degree of independence of the various emirates has, to date, not been fully determined. It is however, led by Abu Dhabi, whose wealth and sheer size make it the most powerful of all the emirates.

The massive oil reserves that lie below Abu Dhabi allowed Sheikh Zayed to make the most of the revenue from his own emirate. With a population of only 15,000 in 1962, there was a lot of wealth to go around amongst a small number of people. Even now, the population of Abu Dhabi, at the last census in 2003, was estimated at 1.6 million, of which only 27% are Nationals (and this in an area twice the size of Belgium!)

HH Sheikh Zayed Bin Sultan Al Nayhan

Paul Thuysbaert
PHOTOGRAPHY

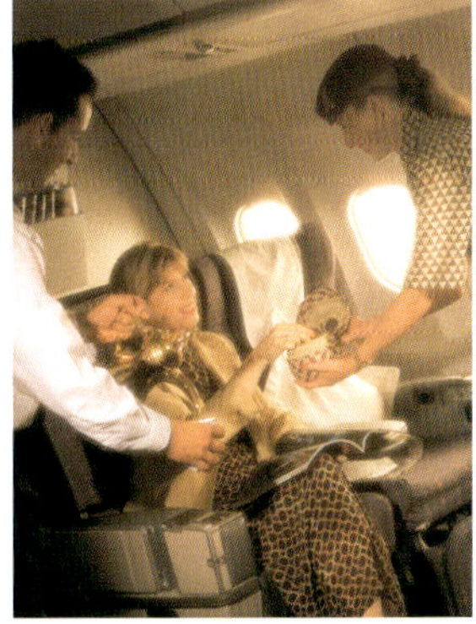

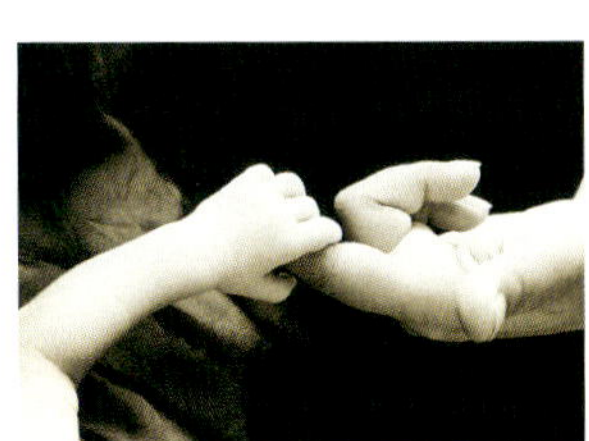

Under Sheikh Zayed's vision and careful guidance, this new found wealth was wisely used to create an economic and social infrastructure, which is the basis of today's modern society. The welfare of his people has always been the most important factor and hence, there are excellent hospitals and a health service that is available for free to the national population and at a very low cost to expatriate residents. Education, roads, housing, and women's welfare are all priorities that continue to be developed under Sheikh Zayed's farsighted leadership. As a result, UAE Nationals have a deep admiration and regard for the leader who brought about such a radical transformation to their way of life.

Economy

UAE Overview

The UAE has an open economy, with one of the world's highest per capita incomes estimated at Dhs.72,500 in 2003 (near US$20,000), although this is far from being spread evenly amongst the population. Its wealth, once chiefly based on the oil sector, now sees an oil contribution of 28% of the country's gross domestic product (GDP). The GDP for 2003 was approximately Dhs.293 billion, compared with Dhs.156 billion in 1995. Abu Dhabi and Dubai contribute around 80% to the country's GDP.

Over 90% of the UAE's oil reserves lie in Abu Dhabi and there is enough at the current rate of production (just over 2.5 million barrels per day) to last a further 100 years. However, although there is a heavy dependence on the oil and gas industry, trade, manufacturing, tourism and construction also play an important part in the national economy. Investment in infrastructure and development projects exceeded an estimated Dhs.3.9 billion in the first half of 2003. The UAE's main export partners are Saudi Arabia, Iran, Japan, India, Singapore, South Korea, and Oman. In 2002, the UAE's trade outflow was Dhs.143.7 billion. The main import partners are Japan, USA, UK, Italy, Germany and South Korea.

Current reports note that the country's economy is roughly 36 times larger than it was in 1971. The UAE has a good GDP growth rate, showing an annual growth of 4.3% since 2000.

The situation in the Emirates is radically different to that of 30 - 40 years ago when the area consisted of small, impoverished desert states. Visitors will find a unified and forward looking state with a high standard of living and a relatively well balanced and stable economy.

Abu Dhabi Overview

Other Options → **Business [p.98]**

Abu Dhabi's traditional economy was based around pearl diving, fishing and cultivating the date palm. However, the discovery of oil brought about a radical change. Exports began five years later and the new wealth, coupled with enlightened leadership, gave a complete turnaround to Abu Dhabi's fortunes. A modern city was created with an infrastructure built virtually from scratch.

Ongoing exploration in Abu Dhabi, both onshore and offshore, has so far identified 10% of the world's known crude oil resources. This makes Abu Dhabi the third largest oil producer in the Gulf after Saudi Arabia and Kuwait. It also has 4% of the

Abu Dhabi Overview

world's known natural gas reserves. Hence, the infrastructure has been expanded considerably to support the marine crude resources and processing oil and gas is now big business. The government runs the Abu Dhabi National Oil Company (ADNOC), which was set up to develop the reserves and to administer the industry.

However, the government is trying to diversify the economy to give less dependence on oil wealth. In Abu Dhabi, both government and private sector investment in agriculture, industry, fishing, water and electricity supply, transport, construction, warehousing and retailing has grown at a breakneck pace. Communications are the responsibility of the federally run Emirates Telecommunication Corporation (Etisalat) which, although currently a monopoly organisation, is continuously building and expanding its services. A plan to privatise this sector is yet to be finalised. Tourism in Abu Dhabi is also expected to play a major part in the future economy. At present, it still lags behind the emirate of Dubai in this respect.

Other initiatives to diversify the economy include the development of Sadiyat Island as a free trade zone. This zone gives investors certain tax and ownership incentives, such as exempting goods being imported or exported into the zone from customs duties. Free zones, such as the Jebel Ali Free Zone in the Dubai emirate, have proved to be a very successful concept and, undoubtedly, Sadiyat will offer the same attractions to foreign businesses.

Really Tax Free?

Taxes? Do they exist in Abu Dhabi? Well, yes and no. You won't pay income or sales tax, unless you purchase alcohol from a licensed liquor store, after which you'll be hit with a steep 30% tax. The main taxes are those set by the municipality, which is 5% on rent, and 10% on food, beverages and rooms in hotels. The rest are hidden taxes in the form of 'fees', such as your car registration renewal and visa/permit fees.

Export of non oil related products has grown threefold since 1990 and continues to rise. Private and overseas investment is actively encouraged.

Do not, however, be blinded by the healthy economy into believing that the average expat coming to work in Abu Dhabi will be on a huge salary. Except for highly skilled professionals, the salary for most employees is dropping and this downward trend is attributed, in part, to the willingness of workers to accept jobs at very low wages. While per capita income was Dhs.72,500 in 2003, this figure included all sections of the community, and the average labourer can also expect to earn as little as Dhs.600 (US$165) per month.

Unemployment levels in the national population are high, partly due to the desire of Nationals to work in the public sector (where salaries and benefits are better) and partly because their qualifications may not match the skills required in the private sector. However, the government is trying to reverse unemployment with a 'nationalisation' or 'emiratisation' programme (this is common to countries throughout the region). The aim is to reduce reliance on an expat workforce by putting the local population to work. This is being achieved by improving vocational training and by making it compulsory for certain categories of companies, such as banks, to hire a determined percentage of Emiratis. Another step taken by the government to make employment in the private sector more attractive to Nationals, is implementing a pension scheme where private companies are now required to provide a pension for their National employees.

Tourism Developments

Other Options → UAE Annual Events [p.40]

Abu Dhabi's economic and social transformation from a breakwater fishing village to an international tourist destination and global marketplace can be credited to the President, His Highness Sheikh Zayed bin Sultan Al Nahyan, who is considered the modern architect and visionary of the emirate and the UAE Federation. Planning department figures show that more than Dhs.100 billion has been pumped into the development of Abu Dhabi, particularly into infrastructure projects, since Sheikh Zayed took over as Ruler in 1966.

Abu Dhabi has recently upgraded a number of its five star hotels, and several more are being expanded, under construction, or at the planning stage. Most hotels have private beaches where guests can indulge in a wide range of water sports with state of the art facilities. The Abu Dhabi National Hotels Company (ADNHC) owns and administers a variety of hotels and resorts in Abu Dhabi and Al Ain. It also supervises the duty free complexes at Abu Dhabi and Al Ain international airports, and provides transport services through Al Ghazal (taxis), a wholly owned subsidiary.

Also active in hotel management is the National Corporation for Tourism and Hotels (NCTH), which is responsible for promoting Abu Dhabi as a tourist and international destination.

With more than 40 airlines touching down at the Abu Dhabi International Airport, Abu Dhabi has become a widely accessible tourist destination. The planning and execution of a $250 million satellite terminal is now underway. This ambitious project, overseen by Sheikh Hamdan bin Mubarak Al Nahyan, Chairman of the Department of Civil Aviation, is expected to be implemented by 2005. The airport intends to double its passenger and cargo capacity (to over 7 million passengers and over 300,000 cargo tonnes annually) with the construction of a new terminal, a second runway and additional facilities.

Abu Dhabi's developing reputation as a trend setting retail paradise can be traced to the opening of the Abu Dhabi Mall and Marina Mall in 2001. Abu Dhabi Mall is located within the Tourist Club area, and boasts the Abu Dhabi Co-op (a 16,000 square metre hypermarket), over 200 retail outlets, restaurants, an extensive food court, coffee shops and a multi-screen cinema. Located near the rapidly developing Breakwater area opposite the Corniche, Marina Mall is another shopping and recreational landmark of Abu Dhabi, attracting crowds with a nine screen megaplex, IKEA and a Carrefour hypermarket. Eventually, the Breakwater will be joined to the nearby manmade Lulu Island which, upon completion, will have a wildlife reserve, fun parks, hotels, restaurants, an aquarium and a museum.

Abu Dhabi is slower than Dubai in developing tourist attractions, but nonetheless, it is still a prominent centre for leisure and sports tourism, and there are plenty of substantial projects in the pipeline.

The Corniche

An imaginative scheme has transformed the 45 square kilometres of Futaisi Island off the coast of Abu Dhabi into a popular tourist resort. Housing fifteen luxurious chalets, two villas and a nature reserve, the club boasts a restaurant, an Arabic Fort, horse riding facilities, beaches and a swimming pool. The venue can also be booked for private functions, such as concerts and gala dinners.

The US$200 million Emirates Palace Hotel (near the Hilton Hotel) is under construction and will be ready for the next GCC Summit. Set within 200 acres of landscaped gardens, it will house the largest conference facilities in the UAE. Also on the Corniche Road, the Dhs.750 million Capital Plaza Commercial Development Project will include a luxury hotel, offices, apartments and retail facilities.

The Abu Dhabi Municipality plans to provide more recreational centres in the capital, thus helping to promote tourism in the emirate. Specific projects include the Khalifa Park and the New Corniche Park.

Due for completion before the end of 2004, the Khalifa Park Project is located on the site of the old airport, near the Al Maqtaa Bridge. The 430,000 square metres of land will be dedicated to promoting tourism and highlighting the emirate's cultural heritage. When completed, it will be the first of its kind in the Middle East, featuring a marine natural history museum, several public gardens and oases, a mosque, a huge open air amphitheatre seating 1,500, a water garden, games and a festival stand. The New Corniche Park will be divided into three themed zones: Family Zone, Central Zone and Heritage Zone.

To date, tourism development in Al Ain has been slow and quiet, but this is set to change. The Al Ain Economic Development & Tourism Promotion Authority has unveiled a new venture in its bid to position Al Ain as an emerging tourist destination in the region. Watch this space!

International Relations

In its foreign relations, the UAE's stance is one of non alignment, but it is committed to the support of Arab unity. The country became a member of the United Nations and the Arab League in 1971. It is a member of the International Monetary Fund (IMF), the Organisation of Petroleum Exporting Countries (OPEC), the World Trade Organisation (WTO) and other international and Arab organisations. It is

also a member of the Arab Gulf Co-operation Council (AGCC, also known as the GCC), whose other members are Bahrain, Kuwait, Oman, Qatar and Saudi Arabia. The UAE, led by Sheikh Zayed bin Sultan Al Nahyan, had a leading role in the formation of the AGCC in 1981 and the country is the third largest member in terms of geographical size, after Saudi Arabia and Oman. All major embassies and consulates are represented either in Abu Dhabi or Dubai, or both.

Government/Ruling Family

The Supreme Council of Rulers is the highest authority in the UAE, comprising the rulers of the seven emirates. Since the country is governed by hereditary rule, there is little distinction between the royal families and the government. The Supreme Council is responsible for general policy matters involving education, defence, foreign affairs, communications and development, and for ratifying federal laws. The Council meets four times a year and the Abu Dhabi and Dubai rulers have effective power of veto over decisions.

The seven members of the Supreme Council elect the chief of state (the President) from among its members. The President of the UAE is HH Sheikh Zayed bin Sultan Al Nahyan who is also Ruler of Abu Dhabi. He has been President since independence on 2nd December, 1971, and ruler of Abu Dhabi since 6 August, 1966. The Supreme Council also elects the Vice President, who is HH Sheikh Maktoum bin Rashid Al Maktoum, Ruler of Dubai. The President and Vice President are elected and appointed for five year terms. The President appoints the Prime Minister (currently HH Sheikh Maktoum bin Rashid Al Maktoum) and the Deputy Prime Minister.

The Federal Council of Ministers is responsible to the Supreme Council. It has executive authority to initiate and implement laws, and is a consultative assembly of 40 representatives who are appointed for two years by the individual emirates. The council monitors and debates government policies, but has no power of veto.

The individual emirates still have a degree of autonomy, and laws that affect everyday life vary between the emirates. All emirates have a separate

The UAE Flag

Abu Dhabi Ruling Family Tree

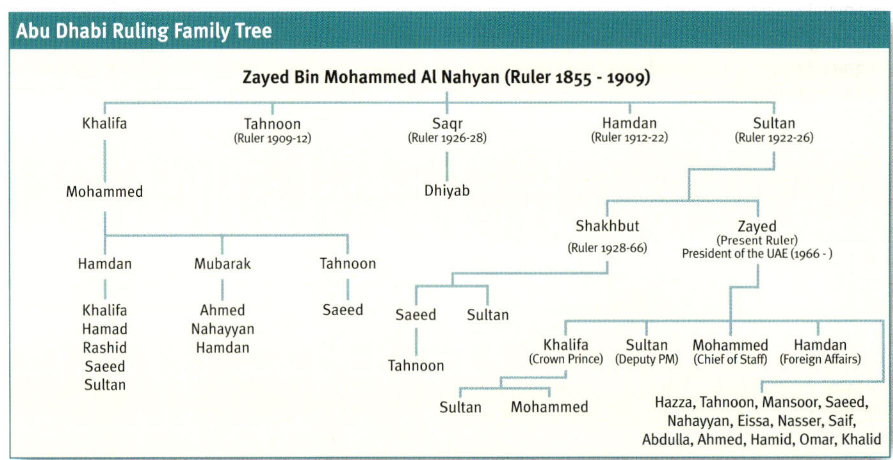

police force, with different uniforms and cars. Additionally it is possible to buy alcohol in Abu Dhabi, but not in Sharjah. Abu Dhabi has consistently been in favour of increasing the strength of the federation and, due to its wealth and size, has always been the most powerful and therefore able to press its point. The current move is towards greater interdependence and increasing the power of the federation, especially in the less oil rich emirates, which are relying more and more on Abu Dhabi for subsidies.

Facts & Figures

Population

Emiratis make up only 20% of the population (according to the most recently available data) and demographic trends within the country are driven by the Emirates' reliance on foreigners to provide the workforce for their growing economy. During the 1990s, the population grew by an average of 6% a year, reaching an estimated 4,041,000 by mid 2003. The boom in oil prices in 1999 and 2000 led to a sharp increase in demand for foreign labour and, as a result, the population rose to 3,488,000 by the end of 2001, a year on year increase of 12%. Recent UN estimates suggest that the UAE's population will double by 2029.

The emirate of Abu Dhabi has the largest population amongst all the emirates, reaching almost 1,600,000 compared with just over 1,200,000 in Dubai and 636,000 in Sharjah. Abu Dhabi also has the highest male to female ratio of 2.53 men to every woman.

According to the United Nations Development Program (UNDP), the UAE has the highest life expectancy in the Arab world at 72.2 years for males and 75.6 years for females.

National Flag

In a nation continually striving for world records, the country's 30th anniversary celebrations on National Day 2001 were marked with the world's tallest flagpole erected in Abu Dhabi and the world's largest UAE flag raised in Dubai. The flag consists of three equal horizontal bands: green at the top, white in the middle and black at the bottom. A thicker vertical band of red runs down the hoist side.

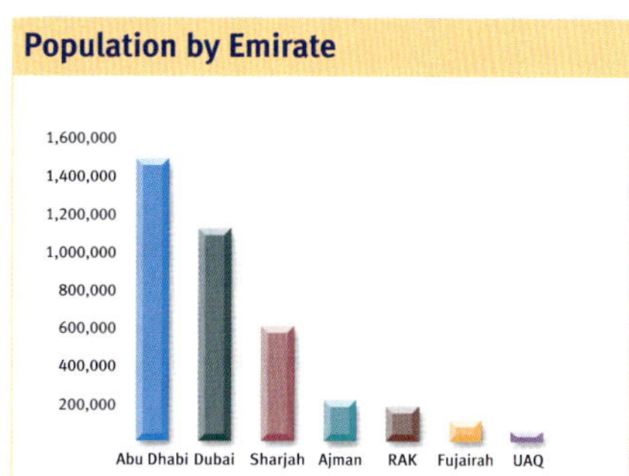

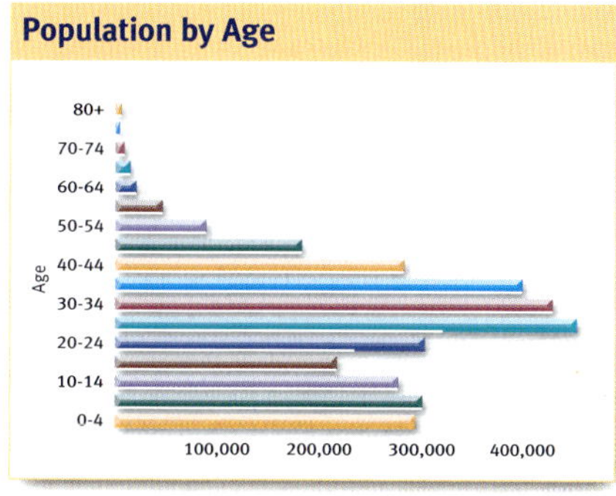

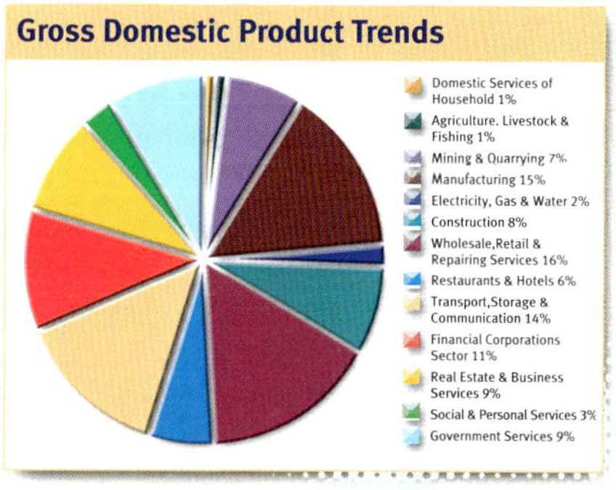

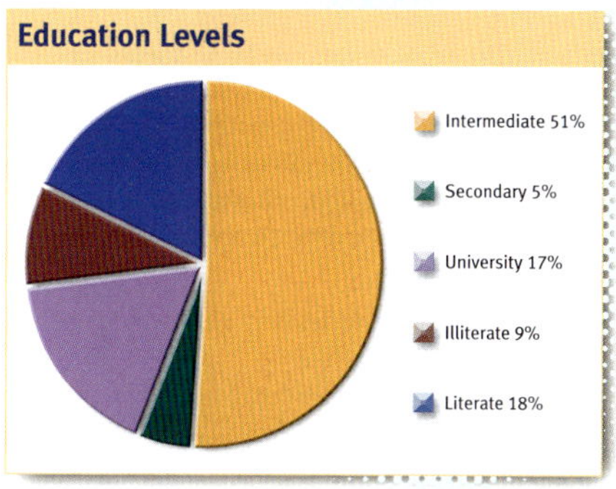

Source: Ministry of Planning

Local Time

The UAE is four hours ahead of UCT (Universal Co-ordinated Time – formerly known as GMT). There is no summer time saving when clocks are altered. Hence, when it is 12:00 midday in Abu Dhabi, it is 03:00 in New York, 08:00 in London, 13:30 in Delhi, and 17:00 in Tokyo (not allowing for any summer time saving in those countries).

Social & Business Hours

Other Options ➜ Business [p.98]

Social hours are very Mediterranean in style – in general, people get up early, often have an afternoon siesta and eat late in the evening. The attitude to time, especially in business, is often very different from the 'time is money' approach in other parts of the world. So, don't be frustrated if your business meeting takes place a day late – the 'Inshallah' (God willing) attitude prevails!

Traditionally, there was no concept of a weekend, although Friday has always been the holy day. In modern UAE, the weekend has established itself on different days, generally according to each company. Until recently, government offices had Thursday afternoon and Friday off. However, a 1998 ruling established a five day week for government offices and schools, which are now closed all day Thursday and Friday. Some private companies still take a half day Thursday and Friday, while others take Friday and Saturday as their weekend. Understandably, these differences cause difficulties, since companies may now be out of touch with international businesses for up to four days. Moreover, families may end up not necessarily sharing the same weekend.

Government offices are open from 07:30 - 13:30, Saturday to Wednesday. In the private sector, office hours vary between split shifts and straight shifts. Split shift days are generally 08:00 - 13:00, with offices reopening at either 15:00 or 16:00 and closing at 18:00 or 19:00. Straight shift days are usually 09:00 - 18:00, with an hour off in between for lunch.

Shop opening times are usually based on split shift hours, although outlets in many of the big shopping malls now remain open all day. Closing times are usually 22:00 or 24:00, while some food shops and petrol stations are open 24 hours a day. On Fridays, a few places are open all day, apart from prayer time (11:30 - 13:30), while stores in shopping malls only open in the afternoon from 12:00 or 14:00.

Embassies and consulates open from 08:45 - 13:30 everyday, but are closed on Fridays and, in most cases, Saturdays as well. However, they generally leave an emergency contact number on their answering machines.

During Ramadan, work hours in most public and some private organisations are reduced by two to three hours per day, and business definitely slows during this period. Many offices start work an hour or so later and shops are open much later at night. The more popular shopping malls are crowded at midnight and parking at that time is tough to find!

Public Holidays

Other Options ➜ Annual Events [p.44]

The Islamic calendar starts from the year 622 AD, the year of Prophet Mohammed's (Praise Be Upon Him) migration (Hijra) from Mecca to Al Madinah. Hence the Islamic year is called the Hijri year and dates are followed by AH (After Hijra).

The Hijri calendar is based on lunar months; there are 354 or 355 days in the Hijri year, which is divided into 12 lunar months, and is thus 11 days shorter than the Gregorian year.

As some holidays are based on the sighting of the moon and are not fixed dates on the Hijri calendar, the dates of Islamic holidays are notoriously imprecise, with holidays frequently being confirmed less than 24 hours in advance. Some non religious holidays, however, are fixed according to the Gregorian calendar.

The different emirates also have some different fixed holidays, such as the accession of HH Sheikh Zayed on August 6, which is celebrated only in Abu Dhabi. The number of days a holiday lasts is shown within brackets in the table. However, this applies to the public sector only,

Public Holidays – 2004

Holiday	Date	
New Year's Day (1)	Jan-01	Fixed
Eid Al Adha (4)	Feb-02	Moon
Islamic New Year's Day (1)	Feb-22	Moon
Propet Mohammed's Birthday (1)	May-02	Moon
Accession of HH Sheikh Zayed (1)	Aug-06	Fixed
Lailat Al Mi'Raj (1)	Sept-12	Moon
Ramadan begins	Oct-15	Moon
Eid Al Fitr (3)	Nov-14	Moon
UAE National Day (2)	Dec-02	Fixed

since not all listed holidays are observed by the private sector and often the public sector gets a day or two more.

Electricity & Water

Other Options → Utilities & Services [p.76]

Electricity and water services in Abu Dhabi are excellent and power cuts or water shortages are practically unheard of. Both of these utilities are provided by Abu Dhabi Water and Electricity Authority (known as ADWEA).

The electricity supply is 220/240 volts and 50 cycles. The socket type is the same as the three point British system. Most hotels and homes have adapters for electrical appliances.

The tap water is heavily purified and safe to drink, but most people prefer to drink the locally bottled mineral waters, of which there are several different brands available. Bottled water is usually served in hotels and restaurants.

Photography

Other Options → Camera Equipment [p.152]

Normal tourist photography is acceptable but, like anywhere in the world, it is courteous to ask permission before photographing people, particularly women. In general, photographs of government buildings, military installations, ports and airports should not be taken.

Environment

Climate

Abu Dhabi has a sub-tropical, arid climate and sunny blue skies, and high temperatures can be expected most of the year. Rainfall is infrequent and irregular, falling mainly in winter – November to March (12 cm per year). Temperatures range from a low of around 10° C (50° F), to a high of around 48° C (118° F) in the summer. The most pleasant time to visit is in the cooler winter months when temperatures are around 24° C (75° F) during the day and 13° C (56° F) at night.

During winter, occasional sandstorms occur when the wind (known as the 'shamal') whips the sand off the desert. More surprisingly, fog occasionally

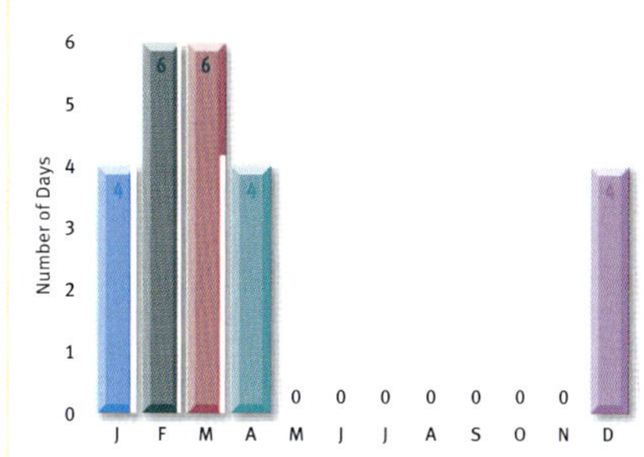

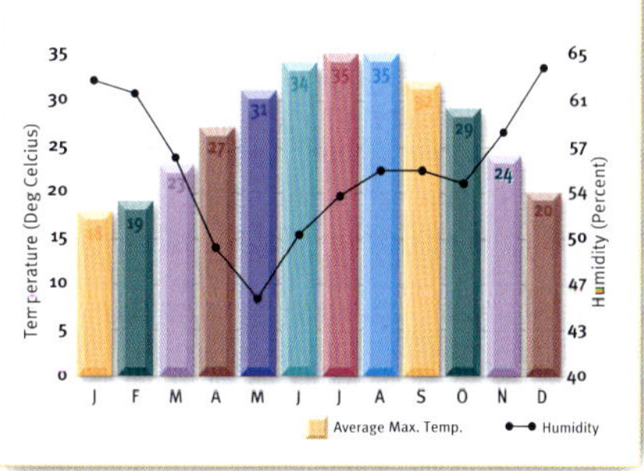

sets in on winter mornings, but by mid morning, the sun invariably burns the cloud away. The humidity can be a killer in the summer, approaching 100% – prepare to sweat!

Flora & Fauna

Other Options → Protection [p.14]
Plants & Trees [p.164]

As you would expect in a country with such an arid climate, the diversity in flora and fauna isn't as extensive as in other parts of the world. A substantial variety of life has, nevertheless, managed to adapt to the high temperatures and little rainfall.

In the city of Abu Dhabi, as in all the emirates to a lesser extent, the local municipality has an extensive 'greening' programme underway. For such an arid region, the areas along the roads are incredibly colourful, with grass, palm trees and flowers being watered around the clock and constantly maintained by an army of workers. The road from Abu Dhabi to Al Ain covers a

distance of 150 km and is green most of the way. The cities also boast a large number of attractive and well kept parks.

Sheikh Zayed was the chief architect behind the greening of the cities, and it is an ongoing process. In the south of the country at the oasis of Liwa on the edge of the Rub Al Khali, the objective is to 'push back' the desert. Each year the tarmac inches forward and each side of the road sees extensive agricultural projects established, that bring in employment, fresh produce and wealth to the region, as well as make for a more fertile and green environment.

Al Ain, the second city of the emirate, has won various international awards for the quality of its parks, gardens and roadsides, often beating far more fertile regions of the world. Without doubt, it lives up to its label as the 'Garden City'.

The entire region has about 3,500 endemic plants – quite amazing, considering the high salinity of the soil and the harsh environment. The date palm is the most obvious of the indigenous flora, and this provides wonderful seas of green, especially in the oases. Heading towards the mountains, flat topped acacia trees and wild grasses give a feel of African savannah. The deserts are often surprisingly green, even during the dry summer months, but it takes an experienced botanist to get the most out of the area.

Arabian Caracal (courtesy WWF)

Indigenous fauna includes the Arabian Leopard and the ibex, but sightings of them are extremely rare. Realistically, the only large animals you will see are camels and goats (often roaming dangerously close to the roads). Other desert life includes the sand cat, sand fox and desert hare, plus gerbils, hedgehogs, snakes and geckos. However, a visit to the Arabian Wildlife Centre in Sharjah guarantees a viewing of all the animals mentioned above.

Birdlife in the city is limited – this isn't the place for hearing a 'dawn chorus', unless you've been lucky in where you live. However, recent studies have shown that the number of species rises each year, due in part to the increasing lushness of the area. This is most apparent in the parks in spring and autumn, as the emirate lies on the route for birds migrating between Central Asia and East Africa.

Off the coast, the seas contain a rich abundance of marine life, including tropical fish, jellyfish, coral, the dugong ('sea cow') and sharks. Eight species of whales and seven species of dolphins have been recorded in UAE waters. Various breeds of turtle are also indigenous to the region, including endangered species of the loggerhead, green and hawksbill turtle. These may be seen by divers off both coasts. The best known local fish is hammour, which is a type of grouper and can be found on most restaurant menus.

Protection

The UAE's, and specifically Sheikh Zayed's, commitment to the environment is internationally recognised. At the Environment 2001 Conference and Exhibition in Abu Dhabi, a statement was made that the UAE would invest US$46 billion on projects related to the environment over the next ten years. Sheikh Zayed set up the Zayed International Prize for the Environment, and has already been awarded the World Wild Fund for Nature's Gold Panda Award.

Various organisations have been formed to protect the environment as well as to educate the population on the importance of environmental issues. The Environmental Research and Wildlife Development Agency or ERWDA (681 7171, www.erwda.gov.ae) was established in 1996 to assist the Abu Dhabi government in the conservation and management of the emirate's natural environment, resources, wildlife and biological diversity. In the GCC's 2002 - 2003 competition, ERWDA won the prize for best environmental achievements.

There is also an active branch of the World Wide Fund for Nature in Abu Dhabi (693 4510, www.panda.org). Working closely with the government, NGOs and businesses, the WWF recently awarded a 'Gift to the Earth' to the first internationally recognised marine protected area in the Arabian Gulf – the island of Qarnein (180 km northwest of Abu Dhabi).

In addition, Sir Bani Yas Island in Abu Dhabi has an internationally acclaimed breeding programme for endangered wildlife. The Arabian Wildlife Centre in Sharjah also has a similar and very successful programme for endangered wildlife, particularly the Arabian Leopard.

The UAE is party to international agreements on biodiversity, climate change, desertification, endangered species, hazardous wastes, marine dumping and ozone layer protection. In addition to emirate wide environmental controls, Abu Dhabi has strictly enforced laws governing the use of chemical insecticides.

Despite all the efforts being made, the UAE still faces some serious environmental issues. With very little rainfall to speak of in the past few years, the water table is at record low levels and desalination plants work overtime to satisfy a thirsty population, whilst also keeping the numerous parks and verges green. Desertification and beach pollution from oil spills are other areas of worry.

See Also: *Environmental Groups [p.210]*

Islam

The basis of Islam is the belief that there is only one God and that Prophet Mohammed (Peace Be Upon Him) is his messenger. There are five pillars of the faith, which all Muslims must follow: the Profession of Faith, Prayer, Charity, Fasting and Pilgrimage. Every Muslim is expected, at least once in his/her lifetime, to make the pilgrimage or 'Hajj' to the holy city of Mecca (also spelt Makkah) in Saudi Arabia.

Additionally, a Muslim is required to pray five times a day and the times vary according to the position of the sun. Most people go to a mosque to pray although it's not unusual to see them kneeling by the side of the road if one is not close by. It is not considered polite to stare at people praying, or to walk over prayer mats.

The modern day call to prayer through loudspeakers on the minarets of each mosque ensures that everyone knows it's time to pray. Friday is the holy day.

Culture & Lifestyle

Culture

Other options → Business [p.98]

Abu Dhabi's culture is firmly rooted in the Islamic traditions of Arabia. Islam is more than just a religion; it is a way of life that governs even the minutiae of everyday events, from what to wear to what to eat and drink. Thus, the culture and heritage of the UAE is tied to its religion. In parts of the world, Islamic fundamentalism has given the 'outside' world an extreme, blanket view of the religion. However, in contrast to this image, the UAE's culture is tolerant and welcoming; foreigners are free to practice their own religion, alcohol is served in hotels and the dress code is liberal. Women face relatively little discrimination and, contrary to the policies of neighbouring countries, are able to drive and walk around unescorted. Among the most highly prized virtues are courtesy and hospitality, and visitors are sure to be charmed by the genuine warmth and friendliness of the people.

Connected!

'Wasta' means connections. If you've got them, all power to you - they'll take you far! However, most people in Abu Dhabi don't have wasta - it is reserved for the select few who have somehow managed to establish the 'right' contacts, either through family or friends. It's pretty much the same as in any other country (very much like an old boys' network), only here it's more pronounced as rules and regulations aren't always set in stone.

The rapid economic development over the last 30 years has, in many ways, changed life in the Emirates beyond recognition. However, the country's rulers are very aware that their traditional heritage faces the danger of being eroded by the speed of development and increased access to outside cultures and material goods. They are, therefore, keen to promote cultural and sporting events that are representative of their past, such as falconry, camel racing and traditional dhow sailing. Ironically though, a large portion of local entertainment focuses less on traditional pastimes and more on shopping! Still, traditional aspects of life are apparent, most obviously in the clothes (see National Dress [p.18]). Arabic poetry, dances, songs and traditional art are encouraged, and weddings and celebrations are still colourful occasions of feasting and music.

Language

The official language of the country is Arabic, although English, Urdu and Hindi are spoken and, with some perseverance, understood. Arabic is the official business language, but English is widely used and most road and shop signs, restaurant menus etc, are in both languages. The further out of town you go, the more Arabic you will find, both written and spoken, on street and shop signs. See the facing page for a quick list of useful Arabic phrases to get you around town.

Arabic isn't the easiest language to pick up – or to pronounce. But if you can throw in a couple of words of Arabic here and there, you're more likely to receive a warmer welcome or at least a smile. Most people will help you out with your pronunciation – they're happy you're putting in the effort, so it certainly won't hurt to try, and definitely helps when dealing with officials of any sort.

Religion

Islam is the official religion of the UAE, but other religions are respected. Abu Dhabi has a variety of Christian churches: St Joseph's Roman Catholic Church, St George's Orthodox Church, St Andrew's Protestant Church, Evangelical Community Church and Arabic Evangelical Church. In Al Ain, there is St Mary's Church.

Mosque at Dusk

Ramadan

In Islam, Ramadan is the holy month in which Muslims commemorate the revelation of the Holy Koran (the holy book of Islam, also spelt Quran). It is a time of fasting when Muslims abstain from all food, drinks, cigarettes and unclean thoughts between dawn and dusk. In the evening, the fast is broken with the Iftar feast. Iftar timings are found in all the daily newspapers.

All over the city, festive Ramadan tents are filled to the brim each evening with people of all nationalities and religions enjoying shisha and traditional Arabic meze and sweets. In addition to the standard favourite shisha cafés and restaurants around town, the five star hotels erect special Ramadan tents for the month.

The timing of Ramadan is not fixed in terms of the western calendar, but each year it occurs approximately 11 days earlier than the previous year, with the start date depending on the sighting of the moon (see Public Holidays [p.12]). In 2004, Ramadan should commence around October 15th.

Non-Muslims are required to refrain from eating, drinking or smoking in public places during daylight hours as a sign of respect. Visitors and new residents should note that in Abu Dhabi, there is no sale of alcoholic beverages whatsoever in restaurants or hotels during the holy month of Ramadan or during any religious festival or holiday. Many venues are actually closed for the full month. In addition, entertainment such as live music is stopped and cinemas limit the daytime screenings of films.

Business hours tend to be shorter during this period, while shops usually open and close later. Expatriate women are advised to be more modest in their dress during this time.

Ramadan ends with a three day celebration and holiday called Eid Al Fitr, or 'Feast of the Breaking of the Fast'. Seventy days later is another Eid holiday and celebration called Eid Al Adha, or 'Feast of the Sacrifice' and this marks the end of the pilgrimage season to Mecca. For Muslims, Eid has similar connotations as Diwali for Hindus and Christmas for Christians.

Basic Arabic

General

Yes	na'am
No	la
Please	min fadlak (m)/min fadliki (f)
Thank you	shukran
Please (in offering)	tafaddal (m)/tafaddali (f)
Praise be to God	al-hamdu l-illah
God willing	in shaa'a l-laah

Greetings

Greeting (peace be upon you)	as-salaamu alaykom
Greeting (in reply)	wa alaykom is salaam
Good morning	sabah il-khayr
Good morning (in reply)	sabah in-nuwr
Good evening	masa il-khayr
Good evening (in reply)	masa in-nuwr
Hello	marhaba
Hello (in reply)	marhabtayn
How are you?	kayf haalak (m)/kayf haalik (f)
Fine, thank you	zayn, shukran (m)/zayna, shukran (f)
Welcome	ahlan wa sahlan
Welcome (in reply)	ahlan fiyk (m)/ahlan fiyki (f)
Goodbye	ma is-salaama

Introduction

My name is...	ismiy...
What is your name?	shuw ismak (m)/shuw ismik (f)
Where are you from?	min wayn inta (m)/min wayn inti (f)
I am from...	anaa min...
America	ameriki
Britain	braitani
Europe	oropi
India	al hindi

Questions

How many/much?	kam?
Where?	wayn?
When?	mata?
Which?	ayy?
How?	kayf?
What?	shuw?
Why?	laysh?
Who?	miyn?
To/for	ila
In/at	fee
From	min
And	wa
Also	kamaan
There isn't	maa fee

Taxi/Car Related

Is this the road to...	hadaa al tariyq ila...
Stop	kuf
Right	yamiyn
Left	yassar
Straight ahead	siydaa
North	shamaal
South	januwb
East	sharq
West	garb
Turning	mafraq
First	awwal
Second	thaaniy
Road	tariyq
Street	shaaria
Roundabout	duwwaar
Signals	ishaara
Close to	qarib min
Petrol station	mahattat betrol
Sea/beach	il bahar
Mountain/s	jabal/jibaal
Desert	al sahraa
Airport	mataar
Hotel	funduq
Restaurant	mata'am
Slow Down	schway schway

Accidents

Police	al shurtaa
Permit/licence	rukhsaa
Accident	Haadith
Papers	waraq
Insurance	ta'miyn
Sorry	aasif(m)/aasifa (f)

Numbers

Zero	sifr
One	waahad
Two	ithnayn
Three	thalatha
Four	araba'a
Five	khamsa
Six	sitta
Seven	saba'a
Eight	thamaanya
Nine	tiss'a
Ten	ashara
Hundred	miya
Thousand	alf

National Weddings

Weddings in the UAE are a serious and very large affair. Homes are lit from top to bottom with strings of white or yellow fairy lights and the festivities last up to two weeks. Men and women celebrate separately, normally in a hotel ballroom or convention centre, depending on the number of guests. High dowries and extravagant weddings may be a thing of the past though, as the government has placed a ceiling of Dhs.50,000 on dowries, and lavish weddings can result in a prison sentence or Dhs.500,000 fine!

The government sponsored Marriage Fund, based in Abu Dhabi, assists Nationals in everything to do with marriage - from counselling and financial assistance (long term loans up to Dhs.70,000 for UAE National men marrying UAE National women) to organising group weddings to lower costs. While marriage between a National man and a non National woman is legally permissible (but frowned upon), National women are not allowed to marry non-National men. One of the main aims of the marriage fund is to lessen the number of foreign marriages by UAE Nationals.

National Dress

On the whole, the national population still chooses to wear their traditional dress. For men this is the 'dishdash(a)' or 'khandura' – a white full length shirt dress, which is worn with a white or red checked headdress, known as a 'gutra'. This is secured with a black cord ('agal'). Sheikhs and important businessmen may also wear a thin black or gold robe or 'mishlah', over their dishdasha at important events, which is equivalent to the dinner jacket in Western culture.

In public, women wear the black 'abaya' – a long, loose black robe that covers their normal clothes – plus a headscarf called the 'sheyla'. The abaya is often of very sheer, flowing fabric and may be open at the front. Some women also wear a thin black veil hiding their face and/or gloves, and older women sometimes still wear a leather mask, known as a 'burkha', which covers the nose, brow and cheekbones. Underneath the abaya, women traditionally wear a long tunic over loose, flowing trousers ('sirwall'), which are often heavily embroidered and fitted at the wrists and ankles. However, these are used more by the older generation and modern women will often wear trousers or a long skirt beneath the abaya.

Sharjah has a Decency Law that penalises those who do not abide by a certain dress code and moral behaviour. 'Indecent dress' includes anything that exposes the stomach, back or legs above the knees. Tight fitting, transparent clothing is also not permitted, nor are acts of vulgarity, indecent noises or harassment. If you have offended the law, you will initially be given advice by the police on what decency is, and then warned to abide by the law in future. If the police find you breaking the law again, a more severe penalty will be imposed.

Food & Drink

Other Options → **Eating Out [p.219]**

Abu Dhabi offers pretty much every type of international cuisine imaginable. While most restaurants are located in hotels and are thus able to offer alcohol, some of the best places to eat are the small street side stands around town. Refer to the Going Out section for more details on everything available to quench both hunger and thirst.

Arabic Cuisine

Modern Arabic cuisine is a blend of many types of cooking, from Moroccan, Tunisian, Iranian, Egyptian to Afghani, but in Abu Dhabi, modern 'Arabic cuisine' invariably means Lebanese food. Sidewalk stands selling 'shawarma' (lamb or chicken sliced from a spit and served in pita bread) and 'falafel' (small savoury balls of deep fried beans) are worth a visit at least once. Generally, this cuisine is excellent for meat eaters and vegetarians alike. A popular starter is a selection of dishes known as 'meze', which is often a meal in its own right. It's a variety of appetisers served with pita bread, a green salad and radioactive pickles! Dishes can include 'humous' (ground chickpeas, oil and garlic), 'tabouleh' (parsley and cracked wheat salad with tomato etc), 'fatoush' (lettuce, tomatoes etc, with grilled Arabic bread) and 'fattayer' (small, usually hot pastries filled with cottage cheese and spinach).

Charcoal grilling is a popular style of cooking. However, a Ramadan favourite is 'khouzi' (whole lamb served on a bed of rice, mixed with nuts), an authentic local dish also served at the 'mansaf', a traditional, formal Bedouin dinner with dishes placed on the floor in the centre of a ring of seated guests. Other typical dishes include 'kibbeh' (deep fried mince, pine nuts and bulgur) or a variety of kebabs.

The meal ends with Lebanese sweets, which are delicious but extremely sweet. The most widely known are 'baklava' (filo pastry layered with honey and pistachio nuts) and 'umm Ali' or 'mother of Ali' in English, a dessert with layers of milk, bread, raisins and nuts.

Pork

Pork is not included on the Arabic menu. Do not underestimate how taboo this meat is to a Muslim. Its restriction is not just in eating the meat, but also in the preparation and service. Thus to serve pork, restaurants need a separate fridge, equipment, preparation and cooking areas etc, while supermarkets need a separate pork area in the shop and separate storage facilities. Images of pigs can also cause offence.

Additionally, in Islam, it is forbidden to consume the blood or meat of any animal that has not been slaughtered in the correct manner. The meat of animals killed in accordance with the Islamic code is known as 'halaal'.

Alcohol

Alcohol is only served in licensed outlets that are associated with hotels (ie, restaurants and bars), a few clubs (such as, golf clubs) and associations. Restaurants outside of hotels that are not part of a club or association are not permitted to serve alcohol.

Nevertheless, permanent residents who are non Muslims can obtain alcohol for consumption at home without any difficulty. All they have to do is get a permit.

See Also: *Liquor Licence [p.56]; Alcohol Outlets [p.149]*

Shisha

Throughout the Middle East, smoking the traditional 'shisha' (water pipe) is a popular and relaxing pastime, usually savoured in a local café while chatting with friends. Shishas are also known as hookah pipes or hubbly bubbly, but are properly called a 'nargile'.

Shishas

Shisha pipes can be smoked with a variety of aromatic flavours, such as strawberry, grape, apple etc, and the experience is quite unlike smoking a normal cigarette or cigar. The smoke is softened by the water, creating a much more soothing effect. This is one of those things in life that should be tried at least once and preferably during Ramadan, under the festive tents set up throughout the city, filled with people of all nationalities and the fragrant smell of shisha tobacco.

Entering Abu Dhabi

Visas

Other options → Residence Visa [p.52]
Entry Visa [p.50]

Visa requirements for entering the UAE vary greatly between different nationalities, and regulations should always be checked before travelling, since the details can change with little or no warning.

All visitors except Arab Gulf Co-operation Council nationals (Bahrain, Kuwait, Qatar, Oman and Saudi Arabia) require a visa. However, citizens of the UK (with right of abode in the UK) will be granted a free visit visa on arrival. Although the visa is stamped for 30 days, you can stay for 60 and renew once for an additional period of 30 days for Dhs.500. For renewal, apply at the Immigration Department on Saeed bin Tahnoon Street in Abu Dhabi (446 2244), and Aditaba Road near Dubai Islamic Bank in Al Ain (03 762 5555/751 0000). After the third month, you have the choice of flying out of the country on a 'visa run' (see below).

> ***Dhs.100 Visa on Arrival***
>
> *Andorra, Australia, Austria, Belgium, Brunei, Canada, Cyprus, Denmark, Finland, France, Germany, Greece, Hong Kong, Iceland, Ireland, Italy, Japan, Liechtenstein, Luxembourg, Malaysia, Malta, Monaco, the Netherlands, New Zealand, Norway, Portugal, San Marino, Singapore, Spain, Sweden, Switzerland, United States and Vatican.*

The visit visa period has recently been reduced for citizens of 33 countries (listed above). These travellers may now enter the UAE without a prior visa for a one month non renewable stay instead of three months. The Cabinet also decided to impose a charge of Dhs.100 per visa to be collected on entry to the UAE through land, seaport and airport entry points.

Expat residents of the AGCC who meet certain criteria may obtain a non renewable 30 day visa on arrival. Residents of Oman of certain nationalities may enter the UAE on a free of charge entry permit.

Tourist nationalities (such as those from Eastern and Western Europe, Thailand, China and South Africa) may obtain a 30 day, non renewable tourist visa sponsored by a local entity, such as a hotel or tour operator, before entry into the UAE. Other visitors may apply for an entry service permit in advance (for 14 days exclusive of arrival/departure days), valid for use within 14 days of the date of issue, or for a 60 day visit visa (renewable once for a total stay of 90 days) sponsored by a local company. This visit visa costs Dhs.120 plus a visa delivery fee of Dhs.10. Allow two weeks for processing.

For those travelling onwards to a destination other than that of original departure, a special transit visa (up to 96 hours) may be obtained free of charge through any airline carrier operating in the UAE.

Visa Renewals

Visit visas may be renewed for a total stay of up to 90 days. Renewals are usually made by paying for a month's extension (Dhs.500) at the Immigration Department, Saeed bin Tahnoon Street in Abu Dhabi (446 2244), and Aditaba Road, near Dubai Islamic Bank in Al Ain (03 762 5555). After the third month, you must either fly out of the country on a 'visa run' (see below) and collect a new visit visa on return to the airport, or leave the country and arrange a new visit visa from your home country.

The Airport

At Abu Dhabi airport, the aircraft are uniquely arranged around a circular satellite, so you won't have to walk far to reach Immigration and the luggage area.

Need cash? There are ATM machines dotted around the airport in both the arrivals and departures areas. Currency exchanges are in the departures area and outside the Customs area in arrivals.

If you're lucky enough to have friends or family collect you from the airport, you'll avoid the hassles of fighting for a taxi with all the other passengers who have just arrived in Abu Dhabi. If not, find the curb and, along with everyone else, shove your way into the first available cab. It costs about Dhs.65 for a trip from the airport into Abu Dhabi city. You can choose to take one of the local taxis queuing outside or, for a more comfortable ride, go to the Al Ghazal Taxi office in the arrivals lounge and travel in a Mercedes to the town centre (you can also pre-book this service on 444 7787).

A multiple entry visa is available for business visitors who have a relationship with a local business. It is valid for six months from the date of issue for visits of a maximum of 30 days, costs Dhs.1,000, and should be applied for after entering the UAE on a visit visa.

Airlines may require confirmation (a photocopy is acceptable) that a UAE visa is held before check in at the airport. If you have sponsorship from a UAE entity, ensure they fax you a copy of the visa before the flight. The original is held at the Abu Dhabi International Airport for collection before passport control. Your passport should have a minimum of three months validity left. Israeli nationals will not be issued visas.

Costs: *Some companies may levy a maximum of Dhs.50 extra in processing charges for arranging visas.*

Note: *Visit visas are valid for 30 or 60 days, not one or two calendar months. If you overstay, there is a Dhs.100 fine for each day overstayed.*

Warning: *If you have an Israeli stamp in your passport you will not be allowed to enter the UAE.*

'Visa Run'

The 'visa run' (or 'visa change' flight) basically involves exiting and re-entering the country to gain an exit stamp and a new entry stamp in your passport. You can simply fly to a neighbouring country and back into Abu Dhabi. Driving over the border into Oman is also an option as you can get your passport stamped at the UAE control post in Hatta.

The flight is invariably to Doha or Muscat and returns an hour or so later. Passengers remain in transit and hence, do not need a visa for the country they fly to. Gulf Air (633 2600) and Qatar Airways (632 5777) fly to Doha daily, with a return ticket costing about Dhs.500. British Airways (622 4540) and Gulf Air fly to Muscat and back, and a return trip costs around Dhs.600. The low price is only offered for the visa run flight and is not available if you want to spend any time in the country to which you are travelling. There is no visa flight service offered from Al Ain.

These flights are the cheapest option for those who need to change their visa status after their residency application has been approved by Immigration.

In February, 2004, regulations changed following a Kish Airlines visa run flight crash, and it is now not necessary to leave the country. Some companies, however, still prefer to send employees out of the country as the alternative option is more expensive.

The visa run is also a classic opportunity to stock up on good value duty free, and there are sales outlets in both the departure and arrival halls of the airports.

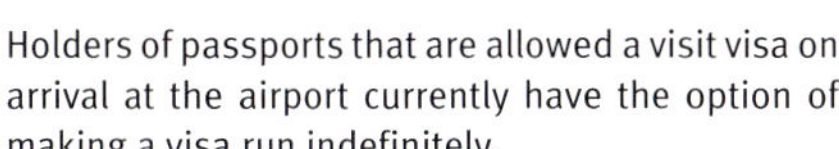

Holders of passports that are allowed a visit visa on arrival at the airport currently have the option of making a visa run indefinitely.

Until 2000, the visa run was an option for all nationalities with sponsors willing to arrange for a new visit visa. Now, unless the situation reverts, a visa run is only possible for nationalities who can gain a visa stamp on arrival at the airport. This was implemented in a crackdown on people working in the country illegally without sponsorship or residency.

Meet & Greet

In keeping with the Arabian tradition of hospitality, meet and greet services are offered at Abu Dhabi airport to assist passengers with airport formalities.

Golden Class Service assists both departing and arriving passengers (575 7466 or fax 575 8070). This can be particularly helpful to passengers who fit the categories of unaccompanied children, the disabled or elderly, although anyone can use the service. Golden Class offer a dedicated check in counter, help with Immigration, and use of facilities in the VIP lounge, which includes use of the health club or secretarial services in the Business Centre. Individual annual membership and company memberships are also available for the year. For individuals, prices range from Dhs.60. For groups of two or more travelling together, the charge is Dhs.45 each, and children from 2 - 12 years are Dhs.25 each for arrival or departure. Entrance to the VIP lounge is a further Dhs.30 per person. Additional offers include a limousine service and fresh flowers for arrivals. This useful service may be booked and paid for at the City Terminal opposite the Beach Hotel.

Customs

No customs duty is levied on personal effects entering Abu Dhabi. It is forbidden to import drugs and pornographic items.

At Abu Dhabi International Airport, after your bags are collected in the arrivals hall, they are x-rayed. Videos, DVDs, CDs books and magazines are sometimes checked, and suspect items, usually movies, may be temporarily confiscated for the material to be approved. Unless it is offensive, it can be collected at a later date. The airport duty free has a small sales outlet in the arrivals hall.

There has been talk of restrictions on the import or export of large amounts of any currency since the events of 11 September 2001. We recommend that you check this out before you try it! Additionally, a new anti money laundering law will also, eventually, come into effect, which not only penalises individuals who violate the law, but also financial institutions. The penalty for money laundering will be a prison sentence of up to seven years or a maximum fine of Dhs.300,000. The limit for undeclared cash that you can carry with you into the country is Dhs.40,000.

Duty Free Allowances

- Cigarettes – 2,000
- Cigars – 400
- Tobacco – 2 kg
- Alcohol (non-Muslim adults only) – 2 litres of spirits and 2 litres of wine
- Perfumes – a 'reasonable' amount

Travellers' Info

Health Requirements

No health certificates are required for entry to the Emirates, except for visitors who have been in cholera or yellow fever infected areas in the previous 14 days. However, it is always wise to check health requirements before departure as restrictions may vary depending upon the situation at the time.

Malarial mosquitoes are not really a problem in the cities, although they do exist, mainly around the wadis and the mountain pool areas where it's damp. Long term residents rarely take malaria tablets, but short term visitors who plan to visit the countryside during mosquito season may be advised to take them. Check out the requirements a month or so before leaving your home country.

Health Care

Other Options → Health [p.84]

The quality of medical care in the Emirates is generally regarded as quite high and visitors should have little trouble obtaining appropriate treatment, whether privately or, in case of an emergency, from the government run hospitals. Tourists and non residents are strongly recommended to arrange private medical insurance before travelling, since private medical care can be very expensive.

There are no specific health risks facing visitors, though the climate can be harsh, especially during the summer months. It's advisable to

drink plenty of water (replace lost salts with energy drinks or salty snacks), and cover up when out in the sun. Use the appropriate factor sunscreen – sunburn, heat stroke and heat exhaustion are quite unpleasant.

Most medicines are readily available at pharmacies and many without prescription – even antibiotics. Each emirate has at least one pharmacy open 24 hours a day. Check the Gulf News for information. Dial 998 or 999 for ambulance service.

Travel Insurance

All visitors to the Emirates should have travel insurance – just in case. Choose a reputable insurer, and a plan that suits your needs and activities that you plan to do while in the UAE. Make sure this insurance also covers 'blood money' (see [p.33]) in the unfortunate event of an accident involving a death where you are found at fault.

Female Visitors

Women should face few, if any, problems while travelling in the UAE. Single female travellers who don't want extra attention should avoid wearing tight fitting clothing and should steer clear of lower end hotels and seedy nightclubs. No matter what, most females receive some unwanted stares at some time or another, particularly on the public beaches. If you can ignore it, you'll save yourself some aggravation! The police are very helpful and respectful – call them if you face any unwanted attention or hassles.

Travelling with Children

Luggage, tickets, passports... kids?

Travelling at the best of times can be stressful. Add the responsibility of looking after the kids and you have a recipe for disaster. Avoid this danger by delegating one parent to be in charge of the bags and the other in charge of the kids – before setting off on your travels.

Abu Dhabi is a great place for kids of all ages. Parks and amusement centres abound, and if that's not enough for the little ones, there's always the beach. The Activities section will give a better idea of what there is to do with kids, as will the *Family Explorer (Dubai & Abu Dhabi)*.

Hotels and shopping malls are well geared up for children, offering everything from babysitting services to kids' activities. Restaurants, on the other hand, have children's menus but tend not to have many high chairs; it's best to check when making reservations. Discounted rates for children are common – just ask.

Disabled Visitors

Most of Abu Dhabi's five star hotels have wheelchair facilities but, in general, facilities for the disabled are very limited, particularly at tourist attractions. Wheelchair ramps are often really nothing more than delivery ramps, hence the steep angles. When asking if a location has wheelchair access, make sure it really does – an escalator is considered 'wheelchair access' to some! The Abu Dhabi International Airport is equipped for disabled travellers (see Golden Class Service [p.21]). As for parking, good luck! Handicapped parking spaces do exist, but are often used by ignorant drivers who don't need the facility.

Hotels with specially adapted rooms for the disabled include: Le Royal Meridien Abu Dhabi, Al Diar Gulf Hotel & Resort, Crowne Plaza, Millennium Hotel, Hotel InterContinental, Hotel InterContinental (Al Ain).

Dress Code

For visitors to the country, lightweight summer clothing is suitable for most of the year, but something slightly warmer may be needed for the winter months. Be sure to take some sort of jacket or sweater when visiting hotels or the cinema, as the air conditioning can be pretty fierce.

Although the attitude towards dress is fairly liberal throughout the Emirates, Abu Dhabi is rather more conservative than neighbouring Dubai. There still isn't much that you can't wear but, as in all countries, a healthy amount of respect for local customs doesn't go amiss, especially when shopping or generally sightseeing. Like anywhere in the world, the rural areas have a more conservative attitude than in the cities. Short or tight clothing may be worn, but it will attract attention – most of it unwelcome. For ladies, it is advisable to wear short sleeved rather than sleeveless tops and dresses, especially if travelling alone by local taxi. During the day, as in any place with loads of sun, good quality sunglasses, hats and buckets of sunscreen are needed to avoid the lobster look!

In the evenings, the restaurants and clubs usually have a mixture of styles – western, Arabic and Asian – anything goes. Again, ladies are advised to take a shawl or jacket, not only for the journey home, but also because of the cold blasts from the air conditioning.

Dos and Don'ts

Do make the most of your stay in Abu Dhabi. Have fun, but don't break the law. It's a simple and easy rule, and common sense will keep you out of trouble. In the UAE, drugs are illegal and carry a jail sentence. If you're caught bringing drugs into the country, you will be charged with trafficking which can result in a life sentence. Pornography of any sort is also illegal and will be confiscated immediately.

The best rule of thumb is to respect the local laws, culture and Muslim sensibilities of the UAE; remember that you are a visitor and treat the local population with the same respect you'd expect back home.

Safety

While the crime rate in Abu Dhabi is very low, a healthy degree of caution should still be exercised. Keep your valuables and travel documents locked in your hotel room or in the hotel safe. When in crowds, be discreet with your money and your wallet; don't carry large amounts of cash on you and don't trust strangers offering to double your money with magic potions. Money and gem related scams are on the increase – be warned!

With a multitude of driving styles converging on Abu Dhabi's roads, navigating the streets either on foot or in a vehicle can be a challenge. Here are some quick tips to make your experience on the streets safer: if your taxi driver is driving too aggressively, tell him to slow down; cross the roads only at designated pedestrian crossings, and before you cross, make sure all cars have actually stopped for you; learn the rules of the road before getting behind the wheel and drive defensively; make sure you have insurance!

Lost/Stolen Property

To avoid a great deal of hassle if your personal documents go missing, make sure you keep one photocopy with friends or family back home, and one copy in a secure place such as your hotel room safe.

If your valuables do go missing, check with your hotel first, or if you've lost something in a taxi, call the taxi company's lost and found department. There are a lot of honest people in Abu Dhabi who will return found items. If you've had no luck, then call the Abu Dhabi Police to report the loss or theft; you'll be advised on the next steps to follow. If you've lost your passport, your next stop will be your embassy or consulate. Refer to [p.104] for a list of all embassies and consulates in Abu Dhabi.

Abu Dhabi Tourist Info

Abu Dhabi does not have any overseas tourist offices. However within their respective areas, the Al Ain Economic Development and Tourism Promotion Authority (03 765 5444) and the Abu Dhabi Chamber of Commerce Information Centre (800 2282) will both be able to provide details of current local events etc.

Places to Stay

Visitors to Abu Dhabi and the UAE will find an extensive choice of places to stay, from hotels to hotel apartments, youth hostels and even an eco-tourist hotel (the Al Maha resort, located among the dunes between Dubai and Al Ain).

The growth in the number of hotels and hotel apartments is constantly on the rise and you can expect excellent service and facilities – at least at the higher end of the market.

Some hotels offer to sponsor those needing an entry visa. However, the visitor is then expected to stay at the hotel for 3 - 5 nights.

Hotels

Although the choice of good quality, cheap hotels, is limited, visitors can be assured of an excellent selection at the higher end of the market.

Hotels in Abu Dhabi are mostly located around the northern end of the island near the Corniche. The journey from the airport to the centre takes about 40 minutes and a taxi ride to most hotels will cost Dhs.70 in specially registered airport taxis. Larger hotels offer an airport shuttle service. Road transport in Abu Dhabi is usually pretty fast and the majority of journeys on the island will only be of 10 - 15 minutes duration, costing about Dhs.5 - 10.

Abu Dhabi City 5 Star Hotels

Abu Dhabi Airport Hotel
Map Ref → 2-B2

Situated at the Abu Dhabi International Airport, this convenient stopover is a great bonus for travellers. Having expanded in 2002, the hotel offers all the facilities you would expect. There are five bars/restaurants, a well equipped children's play area and a Nautilus gym to work out in while you wait for your onward flight.

Al Diar Capital Hotel
Map Ref → 8-B2

Now a part of the Al Diar Hotel Group, the Capital Hotel opened in late 2002. Well positioned in the centre of Abu Dhabi, it offers 140 standard/deluxe rooms and 60 executive suites (with an equipped kitchenette). The hotel also boasts seven bars and restaurants, including the happening nightspot, Rock Bottom Café.

Beach Rotana Hotel & Towers
Map Ref → 4-B3

This luxury hotel has recently undergone major expansion. Now boasting a conference centre and additional luxury sea facing rooms (bringing the total to 558), it also offers a plethora of dining options from Trader Vic's to Italian, Japanese, German and Lebanese. Direct access to the Abu Dhabi Mall is an added bonus.

Crowne Plaza
Map Ref → 8-C1

Situated in the heart of the city and only minutes' walking distance from Abu Dhabi's shopping district, this hotel also won the Quality Excellence Award in 2000. Some of their rooms are equipped for disabled travellers. Restaurants include the popular Heroes Diner, and the rooftop pool offers stunning views of the city.

Emirates Palace
Map Ref → 10-D4

This Arabian style palace will open in December 2004. It will have 12 restaurants, 390 rooms and suites and house the most advanced conference facilities in the UAE. The palace, equipped with first class leisure facilities, will be set within 200 acres of landscaped gardens and situated alongside 1.3 km of sandy beach.

Hilton Baynunah Tower
Map Ref → 9-A2

Undoubtedly one of the most impressive towers on the Corniche, the Hilton Baynunah Tower has the accolade of being the tallest residential complex in Abu Dhabi. Forty storeys of blue glass house deluxe suites, a restaurant/coffee shop, a health club and an indoor pool with stunning views.

Hilton International Abu Dhabi
Map Ref → 10-C2

Conveniently located near Abu Dhabi's financial and business district, the Hilton was refurbished in 2000 and now has 350 guestrooms with first class executive floors. However, it's the Hiltonia Beach Club and the famous Hemingway's and Jazz Bar nightspots, along with nine other restaurants and bars that make this hotel a favourite.

Hotel InterContinental
Map Ref → 10-C1

Adjacent to the marina, this hotel is surrounded by lush parks and gardens. With 5 restaurants, 4 bars and 330 deluxe rooms offering views of the city and the Arabian Gulf, this ageing hotel draws many conference and business visitors. Located out of the city centre, some of the outlets here are definitely worth the trek.

Le Meridien Abu Dhabi
Map Ref → 7-D1

Renovated in 1998, this hotel has a vast choice in accomodation, from the standard five star rooms to studios, residence, diplomatic and deluxe suites, and even a presidential suite. However, the hotel is best known amongst residents for its modern health club and spa, private beach, and Culinary Village with excellent food and beverage outlets.

Le Royal Meridien Abu Dhabi
Map Ref → 8-B2

Recently taken over by Le Meridien Hotels, this landmark, known to most as the Abu Dhabi Grand, has 187 rooms/suites, most of which are Corniche and sea facing. Originally opened in 1993, current refurbishments are due to finish in 2004. Offering spectacular views, it also has the only revolving restaurant in the capital.

Abu Dhabi City 5 Star Hotels

Millennium Hotel
Map Ref → 8-C2

The modern Millennium Hotel, located near the famous Corniche, has great views of the city. It has 325 elegantly decorated rooms and 3 restaurants serving Moroccan, Italian and international cuisine. However, the hotel is more widely known for opening Abu Dhabi's first ever champagne & cigar bar, Cristal.

Sheraton Abu Dhabi
Map Ref → 8-A3

Situated on the Corniche, the Sheraton has recently undergone renovations and is a favourite dining venue in Abu Dhabi with both residents as well as business travellers. Apart from the 259 rooms, most with a sea view, their Italian restaurant, La Mamma, draws many regulars. It also has a private beach and health club.

Sands Hotel
Map Ref → 8-C1

Previously known as the Holiday Inn, this hotel reopened as the Sands Hotel in 1996. Located in the city centre with 253 rooms/suites, it has convenient access to the business district as well as both the Abu Dhabi and Marina Malls. The Sands has six restaurants and bars, including Chequers, La Piazza and Imperial Chinese.

Beach Rotana Hotel & Towers

Al Ain City 5 Star Hotels

Al Ain Rotana Hotel
Map Ref → 14-E4

Set in the heart of the garden city, this hotel allows easy access to Al Ain's tourist attractions. The 100 spacious rooms, suites and chalets are comfortable and the fitness centre is state-of-the-art. On the cuisine front, their restaurants cover everything from Lebanese to the ever popular Polynesian Trader Vic's.

Hotel InterContinental Al Ain
Map Ref → 15-E4

A recent multi-million dollar refurbishment has transformed this hotel into one of the most impressive inland resorts in the UAE. Landscaped gardens, swimming pools, guestrooms, deluxe villas and a Royal Villa with a private jacuzzi, along with many restaurants and bars only make this a great leisure retreat.

Hilton Al Ain
Map Ref → 15-C4

Located near the heart of Al Ain, this ageing hotel, built in 1971, is a base from which to explore the zoo, museum, Jebel Hafeet and the Hili Tombs. The 202 guestrooms, suites and villas look over landscaped gardens, and the five bars and restaurants, floodlit tennis/squash courts, a health club and a nine hole golf course offer plenty to do.

Mercure Grand Jebel Hafeet
Map Ref → 17-B4

Having taken seven years to build, thanks to its precarious location on Jebel Hafeet, the Mercure Grand finally opened its doors in 2002. Simply decorated rooms offer the best views over Al Ain. Diners at Le Belvedere can admire stunning vistas of the city at night, as can those out for a stroll through the hotel gardens below.

Abu Dhabi City 4 Star Hotels

Al Ain Palace Hotel
Map Ref → 8-B3

The Al Ain Palace is one of Abu Dhabi's more established hotels (fondly known as the 'Ally Pally'). It offers international restaurants and theme bars, 110 deluxe rooms and suites plus self contained studios and chalet style rooms. Situated on the waterfront with a private beach, it's a good base from where to discover Abu Dhabi.

Al Diar Dana Hotel
Map Ref → 4-B4

Located in the tourist club district a short way away from the new Abu Dhabi Mall, this hotel has 112 spacious rooms, each with their own kitchenette for self sufficiency coupled with the perks of a hotel. On the dining front, it offers a choice of European pub, pizzeria, karaoke bar, and 49ers (the only Wild West rooftop restaurant and bar).

Al Diar Gulf Hotel & Resort
Map Ref → 1-D3

This resort offers a range of amenities to distinguish it from others. Opened in 1977, it has 273 rooms and 4 restaurants, and boasts the largest beach on the island. The hotel's Palm Beach Club offers every activity imaginable, from numerous water sports to tennis, squash and even mini golf – great for family vacations.

Al Diar Palm Hotel
Map Ref → 5-A2

Situated near the shopping districts, this hotel comprises 72 apartment style suites offering more than just hotel facilities. All rooms are spacious and have a kitchen equipped with a washer/dryer, fridge and cooker – great for extended stays. There's also a coffee shop on the ground floor.

Al Diar Regency
Map Ref → 8-D2

Situated close to the business district, the guestrooms and suites have the option of sea or city view balconies and all are equipped with kitchenettes. A business centre is provided for the high flyers, along with a conference hall. The in-house restaurants and pubs (plus the Karaoke Club) are an ideal retreat from the busy city life.

Al Maha Rotana
Map Ref → 8-B1

Located near the Corniche, these studios and residential suites are modern and good value for money. With all the conveniences of a hotel, they offer an apartment style stay with your own kitchen/microwave and in-room laundry facilities. For a quick coffee, the City Café is a good choice.

Grand Continental Flamingo Hotel
Map Ref → 8-B2

Open for five years, this 'boutique' hotel looks and feels pretty much the same as other four star hotels in Abu Dhabi. The many rooms and the Flamingo Club showcase views of the city, but it may be the popular Peppino's restaurant that attracts the crowds. A pub and international restaurant caters mostly to guests and lunch diners.

Howard Johnson Diplomat Hotel
Map Ref → 8-B2

This hotel is decent value for money. Repackaged as the Howard Johnson in 2000, it has 125 apartment style rooms and 20 suites, all above average in size and each with a kitchenette for self sufficiency – good for longer staying guests. The hotel has over 11 food/entertainment outlets including the European pub, the Cellar.

Khalidia Palace Hotel
Map Ref → 10-E2

This hotel is a kid's holiday come true. Apart from the 120 rooms and suites, they have beach chalets that comprise a kitchen, private garden and direct beach access. The children can enjoy the mini zoo, bouncy castles and go-karts as well as the usual water sports. For the adults, there are four restaurants and a health club.

Mafraq Hotel
Map Ref → UAE-A4

Built in 1996 and conveniently located 10 minutes from Abu Dhabi International Airport, and 20 minutes from the city centre, this quiet hotel featuring 120 rooms and four suites offers relaxed, landscaped surroundings and a decent range of good value restaurants.

Dhs.100 ~ € 22

Hotels

Five Star	Beach Access	Phone	Map	Double	Email
Abu Dhabi Airport Hotel	–	575 7377	2-B2	506	airphotl@emirates.net.ae
Al Diar Capital Hotel	–	678 7700	8-B2	348	adcapthtl@emirates.net.ae
Beach Rotana Hotel & Towers	✔	644 3000	4-B3	858	beach.hotel@rotana.com
Crowne Plaza	–	621 0000	8-C1	522	reservation@cpauh.co.ae
Emirates Palace	✔	n/a	10-D4	n/a	info.emiratespalace@kempinski.com
Hilton Baynunah Tower	–	632 7777	9-A2	766	baynunah@emirates.net.ae
Hilton International Abu Dhabi	✔	681 1900	10-C2	696	reservationsabudhabi@hilton.com
Hotel InterContinental	✔	666 6888	10-C1	1102	auhha-reservation@interconti.com
Le Meridien Abu Dhabi	✔	644 6666	7-D1	1300	reservations@lemeridienabudhabi.ae
Le Royal Meridien Hotel	–	674 2020	8-B2	580	info@leroyalmeridien-abudhabi.com
Millennium Hotel	–	626 2700	8-C2	1032	sales.abudhabi@mill-cop.com
Sands Hotel	–	633 5335	8-C1	406	sandshot@emirates.net.ae
Sheraton Abu Dhabi	✔	677 3333	8-A3	766	reservations.abu-dhabiuae@sheraton.com
Al Ain Rotana Hotel	–	03 754 5111	14-E4	406	alain.hotel@rotana.com
Hilton Al Ain	–	03 768 6666	15-C4	754	mohamed.fathi@hilton.com
Hotel InterContinental Al Ain	–	03 768 6686	15-E4	406	alain@intercont.com
Mercure Grand Jebel Hafeet	–	03 783 8888	17-B4	638	resa@mercure-alain.com
Four Star					
Al Ain Palace Hotel	–	679 4777	8-B3	575	aphsales@emirates.net.ae
Al Diar Dana Hotel	–	645 6000	4-B4	350	danahtl@emirates.net.ae
Al Diar Gulf Hotel & Resort	✔	441 4777	1-D3	350	adglfhtl@emirates.net.ae
Al Diar Palm Hotel	–	642 0900	5-A2	350	diarpalm@emirates.net.ae
Al Diar Regency Hotel	–	676 5000	8-D2	350	regencyh@emirates.net.ae
Grand Continental Flamingo Hotel	–	626 2200	8-B2	754	grndconh@emirates.net.ae
Howard Johnson Diplomat Hotel	–	671 0000	8-B2	290	diplomathojo@hotmail.com
Khalidia Palace Hotel	✔	666 2470	10-B2	350	kphresv@emirates.net.ae
Mafraq Hotel	–	582 2666	UAE-A4	522	mafraq@emirates.net.ae
Novotel Centre Hotel	–	633 3555	8-D2	550	fom@novatel-abudhabi.ae
Al Maha Rotana Suites	–	610 6666	8-B1	348	reservations.almaha@rotana.com
Dhafra Beach Hotel	✔	877 1600	na	638	dafrahtl@emirates.net.ae
Liwa Hotel	–	882 2000	na	350	liwahtl@emirates.net.ae
Mirfa Hotel	–	883 3030	na	255	secmirfa@emirates.net.ae
Al Jazira Beach Resort	✔	562 9100	na	400	info@jaziraresort.net
Al Hamra Residence	–	678 8000	8-B1	350	ahpr@emirates.net.ae
Three Star					
Al Diar Mina Hotel	–	678 1000	8-A2	319	regencyh@emirates.net.ae
International Rotana Inn	–	677 9900	8-A2	232	intlhtl@emirates.net.ae
Emirates Plaza Hotel	–	672 2000	7-E2	350	eph@emirates.net.ae
Zakher Hotel	–	627 5300	8-B2	265	zakhotel@emirates.net.ae
Al Shana Hotel	–	563 8557	na	225	shariah@emirates.net.ae
Saba Hotel	–	644 8333	8-A1	225	rameedxb@emirates.net.ae
Ain Al Fayda	–	03 783 8333	na	165	na

Hotel Apartments

Five Star	Phone	Map	1 B/room (Weekly)	2 B/room (Weekly)	Email
Al Hamra Residence	678 8000		2,450	4,200	ahpr@emirates.net.ae
Al Maha Rotana Suites	610 6666		3,857	n/a	reservations.almaha@rotana.com
Al Rawda Rotana Suites	445 7111		3,045	n/a	alrawda.suites@rotana.com
Beach Rotana Hotel & Towers	644 3000		n/a	n/a	res.beach@rotana.com
Baynunah Residence	632 7777		3,255	5,684	dawood.ismail@hilton.com
Corniche Residence	627 6000		3,240	8,100	cornicheresidence@hilton.com
Corniche Towers Residence	681 0088		1,925	n/a	kassells@kassellsroyalresidence.ae
Khalidia Palace Hotel Apartments	666 2470		4,200	n/a	kphauh@emirates.net.ae
Platinum Residence	634 4463		3,150	n/a	n/a
Sheraton Residence Abu Dhabi	666 6220		5,250	n/a	sherresa@emirates.net.ae
Al Jazira Residence	632 1100		n/a	2,800	ajr@emirates.net.ae
Al Salam Residence	641 7070		1,400	n/a	alsalamresidence@uaemail.com
Al Shurooq Residence	678 6913		1,400	n/a	n/a
Habara House	443 1010		1,400	n/a	n/a
Oasis Residence	641 7000		1,225	n/a	n/a
Park Residence	674 2000		1,400	n/a	parkres@emirates.net.ae

Note The above prices are peak season published rack rates and are inclusive of tax and service charge. Many hotels offer a discount off the rack rate, if asked. Peak or high season is from October - April (except during Ramadan. Refer to Ramadan and Public Hoildays [p.12] for further details).

In the deluxe category, the apartments are often associated with hotels and have excellent recreational facilities. Although many establishments have 2 bedroom apartments they are not typically rented on a weekly basis. Depending on occupancy, establishments may be willing to negotiate a weekly rate. In the standard category it is more usual to find studio apartments rather than 1 bedroom, so expect them to be smaller than those available in the deluxe category.

Sunset over Emirates Palace

In Al Ain there are four main hotels, the Hilton, the InterContinental, the Al Ain Rotana and The Mercure Grand Hotel. Trips from the airport take 15 - 20 minutes to the Hilton, costing Dhs.15 in normal taxis or Dhs.40 by special airport taxi. The Al Ain Rotana is about five minutes nearer the airport, the InterContinental about five minutes further from the Hilton, and The Mercure Grand is situated near the top of Jebel Hafeet and will take about 30 minutes to reach from the airport.

Remember that, as is the case the world over, a discount is often given on the 'rack rate' or published price.

The rates listed on [p.28] are peak season discounted rates (discount off the rack rate). Where applicable, the 16% municipality tax has been included in the listed price.

Beach Rotana Hotel & Towers

Hotel Apartments

A cheaper alternative to staying in a hotel is to rent furnished accommodation. This can be done on a daily/weekly/monthly or yearly basis and there are a number of agencies offering this service. One advantage is that the place can feel far more like a home than a hotel room. Usually the apartments will come fully furnished, from bed linen to cutlery, plus maid service. Additionally, there may be sports facilities, such as a gym and swimming pool in the building.

See Also: *Hotel Apartments – Accommodation (New Residents)*

Youth Hostels

The UAE is not a budget destination. Nevertheless, inexpensive accommodation in hostels is available in most of the emirates. The hostels are networked and they do co-operate as far as advance bookings and other issues are concerned. A Hostelling International membership card is required and if you do not have one, a yearly membership is available for UAE residents and can be purchased only from the Dubai hostel for approximately Dhs.100. Alternatively, you can pay a higher non member rate per night. To apply for membership, you will need to complete an application form and provide a passport copy along with two passport photos.

Accommodation is available for men, women and families. Single women especially should check availability, since the management reserves the right to refuse bookings from single women when the hostel is busy with men. Hostels can be found in Dubai, Sharjah, Fujairah and Khor Fakkan.

UAE Hostels	
Dubai (Al Qusais Road, Nr Al Ahli Club)	04 298 8161
Fujairah (Nr Supreme Council of Youth Sports Office)	09 222 2347
Khor Fakkan (Nr Oceanic Hotel)	09 237 0886
Sharjah (Nr Sharjah Sports Club)	06 522 5070

Camping

Other Options → Sports & Activities [p.177]

There are no official campsites in the UAE, but there are plenty of places to camp outside the cities. Options in Abu Dhabi include the desert dunes on the way to Al Ain or at Liwa. An hour's drive away, in Dubai, is the Jebel Ali beach, a popular place in the cooler months. If you get there early enough, you can have your own shelter and shower right on the beach. Camping on the beach in Dubai now requires a permit. You can apply for free but only through either Dubai Municipality's Website (www.dm.gov.ae) or the Environment Protection and Safety Section through the Municipality's Customer Service Centre. You will need a photocopy of your passport, a labour card (expatriates only), a driving license, a car registration card and two photographs.

While there are many campers around, the majority are UAE residents. It's quite rare for someone to show up at the airport, camping gear in hand, ready to set off on a camping holiday in the Emirates.

Pick up a copy of the *Off-Road Explorer (UAE)* for further information. This guide covers everything, from where to go and how to get there to what to bring and how to prepare.

Getting Around

Other options → **Maps [p.270]**
Exploring [p.113]

The car is the most popular method of getting around Abu Dhabi, Al Ain and the Emirates, either by private vehicle or taxi. There is a reasonable public bus service, but walking and cycling are limited and there are no trains or trams (see Bus [p.34], Car [p.32] and Taxi [p.34] entries). In the next 4 - 6 years, a rapid rail transit system will be introduced in Dubai. Other proposals for transport include a high speed ferry linking Abu Dhabi and Dubai.

Lane Discipline

Lane discipline is yet another challenge to the overall UAE driving experience. As so many different nationalities converge on the roads, there are bound to be some major differences in driving styles, and lane discipline is a particular annoyance of ours! On a highway, the majority of drivers seem to believe that the two far right lanes are reserved for trucks and the two left lanes for cars. This means that with a posted speed limit of 120 km per hour, and drivers flying down the fast lane at sometimes over 200 km per hour, you will find a small car plodding along in the next lane over at far below the speed limit! Now, if you have someone coming up behind you very, very fast, flashing their headlights and swerving dangerously, where do you go?!

The UAE's road network is excellent and most of the roads comprise two, three and sometimes four lanes. In addition, roads are generally well signposted with blue or green signs indicating the main areas or locations out of the city, and brown or purple signs showing heritage sites, places of interest, hospitals etc. For the benefit of both locals and expats, the majority of signs are in Arabic and English.

In Abu Dhabi, a surprising amount of care has been taken to beautify the roads and roundabouts; you will find many tree lined avenues and roundabouts decorated with flowers and shrubs, and sometimes even a dhow or a massive coffeepot sculpture – these often become useful landmarks for getting around.

Visitors should find the UAE's cities relatively easy to negotiate. Be aware though, for people usually rely on landmarks to give directions or to get their bearings, and most often these are shops, hotels, petrol stations or notable buildings. Roads are named with white road signs, but rarely are these referred to regularly. Similarly, while there is a street name/numbering system, few people actually use it. In Abu Dhabi in particular, confusion arises since some streets can be called by their street number, their old name or their nickname! For example Sheikh Zayed the Second Street is also known as Seventh Street, but is also popularly called Electra Street.

Hence, a little bit of insider knowledge and broad facts will help you get from A to B. The island's roads are built on a grid system and linked to the mainland by two bridges – Al Maqtaa Bridge and Mussafah (or Al Ain) Bridge. As you come onto the island, the first areas you'll pass are chiefly residential. Most of the offices, shops, hotels and restaurants are located within four or five blocks of the main Corniche road, which runs along the northern side of the island.

The island is split using New Airport Road as the dividing line. This road runs from Al Maqtaa Bridge in the east (near the mainland) to the Corniche on the northern side of the island. All roads to the east are in Zone 1 (east) and those to the west in Zone 2 (west). Roads that run parallel with New Airport Road are given even numbers, with the numbers increasing as they move away from New Airport Road to either coast. Roads parallel to the Corniche (ie, at right angles to New Airport Road) are given odd numbers in ascending order. What's more, the city is divided into districts and since Abu Dhabi is built on an island, if you ever get lost, you'll never be far from the coast roads.

Al Ain is unusual in that it straddles the border with the Sultanate of Oman. However, checkpoints at the border now restrict those travelling without visas into the Omani part (known as Buraimi).

In comparison to Abu Dhabi, Al Ain has developed in a less organised manner but is nevertheless based on a rough grid system. The city is fairly spread out, consisting of about ten main roads and here too, roundabouts are important landmarks for giving directions (such as Clock Tower in the centre of town). Oases dominate the city; visitors will find walled oases all around and most of these are still farmed. Most famous spots plus any main heritage and hotel sites are highlighted with large brown or purple signs. (But often, these signs are missing when you need them most!)

For further details of the road network in Abu Dhabi and Al Ain, refer to the main map section at the end of the book.

Downtown Abu Dhabi

Car

Other options → Transportation [p.92]

Over the past two decades, Abu Dhabi has built (and is still building) an impressive network of roads. So be prepared to come across lots of roadworks! There are two bridges linking the island with the mainland, with a third bridge well under way. The roads to all major towns and villages are of an excellent standard. Al Ain is about 150 km from Abu Dhabi and takes about an hour and a half to reach. A four lane highway heads north from the city to Dubai, which also takes about one and a half hours to reach.

Driving Habits & Regulations

While the infrastructure is superb, the general standard of driving is not. Apparently, the UAE has one of the world's highest death rates per capita due to traffic accidents. According to the Abu Dhabi Police, one person is killed in a traffic related accident every 48 hours and there is one injury every four hours – not the most positive statistics! Drivers often seem completely unaware of other cars on the road and the usual follies of driving too fast, too close, swerving, pulling out suddenly, lane hopping or drifting happen far too regularly.

One move to help the situation on the roads was a ban on using handheld mobile phones while driving. Predictably, the sales of hands free systems rocketed before people went back to their old bad habits.

In Abu Dhabi, you drive on the right hand side of the road and it is mandatory to wear seatbelts in the front seats. Children under ten years of age are no longer allowed to sit in the front of a car. This ban is now countrywide, even though you'll still see people driving with their child on their lap.

Fines for any of the above violations are Dhs.100 plus one 'black' point on your licence. Speeding fines are Dhs.400 and parking fines start at Dhs.100. Most fines are paid when you renew your annual car registration. However, parking tickets appear on your windscreen and you have a week or two to pay – the amount increases if you don't pay within the time allotted on the back of the ticket.

ZERO Tolerance

The Abu Dhabi Police exercise a strict zero tolerance policy on drinking and driving. This means that if you have had ANYTHING to drink, you are much better off taking a taxi home or having a friend who has consumed nothing drive you home. If you are pulled over and found to have consumed alcohol, you will most likely find yourself enjoying the hospitality of the police station overnight... at the very least!

Also note that, if you are involved in an accident, whether it's your fault or not, and you are found to have been drinking and driving, your insurance is automatically void. Penalties are severe, so the simple message is to be safe: if you're going to drink, don't even think of driving.

Try to keep a reasonable stopping distance between yourself and the car in front. It also helps to have eyes in the back of your head and to practice skilful defensive driving at all times.

If you wish to report a traffic violation, call the Traffic Police's toll free hotline (800 4353). The Abu Dhabi Police Website: www.adpolice.gov.ae offers all information relevant to driving, such as traffic violations, road maps, contact numbers etc. For complete information on Highway Codes, safety and road rules, check out the Safe Driving Handbook available from the Emirates Motor Sports Federation (04 282 7111).

Contact: *Abu Dhabi Police Headquarters (681 2200)*

Speed Limits

Speed limits are usually 60 - 80 km around town, while roads to other parts of the Emirates are

100 - 120 km. The speed is clearly indicated on road signs and there is no leeway for breaking the limit. Both fixed and movable radar traps, and the Abu Dhabi Traffic Police are there to catch the unwary violator and slap them with a hefty Dhs.400 fine!

Driving Licence

Visitors to Abu Dhabi have two options for driving. You can drive a rental or private vehicle with either an international driving licence, or a temporary licence issued by the Traffic Department in Abu Dhabi (applied for by showing your original national licence). However, to apply for these licences, you have to be from one of the countries included in the transfer list (see [p.55]). Although the law permits visitors to drive private vehicles, some insurance companies are unwilling to pay up on claims unless the driver is a resident holding a UAE licence.

Accidents

If you are involved in a traffic accident, however minor, you must remain with your car at the accident scene and report the incident to the Traffic Police, and then wait for them to arrive. Unfortunately, when you have an accident in this part of the world, you become the star attraction as the passing traffic slows to a crawl and everyone has a good gawk.

Stray animals (mostly camels) are another thing to avoid on the roads in the UAE. If the animal hits your vehicle and causes damage or injury, the animal's owner should pay compensation. However, if you are found to have been speeding or driving recklessly, you must compensate the owner of the animal – this can be expensive.

See Also: *Traffic Accidents [p.98].*

Blood Money

If you are driving and cause someone's death, even if the accident was not your fault, you are liable to pay a sum of money, known as 'blood money', to the deceased's family. The limit for this has been set at Dhs.200,000 per victim and your car insurance will cover this cost (hence the higher premiums). Moreover, insurance companies will only pay if they cannot find a way of claiming that the insurance is invalid (ie, if the driver was driving without a licence or, for example, under the influence of alcohol). The deceased's family can, however, waive the right to blood money if they feel merciful.

Non Drivers

In addition to dealing with the nutters in cars, you will find that pedestrians and cyclists also seem to have a death wish! The few cyclists who do brave the roads will often cycle towards you on the wrong side of the road, invariably without lights if it is night time. Pedestrians often step out dangerously close to oncoming traffic, and a lack of convenient, safe crossings makes life for those on foot especially difficult. However, the numbers of pedestrian footbridges and pedestrian operated traffic lights are gradually increasing.

Parking

In most cities of the Emirates, parking is readily available and people rarely have to walk too far in the heat. In Abu Dhabi, however, parking can be quite a problem, particularly in the city centre and the more popular shopping areas. Over the past year, quite a few underground parking areas have cropped up, and several more are under construction. It's worth paying the Dhs.5 fee just to come back to a cool car.

Petrol/Gas Stations

Petrol stations in the Emirates are numerous and run by Emarat, Emirates, EPPCO and ENOC. Most offer extra services, such as a car wash or a shop selling all those necessities of life that you forgot to buy at the supermarket. Likewise, there are plenty of petrol stations on the main roads around the Abu Dhabi emirate, but the ones on the island itself are mostly tucked away and difficult to find. The Abu Dhabi National Oil Company (ADNOC) runs most of the petrol stations in the emirate.

Most visitors will find petrol far cheaper than in their home countries at Dhs.4.75/gallon for Special (unleaded) and Dhs.5.25/gallon for Super (unleaded). In an effort to protect the environment, leaded fuel was replaced by unleaded at the end of 2002. The UAE must be one of the few countries in the world where diesel is actually more expensive than other fuels.

Car Hire

In Abu Dhabi, you will find all the major car rental companies plus a few extra, and it is best to shop around a bit for rates can vary considerably. Still, it's worth remembering that the larger, more reputable firms generally have more reliable vehicles and a greater capacity to help in an emergency (an important factor when handling the trying times following an accident). Depending on the agent, cars can be hired

with or without a driver, and the minimum hire period is usually 24 hours. Prices range from Dhs.140 a day for smaller cars to Dhs.1,000 for limousines. Comprehensive insurance is essential (and make sure it includes personal accident coverage).

To rent a car, you are usually required to produce your passport, two photographs and a valid international driving licence from one of the following countries: Austria, Belgium, Canada, Denmark, Finland, France, Germany, Greece, Holland, Ireland, Italy, Japan, Norway, Spain, Sweden, Switzerland, Turkey, the UK and the US. If you don't have an international license, you may take your national license to the Traffic Department and obtain a temporary driving license which is valid for six months. The process is quick but you have to carry out the application personally – the car rental company is not permitted to do it on your behalf.

Car Rental Agencies	
Abu Dhabi Rent a Car	644 3770
Al Ghazal Transport Co.	634 2200
Avis Rent a Car	621 8400
(24 hour airport branch)	575 7180
Budget Rent a Car	633 4200
DiamondLease	622 2028
Emco	633 8933
Europcar	626 1441
Hertz Rent A Car	672 0060
Inter Emirates Rent a Car	645 5855
Thrifty Car Rental	634 5663
(24 hour airport branch)	575 7400
Tourist Rent a Car	641 8700
United Car Rentals	642 2203
Avis Rent a Car	03 768 7262
Thrifty Car Rental	03 754 5711

Taxi

If you don't have a car, a taxi is the most common method of getting around. Taxis are reasonably priced and plentiful. The more upmarket Al Ghazal taxis must be booked by phone, but individually registered taxis can be flagged down at the roadside, ideally at the special lay bys which have been built for picking up and dropping off passengers. Individual taxis are easily recognised by the green taxi sign on the roof of the white and gold cars. Some driving school cars have similar markings, which can create quite a bit of confusion (and judging by the standard of some taxi drivers, you'll have a hard job distinguishing the real learners anyway!)

Al Ghazal runs two taxi services along with car hire – its luxury cars are white Mercedes with a pale green stripe and the new Express service uses Toyota Camrys. The service is very professional with courteous, uniformed drivers. Stretch limos are also available for hire and ideal for special events.

Taxi Companies	
Al Ghazal Express	444 5885
Al Ghazal Taxis	444 7787
Al Ghazal Express	03 766 2020
Al Ghazal Taxis	03 751 6565

Taxis are metered with fares starting at Dhs.2 (Dhs.5 in Al Ghazal Mercedes) and most trips around the city will cost between Dhs.5 - 10. Al Ghazal taxis always have the meter running but some drivers prefer to negotiate the fare, particularly after midnight. For trips outside the city, it is best to agree on a price before travelling; alternatively, shared minibuses can be flagged down from the side of the road and are reasonably cheap. A journey from the airport to the town centre can cost from around Dhs.40 to Dhs.70 (in specially registered airport taxis).

Since Abu Dhabi has a somewhat unused street address system, most people use landmarks as an aid to get around. Unless your destination is well known, taxi drivers will not necessarily be familiar with where you want to go, so you may have to help with directions. Remember that most Abu Dhabi taxi drivers speak very little English. Start with the area you wish to go to and then choose a major landmark, such as a hotel, roundabout or shopping centre. Then narrow it down as you get closer. If you are going to a new place, try to phone for instructions first – you will often be given a distinctive landmark as a starting point. It's also helpful to take the phone number of your destination with you, in case things get too desperate.

Bus

The Abu Dhabi Municipality operates bus routes all over the emirate, as well as in the city. Attempts are being made to make the service more cost effective and organised, with more readily available route information and timetables. The service operates more or less around the clock and fares are inexpensive at Dhs.1 for travel within the Capital.

The main bus station is on Hazza bin Zayed Road, and the main station in Al Ain is behind the Co-

Operative Society. Buses between the two cities leave daily on a regular basis and cost Dhs.18 for a one day round trip (Dhs.10 one way). Fares are paid to the driver when you board, so try to keep some change ready.

Contact: *Abu Dhabi Transport (443 1500).*

Al Ghazal (toll free – 800 2121) operates daily buses to Dubai and Al Ain. Buses depart every 45 minutes from the Al Ghazal offices on Defence Road starting at 06:45 till 23:45. On Fridays, they leave every 30 minutes with the last bus departing at midnight. Only one way fares are available and fares from Abu Dhabi are cheaper than the return journey. For example, Abu Dhabi to Dubai costs Dhs.20 (Dhs.33 for reverse journey) and Abu Dhabi to Al Ain costs Dhs.20 (Dhs.30 for reverse journey).

Airport Bus

There is a regular bus between the airport and the city centre. The municipal bus service runs 24 hours a day every 30 minutes from 06:00 to 24:00, and every 45 minutes from 24:00 to 06:00. Buses are air conditioned, green and white in colour, and depart from outside the arrivals hall. The fare (Dhs.3) is paid when boarding the bus. Airport bus route maps are available at the Abu Dhabi International Airport.

For the return journey, Gulf Air passengers can check in at the City Terminal (opposite the Beach Rotana Hotel & Towers) up to 12 hours before departure. This means that passengers can check in their luggage early before travelling to the main airport. This service is especially helpful for those with loads of suitcases. A 24 hour courtesy shuttle service runs every 30 minutes from the City Terminal to the airport.

Air

Other options → **Meet & Greet [p.21]**
Airlines [p.101]

The UAE's location at the crossroads of Africa, Asia and Europe makes it an easily accessible destination. London is seven hours away, Frankfurt six, Hong Kong eight, and Nairobi four. Most European capitals and other major cities have direct flights to Abu Dhabi or Dubai, many with a choice of operator.

Abu Dhabi International Airport is located 35 km from the city. Its futuristic satellite passenger hub has been upgraded to handle 11 aircraft simultaneously, with passengers boarding and disembarking via telescopic walkways – a great bonus against the unrelenting summer heat. Annually, the airport handles over 3,500,000 passengers. Plans are also underway for a new terminal that will be similar in design to the existing one.

A variety of facilities are available at the airport, including a hotel and golf course which can be used by transit passengers. The large Duty Free is well known for its raffles – the latest raffle sells tickets for Dhs.1,000 to win Dhs.1,000,000! Abu Dhabi is part owner in Gulf Air along with Bahrain, Oman and Qatar, and is the second biggest hub for Gulf Air outside Bahrain, boasting non stop flights as far as New York and Australia. There are two national airlines: the recently established Etihad Airways operating out of Abu Dhabi, and the long established Emirates Airline which only operates out of Dubai.

Al Ain has its own international airport, which opened in March 1994 and is about 20 km west of the centre. While the number of airlines operating out of here is not huge, the introduction of this airport has eased the pressure on the one in Abu Dhabi by redirecting some of the air traffic.

Boat

Other options → **Boat & Yacht Charters [p.179]**

Opportunities in the Emirates for getting around by boat are limited unless you wish to travel by dhow, in which case your opportunities are limitless. Various companies offer trips by dhow or boat to explore the islands off the coast; alternatively you can try hiring a fishing boat to do this privately. Currently, there are no scheduled passenger services from Abu Dhabi to other countries, or even to Dubai.

Abu Dhabi Marina

Walking & Biking

Other options → Cycling [p.182]
Hiking [p.191]

Cities in the Emirates are generally very car orientated and not designed to encourage either walking or cycling. In addition, the heat in the summer months, with daytime temperatures of around 45° C, makes either activity a rather sweaty experience! However, in Abu Dhabi, the relative compactness of the main commercial area makes walking a pleasant way of getting around. Evenings in the emirate are much cooler and strolling along the Corniche and Breakwater is a popular pastime, even more so in the winter months when temperatures are perfect for the outdoors. Heading back from the Corniche, the first few blocks comprise a range of shopping malls, souks, cafés and cinemas, similar to the central oasis area in Al Ain, and they are both best explored on foot.

Cycling can be quite an enjoyable way to explore the cities – you cover more ground than you would on foot and are still able to see more than you could from a car. This activity is even more appropriate for the quieter areas where the roads are often wide and tree lined, and cars infrequent. With the exception of the Corniche in Abu Dhabi, there are no dedicated bike lanes to encourage cycling and the busier parts of the cities or the dual carriageways are probably best avoided. A lot of care is needed when cycling in traffic, since drivers often seem very unaware of this method of transport. Also, beware the heat in summer, which can easily exhaust the cyclist. Cycling in Abu Dhabi may not be much fun during the day, but it can be quite a pleasant experience at night.

Money

Cash is still the preferred method of payment in the Emirates, although credit cards are now widely accepted. Foreign currencies and travellers cheques can be exchanged in licensed exchange offices, banks and hotels – as usual, a passport is required for exchanging travellers cheques.

There is more confidence in cheques these days; a strict enforcement of laws concerning the passing of bad cheques has helped. It is a criminal offence to write a cheque with insufficient funds in the bank account, and a jail term will result.

Exchange Rates*

Foreign Currency (FC)	1 Unit FC = x Dhs	Dhs.1 = x FC
Australia	2.80	0.36
Bahrain	9.73	0.10
Bangladesh	0.06	16.03
Canada	2.68	0.37
Cyprus	7.34	0.14
Denmark	0.58	1.74
Euro	4.30	0.23
Hong Kong	0.47	2.14
India	0.08	12.07
Japan	0.03	30.03
Jordan	5.12	0.20
Kuwait	12.15	0.08
Malaysia	0.96	1.04
New Zealand	2.28	0.44
Oman	9.53	0.10
Pakistan	0.06	15.76
Philippines	0.07	15.31
Qatar	1.01	0.99
Saudi Arabia	0.98	1.02
Singapore	2.15	0.47
South Africa	0.54	1.85
Sri Lanka	0.37	26.98
Sweden	0.47	2.13
UK	6.44	0.16
USA	3.67	0.27

*Rates valid at the time of print

Local Currency

The monetary unit is the 'dirham' (Dhs.), which is divided into 100 'fils'. The currency is also referred to as AED (Arab Emirate Dirham). Notes come in denominations of Dhs.5, Dhs.10, Dhs.20, Dhs.50, Dhs.100, Dhs.200, Dhs.500 and Dhs.1,000. Coin denominations are Dhs.1, 50 fils and 25 fils, but be warned, for there are two versions of each coin and they can look very

UAE Dirhams

similar. Because 5 and 10 fil coins are rarely available, you will often not receive the exact correct change.

The dirham has been pegged to the US dollar since the end of 1980, at a mid rate of US $1 ~ Dhs.3.6725. Exchange rates of all major currencies are published daily in the local newspapers.

Banks

The well structured and ever growing network of local and international banks, strictly controlled by the UAE Central Bank, offers a full range of commercial and personal banking services. Transfers can be made without difficulty as there is no exchange control and the dirham is freely convertible.

Banking Hours: *Saturday - Wednesday, 08:00 - 13:00 (a few are also open 16:30 - 18:30); Thursday, 08:00 - 12:00.*

Main Banks	
Abu Dhabi Commercial Bank	696 2222
Bank of Sharjah	679 5555
Barclays Bank Plc	627 5313
Citibank	698 2206
Emirates Bank International	645 5151
HSBC Bank Middle East	615 2330
Mashreq Bank	627 4300
Middle East Bank	446 4000
National Bank of Abu Dhabi	611 1111
National Bank of Dubai	639 4555
Standard Chartered	677 7400
Union National Bank	674 1600
Abu Dhabi Commercial Bank	03 755 0000
Mashreq Bank	03 707 7319
Middle East Bank	03 764 2885
National Bank of Abu Dhabi	03 756 1900

ATMs

Most banks operate ATMs (Automatic Teller Machines, also known as cashpoints or service tills) which accept a wide range of cards. For non UAE based cards, the exchange rates used in the transaction are normally extremely competitive and the process is faster with far less hassle than traditional travellers cheques.

Common systems accepted around Abu Dhabi include American Express, Cirrus, Global Access, MasterCard, Plus System and VISA. ATMs can be found in all shopping malls, petrol stations, various street side locations and the airport.

Money Exchanges

Money exchanges are available all over Abu Dhabi, offering good service and reasonable exchange rates, which are often better than the banks. Additionally, hotels will usually exchange money and travellers cheques at the standard hotel rate (ie, poor).

Money Exchange Hours: *Sat - Thurs, 08:30 - 13:00 & 16:30 - 21:00; Friday, 16:30 - 21:00*

Exchange Centres	
Al Ansari Money Exchange	622 7888
Al Fardan Exchange	622 3222
Habib Exchange	627 2656
Lari Money Exchange	622 3225
Thomas Cook Al Rostamani Exchange	672 7717
UAE Exchange Centre	632 2166
Al Ansari Money Exchange	03 751 1225
Al Fardan Exchange	03 766 1010
Lari Money Exchange	03 766 6424
Thomas Cook Al Rostamani Exchange	03 766 5558
UAE Exchange Centre	03 765 4258

Credit Cards

Most shops, hotels and restaurants accept all major credit cards (American Express, Diners Club, MasterCard and VISA). Smaller retailers are sometimes less keen to accept credit cards and you may have to pay an extra five percent for processing (and it's no use telling them that this is

HSBC Bank

a contravention of the card company rules – you either take it or leave it!). You can, however, call your local credit card company to lodge a complaint if you are charged this five percent 'fee'. Conversely, if you are paying in cash, you may sometimes be allowed a discount... it's certainly worth enquiring.

Tipping

Tipping practices are similar to most parts of the world. An increasing number of restaurants include service, although it is unlikely to end up with your waiter. Otherwise, ten per cent is the usual.

Media & Communications

Newspapers/Magazines

Abu Dhabi has three of its own Arabic language newspapers – Al Ittihad, Al Wahda and Al Fajr. Emirates News, the only English language paper produced in Abu Dhabi, has closed down. Also available in Abu Dhabi are other newspapers printed in Dubai and Sharjah; these include the Arabic papers Al Bayan and Al Khaleej, and the English ones, Gulf News, Khaleej Times and The Gulf Today (all Dhs.2, and Dhs.3 on Fridays).

Foreign newspapers, most prominently French, German, British and Asian, are readily available in hotel bookshops and supermarkets, but are more expensive than at home (about Dhs.8 - 12) and slightly out of date. There is also a good supply of hobby magazines, such as computing, photography, sports and women's magazines (expect to find censored portions, or even occasionally whole pages or sections missing). They are expensive, usually costing two or three times more than they would in your hometown at home (between Dhs.30 - 50).

Newspapers and magazines are available from bookshops, supermarkets and hotel shops. Additionally, newspapers are also available at 'corner' shops and sold at major road junctions.

Further Reading

Visitors will find a variety of books and magazines available on the Emirates, from numerous coffee table books to magazines with details of aerobics classes. Monthly publications range from the free Dubai based Out & About to Connector and Aquarius (on health and beauty), to the event focused Time Out and What's On magazines. Many magazines here seem to almost merge into one; they have no clear cut identity and the audience always seems the same, no matter which magazine you pick up. Currently, the only dedicated Abu Dhabi magazine is Time Out; all others tend to throw in a few token pages that cover Abu Dhabi.

Guides to the region include Explorer Publishing's *Dubai Explorer* as well as the Lonely Planet series. Sharjah the Guide, the Spectrum Guide to the United Arab Emirates and Trident Press' informative United Arab Emirates Yearbook also offer more information on the region.

For the finer points on life in the Emirates, refer to books such as the *Family Explorer (Dubai & Abu Dhabi)*, a family guidebook to life in the UAE; the *Off-Road Explorer (UAE)*, the UAE's ultimate outdoor guide; and the *Underwater Explorer (UAE)*, a detailed guide to scuba diving in the area. These can be found in all good bookstores around town.

Post & Courier Services

Other Options → Postal Services [p.81]

Empost, formerly known as the General Postal Authority (GPA), is the sole provider of postal services in the UAE. In addition, plenty of courier companies operate both locally and internationally, such as Aramex, DHL, Federal Express etc. Empost also operates an express mail service known as Mumtaz Express.

Post within the UAE takes 2 - 3 days to be delivered. Mail takes 7 - 10 days to reach the USA and Europe, 8 – 10 days to reach Australia, and 5 - 10 days to reach India. Airmail letters cost Dhs.3 - 6 to send, depending on weight, and postcards cost Dhs.1 - 2. Letters are a dirham cheaper if they are posted unsealed. Aerogrammes can be bought for Dhs.2 each from post offices, which also saves the bother of buying a stamp before posting your letters.

Stamps can be bought from post offices and certain shops – card shops often sell a limited

Main Courier Companies	
Aramex	627 2888
DHL	800 4004
Empost	800 5858
Federal Express	800 4050
TNT	677 1159
UPS	446 1961

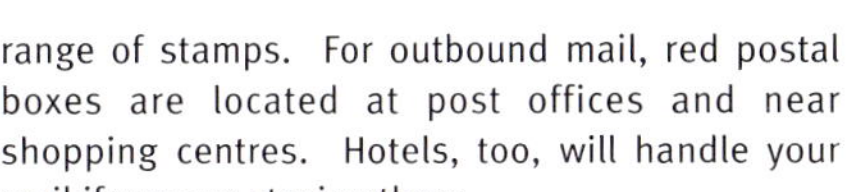

range of stamps. For outbound mail, red postal boxes are located at post offices and near shopping centres. Hotels, too, will handle your mail if you are staying there.

There's no house address based postal service; all incoming mail is delivered to a PO Box at a central location and has to be collected from there.

Radio

The UAE has a number of commercial radio stations broadcasting in a range of languages, from Arabic and English to French, Hindi, Malayalam or Urdu. Daily schedules can be found in the local newspapers.

Operating 24 hours a day, everyday, the English language stations, Dubai FM (92 FM) and Ajman's Channel 4 FM (104.8 FM), play modern music. Operating throughout the UAE, Emirates 1 FM (99.3, 100.5 FM) plays music for a 'younger' audience, while Emirates 2 FM (90.5, 98.5 FM) broadcasts a mixture of news, talk shows and modern music. Sadly, while there are a few current affairs programs in English, most are sorely lacking in depth.

Ras Al Khaimah's Radio Asia (1575 AM) has programmes in Hindi, Urdu and Malayalam, while Umm Al Quwain's Hum FM (106.2 FM) broadcasts mainly in Hindi with a bit of English.

If you want to hear Arabic music, tune in to 93.9 FM, 98.9 FM or 90.5 FM. At times, with the right equipment, the BBC World Service can also be picked up.

Television/Satellite TV

Other options → Utilities & Services [p.76]

Abu Dhabi has thirteen television channels broadcasting mainly in Arabic. It is however, possible to pick up signals from the northern emirates and countries outside the UAE. The local English language channel is broadcast on Channel 48, and you can also tune in to Channel 33, the English language channel in Dubai.

There are a variety of services offered via satellite. Most leading hotels and hotel apartments have satellite television available for residents, and many apartment blocks have dishes preinstalled – residents have to simply acquire a decoder. Satellite programmes that can be received range from international entertainment or films to sports, cartoons and current events.

Telephones

Other options → Utilities & Services [p.76]

Telecommunications are very good, both within the UAE and internationally. All communication is provided by the Emirates Telecommunications Corporation (Etisalat) who, according to recent press statements, will soon lose their monopoly status. Calls from a landline to another landline within Abu Dhabi are free of charge, and direct dialling is possible to over 170 countries. GPRS, WAP, G3 and Hot Spot services are also available in the UAE.

Public payphones are all over the city; a few accept coins, but most require phone cards that are available from many shops and supermarkets. They come in a variety of values, but for international calls, beware... the units vanish at a truly amazing rate! Etisalat has a new generation of prepaid phone cards called 'Smart Cards', which are available for Dhs.30.

Mobile phones are widely used – there are more than 2 million subscribers in the Emirates. Etisalat has a reciprocal agreement with over 60 countries for international GSM roaming service, allowing visitors whose countries are part of the agreement to use their mobile in the UAE. However, if your country is not on the list or you don't have roaming facilities, Etisalat offers a useful prepaid service called 'Wasel'. Bring the phone with you (or buy it here) and purchase a SIM card from Etisalat, which enables you to make and receive calls while in the

Lacking Credit

*If you run out of credit on your mobile and need to get in touch with someone, request a call-back to any mobile number free of charge. Dial *188*, the mobile number of the person you want to call you back, followed by #. The recipient will receive the following SMS. 'You have received a call request from 050 XXX XXXX. Thank you. Etisalat'.*

Telephone Codes

UAE Country Code	+971	Directory Enquiries	181
Abu Dhabi	02	Operator	100
Ajman	06	Fault Reports	171
Al Ain	03	Billing Information	142
Dubai	04	Etisalat Contact Centre	101
Fujairah	09	Speaking Clock	140
Hatta	04	Recharge Al Wasel	122
Jebel Ali	04	Al Wasel Credit Balance	121
Ras al Khaimah	07		
Sharjah	06	To reach a typical Abu Dhabi	
Umm Al Quwain	06	number from overseas it is	
Mobile Telephones	050	00 **971 2** XXX XXXX	

UAE. A local number is supplied and calls are charged at the local UAE rate. Find out more about Etisalat's services on www.etisalat.ae.

Internet

Other options → Internet Cafés [p.256]
Utilities & Services [p.76]

With around one third of the population using the Internet, the UAE is among the top twenty countries in the world in terms of Internet use. Internet or cyber cafés around town provide easy and relatively cheap access.

Etisalat is the sole provider of Internet services within the UAE and in order to maintain the country's moral and cultural values, all sites are provided via Etisalat's proxy server. This occasionally results in frustrated users being unable to access perfectly reasonable sites that, for some reason have been blocked. If you come across such a site, you can report it to Etisalat. Please see [p.41] for helpful sites and numbers.

Most organisations that are connected have up to an eight character email address. Typical email syntax is: user@emirates.net.ae

You can also surf the Internet without being a subscriber. All that's needed is a computer with a modem and a regular phone line. To use this facility, simply call 500 5555. For information on charges, see Dial 'n' Surf on [p.81].

Websites

There are numerous Websites on Abu Dhabi as well as the Emirates in general, and new ones are uploaded all the time. Some are more interesting, successful and relevant than others, and the table on [p.41] lists those that the Explorer team has found to be the most useful – do let us know your suggestions about any new Websites that you feel should be included in the next edition of this guidebook.

UAE Annual Events

Throughout the year, the emirates of Abu Dhabi, Al Ain and Dubai host a number of well established annual events. The events described below are some of the more popular and regular fixtures on the social calendar. However, bear in mind that the following is only a general guide since, for the most part, events are not always promoted until closer to the date and some organisers prefer using the 'grapevine' rather than local press and publications.

Al Ain Flower Festival

The Al Ain Flower Festival, taking place each spring, is a feast of colour. View the stunning landscaping of the park near Jahili Fort, and the amazing flowers and shrubs planted and in bloom for the event. A parade that has most of Al Ain, particularly the children, participating is well worth attending, with the children dressed in colourful flower costumes. Unfortunately, this festival did not take place in 2004 and exact dates for 2005 will be available nearer the time of the event from the Al Ain Municipality (03 763 5111).

Abu Dhabi Shopping Festival

The Abu Dhabi Shopping Festival, held every year in early March, is filled with fantastic bargains, sales and prizes offered by all the shopping malls. Lesser known than the Dubai Shopping Festival in terms of worldwide exposure, it is still a worthy event for those living in the area. The month is filled with competitions and giveaways, and also provides the perfect excuse to make those special purchases you've been waiting for all year.

Camel Racing (www.emirates-heritageclub.com)

Camel racing is a spectacular sport and a trip to a race can be one of the most memorable highlights of any visit to the Emirates. In this traditional sport, ungainly animals ridden by young boys provide an extraordinary sight. Racing camels can change hands for as much as ten million dirhams! Races normally take place on Thursdays and Fridays during the winter months, with additional races on National Day and other public holidays. The main race, a two day event held each year in April, attracts enthusiasts from all over the Emirates. A traditional camel race is held twice a year (February and October); winners are presented with a golden sword. Try to be at the racetracks early on a Friday morning to catch the atmosphere. You can check the local press for details of race dates and times. Races are mostly held at the Sowaihan Racetrack (130 km from Abu Dhabi on the road to Al Ain) and the Al Ain Racetrack (on the road to Abu Dhabi, about 25 km from the centre of Al Ain). Call the Emirates Heritage Club (446 6116) for further information.

Websites

Abu Dhabi Information	
www.abudhabi.com	Online Newspaper-type-site
www.adiamet.gov.ae	Abu Dhabi International Airport Weather Office
www.bayt.com	Recruitment website for the Middle East
www.britishcouncil.org/uae	British Council, UAE
www.doctorelite.com	24 hour doctor/pharmacy/medical service
www.emiratesairline.com	Emirates Airline
www.etihadairways.com	Etihad Airways
www.expatsite.com	Find out what's going on back home
www.explorer-publishing.com	Our site!
www.roomservice-uae.com	Deliveries from your favourite restaurants
www.sheikhzayed.com	His Highness Sheikh Zayed Bin Sultan Al Nahyan's site
www.tenuae.com	UAE news and information
www.uaefilms.com	UAE films
www.uaeinteract.com	UAE Ministry of Information & Culture site
www.uaemall.com	Wide range of goods and services
www.uae-ypages.com	Index of interesting goodies in the UAE
www.weather.com	Weather in the UAE and globally

Business/Industry	
www.adcci-uae.com	Abu Dhabi Chamber of Commerce and Industry
www.adm.gov.ae	Abu Dhabi Municipality
www.adpolice.gov.ae	Abu Dhabi Police
www.auhcustoms.gov.ae	Abu Dhabi Customs
www.dcaauh.gov.ae	Department of Civil Aviation Abu Dhabi
www.eim.ae	Emirates Internet and Multimedia - Internet service provider
www.etisalat.ae	Etisalat - UAE's telephone service provider
www.portzayed.gov.ae	Abu Dhabi Seaport Authority

Embassies	
www.embassyworld.com	Embassies abroad

Hotels/Sports

Hotel details listed in **General Information** [p28], and sporting organisations in **Activities** [p.177]

Wheels	
www.4x4motors.com	A little more sand than tar
www.diamondlease.com	Car leasing/rental
www.valuewheels.com	Buy a vehicle online

Desert Rallies

The UAE deserts provide ideal locations for desert rallying, and many events are organised throughout the year by the Emirates Motor Sports Federation (EMSF) in Dubai. The highest profile event is the Desert Challenge, which is the climax of the World Cup in Cross Country Rallying. It attracts top rally drivers from all over the world and is held in the first week of November. Other events throughout the year include the Spring Desert Rally (4 WD), Peace Rally (saloons); Jeep Jamboree (safari), Drakkar Noir 1000 Dunes Rally (4 WD), Shell Festival Parade, Audi Driving Skills (driving challenge) and Federation Rally (4 WD). For details, call EMSF (04 282 7111). For information on the UAE Desert Challenge call (04 266 9922).

See Also: *Emirates Motor Sports Federation – Rally Driving [p.196]. UAE Desert Challenge [p.43]*

Dhow Racing (www.emirates-heritageclub.com)

Traditional wooden dhows present a very atmospheric sight when racing. The vessels are usually 40 - 60 ft in length and are either powered by men (up to 100 oarsmen per dhow) or the wind. Fixed dhow races take place throughout the year, and some special occasions, such as National Day, will also see a dhow racing event sponsored by the government in its wish to keep traditional heritage alive. Most races take place from September to April. The ones held in Abu Dhabi are short coastal races, and the boats, many of which are old pearling vessels, have a shallow draught which is ideal for sailing closer to the Corniche. In Dubai, longer sea going races take place, particularly the race to Sir Bu Naair Island in April, which sees as many as 80 boats taking part. Keep an eye on the local press for further information.

Dubai Desert Classic – Golf (www.dubaidesertclassic.com)

Incorporated into the European PGA Tour in 1989, this popular golfing tournament attracts growing numbers of world class players. The prestige associated with this event is evident with the past appearance of such players as Tiger Woods, Ernie Els and Thomas Björn.

Dubai Rugby Sevens (www.dubairugby7s.com)

This two day event is a very popular sporting and spectator fixture. With alcohol freely available at the stadium, the party atmosphere carries on until the small hours. Top international teams participate, and the competition also provides a rare opportunity for local teams from all over the Gulf to try their luck in their own games, which run alongside some of the big names in sevens rugby.

Dubai Shopping Festival (www.mydsf.com)

A combination of festival and shopping extravaganza, DSF, as it is popularly known, is hard to miss as buildings and roads are decorated with coloured lights and there are bargains galore in participating outlets. Highlights include a spectacular fireworks show over the Creek each evening, the international wonders of Global Village, and numerous raffles. Other attractions include music, dance and theatrical entertainment from around the world, plus animal shows and a huge funfair. Hotels are at 100% occupancy during this month (mid Jan - mid Feb), and due to its massive success and the resulting traffic congestion that follows in the evenings, it has also been cynically dubbed, the 'Dubai Traffic Festival'

Dubai Summer Surprises (www.mydsf.com)

Similar to DSF but smaller, Dubai Summer Surprises (DSS) is held to attract visitors during the hot and humid summer months. Aimed at the family, DSS offers fun packed activities, which are generally held in climate controlled facilities, such as shopping malls, specially constructed areas and hotels. Events are often based on food, heritage, technology, knowledge, family values, schools etc.

Dubai Tennis Open (www.dubaitennischampionships.com)

Held in the middle of February, the US $1,000,000 Dubai Duty Free Tennis Open is a well supported event. It is established on the international tennis circuit and offers the chance for fans to see top seeds, both male and female, in an intimate setting, battling it out for game, set and match.

Dubai World Cup (www.dubaiworldcup.com)

Now in its ninth year, the Dubai World Cup, taking place in March, is billed as the richest horseracing programme in the world – in 2004 the total prize money was over US $15,000,000. The prize for the Group 1 Dubai World Cup race alone was a staggering US $6,000,000. The event is always held on a Saturday to ensure maximum media coverage in the west, and with a buzzing, vibrant atmosphere, is a great opportunity to dress up and bring out your best hat!

Eid Al Adha

Meaning 'Feast of the Sacrifice', Eid Al Adha is a four day Islamic holiday marking the end of the annual period of pilgrimage to Mecca. The rituals involve slaughtering many animals. This holiday falls 70 days after the first Eid.

Eid Al Fitr

Eid Al Fitr is an Islamic holiday that lasts for three days and celebrates the 'Feast of the Breaking of the Fast'. It is held at the end of the month of Ramadan.

Horseracing (www.adec-web.com and www.uaeequafed.ae)

The Abu Dhabi Equestrian Club provides information on horseracing and show jumping. The season lasts from October to April and horseracing takes place every Sunday night during these months. The racing calendar starts on November 7, 2004 and runs till April 10, 2005. Contact ADEC (445 5500) or check their Website for further details. For endurance horseracing and for further details on horseracing and show jumping, log on to the UAE Equestrian and Racing Federation's Website (www.uaeequafed.ae).

IDEX (www.idexuae.com)

The International Defence Exhibition and Conference is one of the most prestigious of its kind in the world. Suppliers exhibit state of the art weaponry and navies show off their submarines, frigates, minesweepers and more in the specially developed berthing area. The guest list is a worldwide 'who's who' of defence ministers and high ranking chiefs of staff representing most international governments. This biannual exhibition is due to be staged from February 12 - 17, 2005.

Islamic New Year's Day

Islamic New Year's Day marks the start of the Islamic Hijri calendar. It is based on the lunar calendar and should fall on March 21st in 2004.

See Also: *Public Holidays [p.12]*

Lailat Al Mi'raj

This day celebrates the Prophet's ascension into heaven and is expected to occur on September 12 in 2004.

Powerboat Racing

The UAE is well established on the world championship powerboat racing circuit with Formula I (onshore) in Abu Dhabi and Class I (offshore) in Dubai and Fujairah. These events make a great spectacle – take a picnic and settle in with family and friends to be an armchair sports fan for the day. Abu Dhabi plays host to the final round of the Formula One series at the end of the season. ADIMSC organises Formula Four races for the UAE participants, jet ski races and the Al Shwaheef race, which is designed to encourage the younger generation of Emiratis to remain close to their marine heritage. Each season also sees two open regattas for modern sailing boats (including catamarans, lasers and windsurfers), which are open to all ages and nationalities. Abu Dhabi International Marine Sports Club has a water racing calendar, which runs from Oct - May. Contact the Race Co-ordinator on 681 5566.

Powerboat Racing

Terry Fox Run (www.terryfoxrun.org)

Every year, thousands of people around the world run, jog, walk, cycle and even rollerblade their way around for this worthwhile charity. All funds raised go to cancer research programmes at approved institutions around the world. Abu Dhabi's next run is expected to be in February 2005. Al Ain has not had any runs for the last couple of years. For exact dates, check the local media nearer to February, or contact the Ambassador's Office, Canadian Embassy (407 1300).

UAE Desert Challenge (www.uaedesertchallenge.com)

This is the highest profile motor sport event in the country and is often the culmination of the cross country rallying world cup. The event attracts some of the world's top rally drivers and bike riders who compete in the car, truck and moto-cross categories. The race is held on consecutive days over four stages, usually starting in Abu Dhabi and travelling across the harsh and challenging terrain of the deserts and sabkha to finish in Dubai. Call 266 9922 for further details.

Main Annual Events – 2004/2005

August	
6	Accession of the Ruler of Abu Dhabi
27	Dubai Summer Surprises ends

September	
tbc	AUH Rugby Club Summer Fun Sevens (contact 627 5777)
12	Lailat Al Miraj (Accession of the Prophet) (Moon)
13-16	Abu Dhabi 2004 International Hunting & Equestrian Exhibition (ADIHEX) (Contact 444 6900)

October	
tbc	Traditional Camel Race in Suweihan
10	Prologue to UAE Desert Challenge
11-15	UAE Desert Challenge
15	Ramadan begins

November	
14-16	Eid Al Fitr (Moon)

December	
tbc	Dubai Rugby 7s
tbc	AUH Rugby Club Christmas Ball (contact 627 5777)
2	UAE National Day
14-18	Int'l Jewellery Exhibition (contact 679 5444)

Denotes public holidays
tbc – to be confirmed

January	
tbc	Eid Al Adha (Moon)
1	New Year's Day
6-7	Sheraton Mixed Amateur Golf Open (Contact 558 8990)
15	Dubai Shopping Festival starts
21-22	Sheraton Mixed Ladies Golf Open (Contact 558 8990)

February	
tbc	1000 Dunes Rally (contact 282 7111)
tbc	Terry Fox Run (contact 407 1300)
15	Dubai Shopping Festival ends
tbc	Dubai Tennis Championship (Ladies)
tbc	Traditional Camel Race in Suweihan
12-17	International Defence Exhibition (IDEX) (contact 444 6900)
17-18	Sheraton Mixed Juniors Golf Open (Contact 558 8990)

March	
tbc	Dubai Desert Classic
tbc	Dubai Tennis Championship (Men)
tbc	Dubai World Cup
tbc	Islamic New Year (Moon)

April	
tbc	Prophet's Birthday (Moon)
14-15	Sheraton Mixed Men's Golf Open (Contact 558 8990)

Taking on the Challenge

New Residents

EXPLORER

New Residents

UAE Overview

Abu Dhabi, the capital city of the UAE, is one of the Gulf's top destinations for expatriate workers. Life here can definitely be fun... getting things done, however, can be a headache. Emiratis love paperwork and red tape, so to become an official resident of Abu Dhabi, you will need plenty of paper, plenty of patience and a sense of humour!

Still, attempts are continually being made to streamline processes. Government departments are being encouraged to enhance efficiency and creativity, especially focusing on the use of the Internet for issuing documents, such as trade licences or health cards. In fact, 'e-government' is the buzzword everywhere these days, but that said, don't expect to find everything online, and don't expect the paperwork and woes to be at all reduced! This government directive is taking its time (read: years) to filter through to the individual departments, so you can still expect to be sent from counter to counter with your documents. This can be confusing but remember that wherever you go, people are invariably friendly and ready to point you in the right direction if you are well and truly lost.

The following information is meant only as a guide to what you will have to go through in order to become a car owning, phone owning, Internet connected, working resident. Remember, requirements and laws change regularly and often in quite major ways. Changes are generally announced in the newspapers and can be implemented literally overnight – so be prepared for the unexpected while living in the UAE.

The following information applies only to the emirate of Abu Dhabi. The United Arab Emirates is a federation with national laws, but all seven emirates have a degree of independence to make and implement local regulations, so some rules in Abu Dhabi can be quite different to rules in neighbouring Dubai.

The Beginning...

To be resident in Abu Dhabi, you need someone to legally vouch for you. This is usually your employer, who thus turns into your legal sponsor. Once you have residency, you may then be in a position to sponsor your spouse, parents or children, should you wish to do so.

The first step to acquiring residency is to enter the country on a valid entry visa (see Documents – Entry Visa [p.50], Residence Visa [p.52]). Your new employer will usually provide your visa. If you do not already have a job secured, you may obtain a visit visa to enter the UAE for a short time (see also: Visas – Entering Abu Dhabi [p.19]). If you are already in Abu Dhabi and are applying for a visa for a family member or friend, the application form may be collected from the Immigration Department.

The original entry visa documentation must be presented to airport immigration on arrival and your passport will be duly stamped.

Once you have entered the country on the correct visa, the next step is to apply for a health card, which requires a medical test, after which you can apply for residency. This should be done within 60 days of entering the country. To work legally, you also require a labour card. Your employer will usually take care of processing all required documentation for you, and sometimes for your family as well.

Labour cards and residence visas are valid for three years and can be renewed. This does not apply to elderly parents or maids (see: Residence Visa [p.52] and Domestic Help [p.74]). Labour cards for employees on their father or spouse's visa must be renewed on an annual basis. Health cards too, are valid only for one year.

If you are a qualified professional with a degree, or have an established employment history, there should be few difficulties in obtaining the necessary paperwork.

Useful Advice

When applying for a residence visa, labour card, driving permit etc, you will always need a handful of Essential Documents (see below) and countless application forms – invariably typed in Arabic. Don't panic. At most government offices such as the Immigration Department, Labour Office, Traffic Police, Ministry of Health, government hospitals etc, there are small cabins full of typists offering their services in English and Arabic for just Dhs.10 - 15. Most also offer photocopying services and some even take instant passport sized photographs.

Essential Documents

For your ease and to avoid repetition throughout this section, a list of essential documents has been compiled here. These are standard items that you will invariably need to produce when processing

documentation. Additional documents will be referred to in the appropriate paragraph.

- Original passport (for inspection only)
- Passport photocopies (personal details)
- Passport photocopies (visa/visit visa details)
- Passport sized photographs

You will need countless photographs over the next few months. Usually two passport photocopies and two photographs will be required each time you file for something, apply for a job, or even join a gym. To save time and money, ask for the original negative when you order your first set of photos. Duplicate photos can then be made easily. There are many small photo shops that offer this service; look in your local area.

In addition, you will often be required to produce what is commonly known as an NOC, a 'no objection certificate' (or letter) from your employer or sponsor. This confirms who you are and says that they have no objection to you renting a house, getting a driving licence, opening a bank account etc. An NOC should be on company letterhead paper, signed, and stamped with the company stamp to make it undeniably 'official'. Remember to make photocopies of this document for future use.

e-Dirhams

Introduced in late 2001, the credit card sized e-Dirham card, a pre-paid 'smart card', is an electronic payment tool replacing the use of cash payment for procedures done within various federal ministries. Ministries requiring e-Dirham usage that you are likely to visit are the Ministry of Labour & Social Affairs and the Ministry of Health. Private users may purchase fixed value cards from e-Dirham member banks. Currently, the available denominations are Dhs.100, 200, 300, 500, 1,000, 3,000, and 5,000. While they say cash is no longer accepted at these ministries, call ahead before you purchase your e-Dirham card, just in case they have changed the rules and are now accepting cash as well.

Documents

Entry Visa

Immigration rules are the same throughout the Emirates but are subject to frequent change. The Ministry of Information Website (www.uaeinteract.com) states that 'visa regulations and costs are subject to change and should always be checked at the nearest UAE Embassy before travelling'.

In order to initiate your residence visa application process, make sure you enter Abu Dhabi on the correct entry visa. Rules for each type of visa will depend on your nationality.

If you are moving to the UAE to take up a job offer, your employer may have already applied for your employment visa. For many nationalities, UAE immigration and labour laws stipulate that all documentation must be completed in the home country, prior to arrival in the UAE. However, citizens of some countries are allowed to enter the UAE on a visit visa and process their employment and residency applications on arrival. As your sponsor, your employer is responsible for organising this.

Visit visas are issued to certain nationalities at the port of entry. (For a full list of nationalities entitled to an entry permit, see Entering Abu Dhabi [p. 19].) Citizens of other countries are required to obtain a visit visa before entering the UAE. An entry permit entitles the holder to stay for either 30 or 60 days from the date of entry. It is issued without any charge to citizens of the UK when entering the UAE, but other nationalities may be charged Dhs.100. The visit visa can be renewed once by the Immigration department at a cost of Dhs.500. A longer stay requires a 'visa run', back home or an hour long flight to Muscat, Doha, Bahrain in order to get a UAE exit stamp on your passport. It is currently possible for some nationalities to stay in the UAE indefinitely so long as visa runs are undertaken every 60 days.

Note: You are not allowed to work in the UAE whilst on a visit visa.

If you manage to secure work while on a visit visa, you will have to transfer to an employment visa in order to apply for your residence visa and labour card. Your new employer should help you arrange this. You can transfer your visa status through the Immigration Department. You will need the relevant application form (obtainable from the Immigration Department) typed in Arabic, Essential Documents (see [p.49]), a copy of your original labour contract from your new employer and a copy of your sponsor's original passport plus Dhs.100. Alternatively, you can fly out of the country and re-enter on an employment visa.

Office Locations

Abu Dhabi: Immigration Dept, Saeed bin Tahnoon St (446 2244) (Map Ref 3-C2)

Al Ain: Immigration Dept, Aditaba Rd, near Dubai Islamic Bank (03 762 5555)

Health Card

Once you have the correct visa status (see above), the next step to becoming a resident is to apply for a health card, which is valid for one year. This entitles residents to relatively cheap medical treatment at public hospitals and clinics (emergency cases are free). Some employers provide additional private medical insurance and, as in most countries, this is regarded as preferable to state care, although the usual hospital horror stories apply to both sectors.

To apply for your health card, first collect an application form from the Central Hospital or any government clinic. Submit the application form (typed in Arabic) at the hospital of your choice along with the Essential Documents, a letter of employment and Dhs.300. In return, they will issue you with a temporary health card and a receipt for Dhs.300.

You can then go for your medical test. For this, you will need the temporary health card, a copy of the receipt for Dhs.300 and two passport photos. The total cost is Dhs.207, which includes Dhs.7 for typing the application form in Arabic (this is done by the hospital). The medical test includes a medical examination, a chest x-ray and a blood test for aids, hepatitis etc. If you are processing a health card for a maid, you will need to pay an additional Dhs.100 to have him or her vaccinated against hepatitis, and an additional Dhs.10 for typing out the form (refer to Domestic Help [p.74]).

Al Noor Hospital

Your temporary health card will be returned to you, and 2 - 3 days later you can collect your medical certificate. The temporary health card will have a date on it stating when to collect your permanent health card. This can take anywhere from a week to a few months. In the meantime, the temporary health card can be used at government hospitals, should you require treatment.

If you prefer to have your medical test in a private hospital where the conditions tend to be slightly better, you can go to the Al Noor Hospital. At Dhs.650, it's more expensive than going the government hospital route. You will need to present your passport copy and four passport photos along with the fee.

If you intend to apply for a UAE driving licence, you can obtain a certificate showing your blood group at the time of your medical test.

Office Locations

Abu Dhabi: Public Health Dept, Central Hospital (633 1300), entrance on Al Karama St between Al Manhal St (9th) and Sudan St (11th) (Map Ref 5-C2)

Al Noor Hospital (626 5265), Khalifa St (Map Ref 8 C2)

Al Ain: Al Ain Hospital (03 763 5888), Shakhbut bin Sultan Rd

Residence Visa

There are two types of residence visa – when you are sponsored for employment, and when a family member sponsors you for residency only. As stated, the first step to gaining a residence visa is to apply for a health card.

Once a resident, you must not leave the UAE for more than six months without revisiting, otherwise your residency will lapse. This is not relevant to children studying abroad who are on their parents' sponsorship here, as long as proof of enrolment with the educational institution overseas is furnished.

Office Locations:

Abu Dhabi: Immigration Department, Saeed bin Tahnoon St (446 2244) (Map Ref 3-C2)

Al Ain: Immigration Department, Aditaba Rd, near Dubai Islamic Bank (03 762 5555)

Sponsorship by Employer

Your employer should handle all the paperwork and will often have a staff member (who is thoroughly familiar with the ins and outs of the bureaucracy) dedicated for this task alone. After arranging for your residency, they should then apply directly for your labour card (see Labour Card [p.54]). The Ministry of Labour Website (www.mol.gov.ae) outlines the procedures involved in obtaining a labour card, but currently,

the English version of the Website is still under construction. Once complete, it will include a feedback section as well as a facility for companies to process their applications and transactions over the Internet.

You will need to supply the Essential Documents and education or degree certificates. You must have your certificates attested by a solicitor or public notary in your home country, and then by your foreign office to verify the solicitor as bona fide. The UAE Embassy in your home country must also sign the documents. Of course, it would make life much simpler if you could do all this before you've landed in Abu Dhabi! However, there are several courier services, such as DHL and UPS, ensuring fast and secure delivery of your important papers and making the process a lot smoother.

If you are working for a UAE government body, the certificate must also be verified and certified by the Ministry of Higher Education in the UAE.

Family Sponsorship

If you are sponsored and are in turn arranging residency for family members under your sponsorship since your employer will not do so, you will have a lengthy and tedious process ahead. Good luck!

To sponsor your wife or children, you will need a minimum monthly salary of Dhs.3,000 plus accommodation or a minimum all inclusive salary of Dhs.4,000. Only information printed on your labour contract will be accepted as proof of your earnings.

When parents sponsor children, difficulties arise when sons (not daughters) become 18 years old. Unless they are enrolled in full time education in the UAE, they must transfer their visa to an independent sponsor or the parents may pay a Dhs.5,000 security deposit (once only) and apply for an annual, renewable visa. If they are still in education, they may remain under parental sponsorship but again, only on an annual basis.

Babies born abroad to expatriate mothers holding a UAE residency are required to have a residence visa or a visit visa before entering the UAE. The application should be filed by the father or family provider and submitted along with the Essential Documents, a salary certificate and a birth certificate. The residence visa for newborns does not require a security check, so the process promises to be faster than most.

It is very difficult for a woman to sponsor her family, but there are some exceptions to this rule. Those women employed as doctors, lawyers, teachers etc, earning a minimum stipulated salary, may be permitted to sponsor family members. In most cases though, the husband/father will be the sponsor. When sponsoring parents, there are certain constraints depending on your visa status ie, you should be in a certain category of employment, such as a manager, and earning over Dhs.6,000 per month. In addition, a special committee meets to review each case individually – usually to consider the age of the parents that are to be sponsored, their health requirements etc. Even when a visa is granted, it is only valid for one year and is reviewed for renewal on an annual basis.

If you are resident under family sponsorship and then decide to work, you will need to apply for a labour card. You will also need a second medical test – this should be paid for by your employer.

The Process

To become a resident, collect a residency application form from the Immigration Department and have it typed in Arabic. Then submit the application along with the Essential Documents, medical certificate and Dhs.100.

It is essential that you fill out the names of your parents (including your mother's maiden name) in the specified section. Once the application is approved (this may take up to a month), you will be issued with a permit of entry for Abu Dhabi and you must exit and re-enter the country, submitting the entry permit on re-entry to passport control, where your passport will be stamped. You will be required to have an iris scan, which is done by the Immigration Department at Abu Dhabi airport. You should then submit your original passport to the Immigration Department, along with the original passport of your nominated sponsor, your medical certificate, four passport photos and Dhs.300, in order to get your permanent residency stamp. This can take anywhere from ten days to two months or longer. Then you can relax!

Once you have your residency stamp in your passport, your sponsor or employer may insist that they need to keep your passport. This seems to be the accepted practice among many local sponsors. However, there are currently no legal requirements under UAE law for you to hand over your passport. If you aren't comfortable with them keeping it, don't let them! Additionally, you may need it when visiting your consulate, setting up a bank account etc. Other sponsors will keep your labour card in return for you keeping the passport, but this is also a grey area because the law requires you to

produce your labour card immediately if the police ask to see it.

As a fully fledged resident, you are now welcome to take out a bank loan, buy a car, rent an apartment in your own name, get a liquor licence etc.

Labour Card

To work in the UAE, you are legally required to have a valid labour card. This can only be applied for once you have residency. Additionally, expatriate workers who do not renew their labour card will face a penalty of anywhere between Dhs.500 and Dhs.2,000. A fine of Dhs.500 will be imposed for a card expired six months, Dhs.1,000 for a card expired one year and Dhs.2,000 for cards expired longer than one year.

If your employer is arranging your residency, the labour card should be processed directly after residency has been approved. You should not need to supply any further documentation. Before your labour card is issued, you will need to sign your labour contract, which is printed in both Arabic and English. It's a standard form issued by the labour authorities and completed with your details. Unless you read Arabic, it may be advisable to have a translation made of your details, since the Arabic is taken as the legal default if there is any dispute (see Employment Contracts [p.60]).

If you are on family residency and decide to work, your employer, not your visa sponsor, will need to apply for a labour card. Your sponsor will need to supply an NOC (letter of no objection). Sponsored women are not allowed to be employed, even part time, unless they have a labour card. Expat students on their parent's visa who manage to find temporary work during vacations should also apply for a permit allowing them to work legally. Ensure that your employer does supply you with a labour card – the penalties for dependants working without a card are severe and can include jail and deportation.

To get a labour card you will need to supply the Essential Documents (see [p.49]), an NOC, education certificate/s (if appropriate) and usually a photocopy of your sponsor's passport – they may also require the sponsor's original passport.

Office Locations:

Abu Dhabi – Labour & Social Affairs (667 1700) (Map Ref 10-C1)

Al Ain – Labour and Social Affairs (03 762 9999).

Certificates & Licences

Driving Licence

Taking to the roads of the Emirates is taking your life in your hands! The standard of driving leaves much to be desired.

Until you acquire full residency, you can drive a rental car provided you have a valid driving licence from your country of origin (and not from any other country in which you have resided in the past), or an international licence from a country on the transfer list below. Make sure your driving licence details are registered with the rental company.

There is some confusion about who is allowed to drive private vehicles. If you are on a visit visa and have an international licence, the Traffic Police say you can drive a private vehicle, but some insurers dispute this. Other visa categories must apply to the Traffic Police for a temporary Abu Dhabi licence. You will need to fill out the application form and take your Essential Documents and Dhs.10 to obtain a temporary licence that is valid for one month (longer periods are also available). It is probably best to ring the car owner's insurance company and the Licensing Department (419 5558) who issue temporary licences for clarification before venturing onto the roads in a private car.

Once you have your residence visa, you must apply for a permanent UAE licence. Nationals of certain countries can automatically transfer their driving licence, providing the original licence is valid.

Traffic in Abu Dhabi

Automatic Licence Transfer

Australia, Austria, Belgium, Canada, Cyprus, Czech Republic, Denmark, Finland, France, Germany, Greece, Holland, Iceland, Ireland, Italy, Japan, Luxembourg, New Zealand, Norway, Poland, Portugal, Slovakia, Singapore, South Africa, South Korea, Spain, Sweden, Switzerland, Turkey, United Kingdom, United States of America.

Some of these licences will need an Arabic translation from your embassy or consulate – check with the Traffic Police Licensing Department. You may also be required to sit a short written test on road rules before the transfer takes place.

To apply for a permanent driving licence, submit the following documents (see below) to the Traffic Police Licensing Department, plus your valid Abu Dhabi residence visa and Dhs.200. When submitting your documents, you will also be required to take an eye test.

Always carry your Abu Dhabi driving licence when driving. If you fail to produce it during a police spot check, you will be fined. The licence is valid for ten years and if you manage to drive on the UAE roads for that long without going crazy, you deserve a medal!

If you are from a country that falls under the automatic licence transfer list, but your licence has expired, you will have to sit the full driving test. The alternative is to return home, renew your licence and save yourself the hassle.

Driving Licence Documents

- The relevant application form from the Traffic Police typed in Arabic

Plus the following essential documents:

- A copy of your sponsor's passport or a copy of the company's trade licence. Sometimes your sponsor's original passport is requested along with a copy. However, this seems to depend on whim more than anything concrete
- An NOC from your sponsor/company in Arabic
- Your original driving licence along with a photocopy (and translation, if requested by the Traffic Police)
- Certificate or card showing your blood group. Abu Dhabi licences show this information in case of an accident.

Office Locations: *Abu Dhabi Traffic Police Licensing Department, (419 5555) 23rd St, between Eastern Ring Rd and New Airport Rd. (Map Ref 3-B1)*

Note: *The Abu Dhabi Police Website (www.adpolice.gov.ae) contains some (limited) information and an email contact facility.*

Driving Test

If your nationality is not on the automatic transfer list, you will need to sit a UAE driving test to be eligible to drive in Abu Dhabi, regardless of whether you hold a valid driving licence from your country or not. If you haven't driven in your country of origin and need to obtain a driving licence, the following information will apply to you as well.

The first step is to obtain a learning permit – start by picking up an application form from the Traffic Police. You will need your Essential Documents, the driving licence documents and Dhs.40. You will be given an eye test at the Traffic Police department. Then find a reputable driving school – ask around for personal recommendations or check the yellow pages. Several of the establishments listed will simply supply you with phone numbers for individual instructors.

Car Showroom

Some driving institutions insist that you pay for a set of pre-booked lessons. In some cases, the package extends to 52 lessons and can cost up to Dhs.3,000! The lessons must be taken on consecutive days and usually last 30 - 45 minutes. Other companies offer lessons on an hourly basis as and when you like, for about Dhs.35 per hour. Women are traditionally required to take lessons with a female instructor at a cost of Dhs.65 per hour. If a woman wants to take lessons with a male instructor, she must first obtain an NOC from her husband/sponsor and the Traffic Police. That said, if she has previous driving experience, she will have to sit a test with an instructor who could be male before signing up for lessons (no NOCs required for this one!).

When your instructor feels that you are ready to take your test, you will be issued with a letter to that effect and can now apply for a test date. You will need to fill out the necessary application form at the Traffic Police and also hand in your Essential Documents, driving licence documents, and Dhs.35. The time between submitting your application and the test date can be as long as two to three months.

You will be given three different tests on different dates. One is a Highway Code test, another an 'internal' test which includes garage parking etc, and the third is a road test. When you have passed all three tests, you will be issued with a certificate (after about five days), which you should take to the Traffic Police to apply for your permanent driving licence.

Driving Schools

Abu Dhabi Motor Training School	448 4878
Al Harbi Driving School	671 6177
Al Harbi Driving School for Ladies	050 445 4643
Al Nahda Motor Drivers Training School	633 8061
Al Nahda Motor Drivers Training School for Ladies	050 570 8131
Linda Drivers Training School	642 0006

Liquor Licence

Other Options → **Alcohol [p.148]**
Liquor Stores [p.149]

Although Abu Dhabi has a moderately liberal attitude towards the consumption of alcohol by non-Muslims, this should be seen as a privilege, not a right. Anyone arrested for being drunk in a public place faces imprisonment and a fine.

In public, only four and five star hotels, and some social clubs are licensed to serve alcohol.

If you wish to buy alcohol to drink at home, you will need a special liquor licence, which entitles you to buy from a liquor shop (not the local supermarket). Only non-Muslims with a residence visa may obtain a licence. The liquor licence allows you to spend a limited amount on alcohol per month – the allowance is 10% of your monthly salary and can go up to a maximum of Dhs.2500. To apply, collect an application form from your local liquor store or the Police headquarters. Application forms must be typed in Arabic. You must get your employer to sign and stamp the form, then take it to the General Directorate of Police Department (next to the Sharia Court Map Ref 2-C1), along with the Essential Documents and your labour contract (stating your salary). Some nationalities must also supply a letter from their embassy stating that they are not Muslims. The cost of this is Dhs.40.

The licence fee is 20% of your permit value and payment must be in cash. Permits are usually issued on Saturdays and Sundays between the hours of 08:00 - 11:00. Arrive early as there is usually a queue! Once you receive your licence, cross the road to the Al Diar Capitol Hotel on Al Meena Road and step into High Spirits (677 8370), the liquor store located within the hotel. You can now purchase your first month's supply of precious alcohol!

When renewing a liquor licence, the expired licence should be returned. If the residence visa has been issued by a different emirate, a letter will be required confirming that no liquor licence has already been issued elsewhere.

Buying alcohol from liquor shops can be expensive as you have to pay an additional tax of 30% on all items. This amount is not shown on the price tag but included in the total bill. However, the range of alcohol for sale is good. Once you have purchased your liquor, you must head straight home and unload it because it is illegal to drive around Abu Dhabi carrying alcohol, except for the journey from shop to home.

When arriving in Abu Dhabi by air, you are allowed to purchase four bottles of liquor from the airport duty free shop and you do not need a licence to do so.

There are cheaper alternatives for buying alcohol where again, a licence is not required, such as Ajman's 'Hole in the Wall' near the Ajman Kempinski. Umm Al Quwain also has outlets by the Barracuda Resort next to the Dreamland Aqua Park and the Umm al Quwain Beach Hotel. However, if

Zero Tolerance

If you have consumed any alcohol, under no circumstances should you drive. The Authorities in Abu Dhabi have a very strict zero tolerance policy where a jail sentence will be the least of your worries! Also, if you are involved in a traffic accident and found to have alcohol in your bloodstream, your vehicle insurance will be void, even if you did not cause the accident.

A leaflet describing the law and penalties can be found at the liquor shops, which details the law and penalties in very clear terms.

you do decide go for this option, be well aware that it is illegal to transport liquor around the Emirates. This law is enforced, particularly in Sharjah, which is a dry Emirate.

The Abu Dhabi police Website (www.adpolice.gov.ae) has some information on liquor licences and an email enquiry facility.

Birth Certificates & Registration

Every expat child born in the UAE must be registered at the Ministry of Health within two weeks and have a residence visa within 40 days of birth. Without the correct documentation, you may not be able to take your baby out of the country.

The hospital where the baby is delivered will prepare the official 'notification of birth' certificate in English or Arabic upon receipt of hospital records, photocopies of both parents' passports and marriage certificate, and a fee of Dhs.50. Take the notification certificate for translation into English to the Preventative Medicine Department (Central Hospital in Abu Dhabi; Al Ain Hospital in Al Ain), where you will be issued with an application form, which must then be typed in English. You should also take the certificate to be attested at the Ministry of Health (Dhs.10 fee) and the Ministry of Justice and Foreign Affairs (Dhs.50 fee). The father of the baby needs to be present for these procedures.

Once this is done, ensure you register your child's birth at your embassy or consulate. To do this you will require the local notification of birth certificate, both parents' birth certificates, passports and marriage certificate. At the same time, you may want to arrange a passport for your baby. Then, you must apply for a residence visa through the normal UAE channels.

Before the birth, it is worth checking the regulations of your country of origin for citizens born overseas. (See [p.104] for a list of embassies and consulates in Abu Dhabi.)

Marriage Certificates & Registration

Most people prefer to return to their country of origin in order to get married, but if you are planning to marry in Abu Dhabi, you have a number of options.

Muslims

As a Muslim marrying another Muslim, you should apply at the marriage section of the Sharia Court, Sheikh Zayed Court (665 2000). You will need two male witnesses and the bride should ensure that either her father or brother attends as a witness. You will require your passports and copies, and proof that the groom is Muslim. A fee of Dhs.50 will be charged, and you can marry there and then.

For a Muslim woman marrying a non-Muslim man, the situation is more complicated as the man must first convert to Islam. For further information, the Sharia Court can advise. This can be an incredibly long and complicated process (up to six months before the paperwork is complete) and many couples end up returning to their country of origin to marry.

Location: *Sharia Court, off Coast Rd (Map Ref 2-C1)*

Opening Hours: *07:30 - 14:00 & 17:30 - 20:30*

Atheists

Atheists should contact their embassy for information on arranging a local civil marriage.

Christians

Christians can either choose to have a formal ceremony at the church with a congregation, or a small ceremony at the church with a blessing afterwards at a different location, such as a hotel. The cost of a ceremony and church fees is Dhs.250. At the official church ceremony, you will need two witnesses to sign the marriage register. The church then issues a marriage certificate (you will also need to take copies of your passport and residence visa). You can take the certificate and your Essential Documents to your embassy in order to attest the document. If you are Anglican, you will be required to fill out a number of forms stating your intent to marry, that you are not Muslim, and confirming that you are legally free to marry. Documents required are a residency visa for at least one partner, your original passport and photocopies, passport sized photos and a letter

from both sets of parents stating that you are legally free to marry. If you have previously been married, you will need to produce either your divorce certificate or the death certificate of your previous partner.

This marriage is recognised by the government of the UAE, and the chaplain's signature may be authenticated after the ceremony by taking an Arabic translation of the marriage certificate to the Ministry of Justice and Foreign Affairs. Filipino citizens are required to contact their embassy before the court will authenticate the marriage certificate. Contact the multi-denominational church of St Andrews (446 1631) for more information.

Catholics must also undertake a marriage encounter course, which usually takes place on weekday evenings. You will need to fill out a standard form, and at the end of the course you are presented with a certificate. You should then arrange with the priest to undertake a pre-nuptial ceremony and again, you are asked to fill out a form. You will need to take your birth certificate, baptism certificate, passport and passport copies, as well as NOC from your parish priest in your home country. If you are a non-Catholic marrying a Catholic, you will need an NOC from your embassy/consulate stating that you are legally free to marry. A declaration of your intent to marry is posted on the public noticeboard at the church for three weeks, after which time, if there are no objections, you can set a date for the ceremony. Contact St Josephs church (446 1929).

Hindus

Hindus can be married through the Indian embassy – for further details, contact the marriage section (449 2700). They publish a booklet with guidelines on how to get married and you'll have to fill out an application form on the premises. Formalities take a minimum of 45 days.

Death Certificates & Registration

In the unhappy event of a death of a friend or a relative, the first thing to do is to notify the police. On arrival, the police will make a report and the body will be taken to a hospital, where a doctor will determine the cause of death. A post mortem examination/inquest is not normally performed, unless foul play is suspected or the death is a violent one. Contact the deceased's embassy or consulate (see list on [p.104]) for guidance.

The authorities will need to see the deceased's passport and visa details. The hospital will issue a death certificate declaration on receipt of the doctor's report for a fee of Dhs.50. Make sure that the actual cause of death is stated. Then take the declaration of death and original passport to the Al Asima police station, next to Al Khalidiya Spinneys. The police will give permission to release the body in a letter which, along with the death declaration, original passport and copies, should be taken to the Department of Preventative Medicine. In Abu Dhabi, this is at the Central Hospital. In Al Ain, go to the Al Ain Hospital/Al Jimi. The actual death certificate is issued here for a small fee. If you are sending the deceased home, you should also request a death certificate in English (an additional Dhs.100) or apply to the legal profession for translation into other languages.

Then take the certificate to the Ministry of Health and the Ministry of Foreign Affairs for registration. Notify the relevant embassy/consulate for the death to be registered in the deceased's country of origin. They will also issue their own death certificate. Bring the original passport and death certificate for the passport to be cancelled.

The deceased's visa must also be cancelled by the immigration department. Take the local death certificate, original cancelled passport and the embassy/consulate death certificate.

To return the deceased to their country of origin, contact the cargo section of Omeir Travel (631 9997). Apparently, they have had the most experience in arranging this and will give you all the necessary information along with the procedure to follow.

The body will also need to be embalmed and you must obtain a letter to this intent from the police. Embalming can be arranged through the Central Hospital for Dhs.1,000, which includes the embalming certificate (there should be no charge if a copy of the deceased's medical card is supplied). The body must be identified before and after embalming.

The following documents should accompany the deceased overseas: the local death certificate, a translation of the death certificate, the embalming certificate, NOC from the police and the embassy/consulate death certificate and NOC, and the cancelled passport.

A local burial can be arranged at the Muslim or Christian cemeteries in Abu Dhabi. The cost is Dhs.1,000 for an adult and Dhs.250 for a child. As there are no undertakers in the city, you will need

to arrange for a coffin to be made as well as transportation to the burial site. The hospital will advise on this. Advice and guidance for burial in the Christian and non-Muslim cemetery can be obtained from the Parish Clerk at St Andrews Church (446 1631). Only Hindus may be cremated with the permission of the next of kin.

See also: *Support Groups [p.89]*

Work

Working in Abu Dhabi

Working in Abu Dhabi is very different from working in Asia, Europe or North America. The greatest advantage is the general proximity of everything – there are no stuffy trains to catch, no real distances to commute... and it's always sunny!

Expat workers share a common mission – to seek a better quality of life. They come from various countries and lifestyles, and many are skilled, educated and have a lot to contribute. There are those who have been seconded by companies based in their home country and those who have come to UAE in search of the expat lifestyle. However, don't be fooled – it's not all coffee and sunshine. Setting up life here and establishing a network is still hard work. Additionally, you only have developing labour laws to protect you.

Working Hours

Working hours vary quite dramatically within the emirate, and are based on straight shift and split shift timings. Split shifts allow for an afternoon siesta and timings are generally 08:00 - 13:00 and 16:00 - 19:00. Straight shift timings vary from government organisations (07:00 - 14:00) to private companies (09:00 - 18:00).

The working week for many companies is based on a traditional five and a half day week with Thursday afternoon and Friday off, although more are adopting a two day (Thursday/Friday) weekend. Some private companies have a two day, Friday/Saturday, weekend, although this is more common in Dubai than in Abu Dhabi. Government offices and schools have a two day, Thursday and Friday, weekend.

Public holidays are set by the government and religious holidays are governed by the moon. During Ramadan, organisations are meant to reduce working hours for their Muslim employees with the public sector working a six hour day. For more details on Public Holidays, see [p.12].

Finding Work

If you do not have employment on arrival, the best way to find a job is to register with the recruitment agencies and to check the small ads and employment pages in the main newspapers. An employment supplement is published in Gulf News on Sundays, Tuesdays and Thursdays, and in Khaleej Times on Sundays, Mondays and Wednesdays.

A note of caution concerning the use of the words 'UK/US educated' in the papers. It would seem that this is an 'accepted' form of discrimination. Basically, it should read 'white, western educated'. Ironically, the UAE government is strongly encouraging the private sector to give preference to Nationals when employing staff for white collar, management positions. While, at this time, there are no precise laws to force the private sector to employ Nationals, a quota system for international companies is under discussion. This, of course, will make it more difficult for even well qualified expat workers to find a job in the UAE.

Social Life

Circle of Friends

Try to be open minded and make an effort to get to know people from all backgrounds. Diversity is the spice of life.

The Rumour Mill

Abu Dhabi has a very healthy grapevine and quite often you'll know of people even before you meet them. In the end, everyone knows what's going on! If possible, use it to your advantage, but remember... even walls have ears.

Live it Up!

Get ready to live the high life with five star hotels galore. In the Emirates, you can do more for less, so you've no excuse to stay at home.

Recruitment Agencies

There is a big number of recruitment/employment agencies in Abu Dhabi and Dubai that offer recruitment consultancy for Abu Dhabi and Al Ain. To register, check with the agency and find out if they take 'walk ins'. These days, many agencies only accept CVs via email and then contact you for an interview. For the interview, you will need both your CV and passport photographs. Invariably, you will also have to fill out an agency form

summarising your CV. The agency takes its fee from the registered company once the position has been filled. It is illegal for a recruitment company to levy fees on candidates for this service.

Don't rely too heavily on the agency finding a job for you; more often than not, they depend on you spotting a vacancy that they have advertised in the paper and telephoning them to submit your interest. Should you be suitable for the job, the agency will mediate between you and the employer and arrange all interviews.

Below is a list of recruitment agencies operating in the UAE. Some of these agencies have branches throughout the Emirates and some are specialised for certain industries, so do your research and register accordingly. Good luck!

Main Recruitment Agencies	
ABC Recruitment Agency	676 8558
Jobscan	627 5592
Nadia	677 4031
Resources	644 2868
SOS Recruitment Consultants	626 7700
Clarendon Parker	04 391 0460
Kershaw Leonard	04 343 4606

Employment Contracts

Never sign a contract on the spot. You will be thanking us all the way to the bank! Take a copy of the proposed contract home for overnight reflection (and perhaps interjection by a well intentioned friend). This is a binding and legal contract, and severely affects your life in Abu Dhabi, so before you leap in, make sure it's the job that you really want. You can even opt to put an initial three month introductory period into your contract before processing your visa under the company. Once you have accepted a job offer, you may be asked to sign a copy of your contract in Arabic as well as in English. Be sure to check the Arabic translation before you sign, as this is taken as the legal default if there is a dispute. There have been instances of the Arabic reading differently from the English. You should also refer to a copy of the UAE labour law (see below) for details of other benefits and entitlements.

If you are sponsored by your spouse and wish to work, you will need to obtain an NOC (no objection certificate) from him/her before signing a contract with your new employer. Your employer will then apply for your labour card. This card is very important; if an officer asks you to show your card and you are unable to produce one, you can be fined Dhs.1,200 and be sent to jail.

Labour Law

The UAE Labour Law is a work in progress; the most recent version available is from 1980, though updates and amendments occur frequently. The Labour Law outlines everything from employee entitlements (end of service gratuity, workers' compensation, holidays etc) to employment contracts and disciplinary rules. The law tends to favour employer rights but it also clearly outlines those employee rights that do exist in the UAE.

Labour unions are illegal, as are strikes. Recent moves have been made by the Ministry of Labour to assist workers (particularly labourers) in labour disputes against their employers. The Ministry now punishes companies who do not comply with the Labour Law – licences can be withdrawn if warnings are not heeded. Non payment of salaries is a common problem, hopefully to be sorted out one day. However, if you are facing this ugly dilemma, you do have rights. You can file a case with the UAE Labour Department who will then follow up with your employer on your behalf and pressure them to pay you your due wages. You may opt to get a lawyer, which can be less confusing than dealing with a governmental agency, but more expensive as fees can accrue. For recommendations, referrals and consultation, call your embassy.

A copy of the UAE Labour Law may be available from your employer or it can be obtained through the Ministry of Labour & Social Affairs (667 1700). The UAE Labour Guide, published by the Ministry in 2002, also outlines workers' rights.

'Banning'

While it is natural to seek out better work opportunities, many expats live in fear of being banned if they change employer. This is one area of the law that seems to change on a monthly basis. Hence, it's best to check with the Labour Department or someone who's in the know for the latest version. No matter what, in most cases, red tape and visa transferring hassles apply, so check out all options before making any moves.

The government's aim is to stop people from job hopping, and the visa laws favour the educated, degree holding specialist. Unless you work in a free zone, hold a Master's degree, or are in a special category of employment, if you resign from your job, you could potentially receive a six month ban from working elsewhere in the UAE. This stands even if you have an NOC letter from your previous employer. It helps your case if you've worked in your company at least one year, but until the law is set in stone once and for all, this area really is up in the air.

People resigning from a job fall into three groups...

- Those who resign to return to their own country: The residence visa will be cancelled. If they wish to live/work here in the future, they must find a new sponsor and go through the application procedures for residency etc, from the beginning.
- Those who resign to look for other work: If they are lucky, their old company will supply an NOC and their residency can be transferred, so long as they have been employed by the company for over one year and that they fall into certain categories of employment.
- Those who resign to work for another company: People in this category run the risk of a labour ban and residence visa cancellation. This applies where the person was employed on a specified term contract and leaves before the end of the term. Those on an unlimited contract may only risk an immigration ban.

For details of the employee categories that cannot currently be banned, refer to the most recent version of the UAE Labour Law.

Company Closure

Some people and companies move around and see the UAE as a place to make money and run. Employees who face the unlucky situation of bankruptcy or company closure are entitled under UAE Labour Law to receive their due gratuity payments, holidays etc. But claiming your rights will not be easy (the Ministry of Labour can advise on proper procedures). Additionally, no employee of a firm which has been closed is allowed to transfer sponsorship to their new employer unless an attested certificate of closure by their previous employer is issued by the court and submitted to the Ministry of Labour. If you are unfortunate enough to have to deal with this, consult the appropriate government offices or get legal representation in order to get your paperwork right.

Financial & Legal Affairs

Banks

Abu Dhabi is not short of internationally recognised banks offering standard facilities, such as current, deposit and savings accounts, ATMs (otherwise known as automatic teller machines, service tills or cashpoints), chequebooks, credit cards, loans and more. There are plenty of ATM machines around Abu Dhabi (location details can be obtained from the bank) and most cards are compatible with other Abu Dhabi based banks (a few also offer global access links).

In most banks in Abu Dhabi, to open a bank account, you need to have a residence visa or have your residency application underway. You will need to present the banking advisor with your original passport, copies of your passport (personal details and visa) and an NOC from your sponsor. Some banks set a minimum account limit (this can be around Dhs.2,000 for a deposit account and as much as Dhs.5,000 for a current account).

Without a residence visa, Middle East bank, known as ME bank, will open an account for you and provide an ATM card, but not a chequebook. ME bank also allows you to apply online for a bank account at www.me.ae.

Opening Hours: *Saturday - Wednesday 08:00 - 13:00; Thursday 08:00 - 12:00. Some banks such as Mashreq and Standard Chartered also open in the evenings from 16:30 - 18:30.*

National Bank of Abu Dhabi

Cost of Living

Drinks	
Beer (pint/bottle)	Dhs.25
Fresh fruit cocktail	Dhs.10
House wine (glass)	Dhs.20
House wine (bottle)	Dhs.90 - 120
Milk (1 litre)	Dhs.3
Water	
1.5 litres (supermarket)	Dhs.2
1.5 litres (hotel)	Dhs.10 - 18

Food	
Big Mac	Dhs.9
Bread (large)	Dhs.4 - 8
Cappuccino	Dhs.7 - 15
Chocolate bar	Dhs.1.50 - 2
Eggs (dozen)	Dhs.5
Falafel	Dhs.2
Fresh fruit	Dhs.1-19/kg.
Fresh meat	Dhs.6-40/kg.
Sugar	Dhs.3.5/kg.
Shawarma	Dhs.3
Tin of tuna	Dhs.3

Miscellaneous	
Cigarettes (per packet)	Dhs.6
Film	Dhs.20
Film processing (colour, 36 exposures)	Dhs.35 - 45
Hair cut (female)	Dhs.100+
Hair cut (male)	Dhs.40
Postcard	Dhs.2

Getting Around	
Car rental (compact)	Dhs.90/day
Taxi (airport to city)	Dhs.40 - 50
Taxi (airport to beach)	Dhs.70 - 80
Taxi (+ Dhs.1.25 every km)	Dhs.3 drop charge
City tour (half day)	Dhs.110
Bus from airport to downtown	Dhs.3
Desert safari (half day)	Dhs.270

Entrance Fees	
Beach club (may include lunch)	Dhs.60 - 200
Cinema	Dhs.25 - 30
Museum	Dhs.2 - 10
Nightclub	Dhs.50 - 100
Park	Dhs.3 - 5

Sports	
Fishing (two hours)	Dhs.200
Go Karting (10 mins)	Dhs.30
Golf (18 holes)	Dhs.80 - 375
Jet ski hire (30 mins)	Dhs.100

Financial Planning

Planning for the financial future (unless you take the head in the sand approach!) is an important aspect of modern day life and especially necessary for expats.

Before you do anything, you should contact the tax authorities in your home country to ensure that you are complying with the financial laws there. Most countries will consider you not liable for income tax once you prove your UAE residence or your non residence in your home country (a contract of employment is normally a good starting point for proving non residence). As a non resident, however, you may still have to fulfil certain criteria (such as only visiting your home country for a limited number of days each year).

Generally, the main reason for accepting an expat posting is to improve your financial situation. It is recommended not to undertake any non cash investments until you know your monthly savings capacity, even though this may take up to six months to ascertain. In fact, the first steps you should take with your new earnings are to begin paying back as much debt as possible (starting with your credit card/s!).

If you have a short term contract, stay away from long term investment contracts. Once you have decided that the expat life is for you and that you are ready to plan for the future, you might want to establish the following: emergency cash buffer (3 - 6 months salary), retirement home, retirement income, personal and family protection (life insurance, health coverage) etc.

When selecting a financial planner, use either a reputable name or at least an institution regulated by the UAE Central Bank. If another authority is 'regulating' your advisor, you cannot expect the principal UAE authority to be of assistance to you, and your chances of recourse in the event of a problem may be severely hampered. For financial planners, we recommend word of mouth or any of the major international companies.

Taxation

The UAE levies no personal income taxes or withholding taxes of any sort. The only noticeable taxes you are obliged to pay as an

expat are a 30% tax on alcohol bought at liquor stores and a 15 - 16% service tax in hotel food and beverage outlets (these are no longer shown separately on the bill).

Legal Issues

The UAE is governed by Sharia law. This is Islamic canonical law based on the traditions of Prophet Mohammed (PBUH) and the teachings of the Koran, and only a graduate of a Sharia college can practice in court here. All court proceedings are conducted in Arabic, so it is important to hire legal representation that you trust.

For most people, any sort of brush with the 'wrong' side of the law can be a worrying experience, but in a foreign country and with an alien language, this can be particularly unnerving. If you are in serious difficulties, you should contact your embassy or consulate as soon as possible and follow their advice plus find yourself a good lawyer.

Warning: do not fall for any fantasies of opiate nights in the Middle East – such things are highly illegal here and sometimes even your embassy cannot get you out of trouble with the local authorities. For a list of legal consultants in Abu Dhabi, refer to [p.106].

Housing

Housing in Abu Dhabi

In the Abu Dhabi and Al Ain property markets, 'rental' is the name of the game. Unless you are born a UAE national or are a national of another GCC country, owning property or land in Abu Dhabi is not an option.

New residents arriving in Abu Dhabi on a full expatriate package may very well have accommodation included, but don't be fooled by the charm of the 'expat lifestyle' – life here can be expensive.

Search Tips

A Des. Res.?
In potential homes, check the proximity to mosques (the call to prayer five times a day starts before dawn), rubbish bins (very smelly), schools and government departments (traffic congestion and parking problems).

New Buildings
Look out for buildings under construction - it's often a good way to find a place you like and be one of the first on the waiting list. The guys on site should be able to give you the name of the real estate agent or landlord.

Noise Control
In the less built up areas, beware the area around your new home for it could be ripe for development - few people really appreciate a noisy building site just a few metres from their bedroom window! Construction work starts at about 06:00 and finishes by 21:00 or 22:00 with the odd 01:00 concrete pour, often seven days a week.

Renting a Home

In Abu Dhabi, rents over the past few years have consistently risen and in general, are very high. Whilst there are always new apartment blocks under construction, demand for medium to higher end properties has continued to outstrip supply. If your company does not provide accommodation, it can take time to find a suitable property. A few brave souls rent in Dubai and drive to Abu Dhabi to work, but the nightmare daily journey along Sheikh Zayed Road deters most expats from this option.

Rents are always quoted for the year, unless otherwise stated.

Real Estate Glossary

If you need to find your own accommodation, it is generally best to go through a real estate agent as they will handle all the paperwork for you. Most of the ads for the larger, reputable companies who advertise in the property sections of the newspapers will say 'No Viewing Fee'. However, many of the individuals who act as agents will try to charge you a Dhs.50 - 100 fee for every property they show you, even if it is totally unsuitable. Always check before agreeing to view any property.

It's worth noting that occasionally, single women still have difficulty renting apartments and may need to put their employer's name on the lease.

Housing Abbreviations

BR	*Bedroom*
Ensuite	*Bedroom has private bathroom*
Fully fitted	*Includes appliances (oven,kitchen refrigerator, washing machine)*
L/D	*Living/dining room area*
W/robes	*Built in wardrobes (closets)*
Hall flat	*Apartment has an entrance hall (ie, entrance doesn't open directly onto living room)*
D/S	*Double storey villa*
S/S	*Single storey villa*
C.A/C	*Central air conditioning (usually included in the rent)*
W.A/C	*Window air conditioning (often indicates an older building)*
S/Q	*Servant quarters*
Ext S/Q	*Servant quarters located outside the villa*
Pvt garden	*Private garden*
Shared pool	*Pool is shared with other villas in compound*

The Lease

To take out a lease personally, you need to be a resident. The real estate agent will need a copy of your passport and visa, a no objection letter (NOC) from your company, a copy of your salary certificate and an initial signed rent cheque (plus up to three post dated cheques covering the remaining period of the lease). Unlike elsewhere in the world, rent cheques have to be paid to the landlord upfront and not on a monthly basis. This can cause problems as many new residents do not have the cash available to pay this sort of lump sum in advance. Needless to say, banks are quick to offer loans. To rent through your company, you require a copy of the company trade licence, a passport copy of whoever is signing the rent cheque and, of course, the actual rent cheque/s.

Renters' Nightmare

The majority of leases in Abu Dhabi are fixed for one year and, unless you find a really nice landlord who offers you an opt out clause, you are locked in till the end of the year. And the penalty for breaking your contract? You might not get your deposit back and you certainly won't get the remainder of your rent back.

Be careful when you sign your lease. Make sure the apartment or villa you've just found is really the one you'd like to make your home for the next year.

If the contract is written only in Arabic, or in both Arabic and English, get the Arabic version translated before you sign. It has been known for dual versions of legal documents to differ and Arabic documents are always taken to be the correct version in the event of any dispute.

If you do have any problems with your lease agreement, rent disputes etc, the Department of Social Services and Commercial Buildings (615 1394) may be able to give advice. They are located in the Union National Bank Building on the Corniche.

Main Accommodation Options

Apartment/Villa Sharing

For those on a budget, the solution may be to share an apartment or villa with colleagues or friends. Check the noticeboards in supermarkets such as Abela and Spinneys, or sports clubs for people advertising shared accommodation. The classifieds section in the local newspapers also advertises accommodation.

Standard Apartment

There are generally two types of apartments available for rent – those with central air conditioning (A/C) and those with noisier window A/Cs where the unit is in the apartment wall. Central A/C accommodation is always more expensive although, in some buildings, the charge for A/C is absorbed into the rent. Top of the range, central A/C apartments often come semi-furnished (cooker, fridge and washing machine), boast 24 hour security, satellite TV, covered parking, gym, pool etc. Normally, the more facilities that come with the apartment, the more expensive the rent.

Villa

The same procedure applies to leasing villas as for apartments. Value for money villas are very hard to find in central Abu Dhabi and where you used to be able to find older, cheaper villas in some parts of Al Karama and Al Bateen, many are being demolished for redevelopment. As with apartments, villas differ greatly in the quality and facilities that are provided.

Hotel Apartments

An alternative option is to rent a hotel apartment – ideal if you require temporary, furnished accommodation, although they are expensive.

Apartments can be rented on a daily/ weekly/monthly or yearly basis. They come fully furnished (from sofas to knives and forks) and serviced (maid service) with satellite TV, and are often complemented by sports facilities (pool and gym etc). Water and electricity are also included in the rent. If you can, call around first because rates vary hugely according to the area and facilities provided. Rates at many hotel apartments also vary as they follow the resort hotel high and low season rates.

Help for Renters

The Khalifa Committee (www.ejarat.ae)

When seeking accommodation, this is one of the best sources in town. Commonly known as the Khalifa Committee, their proper name is The Department of Social Services and Commercial Buildings. This government organisation acts as a commission free clearing house for flats, villas and other real estate rentals. Reasonable in English, friendly and computerised, they list hundreds of properties and can provide pricing details, the owners' names and contact numbers, and detailed maps. Mind the government hours though, and be prepared for some quirky frustrations. But given the scandalous rental agencies that abound in Abu Dhabi, this office is a godsend.

Location: 5th floor, Union National Bank Building on the Corniche.

Residential Areas

As in all cities, there are obvious areas of desirable residence. The more upmarket area for villas is Al Khalidiya with cheaper options in Rhoda, Al Karama and Al Bateen, and the mainly Arabic areas of Muroor and Al Dhafra. The most popular areas for apartments tend to be along the Corniche and Al Khalidiya, with cheaper alternatives found more centrally on Sheikh Hamdan Street, Najda Street (Bani yas Street) and Sheikh Zayed 2nd Street as well as further out of the town centre on Airport Road and New Airport Road. A glance through the property pages in the newspapers will give you an idea of what's available where and for how much. However, the best deals are often still found by word of mouth. If you find an apartment building you like, you can ask the security guard if there are currently any vacant apartments.

Check out the following areas plus the maps at the back of the book to get a feel for the layout of the city.

Airport Road

Map Ref → 1-D4, 2-C2, 3-C1

- Mix of old and new high rise apartments
- Lower rents in this area
- Wide mix of nationalities
- Early morning traffic congestion

New Airport Road

Map Ref → 2-B3/C3, 3-B1/B3

- Mainly less expensive tower blocks alongside a few newer, pricier ones
- Good mix of nationalities
- Possible parking problem if not included in rent
- Early morning traffic congestion

Al Bateen

Map Ref → 6-A2,/C3, 9-C1

- Very popular, prestigious and quiet area
- Larger villas and more expensive low rise apartment blocks
- Mainly expat Arabs and UAE Nationals
- Roadside parking usually available

Abu Dhabi Apartment Blocks

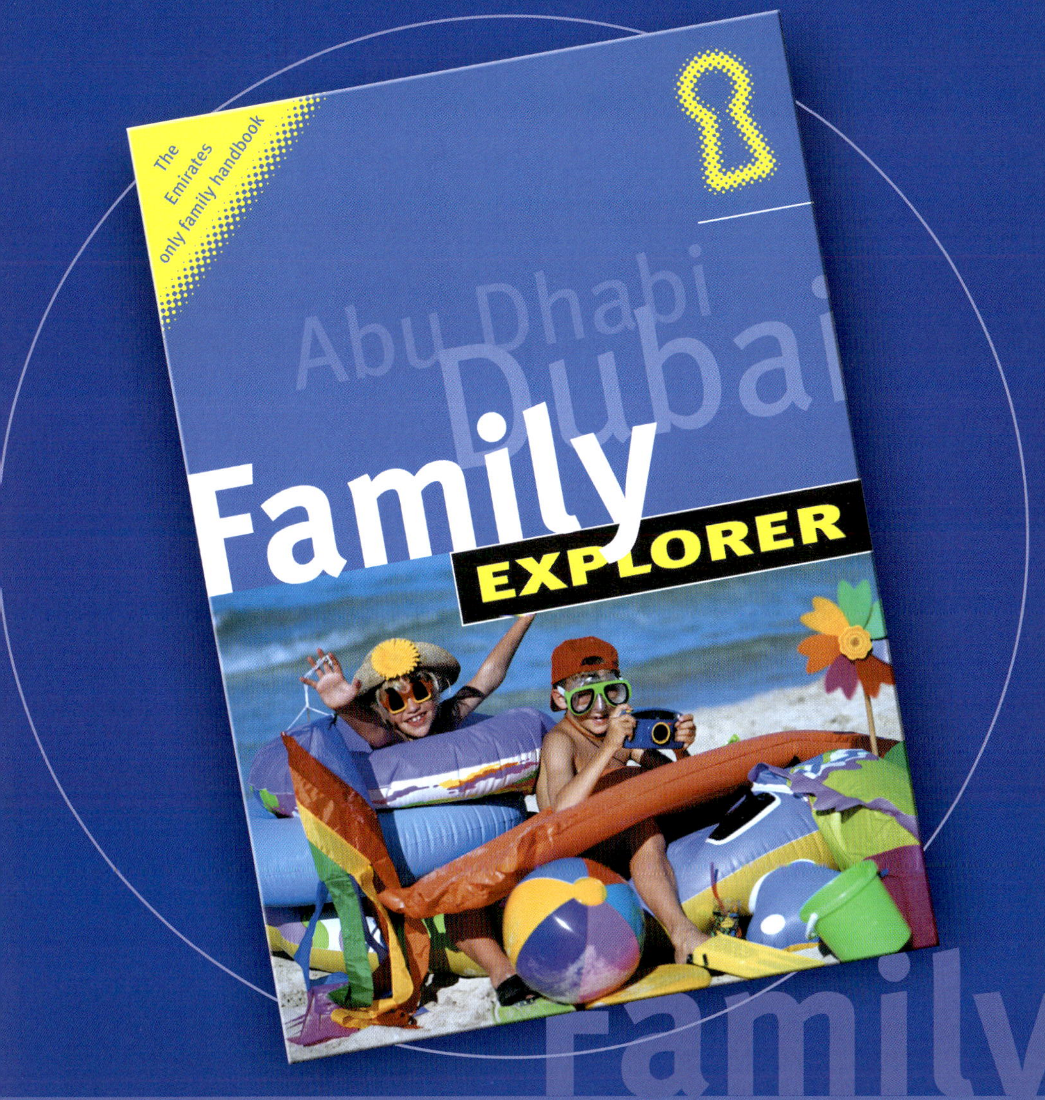
The Emirates only family handbook
Abu Dhabi
Dubai
Family
EXPLORER
Family

Annual Rent

B/R	Apartments	Villas
1	30,000 – 45,000	na
2	40,000 – 80,000	na
3	70,000 – 130,000	90,000 – 160,000
4	90,000 – 175,000	110,000 – 250,000

Corniche — Map Ref → 8-A3/B3

- Very expensive, modern, high rise apartments with beautiful sea views
- Parking difficult to find unless your building has underground parking
- Major road works and construction scheduled along Corniche until 2005

Electra (Nr Town Centre) — Map Ref → 8-A1/D1

- Plenty of hustle and bustle within this mix of commercial and residential towers
- Mainly older towers with some newer executive apartment blocks
- Possible parking problem if not included in rent
- Traffic congestion most of the day
- Mainly Asian men and expat Arabs

Hamdan Street — Map Ref → 8-B2/D2

- A lively mix of commercial and residential towers
- Mainly older towers but some newer, more expensive apartments
- Possible parking problem if not included in rent
- Traffic congestion during rush hour
- Good mix of nationalities

Al Karama & Old Mushrif — Map Ref → 3-C4, 5-C1, 3-D3

- Much sought after, long established expat areas
- Mainly low rise flats and older villas
- Near British and International Schools
- Leafy trees and shrubs give pleasant feel to neighbourhood
- Mainly Western expats and Nationals

Al Khalidiya — Map Ref → 9-D1

- Very expensive, large villas and high rise luxury apartments
- Mainly Western expats, Nationals and expat Arabs
- Near or on the famous Abu Dhabi Corniche
- Quiet, peaceful area
- Near the American Community School

Manaseer — Map Ref → 6-A2

- Much sought after older apartments
- Low rise apartments; not cheap but never vacant for long
- Quiet, open area with ample greenery
- Palaces and embassies as neighbours!

Muroor — Map Ref → 3-B2

- Well out of town, hence lower rents
- Low rise buildings and large villas along the main roads
- Near the American International School
- Mix of Asians, expat Arabs and Nationals

Rhoda — Map Ref → 5-D2, 6-A2

- Villas much sought after by Western expats
- Located near Embassy Road
- Quiet, lush, green, open area

Other Rental Costs

Extra costs to be considered are:

- Water and electricity deposit (Dhs.2,000 for villas and Dhs.1,000 for apartments) paid directly to Abu Dhabi Water & Electricity Authority (ADWEA)
- Real estate commission – 5% of annual rent (one off payment)
- Maintenance charge – 5% of annual rent

The Corniche

- Municipality tax – 5% of annual rent
- Fully refundable security deposit – Dhs.2,000 - 5,000)
- Some landlords also require a deposit against damage (usually a fully refundable, one off payment).

Real Estate Agents

Asteco	626 2660
Hyatt Real Estate	633 2959
Homestyle Property	**672 3220**
	050 444 9937
Silver Lake Property Management	676 2461

If you are renting a villa, don't forget that you may have to maintain a garden and pay for extra water etc. To avoid massive water bills at the end of every month, many people prefer to have a well dug in their backyard for all that necessary plant and grass watering. Expect to pay around Dhs.1,500 – 3,000 to have a well dug and a pump installed.

Renting the Smart Way

Like anywhere else in the world, Abu Dhabi has its fair share of cons. To avoid falling into a landlord trap, it is advised that both parties produce a written agreement. This contract reduces the risk of either party falling out on the rental terms discussed.

Do remember to ask for a copy of the estate agent's identification card and make sure you save copies of all receipts, contracts and other documents.

Some of the older villas may also need additional maintenance, which the landlord may not cover. Often, the more popular accommodations have waiting lists that are years long. To secure an immediate tenancy many people offer the landlord 'key money', a down payment of several thousand dirhams to secure the accommodation.

Real Estate Websites

Asteco	www.astecoproperty.com
Hyatt Real Estate	www.hayattrealestate.co.ae
Homestyle Property	**www.homestyle-property.co.ae**
Silver Lake Property Management	www.silverlakeuae.com

Moving Services

Two main options exist when moving your furniture and personal effects either to or from Abu Dhabi: air freight and sea freight. Air freight is a better option when moving smaller amounts but if you have a larger consignment, sea freight is the way to go. Either way, make sure your goods are packed by professionals. The cargo section of Omeir Travel (631 9997) handles local freight and is a good option.

Unless you send your personal belongings with the airline you are flying with, you will need to use the services of a removal company. A company with a wide international network is usually the best and safest option but more importantly, you must trust the people you are dealing with. Ensure they are competent in the country of origin and have reliable agents in the country to which you are shipping your personal belongings. Most removal companies offer free consultations plus advice and samples of packing materials – call around.

When your belongings arrive in Abu Dhabi, you will be called to customs to be present while the authorities open your boxes to ensure nothing illegal or inappropriate is being brought into the country. Assisting in this process can be exhausting; the search may take place outdoors over a few hours with your belongings thrown on the ground. After this, depending on the agreement you have with the removal company, either their representative in Abu Dhabi will help you transport the boxes to your new home or you can make the arrangements locally.

Moving Tips

- *Book moving dates well in advance*
- *Don't forget insurance; purchase additional insurance for irreplaceable items*
- *Make an inventory of the items you want moved (keep your own copy!)*
- *Ensure everything is packed extremely well and in a way that can be checked by customs and repacked with the least possible damage; check and sign the packing list*
- *Keep a camera and film handy to take pictures at each stage of the move (valuable in case of a dispute)*
- *Do not pack restricted goods of any kind*
- *If moving to the UAE, ensure videos, DVDs and books are not offensive to Muslim sensibilities*

Relocation Experts

Relocation experts offer a range of services to help you settle into your new life in Abu Dhabi as quickly as possible. Practical help ranges from finding accommodation or schools for your children to connecting a telephone, or even information on

medical care. In addition, they will often offer advice on the way of life in the city, putting people in touch with the social networks to help them establish a new life.

Moving Services

Relocation Companies	
Crown Relocations	674 5155
In Touch Relocations	04 332 8807
Virginie Belamaric	050 622 5041

Removal Companies	
Allied Pickfords	677 9765
Al Moherbie Clearance and Transport	672 2004
Crown Relocations	674 5155
Gulf Agency Company (GAC)	673 0500

Furnishing Accommodation

Other Options → **Home Furnishings & Accessories [p.158]**

Readymade, good quality furniture and household items are easily available and at reasonable prices here. The most popular 'western style' furniture outlets in Abu Dhabi are IKEA in Marina Mall (Map Ref 10-B4), THE One on Sheikh Zayed 1st Street, Home Centre on Umm Al Nal Street, Homes R Us in Madinat Zayed Centre, 2XL in Meena Mall and Pan Emirates on Airport Road.

Moving within Abu Dhabi

When moving from once place in Abu Dhabi to another, you can either opt for a moving company or rent a truck and do it yourself. If you like taking the lead, the latter is a cheaper option. The classifieds sections of local papers carry ads like 'shifter with van'. Alternatively, ask the watchman at your apartment building to recommend someone. These men can also be of great help in getting bargain rates for new furniture delivery from the shops to your flat.

Favourites for Indian teak and wrought iron are Marina in Abu Dhabi Mall and Heritage Touch in Marina Mall – ask here for directions to their huge warehouse in Meena Port Area.

The souks have plenty of shops selling inexpensive, basic furniture, pots, pans and ironing boards etc.

You can also often buy cheap second hand furniture from the previous tenant.

Many people sell off their furniture when they leave Abu Dhabi, often leaving behind barely used, good quality items that are sold cheaply, so check out ads on noticeboards at Spinneys and Abela supermarkets, or small ads in the Gulf News and Khaleej Times.

Garage Sale

One man's trash is another man's treasure. Garage sales are common in Dubai and are beginning to gain popularity in Abu Dhabi. With so many expats moving in and out, you can find almost anything at these sales. Read supermarket noticeboards and the small ads in the local papers for the latest happenings.

If you're leaving the Emirates and have some items that you don't want to ship back home, hold your own garage sale. It's a great way to earn some cash while getting rid of all the junk that you couldn't fob off on friends! Ask your neighbours if they have some unwanted treasures to dispose of, and then advertise the sale on local supermarket noticeboards and the classifieds of daily newspapers. If permitted, post some easy to follow directions with arrows marking prominent locations. On the day of the sale, make sure you have plenty of plastic bags, old newspapers for wrapping glass items and loads of change. Clearly mark the goods with prices... then be prepared to haggle hard!

Household Appliances

Carrefour, Jashanmal, Jumbo Electronics and Plug Ins have a decent selection of heavy household appliances. Do make sure that your purchases come with a warranty! All the main brands are available in the UAE. The fittings are made for the European market and thus, North American makes can be harder to find.

Prices are quite reasonable for new appliances, but if you wish to buy items second hand, have a look at the noticeboards at the various supermarkets around town. Of course, there is no guarantee with second hand goods, so beware the souped up junk sellers!

Household Insurance

No matter where you live in the world and how 'safe' a place appears to be, it's always wise to insure the contents of your home. There are many internationally recognised insurance companies operating in the UAE – check the yellow pages for details.

When forming your policy, the general information that insurance companies need is your home address in Abu Dhabi, a household contents list and valuation, and invoices for items over Dhs.2,500. Cover usually extends to theft, storm damage, fire etc. For an additional fee, you can

insure personal items outside the home, such as jewellery, cameras etc.

Most companies allow you to pick and choose the renter's insurance best suited to you. A good coverage gives you flexibility, so you can rest easy when you go on that long vacation or business trip. Coverage generally includes home contents, decorations, personal belongings and more, for you and family members residing with you. Call around for the best rates and options.

Laundry Services

Whilst there are no self service launderettes in Abu Dhabi there are many small outlets, plus larger supermarkets, some hotels and The Club (673 1111) that offer laundry and drycleaning services at reasonable rates and next day delivery. You can also choose to simply get your clothes ironed at approximately Dhs.1 per item. It's always a good idea to speak to the laundry man himself if you have a preference on how you want an item ironed (or if you would like to avoid the 'shiny' look!).

Domestic Help

Although you may never have considered hiring a domestic helper before, many people in Abu Dhabi do employ live in help. For the busy or the lazy, it means the house is spotless and the shirts are always pressed.

If you do decide to go for a maid, take your time and make your decision wisely. The government is tightening the rules in an attempt to both improve working conditions and to reduce the amount of 'maid hopping'. It can, therefore, prove quite difficult for both you and the maid should she not be suitable. No objection certificates will no longer be accepted by the Ministry of Interior for housemaids transferring sponsorship and there will be an automatic six month ban. The worker will then have to re-enter the country on a new visa. Employers who change housemaids frequently or have complaints filed against them for mistreatment will be unable to sponsor housemaids in the future.

Domestic Help Agencies	
Delight Cleaners	678 9216
Solutions	641 9227
Wilson International	667 1200

It's normally best to find a maid through an agency dedicated to hiring domestic helpers, as they will be aware of the frequent changes and updates to the regulations governing sponsorship of domestic staff. You will be asked to sign a contract stating that you will pay your employee a minimum salary of about Dhs.750 each month, with an airfare home once a year.

It is also possible to find a maid through personal recommendation or by advertising in the domestic help section of the local papers.

To employ the services of a full time, live in domestic helper, the sponsor must have a minimum monthly salary of Dhs.6,000. The helper cannot be related to you or be of the same nationality as you. As the employer, you must sponsor the person and deal with all residency papers, including the medical test etc. Singles and families in which the wife isn't working may face difficulties sponsoring a helper. The residence visa for a maid will cost around Dhs.5,000 (Dhs.4,800 for the government fee, Dhs.100 for the residence visa and Dhs.100 for the labour card). Residency is valid only for one year.

You can obtain a residence visa card through the normal channels after which some embassies (eg, the Philippines) require to see the labour contract of your newly appointed maid. This is to ensure that all paperwork is in order and that the maid is receiving fair treatment. It is illegal to share a maid with another household. Employers caught borrowing or lending a housemaid may be fined up to Dhs.50,000, and will not be permitted to sponsor a housemaid again. Moreover, the housemaid will be deported and banned from entering the UAE for a period of one year.

An alternative and cheaper option is to have part time home help. There are a lot of agencies in Abu Dhabi that offer domestic help on an hourly basis. The standard rate is about Dhs.20 - 25 per hour with a minimum of two hours per visit. The service includes general cleaning, washing, ironing and sometimes babysitting, but your mess level will determine the hours they spend cleaning.

It's also possible to find part time help through friends or neighbours, or check out the noticeboards at Spinneys and Abela supermarkets. A word of warning – if your part time helper does not have the correct labour card and papers, and if they are caught by the police in one of the periodic clamp downs on illegal workers, you will be liable for punishment too.

Pets

Bringing Your Pet into Abu Dhabi

Bringing a pet into the UAE is usually possible but, depending on the animal and its country of origin, several rules and restrictions may apply. These have been in place for some time but are now being enforced more stringently by ground staff at the airports.

All pets arriving in the UAE require an import certificate. They also require health and vaccination certificates from the country of origin. Animals that have been brought in without the correct documentation are confiscated and kept at the airport for a three week quarantine period or until the paperwork is obtained. This is at the owner's expense.

There is no automatic quarantine period for animals arriving from most countries, but animals may be quarantined if the UAE has concerns regarding health issues in their country of departure.

The British Veterinary Centre (665 0085 or www.britvet.com) offers a complete service to ensure a trouble free arrival for your pet. They can organise the flight, obtain an import permit, customs clearance and collection from the airport, and arrange delivery and/or boarding of your pet if required. If you choose not to use their services, do check the latest regulations carefully. The airline carrying the pet or the originating country's local embassy should be able to advise you of the necessary requirements.

Family Pet

Taking Your Pet out of Abu Dhabi

You can also take your pets with you if you relocate. The regulations for 'exporting' your pet depend on the rules of the country to which you are moving.

Basic requirements are:

- A valid vaccination card, not older than one year but not less than 30 days
- A health certificate that can be obtained from the Ministry of Agriculture (cost Dhs.100). This is normally issued one week before departure
- A travel box, normally wooden or fibre glass, that meets airline regulations.

Your local vet or the airline you are travelling on can inform you of specific regulations pertaining to your destination, such as blood tests and quarantine. Again, the British Veterinary Centre can provide a complete door to door service for your pet – one less thing to worry about through the chaos of relocation.

Getting a UAE Pet Health Certificate

To obtain a UAE pet health certificate, you will need to go to the Ministry of Agriculture and Fisheries and do the following:

1. Get an import application form from the Ministry of Agriculture

2. Submit a copy of the pet owner's passport including the residence visa page

3. Submit a copy of the pet's vaccination booklet along with Dhs.200 (processing fee).

Veterinary Clinics	
American Veterinary Clinic	673 3337
British Veterinary Centre	665 0085
New Veterinary Clinic	672 5955

Cats & Dogs

In the Middle East, animals are generally treated with a lot less sympathy than you may be used to. It is best to keep your animals indoors as the heat, traffic and attitude of the people here towards animals may be what you would consider cruel. The municipality controls Abu Dhabi's huge stray population by trapping, sterilising and practicing euthanasia. If your pet is trapped without an ID disc, it will be treated as a stray. All pets should also be sterilised and kept safely on your premises. Once sterilised, they will wander less and will therefore be less exposed to the dangers of traffic and disease. If you feed the stray cats around your home, you will encourage a growing

stray population and simply create a problem for yourself and your neighbours. To do something proactive, report or assist an injured or stray animal, contact Feline Friends or K9 Friends (for details, see below).

Pet Shops

Though regulations governing the sale of animals in pet shops exist, they are rarely actively enforced. Animals are often underage (although their papers state differently), sick or even pregnant, and the conditions in which they are kept leave a lot to be desired. Rather than encouraging this trade, you would do better to give a home to one of the many stray animals in Abu Dhabi. Contact Feline Friends or K9 Friends to see who needs a home, or check out the special Animal Page in the Saturday edition of the Gulf News.

Animal Souks

The main animal souk in Abu Dhabi is in the Meena area on the way to The Club. Animal souks are a negative mark on the UAE – a nation that prides itself on being a clean, safe and regulated nation, and an up and coming tourist destination. Much more needs to be done to eradicate this sick trade. The CITES protected list is disregarded in these souks and wild animals are still captured and sold here. Most of the animals are smuggled into the country from Asia and other places, and the conditions in which they are housed are not to be witnessed by the faint of heart. The animals are kept in cramped, overcrowded cages and are often diseased. The sellers may promise 'if you want it, we'll get it for you' but don't get carried away by the thought of a nearly extinct cat or monkey sitting in a cage in your kitchen, even if they do supply one – the misery of an animal in captivity is most definitely not worth that moment of novelty. No vet will be able to give proper care to the animal should you buy it, and most of these sad creatures are destined for a miserable death.

Help!

If you see a stray cat or dog that is injured or in distress, please try to take it to the nearest vet (see table). Most have 24 hour mobiles or pagers. If you need further assistance, call either Feline or K9 Friends, but remember that they are both run by volunteers and would very much appreciate if others would also be 'animal responsible' and help out. Contact Feline Friends (665 5297 or www.felinefriendsuae.com) and K9 Friends (04 347 4611 or k9@emirates.net.ae) if you'd like to offer time, assistance or support.

Utilities & Services

Electricity & Water

These services are provided by the government and run by Abu Dhabi Water and Electricity Department (commonly known as ADWEA). The service is excellent; power cuts and water stoppages are extremely rare.

There is a deposit of Dh.2,000 for villas and Dhs.1,000 for apartments when you register. If the property has been leased through your company, they may arrange the deposits and/or settle the bills. Water and electricity deposits as well as monthly bills can be paid at any ADWEA office or through various banks. Those offering this service are listed on the reverse side of the bill. Bills are 'assessed' one month and the meter read the next month.

Locations:

Abu Dhabi – Headquarters Madinat Zayed (642 3000), (Map Ref 4-D4)

Al Ain – Behind Municipality (03 763 6000).

Opening Hours: *Sat - Wed 07:00 - 19:00 (bill payments); 07:00 - 14:00 (inquiries); Thursday 07:00 - 17:00 (bill payments) and 07:00 - 19:00 (inquiries).*

Electricity

There's plenty of it! The electricity supply in Abu Dhabi is 220/240 volts and 50 cycles. The socket type is identical to the three point British system but most appliances here are sold with two pin plugs. However, adapters can be purchased at any grocery or hardware store.

Water

More expensive than oil! The tap water is safe to drink but not always pleasant and visitors generally prefer the locally bottled mineral water, which is widely available. Bottled water is usually served in hotels and restaurants.

Buying 20 litre water bottles rather than small one and a half litre bottles is more environmentally friendly and can make a considerable cost saving. The bottle deposit is usually Dhs.25 - 35 and every refill is Dhs.7 - 8. These large bottles can be used with a variety of methods for decanting the water. Choices include a hand pump, which is available at supermarkets and costs about Dhs.3, or a fixed pump, which can be bought for about Dhs.60. Refrigeration units are also available, some delivering hot as well as cold water. Prices vary

depending upon the model, but the average cost is about Dhs.300 - 400.

Water suppliers have regular van rounds (usually once a week) and will deliver to your door, thus saving you some serious backache.

Do make sure you buy your bottled water from a reputable source and check the seals before use – it is not unknown for unscrupulous traders to refill water bottles with tap water.

One of the slightly crazy aspects of life in the Emirates is that, during the summer months, if your water tank is on the roof, you won't need to heat water – it's already hot when it comes out of the cold tap! In fact, the only way to have a cold(ish) shower is to keep the immersion heater off and use the hot tap for cold water.

Water Suppliers	
Abu Dhabi: Oasis Water	558 2030
Al Ain: Oasis Water	03 782 5181

Gas

There is no mains gas supply in Abu Dhabi. Some newer apartment buildings supply gas for cooking from central storage tanks situated on the rooftop or underground.

For residents of older buildings and those living in villas, there is the option of buying individual gas canisters for cooking. These can be connected to a gas oven by the gas supplier, and generally cost about Dhs.220 to purchase the new canister and Dhs.25 - 30 for a refill. If you live away from the centre of town, you can hear the gas delivery van's bell ringing in the morning and afternoon as it goes on the rounds.

Gas Suppliers	
Al Ruwais Industrial Gases	555 3809
Zubair Gas Distribution	679 2205
Majed Gas	03 762 2199

Telephone

Emirates Telecommunications Corporation (known as Etisalat, meaning communications) is currently the sole telecommunications provider in the Emirates. Plans have recently been announced to open up the market but potential new service providers will still be 60% government owned. The Abu Dhabi Headquarters is located on Airport Road next to the Fotouh Al Khair Centre, but all phone applications, bill paying etc, is now defalt with at the New Etisalat Building, which is located further along Airport Road on the opposite side of the dual carriageway. If you are going to Etisalat by taxi, do make sure you tell the driver that you want to go to the 'New Etisalat Building', otherwise you'll have to go through a hazardous road crossing experience to get to the correct building. Both buildings are topped by the Etisalat huge trademark golf ball on the roof.

Etisalat is responsible for telephones (both landlines and mobiles) and Internet (through its sister company, Emirates Internet & Multimedia). Etisalat is generally an efficient and innovative company, constantly introducing new services and even cutting bills to the consumer from time to time. You should have few problems in processing paperwork, receiving services or rectifying problems. Full information on all services can be obtained from the Etisalat Website (www.etisalat.co.ae)

Location: *Airport Road (Map Ref 8-E1)*

Hours: *Saturday - Wednesday 07:00 - 15:00. Bill payments only, Saturday - Wednesday 15:00 - 19:00; Thursday 08:00 - 13:00*

Landline Phones

To install a regular landline phone connection in your home, you need to apply directly to Etisalat with the following:

- An Etisalat application form in English (hand written is acceptable)
- A copy of your passport and residence visa
- NOC from employer
- A copy of your tenancy agreement
- Dhs.250 (fee).

Once the application is submitted, a phone connection will be installed within 2 - 3 days. Etisalat will provide a phone handset. If you require additional phone sockets, order them at the same time. You will have to pay a further Dhs.50 for the first socket and Dhs.15 per socket thereafter. The procedure is usually extremely efficient and streamlined.

Etisalat offers many additional services, such as call waiting, call forwarding, a 'follow me' service etc. For more information, contact your nearest Etisalat branch or check the Etisalat home page (www.etisalat.co.ae).

Quarterly rental: Standard landline (for all sockets) is Dhs.45. All calls made within Abu Dhabi on and to a landline are free. For international and mobile rates, check the phone book.

Discount long distance rates: Standard landline – all day Friday and government declared national public holidays; weekdays 21:00 - 07:00 (outside GCC), 19:00 - 07:00 (GCC only).

Missing Mobile

If you lose your mobile or it is stolen from you, call 101 to disconnect your number temporarily. You might need to know your passport number for security.

Mobile Phones

Mobile phones are an integral part of Abu Dhabi life. Mobiles can be purchased from Etisalat, specialised telecommunications shops, most electronics shops and large supermarkets such as Carrefour. A word of caution: when comparing prices, do check the specs carefully since some outlets have stock of ancient units that, at first glance, look remarkably similar to later, more sophisticated, models. Contact the Etisalat GSM assistance telephone service (dial 101 for enquiries).

Non Resident

If your visa is not fully processed or if you're visiting the country and want to use your mobile, your only option is the Wasel GSM service.

This is a popular variation of the GSM service that is available to both non residents and residents. It lets you control the amount of outgoing calls that can be made on your phone and allows unlimited incoming calls. This service also provides international roaming for incoming calls (you will be charged the international rate).

Etisalat Building

The subscription is for one year and payment for outgoing calls needs to be made in advance. The cost is Dhs.185 for one year's subscription and you can apply at any branch office. The annual renewal charge is Dhs.100 and if you do not renew your subscription, you will be cut off. Fill out the application form and provide your Essential Documents, although, as mentioned, you do not need to be a resident to avail this service. The service includes a connection, one year's rental, SIM card charges and Dhs.10 worth of free credit. You may 'recharge' your card for outgoing calls in Dhs.30 units. These cards can be purchased from most grocery stores and garages, or recharged at an Etisalat machine where the minimum charge is Dhs.50.

Resident

If you are a resident, you can apply for a standard mobile phone connection with payment by monthly bill. To get connected, collect an application form from any Etisalat office and submit it along with a copy of your passport and residence visa, and Dhs.215. This amount includes rental for the first quarter. You should receive your SIM card there and then, and once installed, you're ready to dial.

Rental Charges: Quarterly rental charge for the standard mobile phone service is Dhs.90.

Local Rates: Peak rate – 30 fils per minute (06:00 - 14:00 & 16:00 - 24:00); off peak rate – 21 fils per minute.

International Discount Rates: All day Friday and government declared national public holidays; weekdays 21:00 - 07:00 (outside GCC) & 19:00 - 07:00 (GCC only).

An alternative to the standard mobile phone agreement is to apply for the Wasel GSM service (see above). Residents also have the option of using the Wasel4Me service, an online facility that allows you to register for your new number online and even have it delivered straight to your door. Check out this service at www.e4me.co.ae.

Internet

Other Options → **Internet Cafés [p.256]**
Websites [p.40]

For connection to cyberspace, Etisalat's sister company, Emirates Internet & Multimedia (EIM) is the sole provider of Internet services through its

UAE proxy server. With the proxy server in place, some sites are restricted. However, if you find a blocked site that you believe is perfectly reasonable, you can report it to Etisalat on watch@emirates.net.ae. You can access Emirates Internet from any standard telephone line using an appropriate modem at speeds in excess of 56 kbps. If you require higher speed access, you can apply for an ISDN line (64 Kbps) or an ADSL line (128 Kbps). For more information, contact Etisalat (800 6100). Check out the Website listing on [p.41] for sites that contain information about the UAE.

To get yourself connected to the Internet, you will require a landline in your name or your company's name, a copy of your passport and residence visa, and the Internet application form from Etisalat.

Registration Charge: Dhs.100 for dialup or ISDN; Dhs.200 for ADSL (plus Dhs.100 for optional software installation by the Etisalat technician).

Rental: Standard Internet connection – Dhs.20 per month; ISDN line – Dhs.60 quarterly; ASDL line Dhs.250 per month.

User charge: For the standard and ISDN connection, there is an additional user charge: peak rate Dhs.1.8 per hour (06:00 - 01:00); off-peak rate – Dhs.1 per hour. With an ASDL line, you are logged on 24 hours a day and pay no further charges.

Dial 'n Surf

This facility allows you to surf without subscribing to the Internet service. All that's needed is a computer with a modem, and a regular phone (or ISDN) line – no account number or password is required. In theory, you then simply dial 500 5555 to gain access. However, in practice it may not be quite so straightforward, since there are different set ups depending on your software. If you have difficulties, contact the help desk (800 6100).

Charges: A charge of 15 fils per minute is made for the connection and billed to the telephone line from which the call is made.

Internet Help

abuse@emirates.net.ae - report hacking, illegal use of the internet, spamming etc

watch@emirates.net.ae - report inappropriate sites

custserv@emirates.net.ae - comments, billing disputes and general Internet inquiries

help@emirates.net.ae - technical support

www.emirates.net.ae - Etisalat homepage and Emirates Internet & Multimedia products and services, billing inquiries, online change of passwords and change of ISDN access speed

800 6100 - Internet help desk

Internet Cafés

A cheaper option for accessing the World Wide Web is to step out and use an Internet café. Lots and lots of Internet cafés exist, from the chic and sleek to the down and dirty. Rates vary dramatically from Dhs.5 - 15 per hour. Also, check if the café provides food for some joints let you cruise the Internet for free if you order a meal.

Bill Payment

Bills are mailed monthly and are itemised for international and mobile calls, SMS (short message service) and service charges. For all bill payments, it's possible to pay at Etisalat branch offices, on the Internet and at certain banks such as Emirates Bank and HSBC (details can be obtained through Etisalat). Etisalat also has cash payment machines at several sites, which saves you the hassle of queuing at the Etisalat office or the bank.

If you don't pay your telephone bill within fourteen days of the account date, your outgoing calls will be cut off and you will only receive incoming calls for up to 15 days before complete disconnection. Etisalat very kindly automatically calls landlines and sends SMS reminders to people to pay up.

Bill Enquiry Service

Etisalat provides a useful bill enquiry service enabling customers to obtain the current amount payable on their phone/s up to the end of the last month. The aim is to help customers budget their calls and to facilitate prompt settlement of bills, leading to fewer disconnections.

The information is only available for the phone that the call is made from and the cost of the call inquiry is charged at the normal rate. To use the service, dial 142 (English) or 143 (Arabic). You may also use Etisalat cash payment machines for this service and Etisalat's online billing service to pay Internet bills.

Postal Services

Other Options ➜ **Post & Courier Services [p.38]**

The postal service is fast and reliable but there is no house address based mailing system in the UAE – all mail is delivered to the Central Post Office and then distributed to centrally located post office boxes. While many residents direct their mail to a company mailbox, it is also possible to rent a personal PO Box. To apply for one, you require an

application form from the Central Post Office and Dhs.160. You can then select a PO Box at a convenient location near your home (if available).

Emirates Postal Service (Empost) will send you notification by email when you receive registered mail or parcels in your PO Box. There is no charge for this service but you do have to register your email address and details with Empost. They will tell you the origin, arrival date, type of mail and location, and for Dhs.9 payable cash on delivery, you can have your parcel or registered mail delivered to your door. However, there may be a Customs charge on international parcels, usually about Dhs.15.

Locations:

Abu Dhabi – Central Post Office (621 5415), East Road, Madinat Zayed area (Map Ref 5-A4)

Al Ain – Central Post Office (03 764 2200), Main Street nr Clock Tower

Opening Hours: *Saturday - Thursday 08:00 - 20:00; Friday 17:00 - 21:00*

Television

UAE television is divided amongst the emirates with Dubai, Abu Dhabi, Sharjah and Ajman all broadcasting terrestrially and via satellite. Dubai has four channels – Dubai 2, 10 and 41 show Arabic programmes while Dubai 33 broadcasts mainly in English. A mixture of serials, documentaries and films (chiefly American, British and Australian) are offered as well as films from 'Bollywood'. Programme details are published daily in the local press.

Emirates Dubai television broadcasts by satellite throughout the world in Arabic and English. Abu Dhabi has an English language channel, while Sharjah and Ajman TV transmit mainly Arabic programmes, with some in English.

There are numerous video/DVD rental stores around and the latest releases from Hollywood and Bollywood are widely available, usually in English or Hindi with Arabic subtitles. Anything that offends the country's moral code is censored – be prepared for some interesting continuity!

The Emirates Cable TV & Multimedia (E-Vision) is UAE's cable TV network and a subsidiary of Etisalat. There are approximately 70 Arabic, Asian and western channels to choose from, though this will rise to 100 channels in the future. The basic subscription fee is Dhs.50 and for an extra charge, you can add pay satellite channels. For further information, contact 800 5500 or log on to www.evision.co.ae.

Satellite TV

The digital home entertainment revolution is sweeping through the Middle East, and Abu Dhabi is its epicentre, judging by the number of satellite dishes in the city! Satellite TV offers viewers an enormous number of programmes and channels to watch, and the choice and options available can be rather confusing. Most leading hotels offer satellite in their rooms, showing news, sports, movies, documentaries, cartoons and more.

Considering the diversity of people watching, it's not surprising that programmes of all hues, flavours and tastes are available. Couch potatoes first have to decide what kinds of programmes they want to watch and then how much they're willing to pay for them.

Satellite Dealers	
Eurostar	634 7357
Hayat Electronics	676 6094
Star Distributions – Orbit – Bond Communications	633 3377
1st Net	03 766 1144
Star Distributions – Orbit (Digital) – Bait Al Ezz	03 751 2831

The various channels available can be split into two types:

Pay TV Satellite Channels

These are channels that require payment for installation and equipment, such as the decoder, dish etc, followed by a viewing subscription for the channels you choose to watch. Generally, subscriptions can be paid monthly, quarterly or annually. Take your time making the right choice because the Middle East has a competitive pay TV market with four pay TV networks all offering a range of channels.

Free to Air Satellite Channels

These are channels that require payment for the installation and reception equipment, but there is no viewing subscription. There are more than 200 of these types of channels.

Equipment

Equipment can be bought from electrical shops, second hand shops and classified ads or directly from the main dealer. The majority of dealers offer installation. For apartment blocks or buildings with a

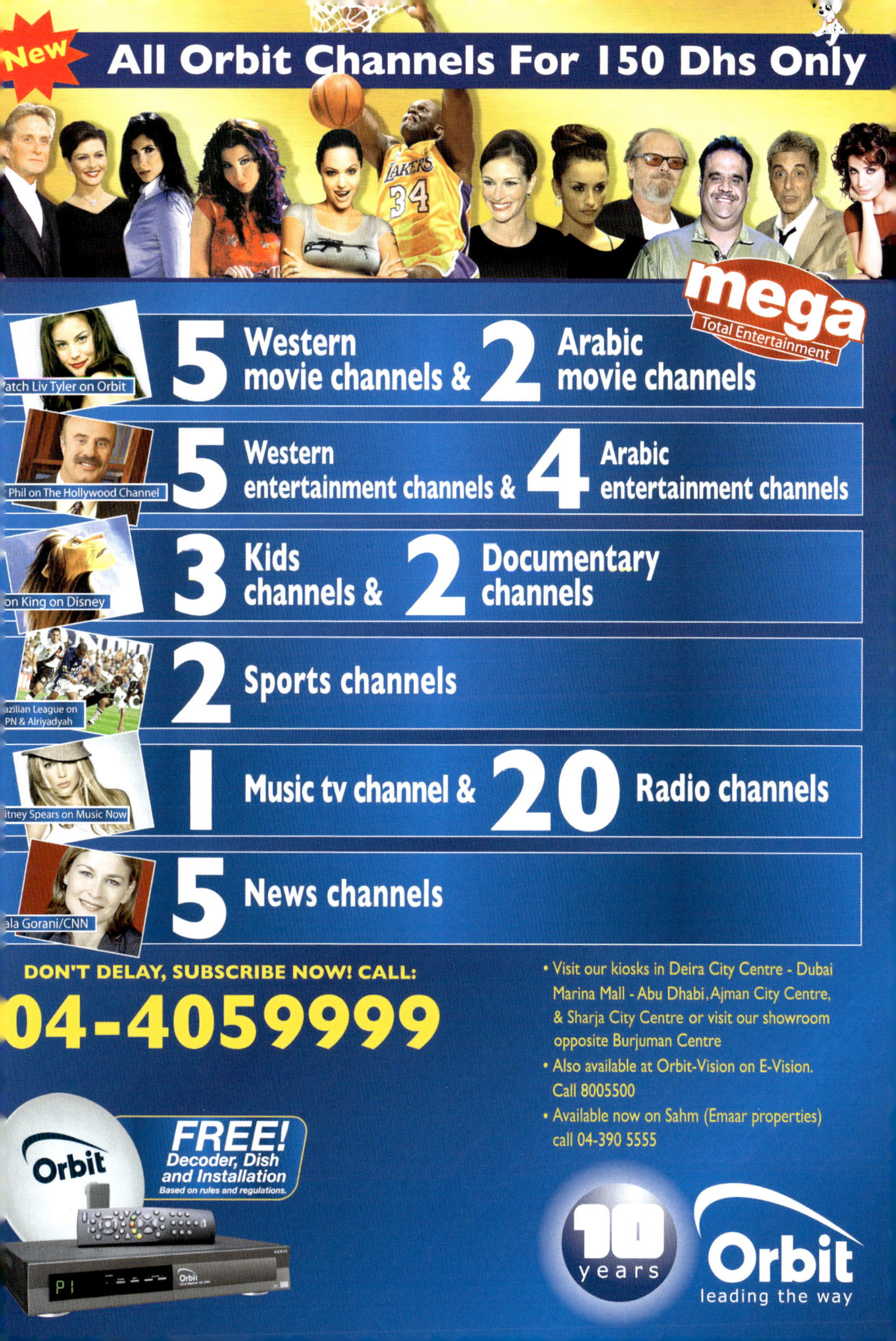
New
All Orbit Channels For 150 Dhs Only
mega
Total Entertainment
atch Liv Tyler on Orbit
5 Western movie channels & 2 Arabic movie channels
Phil on The Hollywood Channel
5 Western entertainment channels & 4 Arabic entertainment channels
on King on Disney
3 Kids channels & 2 Documentary channels
azilian League on
PN & Alriyadyah
2 Sports channels
itney Spears on Music Now
1 Music tv channel & 20 Radio channels
ala Gorani/CNN
5 News channels
DON'T DELAY, SUBSCRIBE NOW! CALL:
04-4059999
• Visit our kiosks in Deira City Centre - Dubai Marina Mall - Abu Dhabi, Ajman City Centre, & Sharja City Centre or visit our showroom opposite Burjuman Centre
• Also available at Orbit-Vision on E-Vision. Call 8005500
• Available now on Sahm (Emaar properties) call 04-390 5555
Orbit
FREE! Decoder, Dish and Installation
Based on rules and regulations.
10 years
Orbit
leading the way

large number of viewing points, a central system is recommended making it economical as well as offering more choice. Persuade your landlord to install the system if the block does not already come with satellite receiving equipment.

Health

General Medical Care

The quality of medical care in the Emirates is generally regarded as quite high and visitors should face little trouble in getting the appropriate treatment for both private and government run hospitals have emergency services. Tourists and non residents are strongly recommended to arrange private medical insurance before travelling as private medical care can be very expensive, and public hospitals will only treat Nationals or resident expats at nominal rates.

Even though the climate can be harsh, especially during the summer months, there are no specific health risks facing visitors. It is advisable to drink plenty of water (and replace lost salts with energy drinks or salty snacks), cover up when out in the sun, and use the appropriate factor sunscreen – sunburn, heat stroke and heat exhaustion can be very unpleasant.

At present, UAE nationals and expatriate residents are allowed healthcare for a minimal cost at the government hospitals and clinics, but of late, the price of some treatments has risen considerably and there is a possibility that, in future, legislation will force all expats to take out private medical insurance.

Shaikh Khalifa Bin Zayed Hospital

In Abu Dhabi, the Department of Health and Medical Services runs the Abu Dhabi Central Hospital, the Corniche Maternity Hospital and the Al Jazeera, the latter is used by Nationals only. Al Ain has the Al Jimi and Tawam hospitals.

Also, various private hospitals and clinics offer a wide array of services and facilities. Those with an A&E department are indicated on the list below.

The system for getting non emergency treatment can be confusing for a new resident, especially since most people are not feeling their best when they first encounter it. In Abu Dhabi, you do not register with a clinic or surgery on arrival to the city. If you are unwell, you can ring any hospital or clinic of your choice for an appointment, or you can just turn up and be seen by a duty doctor who will almost invariably send you to a specialist for a second opinion and tests. This might be within the clinic or hospital, or you may be referred to the Gulf Diagnostic Centre. All clinics are required to display a price list for patients in both Arabic and English. You will be given a bill for your treatment which you should pay and claim from your insurance. Government run clinics operate in a similar way but with lower costs and the facilities tend to be more basic. You will however, need to produce your health card on arrival. Personal recommendations are the best way to find out which hospitals offer the best service, but if you're new to the city and do not know who to ask, try the Dr. McCulloch Clinic, centrally located on Umm Al Nar Street (Map Ref 8-B1). They offer sound advice in English, Urdu, French and Arabic, British GP style consultations, and a range of services. Call 633 3900 or log on to www.mcclinic.inuae.com.

Some hospitals operate informative English language Websites that detail the services provided by them. Among these are the Gulf Diagnostic Centre (www.gdcuae.com), New Medical Centre (www.nmc.com) and Al Noor Hospital (www.alnoorhospital.com).

If you have company medical insurance, check if they have an agreement with a particular clinic or hospital.

Each emirate has at least one pharmacy open 24 hours a day. The location and telephone numbers are printed in the daily newspapers. The pharmacies attached to Al Noor and New Medical Centre are open 24 hours a day, as is the Al Rizi Pharmacy at the Hamdan Centre.

> ***Opening Times:*** *Saturday - Thursday 08:30 - 13:30 & 16:30 - 22:30; Fridays 16:30 - 22:30. Some pharmacies may open Friday mornings between 09:00 - 13:00.*

Hospitals

Al Noor Hospital Emergency	626 5265
Corniche Hospital (maternity only) Emergency	672 4900
Golden Sands Medical Hospital	642 7171
Mafraq Hospital Emergency	582 3100
National Hospital Emergency	671 1000
New Medical Centre Hospital Emergency	633 2255
Al Ain Hospital (Al Jimi) Emergency	03 763 5888
Emirates International Hospital	03 763 7777
Oasis Hospital Emergency	03 722 1251
Tawam Hospital Emergency	03 767 7444

Emergency Denotes 24 hour Emergency Service

Private Centres/Clinics

Centre Medical Franco – Emirien Emergency	626 5722
Gulf Diagnostic Centre	665 8090
Al Aheed Medical Centre	03 764 2791
Al Dhahery Clinic	03 765 6882
Emirates Medical Clinic Centre	03 764 4744
Family Medical Clinic	03 766 9902
Hamdan Medical Centre	03 765 4797
New Al Ain Medical Clinic	03 764 1448

Emergency Denotes 24 hour Emergency Service

Maternity

As part of the drive towards 'Emiratisation', the government is actively encouraging Emirati women to have at least six children, so delivering babies is a major part of hospital services in Abu Dhabi! Expatriate mothers-to-be can choose to have their baby in the Corniche Hospital, which is the public hospital, or to book into one of the private hospitals that offer obstetric services. Most seem to choose the Corniche because it is widely acknowledged to be a centre of excellence, delivering over 15,000 babies a year to women of all nationalities. If you choose to go to the Corniche, you will need to show your health card and prove you're a resident to be entitled to low cost care. At the moment, the cost of one night's stay in the hospital with free medical care is Dhs.200. If you choose the private route, do check details of your private medical care plan to see exactly what is covered by the policy during pregnancy and delivery. If you choose to have your baby at a private clinic and problems develop, you will be transferred to the Corniche in order to benefit from their specialised equipment and experience.

Because the Corniche hospital is run by the government, Islamic traditions tend to be upheld. Husbands are usually allowed to accompany their wives into the delivery room, but may not be allowed to stay during for the actual delivery of the baby. However, these rules are not so hard and fast, and many western midwives use their discretion over what is allowed and what is not.

The Corniche offers a full range of antenatal and postnatal clinics at a cost of Dhs.50 per visit, but waiting time is long, so many women choose to attend antenatal clinics at one of the private places and go to the Corniche for delivery. Men are not allowed in these private clinics. After the baby is born, you can go to the Corniche for a range of support, including exercise classes and breastfeeding support groups. Home visits by midwives and health visits are also provided.

Mums and Toddler Group (see details in Support Groups [p.89]) welcomes pregnant ladies, so you can visit even before you've had your baby and get valuable advice from mums who have actually been through it. You can of course, return for more advice and support once your little bundle of joy is in your arms.

Ante Natal/Post Natal Care

Al Noor Hospital	626 5265
Corniche Hospital	672 4900
Dr McCulloch Clinic	633 3900
Gulf Diagnostic Centre	665 8090
New Medical Centre	633 2255
Emirates International Hospital	03 763 7777
Oasis Hospital	03 722 1251
Tawam Hospital (Ante Natal only)	03 767 7444

Paediatrics

The Corniche hospital has paediatric doctors on hand to treat any newborns with problems. However, any difficulties occurring after will require you to find a paediatrician. Your kids deserve the best, so choose wisely and be nosey. Call around and ask for the experience and qualifications you are after, or think your child may need. Ask other parents for recommendations. There are also specialists, such as paediatric surgeons and neurodevelopment therapists, and doctors that care for children with special needs and learning difficulties.

Gynaecology & Obstetrics	
Al Noor Hospital	626 5265
Corniche Hospital	672 4900
Gulf Diagnostic Centre	665 8090
New Medical Centre	633 2255

Al Ain Hospital (Al Jimi)	03 763 5888
Emirates International Hospital	03 763 7777
Oasis Hospital	03 722 1251
Tawam Hospital	03 767 7444

Dentistry & Orthodontics

The standard of dentistry in Abu Dhabi is generally very high. Practitioners and specialists of all nationalities offer services on par with or better than those found 'back home'. Note that there is currently no legislation in place covering dental costs, so prices vary widely and high costs are not always an indication of superior service. Most health insurance packages do not cover dentistry, unless it is emergency treatment as the result of an accident. The health card entitles expats to dentistry services at public clinics but there is a Dhs.50 charge for the visit, plus a charge for any treatment performed such as cleaning, filling etc. Services are generally professional but the cost may not be any lower than that of a private dental practice. Word of mouth works particularly well for finding a suitable dentist. Alternatively, phone around and enquire after the methods and equipment used at the various clinics.

Opening Hours: *Timings vary but several practices operate 'Arab hours', closing during the afternoon and re-opening for evening appointments.*

Private Dentists-Orthodontists	
Advanced Dental Clinic	681 2921
American Dental Clinic	677 1310
Austrian Dental Clinic	621 1489
Barbara Dental Clinic	626 9898
British Dental Clinic	677 3308
Dr Elisabeth Dental Clinic	626 7822
Dr Firas Dental Clinic	633 5988
Gulf Diagnostic Centre	665 8090
Faxius Dental Clinic	672 3445
International Dental Clinic	633 3444
Maher Dental Clinic	666 3588
Swedish Medical Centre	666 5444

Al Bahri Dental Clinic	03 764 3273
Canadian Dental Clinic	03 766 6696
City Dental & Medical Centre	03 764 2252
Gulf Dental Clinic	03 765 4373
Modern Dental Centre	03 766 4764
New Al Ain Dental Clinic	03 766 2059
Swedish Dental Clinic	03 766 6227

Alternative Therapies

The vast number of UAE residents that come from countries practicing traditional, herbal and alternative therapies has given Abu Dhabi a well balanced choice of western and holistic treatments. So, in addition to the more conventional approach to medicine, residents can choose from a range of healing methods. Prices vary but are usually comparable to western medicine charges. However, most insurance companies will not cover the cost of alternative treatments. The UAE Office of Complementary & Alternative Medicine governed by the Ministry of Health carries out inspections and grants licences to qualified practitioners of alternative medicine. This legal process helps weed out the quacks. Still, there is a grey area where beauty therapies and massages overlap with therapeutic healing techniques. Beauty salons or spas are not yet subject to the same stringent regulations as healing clinics.

Natural medicine can be quite specialised, so ask questions, explain your needs and expectations, and talk about your medical history, if necessary, to ensure the practitioner can help with your situation. The following are some of the services offered and the main practitioners in Abu Dhabi but, as always, word of mouth is the best way of establishing who might offer the most appropriate and effective treatment.

Additionally, the Dubai Herbal & Treatment Centre (04 335 1200) offers a full range of Chinese, Indian and Arabic herbal medicines. This facility, which is unique in the GCC region, currently offers out-patient services with plans of expansion to include in-patient treatment as well.

Acupressure/Acupuncture

Among the oldest healing methods in the world, acupressure involves the systematic placement of pressure with fingertips on established meridian points on the body. This therapy can be used to relieve pain, soothe the nerves and stimulate the body as determined necessary by the therapist.

Acupuncture is an ancient Chinese technique that uses needles to access the body's meridian points. The technique is surprisingly painless

FJ
Dr. FIRAS DENTAL CLINIC
Waterlase YSGG
The # 1 Dental Laser
Free online consultation
Book appointment online and get 10% discount
Visit
www.firasdental.com
el.: 02 6335990 / 6335988
u Dhabi, Hamdan Str., Liwa Center. Tower B,

and is quickly becoming an alternative or complement to western medicine as it aids a range of ailments and diseases, including asthma and rheumatism and even as a treatment to help people give up smoking!

Acupressure – Acupuncture	
Abu Dhabi Health and Fitness Club	443 6333
Gulf Chinese Medical Centre	634 3538
Gulf Diagnostic Centre	665 8090

Homeopathy

Homeopathy strengthens the body's defence system. Natural ingredients are used to address physical and emotional problems. The discipline extracts elements from traditional medicines of various origins, but was recently organised into a healthcare system in Europe. Practitioners undergo disciplined training and some are also western medical doctors. Currently, in the UAE, only the Holistic Healing Medical Centre (Dubai, 04 228 3234) has licensed homeopaths.

Massage Therapy/Reflexology

Reflexology is a detailed scientific system with Asian origins which outlines points in the hands and feet that impact other parts and systems of the body. In addition to stress reduction and improved health, the pressure applied to these points directly addresses issues in those specific corresponding parts of the body. While many spas and salons offer massages and some offer reflexology, the following centres have a more focused approach to the holistic healing qualities of reflexology and massage therapy. For a listing of spas that offer massages for relaxation and beauty, see Activities [p.174].

Massage Therapy – Reflexology	
Abu Dhabi Health and Fitness Club	443 6333
Eden Spa & Health Club, Le Meridien	644 6666
Gulf Chinese Medical Centre	634 3538
Gulf Diagnostic Centre	665 8090

Aromatherapy

Essential oils derived from plants and flowers can be used in a myriad of ways to add balance to your health. Specialists use such oils when delivering massages as well as in a number of other methods that address your needs. While no certification is required to practice aromatherapy, it's a healthy decision to make sure your practitioner has studied plants and can make the best choices for you. For cosmetic and relaxation purposes alone, it is nice to have an aromatherapy facial or massage which is offered by many spas and salons around the city. While these are intended to be for pleasure rather than medical, they can work wonders on your soul!

Back Treatment

Without a strong and healthy back, you're nothing! Luckily, treatment is widely available in the UAE with top notch specialists from all around the world practising here.

Chiropractic and osteopathy treatments concentrate on manipulating the skeleton in a non intrusive manner to improve the functioning of the nervous system or the blood supply to the body. Chiropractic is based on the manipulative treatment of misalignments in the joints, especially those of the spinal column, while osteopathy involves the manipulation and massage of the skeleton and musculature.

Craniosacral therapy aims to relieve pain and tension by gentle manipulations of the skull to balance the craniosacral rhythm. Pilates is a form of exercise, which is said to be the safest form of neuromuscular reconditioning and back strengthening available, so no wonder it's fast gaining popularity.

Back Treatment	
Abu Dhabi Health and Fitness Club	443 6333
Chiropractic Speciality Clinic	634 5162
Gulf Diagnostic Centre	665 8090
Pilates Classes	
Abu Dhabi Health and Fitness Club	443 6333
The Club	673 1111

Mental Health

Everyone needs to talk. Instead of dwelling on your imperfections, why not call someone that can give you an objective opinion? Even the most resilient of personalities can be affected by culture shock (maybe the mountain of heat here that sticks to your every move is just weighing you down!). Whatever the origin of the stress, a new environment and the natural adjustment period can be demanding on your nerves. Couple this with a few personal problems and it may be best to talk it over with someone who can give you some sound advice.

There is a range of mental health services on offer in Abu Dhabi but cultural differences and language difficulties can make it hard to find the most appropriate service for your particular needs in this sensitive area of medical care. If you contact Dr McCulloch's Clinic for a GP style consultation, their doctors will be able to refer you to an appropriate specialist. They also have a list of counsellors who work in Abu Dhabi. The Gulf Diagnostic Hospital seems to operate the most comprehensive mental health department with a permanent psychiatrist on the staff. Ring for an out patient appointment. Patients requiring a psychologist can contact the clinic for references and contact details.

Help on the Web

A Website run by doctors and health professionals in the UAE (www.doctorelite.com) contains a host of information, including tips on where to find a doctor who speaks your language, health advice, a listing of pharmacies that are open late at night etc. Basically, the main function of the Website is to provide a search engine that allows you to look for practitioners within the UAE and internationally. It details their qualifications, specialities, medical degrees, etc - very helpful!

In Al Ain, the Al Jimi public hospital offers psychiatric services. Their doctor can put patients in touch with other specialists as required.

Farther away, but worth a phone call at least, is the Dubai Community Health Centre offering workshops and other psychiatric services to all nationalities free of charge. The centre is the GCC region's first dedicated mental health centre and is affiliated to the Dubai Police. For details on the range of services on offer, call 04 395 3939 or fax them at 04 395 4343. Future plans for the Centre include setting up a Website that offers a 24 hour advice and consultation line.

Support Groups

Abu Dhabi can be a challenging place to live in, and with many residents originating from overseas, there is often a lack of the family support that many people are used to. Making the first step of reaching out for help can be tough; however, there are groups out there that are more than willing to offer a hand through the difficult patches.

Check out the list above, or look in any of the monthly health focused magazines that are usually available in surgeries, nutrition stores etc, for updates of support groups. If possible, get personal recommendations first as standards can vary enormously, especially if a group or workshop is linked to a business. Be wise and use your discretion.

Support Groups in Abu Dhabi:

- Al Anon Family Groups (050 668 4640). Meet Saturdays at 18:00.
- Alcoholics Anonymous (AA) (443 6325 – hotline). Website www.aainarabia.com. Meet every Saturday, Monday and Wednesday at 20:00, and Friday at 10:00.
- Overeaters Anonymous (050 668 4640). Meet Mondays at 18:30 at St Andrews Church Hall.
- Twins, Triplets or More! (050 312 5068 – Klara). Website http://uk.groups.yahoo.com /group/TTOM. Community support, advice and information for families of multiples.
- Abu Dhabi Mums. Website www.abudhabimums.ae. A voluntary organisation providing support and activities for parents and children.
- Mums and Toddler group (681 4913 Michiko Daniels). Meet every Monday, Wednesday, Thursday and Saturday from 10:00 - 12:00 at St Andrews Church Community Hall.
- Abu Dhabi Ladies (050 3133602, 446 0516 Sue Brown). A support group open to ladies of all ages, find new friends. Offers many activities on a very informal basis. Meet every Wednesday 10:00 - 12:00 at the Sands Hotel.

In addition, the following Support Groups operate in Dubai:

- Adoption Support Group (04 394 6643). Meetings are held once a month at different locations.
- Diabetic Support Group (04 309 6876). Meets every three months on a Wednesday evening at 17:30. Based at the American Hospital, Dubai.
- Still Birth and Neo Natal Death Society (SANDS) (04 884 6309 – June Young). Meetings are held approximately once a month.

Education

Due to the diverse expat culture, the education system in Abu Dhabi is extremely varied and there are many private international schools from which to choose, all of which charge fees. It's always best to seek advice from friends or colleagues about a school's reputation. Many schools operate a waiting list and families are not necessarily able to enrol their child at their preferred school.

Abu Dhabi Municipality has recently started more vigorous inspection procedures for schools and the Ministry of Education has warned secondary students from enrolling in schools that are not accredited. For a listing of Ministry approved institutions, log on to www.uae.gov.ae/mohe. For more information on the education system, schools, fees etc, refer to the *Family Explorer (Dubai & Abu Dhabi)*.

School terms: Autumn (mid September - mid December), spring (early January - early April) and summer (mid April - early July). Exact timings of school terms vary according to dates of Islamic religious celebrations.

Generally, to enrol your child at a school, the following information is needed:

- A school application form
- Copies of student's and parents' passports (including the information page/s and residence visa stamp page)
- Passport size photos (usually eight)
- Copies of student's birth certificate
- School records for the past two years
- Current immunisation records and medical history
- An official transfer certificate from the student's previous school detailing his/her education
- Some schools also require a student questionnaire to be completed.

Original transfer certificates must contain the following details:

- Date of enrolment
- Year of placement
- Date the child left the school
- School stamp
- Official signature

The Ministry of Education also requires the following documentation for any student enrolling at any school in the emirate:

- Original transfer certificate (to be completed by the student's current school)
- Most recently issued original report card.

If the student was attending a school in any country other than the UAE, Australia, Canada, European nation or USA, the transfer certificate and the most recently issued original report card must by attested by the Ministry of Education, Ministry of Foreign Affairs and the UAE embassy in that country.

Nursery & Pre-School

Age: Babies – 4 1/2 years. (Some nurseries only take children aged 3 - 4 1/2 years)

Nursery schools usually like to interview a child before accepting him or her. Most nurseries adopt English as their common teaching language and annual fees can vary dramatically. Call around to find the one that's right for you.

Hours: *Most nurseries run for 4 - 5 hours in the morning*

Fees: *Approximately Dhs.3,000 - 12,000 per annum*

Nursery & Pre-School	
The British School Al Khubairat	446 2280
First Steps Kindergarten	445 4920
Giggles	641 6255
Humpty Dumpty	666 3277
Sesame Street Private Nursery	641 2300
Stepping Stones	681 5583
Al Adhwa'a Private School	03 766 7667

Primary & Secondary School

Age: $4^{1}/_{2}$ - 11 years / Age: 11 - 18 years

Some primary schools operate a nursery class for children aged three years and over. Not all secondary schools cater for pupils in Grades 12 and 13 (aged 16+ or A Level). The British School Al Khubairat operates through the whole age range (446 2280, www.britishschool.sch.ae).

Most schools require proof of your child's previous school academic records. You will also need an official letter from the school in your home country detailing your child's education to date. Some schools even ask for a character reference! The child may also be required to take a short entrance exam and there may be a physical examination as well as a family interview.

Depending on your nationality and educational requirements, most national curriculum syllabuses can be found in Abu Dhabi schools, covering GCSE's, A levels, French and International Baccalaureate and CNEC as well as the American and Indian equivalent.

Standards of teaching are usually high and schools have excellent facilities, with extracurricular activities on offer. The Ministry of Education regularly inspects schools to ensure rules and regulations are being upheld, and most schools insist on a school uniform. Some

school fees include books and transport to school by bus but mostly, fees only cover the basic education.

Hours: *Saturday - Wednesday from 08:00 - 13:00 or 15:00.*

Fees: *Primary, approximately Dhs.10,000 - 20,000 per annum. Secondary, approximately Dhs.15,000 - 43,000 per annum. Other costs may include a deposit or registration.*

Primary & Secondary Schools	
Al Nahda National School	445 4200
Al Rabeeh	448 2856
American Community School	681 5115
American International School	444 4333
Cambridge High School	552 1621
International School of Choueifat	446 1444
The British School Al Khubairat	446 2280
Al Ain English Speaking School	03 767 8636
Al Dhafra Private School	03 767 1123
International School of Choueifat	03 767 8444

University & Higher Education

Most teenagers at university or higher education level return to their 'home' country to enrol in further education there. However, for those who wish to stay in the Emirates, a few choices do exist.

A number of universities and colleges around the UAE with American, Australian and European affiliates offer degree and diploma courses in Arts, Sciences, Business & Management, and Engineering & Technology. Many commercial organisations also offer higher education courses for school leavers, mature students and adults. Details of these establishments can be found in the Hawk Business Pages or the Yellow Pages. However, do check out affiliation and accreditation of your chosen establishment carefully before embarking on an expensive and lengthy degree course.

Universities	
Ajman University – Abu Dhabi Branch	626 6664
Higher Colleges of Technology Abu Dhabi Mens	445 1514
Higher Colleges of Technology Abu Dhabi Womens	641 3839
Zayed University	445 3300
Ajman University – Al Ain Branch	03 755 1100
Higher Colleges of Technology Al Ain Mens	03 782 0888
Higher Colleges of Technology Al Ain Womens	03 782 0777
UAE University	03 754 2500

Special Needs Education

If you have a child or children with special needs, then before embarking on your adventure in the Emirates, we recommend that you first contact one or more of the following schools/centres, as student spaces are limited. All centres are charities rather than government run and thus, rely on donations, sponsorship, grants and a certain amount of voluntary work from outside helpers. Entry into most is generally between the ages of 3½ to 5, unless the child was in a special needs school previously. Most of the teaching is generally in English but Arabic language instruction is also available and in most cases, each child receives an individual programme. However, the concept of special educational needs is still relatively new in the Arab world, so levels of expertise and specialised programmes may not be comparable to those offered in your home country. It is strongly advised that you visit the establishments and thoroughly check out the programmes first before enrolling your child. All charge tuition.

- Al Noor Speech, Hearing and Development Centre (449 3844) is partially a charity organisation as it takes in students who cannot afford to go to other centres in Abu Dhabi. Students are accepted with all types of disabilities and are of all ages. The centre provides formal and informal education and also vocational training, which may further help the students to be self dependent. The staff there is mainly Arab with a few staff members of other nationalities.
- Future Centre (445 3324) is a 'not for profit' charitable institution for all nationalities between the ages of 3 and 20. Classes exist for students with ADD/behavioural disorders, Downs Syndrome, cerebral palsy and traumatic brain injury. There is also a small autism unit. The combination of education, therapies and care enables specialised and holistic services to be offered to children and young people with complex needs, degenerative conditions and additional sensory impairments whilst also supporting the rest of the family. Check out their Website (www.future-centre.com) for more information.

- Riding for the Disabled (04 336 6321) is a therapeutic horse riding programme in Dubai for children with special needs, but this only involves a weekly appointment rather than a full time programme.

Note that in general, the UAE is not yet set up for those with special needs, and you won't find many wheelchair ramps around. Those ramps that we have seen appear to be there to assist with construction rather than with wheelchairs, as they all seem to be at a 60 degree angle. When considering employment in the Emirates, check with your future employer to see if the medical insurance programme they offer covers special needs children, as many do not.

See also: *Disabled Visitors [p.22]*

Learning Arabic

Can you speak the local lingo and know that corner store jive? While it's relatively easy to pick up a few words of greeting, expand your horizons and learn more. There are quite a few private institutions that offer very good Arabic language courses. Refer to Language Schools [p.211].

If you want just a few words to help you get by, have a look at the Arabic expressions table on [p.17].

Transportation

Other Options → **Car [p.32]**
Car Hire [p.33]

Cars are the most popular mode of transport in Abu Dhabi and those who have a licence and can afford one, generally have one. The main options, if you wish to drive here for any length of time, are to buy a vehicle (for which you will need residency) or to lease. Visitors (short or long term) have the option of renting a vehicle from one of numerous rental companies, provided they have a valid licence.

The following section covers leasing, buying (new or used vehicles), registration, fines, insurance and traffic accidents.

The Traffic Department recorded information line (9000 1234) in English/Arabic gives some information about fines, speeding tickets, registering vehicles, applying for driving licences, emergency numbers, suggestions etc.

Office Locations:

Abu Dhabi – Traffic Police HQ/Traffic Department, off Eastern Ring Road (419 6666) (Map Ref 3-B1)

Traffic Police Licensing Department, on 23rd Street between Eastern Ring Road and New Airport Road (Map Ref 3-B1)

Al Ain – Traffic Police, Zayed Al Awwal Street (03 707 3500)

Vehicle Leasing

Leasing a vehicle has many advantages over buying. Not only is it a more financially viable option for shorter periods, but there are also fewer hassles involved when it comes to breakdowns, re-registration etc, as the leasing company deals with everything. All services are provided inclusive of registration, maintenance, replacement, 24 hour assistance and insurance (comprehensive with personal accident is advisable). You may find that your employer has connections with a car hire company and can negotiate better rates for long term hire than you can on an individual basis.

Leasing is generally weekly, monthly or yearly. All sizes and makes are available, with monthly lease prices ranging from Dhs.1,600 for a small vehicle and Dhs.1,800 - 3,000 for larger cars to Dhs.5,500 - 7,500 for a 4 wheel drive. As the lease period increases, the monthly rental price decreases.

For short term rental, there are many companies offering daily services – there are booths at the airport and most of the major hotels and numerous shops dotted throughout the city. You could also check out the Yellow Pages to ring around for the most competitive rates. To hire any vehicle you will need to provide a passport copy, credit card and a valid driving licence from your home country or a valid international driving licence.

Vehicle Leasing Agents	
Al Ghazal Rent a Car	634 2200
Avis	621 8400
Budget	633 4200
Diamond Lease	622 2028
Europcar	626 1441
Eurostar	645 5855
Fast Rent a Car	632 4000
Thrifty	634 5663
Avis	03 768 7262
Fast Rent a Car	03 768 8640

Buying a Vehicle

In Abu Dhabi, the car rules as the most popular method of getting around and buying one gives you far greater flexibility than relying on other means of transport. Choosing a car here can be a tough decision as the market is huge – should it be new or second hand, a 4 wheel drive, which one has a good a/c, does white really reflect the heat of the desert sun...?

Only those with a residence visa can own a vehicle in the UAE. Most people will find that cars are far cheaper here than in their home countries, and with the low cost of petrol and maintenance, they can afford something a little more extravagant than they would otherwise think of buying. However, do your research before making a purchase; less stringent regulations here mean that manufacturers will often 'de-spec' vehicles for the UAE market.

New Vehicles

If you decide to invest in a brand new vehicle, you will find most models available through the main dealers.

New Car Dealers		
Audi	Ali & Sons	681 7770
BMW	Abu Dhabi Motors	558 2400
Cadillac	Al Otaiba Group	444 3333
Chevrolet	Al Otaiba Group	444 3333
Chrysler	Trading Enterprises	633 3408
Dodge	Trading Enterprises	633 3408
Fiat	Al Jallaf Trading	677 3030
Honda	Trading Enterprises	676 3300
Jeep	Al Jallaf Trading	631 2345
Lancia	Al Jallaf Trading	677 3030
Land Rover	Al Otaiba Group	558 8777
Lexus	Al Futtaim Motors	419 9888
Mazda	Galadari Automoblies	677 3030
Mercedes-Benz	Emirates Motor Company	444 4000
Mitsubishi	Elite Motors	642 3686
Nissan	Al Masaood Automobiles	677 2000
Porsche	Ali & Sons	681 7770
Toyota	Al Futtaim Motors	419 9999
Volkswagen	Ali & Sons	681 7770
Volvo	Trading Enterprises	621 3400
Audi	Ali & Sons	03 721 0066
Cadillac	Al Otaiba Group	03 721 8888
Chevrolet	Al Otaiba group	03 721 8888
Chrysler	Trading Fnterprises	03 721 1838
Dodge	Trading Enterprises	03 721 5504
Honda	Trading Enterprises	03 721 1838
Land Rover	Al Otaiba Group	03 721 8888
Lexus	Al Futtaim Motors	03 721 0888
Mercedes-Benz	Eastern Motors	03 721 7777
Mitsubishi	Elite Motors	03 721 6252
Porsche	Ali & Sons	03 721 0066
Toyota	Al Futtaim Motors	03 722 0888
Volkswagen	Ali & Sons	03 721 0066
Volvo	Trading Enterprises	03 721 1838

Used Vehicles

Where can you go to buy a second hand vehicle? Due to the relative cheapness of cars and the high(ish) turnover of expats in the Emirates, there is a thriving second hand market. The best area for second hand car dealers is Mussafah. Airport Road (both sides of the road between 15th and 19th streets) also has a decent selection of second hand car dealers. Expect to pay a premium of about Dhs.5,000 for buying through a dealer, since they do offer a limited warranty, insurance, finance and registration, unlike some of the less 'official' sales. Sometimes the main dealers will offer good deals on demonstration cars, which are basically new but have been used by the showroom for test drives.

Used Car Dealers	
Abu Dhabi 4X4 Motors	664 9942
Ali & Sons	665 8000
Automall	699 3215/050 565 0351
Reem Automobile	446 3343
Al Jimi Car Showroom	03 721 9118
Technical Centre for Cars	03 721 6386

Some Abu Dhabi residents venture up to Dubai to purchase second hand cars from the Dubai Municipality Used Car Complex at Al Awir/Ras Al Khor, where all the cars have been checked by EPPCO's Tasjeel service. It is certainly possible to find a bargain but be aware of the additional hassle involved when you try to register a vehicle from another emirate (see below).

If you decide to buy privately, there are a number of options. Check out the classifieds in the Gulf News and Khaleej Times, noticeboards at Abela and Spinneys supermarkets, St Andrews Church and many of the sports clubs. Alternatively, log on to www.valuewheels.com.

Before buying a second hand car, it is advisable to have it checked by a reputable garage, just to 'make sure', especially 4 wheel drives which may have been driven off-road rather adventurously! Expect to pay around Dhs.300 for this service and it is best to book in advance. All the garages in Abu Dhabi are located out of the city in Mussafah. To get to Mussafah, take the Coast Road out of the city over Mussafah Bridge and keep going.

All transactions for vehicles must be directed through the Traffic Police. A Dhs.3,000 fine is imposed on both buyer and seller for cars sold unofficially.

Ownership Transfer

To register a second hand car in your name, you must transfer vehicle ownership. You will need to collect an application form from the Traffic Police and submit

it along with an NOC from the finance company, the original licence plates, the valid registration card, the insurance certificate and Dhs.10. The previous owner must also be present to sign the form.

Vehicle Import

Cars imported by individuals or private car showrooms that were manufactured after 1997/98 require an NOC from the official agent in the UAE or from the Ministry of Finance and Industry if no official agent exists in the emirate. Officially, this is to ensure that the car complies with GCC specifications (or rather that the local dealers are not outdone by any neighbouring competition!).

Moreover, believe it or not, if you are buying a vehicle from another emirate, you will first have to import it. This means lots of paperwork and lots of hassle. You will need to take the Essential Documents, the sale agreement, current registration and Dhs.60. in order to be issued with a set of temporary licence plates, which are valid for a few days, giving you a chance to submit a new registration application in the emirate where you hold your visa.

Vehicle Insurance

Before you can register your car, you must have adequate insurance and many companies offer this service. The insurers will need to know the year of manufacture and may wish to inspect the vehicle. Take along a copy of your Abu Dhabi driving licence, a copy of your passport and a copy of the vehicle's existing registration card.

Annual insurance policies are for a 13 month period (this is to cover the one month grace period that you are allowed when your registration expires). Rates depend on the age and model of your car and your previous insurance history. The rates are generally 4 - 7% of the vehicle value or 5% for cars over five years old, but prices are rising due to the number of accidents and the increase of the 'blood money' payment to Dhs.200,000 if you kill someone whilst driving. Fully comprehensive with personal accident insurance is highly advisable. For more adventurous drivers, insurance for off-road accidents is also recommended. For details of insurance companies look in the Yellow Pages or the Hawk Business Pages.

It is wise to check whether your insurance covers you for the Sultanate of Oman as within the Emirates, you may find yourself driving through small Omani enclaves (especially if you are off-road, for example near Hatta, through Wadi Bih and on the East Coast around Dibba). Insurance for a visit to Oman can be arranged on a short term basis, usually for little or no extra cost.

Registering a Vehicle

All cars must be registered annually with the Traffic Police. If you have the energy to do it yourself, expect to be pushed from counter to counter, filling in form after form. If you do not wish to battle through the red tape, some companies offer a full registration service.

There is a one month grace period after your registration has expired during which time you can have your car re-registered (hence, the 13 month insurance period).

Registration Services	
AAA Service Center Central Office	04 266 9989
Midland Cars Dubai	04 396 7521

The Process

In order to obtain licence plates for the vehicle, it must first be tested, then registered with the Traffic Police. If you have purchased your vehicle brand new from a dealer, they may agree to carry out the registration for you (for a fee). A new vehicle does not need to be tested for the first two years, though it must be re-registered after the first year.

The test involves a technical inspection, checking lights, bodywork, fire extinguisher, emissions etc. Once the car has been 'passed', you will receive a certification document.

Once your vehicle is insured, you must submit the insurance documents (valid for 13 months), the proof of purchasing agreement and the vehicle 'passing' certificate to the Traffic Police along with the Essential Documents and Dhs.360.

Before starting the registration procedures, check that you do not have any traffic offences and fines against your car number because the registration procedure cannot be completed until these have been settled (a potentially expensive business!) You can check for fines by logging on to

Beware!

Beware some second hand dealers selling cars that, under normal circumstances, would not pass the annual vehicle testing. However, with 'friends' at the test centre, these dealers are able to get the car 'passed', leaving you stuck when you come to do it yourself the following year.

the Abu Dhabi police Website (www.adpolice.gov.ae) or calling the information line (9000 1234).

Traffic Fines & Offences

Traffic Police in Abu Dhabi drive red and white police cars and motor bikes.

If you are caught driving or parking illegally, you will be fined (unless the offence is more serious). You can also be fined Dhs.50 on the spot for being caught driving without your licence. If you are involved in an accident and don't have your licence with you, you will be given a 24 hour grace period in which to present your licence to the police station. If you don't, you risk having your car impounded and going to court.

No Black Points

As you drive around the UAE, be aware that traffic regulations (and the enthusiasm with which they are implemented on the roads of the seven emirates) vary considerably. Dubai has an excellent Traffic Police Information Line (04 268 5555 or www.dbxtraffic.gov.ae) that tells you all you could possibly need to know about regulations, fines, speeding tickets etc, but the information only applies to the Dubai emirate. They also operate a black point penalty system for certain offences.

Fines picked up for offences in other emirates also find their way through the system to your car registration number. Latest information available at the time of going to press is that black points gathered in Dubai have no meaning or penalty in Abu Dhabi because the system is not in place here (yet!).

There are a number of police controlled speed traps, like fixed and mobile radar cameras around Abu Dhabi. There is no leeway for breaking the speed limit – not that it seems to bother many people. The fine for speeding is usually Dhs.400 but the amount can increase if you are driving very fast. The police also have the power to confiscate vehicles and occasionally this does happen.

Parking tickets are Dhs.100 and up. You do not receive any notification when you are caught on camera, so it can be quite a shock when you re-register your car and collect all the fines in one go, especially since there is also an additional fine of Dhs.10 a month for non payment. Keep a check on the number of fines against your vehicle by telephoning the traffic information dialling system. You will need to know the licence plate number and colour of your car. If you can leave a fax number, you will be faxed a list of offences, when they were committed and the fine. You can pay online or go to the Traffic Fines section of the Traffic Police.

Tinted Car Windows

Currently, government regulations allow you to avoid the sun somewhat by tinting your vehicle's windows up to 30 percent. Tinting is a simple stick on job, similar to applying a transfer to the insides of your windows. There are several pull in shops along Al Salaam Street (Map Ref 4-C2) who will black your car up for about Dhs.100. They will be prepared to tint your car windows as dark as you like - but don't get carried away and remember to stick to the limit. Random checks take place and fines are handed out to those caught in the dark! Again, rules vary in different emirates - tinting in Sharjah is allowed for a fee of Dhs.100 and Ajman residents may tint for Dhs.200 per annum, but only if they are women.

Breakdowns

In the event of a breakdown, you will usually find that passing police cars stop to help or at least to check your documents. We recommend that you keep water in your car at all times – the last thing you want is to be stuck in the middle of summer with no air conditioning, nothing to drink and lots of time to kill waiting for help. Traffic Police recommendations are that you should pull your car over to a safe spot, but if you are on the hard shoulder of a highway, it is suggested that you pull your car as far away from the yellow line as possible and step away from the road until help arrives.

Car Trouble

The Arabian Automobile Association (AAA – 285 8989) offers a 24 hour roadside breakdown service for an annual charge. This includes help in minor mechanical repairs and battery boosting, if you run out of petrol, get a flat tyre or lock yourself out. The more advanced service includes off-road recovery, vehicle registration and a rent a car service. It's a similar concept to the AA in Britain or AAA in the States.

Recovery Services – Towing	
Ghazal Al Wadi	554 0000
IATC Recovery	632 4400
Ghazal Al Wadi	03 721 5444

Traffic Accidents

Bad luck! If you have a serious accident, dial 999 for emergency help. For minor collisions that do not require emergency services to attend, call 446 2462 (Al Ain 03 707 9999) and wait for the police to arrive. In this part of the world, if you have an accident, you are the star attraction of a million rubber neckers who will offer advice and further block the road with their vehicles.

If there is only minor damage to the vehicles involved in the accident, the Traffic Police instruction is to move the vehicles to the side of the road since drivers involved in minor accidents can be fined for leaving vehicles blocking the road. However, there is no clear definition as to what constitutes 'minor damage' and you can also be fined for illegally moving your vehicle after an accident! If there is any doubt as to who is at fault, or if there is an injury (however slight), do not move the cars, even if you are blocking the traffic. It is also widely rumoured, and generally believed, that if you help or move anyone involved in an accident, the police may hold you liable should anything then happen to that person.

Once the police arrive, they will assess the accident and apportion blame on site (and if you disagree with their judgement, well... tough!) The police then document the necessary details and give you a copy of the accident report. Submit the paper to your insurance company to get the vehicle repaired. A pink accident report means you are at fault, and green means you are not to blame. The police may retain your driving licence until you obtain the necessary documentation from the insurance company saying the claim is being processed. Your insurers will then give you a paper that entitles you to retrieve your licence from the police.

Repairs

By law, no vehicle can be accepted for repair without an accident report from the Traffic Police. Even if you just drive into a concrete post, you must call the police and obtain the necessary accident report. Usually, your insurance company has an agreement with a particular garage to which they will refer you. The garage will carry out the repair work and the insurance company will settle the claim. Generally, there is a Dhs.500 excess deductible for all claims, but check with your insurance company for details of your policy.

Business

General Business Information

Strategically located between Europe and the Far East, Abu Dhabi is one of a few cities of choice for both multinational and private companies wishing to tap the lucrative Middle Eastern, Indian and African markets (a combined population of over 1.4 billion people).

Customs

Imports to Abu Dhabi (and the UAE) are subject to 5% customs duty, which is applied at the time of delivery at the port or airport; there are no duties on

Abu Dhabi Office Buildings

Heads Up!

Although there are no direct taxes in the UAE, the government has a large number of pricy fees for residence visas, trade licences, and office and apartment rental taxes. Always be wary and ask questions before committing to a contract or agreement.

the import of personal effects. No customs duties are payable on goods that do not leave a free zone.

At the beginning of 2003, the Gulf Co-operation Council's GCC Customs Union went into effect. Under the terms of this agreement, all six GCC countries now apply the same rate of 5% to imports.

Taxation

Although UAE law provides for taxation, no personal income taxes or corporate taxes are actually levied and collected, either in the city or in the free zones; the free zones offer additional guarantees to companies concerning their future tax free status. The UAE has double taxation treaties with various countries, although the effectiveness of these treaties is limited given that the effective tax rates in the UAE are nil.

The only corporations subject to income taxes in the UAE are courier companies, oil companies, and branches of foreign banks.

Exchange Controls

The UAE Dirham (Dhs.) is pegged to the US Dollar at the rate of about 3.67 dirhams per dollar and never fluctuates significantly from this level. Due to the strength of the local economy, the large foreign currency reserves, the lack of advanced financial currency products and restrictions on foreign share ownership, the dirham has not been attacked by foreign speculators and is generally perceived to be a safe currency.

There are no foreign exchange controls and there are generally no restrictions on repatriating capital and/or earnings. In an attempt to control problems of money laundering, banks are supposed to report all transactions in excess of Dhs.40,000 to the government, although pre-approval is not required.

September 11 changed things considerably and now, the Central Bank keeps an eye on all kinds of bank transactions. Background checks are carried out even when you open a bank account.

White Collar Crime

Like everywhere in the world, there are instances here of white collar crime, so companies must establish proper audit controls. However, companies exert a greater level of control over their employees because most are expatriates, with some employers even holding passports belonging to staff.

In the UAE, it is considered a crime to issue a cheque for which insufficient funds exist in the bank account – penalties for this offence range from a fine to imprisonment. The authorities tend to favour the more extreme punishment for this crime – be warned!

Infrastructure

The fuel for development is investment in infrastructure. Abu Dhabi continues to invest a large percentage of its oil revenues in both the basic and advanced infrastructure required to make the city attractive to local and foreign investors. Equally important, the government maintains low tariffs, which further stimulates demand. This is how a nation converts natural resources into human, intellectual and

Abu Dhabi Planning Department

technological capital, and creates real wealth. The government of Abu Dhabi, under the wise guidance of Sheikh Zayed, remains committed to developing the infrastructure of the emirate and improving the lot of all inhabitants. Basic initiatives, such as water, food and housing to more advanced initiatives, such as genetics, robotics etc, are all links in the same chain.

International banks, such as HSBC, Citibank, Standard Chartered Bank and Lloyds TSB offer advanced financial products for trade and commerce, while the government controlled Etisalat offers a full range of advanced voice and data telecommunication services. Most government departments have at least begun to develop Websites offering some services online, but not all are fully functioning at the present time.

Housing

Private companies supply the housing needs of expat workers from modern, high rise, glass sided apartment blocks along the Corniche to older, low rise dwellings away from the city centre. All these properties are built to rent because only Nationals may buy property in Abu Dhabi.

Among various other housing development programs, the Abu Dhabi Department of Social Services and Commercial Building, more commonly known as the Khalifa Committee (02 615 1394), oversees the most significant housing initiative. Up to the end of 2000, the Department had spent a total of Dhs.33 billion to build around 6000 buildings with over 93,000 apartments. These have been allocated to citizens and in most cases, the Department also undertakes management of these buildings.

Land Ownership

Currently, foreign companies and non Nationals are not permitted to own commercial land in the UAE, except in free zones where leasehold ownership is offered. Commercial property must be rented and rates tend to be very high. In Dubai, the year 2002 witnessed significant changes in land ownership rules for residential properties with leasehold and freehold ownership opportunities offered to non Nationals, but it seems unlikely that Abu Dhabi has any plans to follow this lead.

Public Transportation

There are a few public buses operating within Abu Dhabi but the only significant services are those that run to Dubai and Al Ain.

Nearly everyone who does not own a vehicle gets around the city by taxi. The white and gold city taxis, owned by Nationals but operated by expats, are cheap and plentiful. They can be flagged down on the streets and fares start from Dhs.2. Additionally, there are two taxi fleets – Al Ghazal and NTC – who have struck deals with hotels, social clubs and the airport and gained exclusive rights to picking up customers from their premises. You can also phone and ask for a taxi to collect you (Al Ghazal – 444 7787, NTC – 622 3300)

Electricity and Water

The UAE has the second largest per capita water consumption in the world after the United States. Provision of electricity and water remain top priorities. The Abu Dhabi Water & Electricity Authority (ADWEA) has continued to successfully meet the challenges of an ever increasing demand and, as in other developed countries, the buzzword is privatisation. ADWEA has been proactively soliciting domestic and international private sector investment and the reward is an uninterrupted supply of electricity and water at affordable rates.

Seaports and Shipping

The UAE is a maritime nation with 800 kilometres of coastline and, in Abu Dhabi, the main general cargo port is Mina Zayed. The oil industry related marine terminals of Jebel Dhanna, Ruwais, Umm Al Nar, Das Island, Zirku and Mubarraz make up the other major terminals. Dry docks and shipbuilding are other successful initiatives of the Abu Dhabi government.

Airports

ISO certified Abu Dhabi International Airport (ADIA) is rated as one of the most modern airports in the Middle East. ADIA is equipped to receive all types of aircraft and provides a full range of services and management.

Free Zones

Jebel Ali Free Zone Authority (JAFZA), established in 1985 at an estimated cost of over US$2 billion, has become a runaway success. Today, the port is home to almost 2,500 companies from about 100 different countries. The signboards dotting the free zone are a who's who of both Fortune 500 companies and local business houses. The original area between the port and Sheikh Zayed Road is almost full, and massive efforts are

underway to develop the desert on the other side of the road. JAFZA offers investors 100% control of their business, duty free import of products (for manufacturing/transit/export), leasehold land ownership, and guaranteed freedom from corporate taxation.

The success of JAFZA has spawned competing facilities in Sharjah, Ajman, Fujairah, and Ras al Khaimah. Each of these free zones also offers investors 100% control of their business. Abu Dhabi has a Free Zone Authority but, as yet, no significant free zone area. As long ago as 1999, plans were made to establish a Free Zone in Abu Dhabi on Saadiyat Island, but the development has not materialised.

Free Zones	
Ajman Free Zone Authority	06 742 5444
Dubai Airport Free Zone Authority	04 299 5555
Dubai Media City	04 391 4615
Dubai Internet City	04 391 1111
Fujairah Free Zone	09 222 8000
Hamriya Free Zone Authority – Sharjah	06 526 3333
Jebel Ali Free Zone Authority	04 881 5000
RAK Free Zone	07 228 0889
Sharjah Airport Free Zone	06 557 0000
Umm al Quwain Ahmed Bin Rashid Free Zone Authority	06 765 5882

A useful Website, www.uaefreezones.com lists the Websites of all the free zones operating in the UAE. It also carries a range of news and information about business in the UAE.

Dubai Media City

Business Climate

The pace of economic growth over the past 20 years has been incredible and the emirate stands poised for future strong growth with a multitude of new businesses and financial ventures. With the vision of the rulers of the UAE, both the legislation and government institutions were designed to minimise bureaucracy and create a business friendly environment. However, as new rules are introduced to regulate the expanding business and commercial sectors, the Emirati's love of red tape becomes increasingly noticeable. Government officials take an active role in promoting investment in the emirate and decisions can be taken (and implemented) swiftly. This sometimes means that rules concerning employees, sponsorship, partnership arrangements etc, can change overnight. Government departments have also, in recent years, placed increasing importance on improving customer service levels, but traditional attitudes prevail in many areas, so patience is always required in all dealings with the Ministries.

The commitment of the rulers to economic development is pioneering in the Middle East and is seen by many as a model for other governments in the region. While Abu Dhabi is among the more expensive business locations in the Middle East, many companies pay this premium to reap the rewards offered. These include no tax collection and low business fees, a high degree of political stability, steady, strong economic growth rates, excellent infrastructure and a high quality of life for expatriate residents.

Doing Business

Aside from Agency Law (see [p.106]), which is in many cases avoidable by establishing oneself in one of the various free zones, the UAE can be an enjoyable and rewarding place to live and do business. There are still a range of exciting business opportunities for companies and entrepreneurs to serve an increasingly sophisticated and growing market.

Business Groups & Contacts

In addition to various government departments specifically responsible for providing commercial assistance to enterprises in Abu Dhabi, there are various chambers of commerce and other business groups that help facilitate investments and provide

You choose the destination
- We fly you there.
Daily Worldwide
from Abu Dhabi.
"With over 755 destinations in more than 132 countries and over 14,000 daily flights, Lufthansa and its 15 Star Alliance Partners offer you the best connections around the Globe. Along with an award winning on-board service and the Miles & More frequent flyer program, there is simply no better way to fly. For more information on Lufthansa and Star Alliance visit www.uae.lufthansa.com, call 02-639 4640 or visit your nearest Travel Agent."
There's no better way to fly.
Lufthansa
A STAR ALLIANCE MEMBER

opportunities for networking with others in the community. Some groups provide information on trade with their respective country, as well as on business opportunities both in Abu Dhabi and the other emirates. Most also arrange social and networking events. Refer to the Abu Dhabi Yellow Pages and Hawk Business pages for details. Both directories are available on line www.yellowpages.net.ae, www.hawkpages.com . Another useful Website is The Emirates Network (www.theemiratesnetwork.com) – an online facility that allows you to access the specialised business directories in the UAE.

Listed below are some of the embassies located in Abu Dhabi. A full list can be obtained from either the British Embassy or the Hawk Business Pages.

Embassies/Consulates

Country	Phone	Map ref
Australia	634 6100	8-E1
Bahrain	665 7500	4-E4
Bangladesh	446 5100	6 B4
Canada	407 1300	3-D4
China	443 4276	5-D1
Egypt	444 5566	2-C2
France	443 5100	3-D4
Germany	443 5630	3-D4
India	449 2700	2 C3
Iran	444 7618	2-C2
Japan	443 5696	3-E4
Jordan	444 7100	2-C3
Kuwait	444 6888	2-C3
Lebanon	449 2100	2 C3
Malaysia	448 2775	6-B1
Netherlands	632 1920	8-C2
Oman	446 3333	3-C2
Pakistan	444 7800	2-C3
Qatar	449 3300	2-C3
Saudi Arabia	444 5700	2-C2
Sri Lanka	642 6666	6-A4
Switzerland	627 4636	8-B2
Syria	444 8768	2 C2
Thailand	642 1772	3-D4
UK	610 1111	9-A2
USA	414 2200	2 C3
Yemen	444 8454	2 C3

Business Councils

American Business Council	671 1141
British Business Group	445 7234
British Council	665 9300
Canadian Business Council	407 1300
South African Business Group	633 7565
Australian Business in the Gulf (ABIG)	04 395 4423

Trade Centres and Commissions

Australlian Trade Commission	634 6100
British Embassy – Commercial Section	610 1111
Canadian Trade Commission	407 1300
Egyptian Trade Centre	444 5566
Romanian Trade Representation	666 6346
Sultanate of Oman Office	446 3333
Thailand Trade Centre	642 1772
Trade Representative of the Netherlands	632 1920
USA Consulate General	414 2200
Cyprus Trade Centre	04 228 2411
Danish Trade Centre	04 222 7699

Business Culture

Customs

Despite its cosmopolitan outward appearance, Abu Dhabi is an Arab city in a Muslim country and people doing business in Abu Dhabi must remember this fact. Even if your counterpart in another company is an expatriate, the head decision maker may be a UAE national who might take a different approach to business matters. Your best bet when doing business in the UAE for the first time, is to observe closely, have lots of patience, and make a concerted effort to understand how the customs and culture still affect the modern business environment. Once you understand the customs and culture, follow them (and keep a hold of that patience!)

Although women have not made significant inroads into mainstream business, there are both National and expatriate women in the UAE who have risen to positions of prominence.

Remember, as in any community, networking is critical even across industries. Abu Dhabi is a very small community within the setting of a large urban city. Business acumen here can at times, be more important than specific industry knowledge. Keep your finger on the pulse of activity by attending business events and trade shows. Make friends in government departments where your business has direct interfaces and this will often land you in the front line of opportunities. Likewise, bad news is rarely made public here, so staying in tune with the grapevine can help prevent wrong decisions.

Etiquette

Tea and coffee are a very important part of Arabic life and it may be considered rude to refuse this offer of hospitality whilst in a meeting or waiting for it to start. Tilting the small Arabic coffee cup back and forth several times with your fingers will signal that you do not want another refill.

Although proper dress is important for all business dealings, the local climate has dictated that a shirt and tie (for men) is sufficient for all but the most important of business encounters; women usually choose a suit or a skirt and blouse that are not excessively revealing.

In Arab society, a verbal commitment once clearly made, is ethically if not legally binding, and reasonable bargaining is an important part of reaching any such agreement. Finally, it is important to remember that Abu Dhabi is still a relatively small business community, and so confidentiality and discretion are of the utmost importance in all business dealings.

Meetings

A strong handshake should not only start off each meeting but also end the encounter – a longer handshake at the end is an indication that the meeting has gone well. It is always preferable to start a meeting with a non business discussion but avoid enquiring after somebody's wife, even if you know the wife. General enquiries about the family are more appropriate.

Don't be surprised if other people walk in and out during the meeting to discuss unrelated matters and be prepared for the meeting to run longer than expected.

While meeting agendas might be important to ensure that all relevant matters are discussed, they are better used as a checklist (at the end) instead of a schedule for discussions during the meeting. Sometimes it will become obvious during the course of the meeting that it is simply not a good day for a particular discussion. In this event, it is better to move on and return to the difficult subject another day.

It is also a good idea not to jump to conclusions at the end of a meeting. Try to do background work on the people you are meeting to understand how much influence they actually wield in the decision making process. Due to cultural norms, it is rare for an Arab to admit just how little or how great their influence is on the result of a business decision.

Time

While your punctuality for meetings is very important, if the host is delayed due to an unforeseen (and possibly more important!) other visitor or event, you must always remember to be patient. Remember traffic accidents are a very predictable event (they happen every day), so plan ahead and don't be forced to use them as an excuse for being late.

Business Hours

Abu Dhabi has no business hours (or even fixed working days for that matter) that are set in stone. Government departments generally work between 07:00 - 14:00 from Saturday to Wednesday, although departments providing services to the public sometimes offer extended hours. Many multinational companies prefer the Sunday to Thursday work week, allowing them a greater overlap with other international offices, while other companies work a straight six day week (Saturday to Thursday). Private sector offices normally work from 08:00 - 17:00 or 09:00 - 18:00, though some take advantage of the Labour Law guidelines and make the most of their employees' time with an 08:00 - 18:00 work day.

Banks remain open until about 13:30 on weekdays but close early on Thursdays, while large supermarkets generally maintain hours between 8:00 and midnight throughout the week. Shopping

Highrises in Abu Dhabi

malls are open for about 12 hours starting from 10:00 (later in the day on Fridays), while many other shops in the city still close between 13:00 and 16:30.

During the holy month of Ramadan, working hours for government and some private sector companies are reduced by two hours, while shops and malls open later in the day and stay open till much later in the evening – call ahead to avoid frustration.

Business Laws

Laws & Regulations

As with many countries in the Middle East, UAE law requires that companies have a local (UAE National) participant holding at least 51% of the shares. While there has been discussion of easing, or even removing, these ownership restrictions, no change in the regulations is imminent.

100% foreign ownership is permitted for the following:

- A company located in a UAE free zone (see below)
- A company with activities open to 100% GCC ownership (Gulf Co-operation Council – Saudi Arabia, Oman, Kuwait, Qatar and Bahrain)
- A company in which wholly owned GCC companies enter into partnership with UAE Nationals
- A branch or representative office of a foreign company registered in Abu Dhabi
- A professional or artisan company practising business activities that allow 100% foreign ownership.

Legal Consultants	
Afridi & Angell	627 5134
Al Tamimi & Co	674 4535
Denton Wilde Sapte	626 6180
Emirates Advocates	639 4446
Simmons & Simmons	627 5568
Trowers & Hamlin	626 7274

Agency Law

By law, foreign nationals intending to set up a company such as a sole proprietorship, a branch of a foreign company or a professional company must find a National agent and sign a local (National) service agency agreement with him. The local agent is usually referred to as a 'sponsor'.

A sponsor may be a UAE National or a company fully owned by UAE Nationals. The choice of a sponsor can be of significant importance, particularly for a larger company. Appointing a sponsor who is considered prominent and influential can open many doors that might otherwise be extremely difficult to access. Local sponsors may be paid a lump sum and/or a percentage of the profits or turnover.

The sponsor does not have any responsibility for the business, but he is obliged to assist with all government related procedures, such as obtaining government permits, trade licences, visas and labour cards. His signature will be required on most application forms. Once the company is up and running, many sponsors become 'sleeping partners', simply taking a share of the profits. Whilst this practice has previously been encouraged by the government because it is a good source of income for Nationals, there have been cases where the foreign partner has acted fraudulently and then left the country, leaving the National with debts. Trade licences have also been misused to bring in expat workers.

A foreign national looking to establish a business in Abu Dhabi must place a lot of trust in this system. Before choosing an agent, it is highly advisable to first investigate his reputation in the market and agree on each party's rights and responsibilities. Once a is business established, it is very difficult to break an agency agreement, except in case of cessation of activity.

Abu Dhabi Municipality & Road Planning Department

Commercial Agent

If a foreign company wants to supply goods and/or services from abroad without establishing a physical presence in the UAE, it can appoint a commercial agent as a distributor for its goods and/or services here. The agent is entitled to exclusive rights to distribute and market specific products and services within a specific territory. The company is not allowed to distribute these products in that territory. If the company does assist in a sale, its commercial agent is entitled to a commission.

Such a commercial agency also covers franchises, distributorships and commission arrangements. The agent must register the agency agreement with the Ministry.

Disputes

The UAE legal system has its roots in French and Egyptian law. In the event of a dispute, it is highly advisable that you undertake good legal counsel. Generally, you can measure the 'wasta' a consultant has by the cases he handles (wasta – a very important term in business here; essentially referring to the 'influence' that one has over the powers that be).

Financial Issues

The primary dispute that you will encounter in the UAE is the flow of payments for goods and services. At present, there is no credit measurement system in the UAE that helps determine creditworthiness. Credit granting decisions are taken on history, reputation and legacy (bad criteria at times for judging creditworthiness!).

Be wary of extending credit and be sure to ask around in the banking community about the reputation of potential customers. Additionally, run the gamut in your industry and collect information on your potential customer. You'll be able to find a semblance of their reputation (rumours filtered out).

Also, talk to your competitors and see what you can get from them (a little difficult, but you may find a sympathetic ear from those who've been burned before).

A solid way to measure the financial depth of your customer is to get an understanding of how willing they are to put up deposits or provide post dated cheques. Post dated cheques are the securest form of payment here as there is criminal recourse for not clearing them. Some banks are willing to offer you a discount for payments prior to maturity (also depending upon company and reputation). The key here is not to wave the legal flag too quickly. Be patient and work with your customers; it's a vicious circle and quite possibly, their money could be held up by non payment from their customers. Additionally, the chance of legally seeing a quick return on your dues is slim. Courts here pass judgement on the ability to pay; not amounts owed (ie, a Dhs.1 million debt could be settled for Dhs.1,000 a month, as long as the defendant can prove inability to pay).

The UAE Labour Law

Other Options → 'Banning' [p.60]

The UAE Labour Law is very employer friendly. Labour issues are administered by the Federal Ministry of Labour and Social Affairs. The law is loosely based on the International Labour Organisation's model and deals with employer/employee relations, such as working hours, termination rights, benefits and repatriation. Little recourse for employees exists and exploitation does occur, particularly amongst blue collar workers and labourers. At the moment, trade unions do not exist and strikes are forbidden, but there are GCC wide discussions under way about issues concerning the basic human rights of employees.

Government workers and employees of quasi-government institutions are not necessarily subject to the UAE Labour Law. Some free zones have their own labour rules and disputes are settled by the free zone authority without recourse to the Federal Ministry.

A copy of the UAE Labour Law can be obtained from the Abu Dhabi offices of the Ministry of Labour (667 1700). The law applies to all staff and employees working in the United Arab Emirates, whether UAE National or expatriate, barring a few exempt categories. The law also deals with all aspects of employee-employer relationships: the contracts, employment restrictions on women and children, salaries, working hours, leave, employee protection, medical care, benefits and compensation.

Copyright Law

Introduced in 1993, the UAE Copyright Law was most recently updated in 2002 with the development of Federal Copyright Law No.7. This law, which is overseen by the Ministry of Information and Culture, protects the rights of creators, performers, producers of audio recordings as well as broadcasting and recording corporations.

Trademark Law

The UAE federal government first introduced its trademark law in 1974 and then updated it in 1993. Throughout, the government has continually improved its efforts to protect registered trademark owners. Trademark registration in the UAE is done through the Ministry of Economy and Commerce. The entire registration process can take anywhere from 12 to 18 months. Under the UAE trademark law, trademark owners can now protect their marks and count on government assistance to penalise those infringing upon their trademark.

Legal Eagle

If you are working with intellectual property (ie, music, publishing, software etc), be sure to register your trademarks and copyrights with the Chamber of Commerce and Industry. This ensures you have legal recourse in case there are any illegal attempts to resell your material. Without this registration, you will not be recognised as the owner!

Setting Up

It is difficult to provide 'hard and fast' rules for those wishing to set up a business in Abu Dhabi. The main difficulty in providing this information arises from the amount of variables involved. Rules depend on nationality, business activity, capital amounts, partners, products etc, and the laws and/or regulations change on a regular basis. Check with the relevant government department(s) before proceeding.

You will need to find a reliable UAE national to sponsor the business (see Agency Law [p.106]).

Be wise... Get a PRO

Although laws exist, there is always some preferential treatment for a special segment of the population. It is strongly advised to hire a Public Relations Officer (PRO) who is preferably an Arabic speaker. Selection of a PRO should be done carefully to avoid any bad deals (selecting a PRO by referral is recommended).

Trade Licence

In order to obtain a trade licence, membership with the Abu Dhabi Chamber of Commerce & Industry must first be obtained. An application for a trade name is submitted as the first step in the membership procedure. Once approved by the Chamber of Commerce & Industry, a copy is then submitted to the Abu Dhabi Municipality along with an application form and all related documents. On the Municipality's approval, a membership letter will be sent by the Municipality to the Chamber of Commerce & Industry. The Abu Dhabi Chamber of Commerce & Industry will assist with this procedure.

After obtaining a trade licence, there are generally five set up options for non GCC nationals. These are: setting up a branch of a foreign company; a limited liability company (LLC); a sole proprietorship; a professional company; and setting up in a free zone.

Branch or Representative Office

Established foreign companies may set up a branch or a representative office of their firm in Abu Dhabi. The branch will be considered a part of the parent company and not a separate legal entity. A representative office, unlike a branch office, is permitted to practice promotional services for the company and products and also facilitate contacting potential customers.

Limited Liability Company (LLC)

An LLC is a business structure that is a hybrid of a partnership and a corporation. Its owners are shielded from personal liability; the liability of the shareholders is limited to their shares in the company's capital.

This company type suits organisations interested in developing a long term relationship in the local market. Responsibility for the management of an LLC can be vested in either the National or foreign partners, or in a third party.

Sole Proprietorship

A sole proprietorship by definition, means 'one owner'. This is the most basic company form where the owner has a trade licence in his name and is personally held liable for his accounts ie, he is responsible for the company's financial and legal obligations. The proprietor can conduct business in the commercial, professional, industrial or agricultural industries.

Nationals and GCC nationals are permitted to set up a sole proprietorship with few restrictions. Stricter conditions apply for non GCC nationals.

A non GCC national setting up a sole proprietorship is restricted in the type of activities he may perform. The company should be in a service or knowledge based industry.

Professional Company

Also referred to as a business partnership, a professional business company or a consultancy business, a professional company type falls under the civil code rather than under commercial law. This differentiation is unique to the UAE. Such firms may engage in professional or artisan activities but the number of staff members that may be employed is limited and a UAE national must be appointed as a local service agent.

An important part in applying for the licence is showing evidence of the credentials and qualifications of the employees and partners.

Free Zones

Other Options → Free Zones [p.109]

If you decide to set up your business in a Free Zone, usual UAE laws will not apply. Each Free Zone has different regulations. Check out Websites for details.

Staffing

For companies operating outside free zones, the Ministry of Labour will set a maximum number of expatriate staff that may be hired according to the size of the business and the business activity. In some cases such as banks, the Ministry will state that a minimum percentage of the organisation's employees must be UAE Nationals.

Recruitment of staff is an entirely separate challenge. Various agencies can assist with the recruitment of labourers from the Indian subcontinent, while other local recruiters specialise in searches for professional and managerial positions. In reality however, many positions in Abu Dhabi are filled through word of mouth between friends and business colleagues, and also through 'wasta' (connections).

Work Permits

Other Options → Visas [p.19]
Residence Visa [p.52]
Labour Card [p.54]

The employer is responsible for all work permits and related immigration procedures; this can be quite a tedious endeavour so be warned and start the process early. If setting up in a free zone, the free zone authority will handle all immigration related procedures, which simplifies the process dramatically but costs slightly more. The company must cover all costs (visa, medical test etc) involved in hiring an employee. Costs for family members are the employee's responsibility, unless otherwise stated in the employment contract.

Labour Contracts

When applying for a work permit, the Ministry of Labour provides a model labour contract in Arabic. It is advisable to draft an additional contract with further employment and benefit details, particularly for senior staff. The employment contract is enforceable in a court of law (except in the case of some free zones) as long as it does not contravene the Labour Law, and the Arabic version of the contract will prevail.

Al Maqtaa Bridge

Exploring

EXPLORER

Exploring

Abu Dhabi City

Abu Dhabi Areas

Exploring

Abu Dhabi is a growing city with high rise buildings and well manicured green patches. The modern look conceals the reality that just forty years ago, before the discovery of oil, Abu Dhabi was little more than a village consisting of the ruler's stone fort and a scattering of barasti (palm) huts. The changes that have occurred as the barren desert of the past has been transformed into an urban sprawl have been remarkable. Judging from the construction sites around Abu Dhabi, the rapid development and expansion looks set to continue. However, with life in the federal capital unfolding at a slower pace than that of neighbouring Dubai, Abu Dhabi is often referred to as Washington to Dubai's New York. Certainly, Abu Dhabi constitutes the heart of UAE national politics and major decisions continue to be taken in the informal settings of the 'Majlis', which remains the cornerstone of Emirati political culture.

Due to its unique position on an island, this modern capital is compact with clearly marked areas. Skyscrapers boasting coloured glass and sleek, imaginative designs pack the main 'downtown' streets near the Corniche. Further inland, the streets are quieter and house magnificent government buildings and homes or palaces tucked behind high walls to deter unwanted scrutiny. Many of the roundabouts here are decorated with giant coffee cups, clock towers, forts and falcons offering excellent photo opportunities. Canon Square, situated near the Clock Tower, has a huge cascading water fountain and enormous concrete replicas of traditional Arabic artefacts.

Souks were, and still are, an integral part of life in the Middle East, and a visit to Arabia is not complete without experiencing the hustle and bustle of this traditional and busy marketplace. Originally, the souks were also the place where locals used to meet with friends, catch up on gossip, and for the men to sit in adjoining cafés and smoke shisha. Abu Dhabi has a number of thriving souks, selling everything from plastic buckets and fresh fish to carpets from Afghanistan. If you are prepared to explore then you are guaranteed to find a few unexpected bargains on your souk expedition (refer to Souks [p.173]).

The following section deals with what there is to see and do in Abu Dhabi and Al Ain – interesting places to visit, such as museums and heritage sites, parks and beaches. The list is by no means exhaustive and should be read in conjunction with the rest of the book, and, in particular, with the Organised Tours section [p.132]. This section gives information on tour operators, prices and descriptions of various tours that are on offer. Unless otherwise marked for Al Ain, the activities in the book are for Abu Dhabi.

The city of Abu Dhabi grew and developed along the waterfront on the northern side of the island and to date, the waterfront is still the main centre of activity. Most of the hotels, restaurants and places of interest are within four or five blocks of the sea (although this is still quite a wide area). However, since the sea and fishing played an important part in the early lives of the local people, we suggest you start your exploration of Abu Dhabi at the Corniche and Breakwater, then work your way along the coast or inland.

The Corniche

Visitor's Checklist

The following is our list of 'must dos' for you to make the most of your stay in Abu Dhabi. This checklist will help you plan your schedule, tell you where to go and what to see and do. There is still enough culture and heritage in Abu Dhabi to provide you with plenty of options other than shopping or lounging by the hotel pool. So while you're topping up on your tan, sit back, read on and tailor your own memorable tour of this fascinating emirate.

Culture Buffs

The Old Fort, which dates back to 1793, is a rare display of authentic Abu Dhabi heritage. It is located on the same grounds as the Cultural Foundation, which organises a number of events, from international dance ensembles to arts exhibitions.

Liwa [p.135]

Watching the sunrise over untouched golden desert dunes is not an activity most of us engage in on a regular basis, so grab this opportunity to visit Liwa and prepare to be amazed.

Desert Delights [p.133]

A number of organised tour companies offer you the chance to experience the attractions of the Arabian desert in style and comfort. Prepare to be entertained by Arabian dancers under the star-lit desert sky.

Abu Dhabi Corniche [p.117]

Although parts of the Corniche are more of a building site these days, this stretch of Abu Dhabi, nonetheless, offers you a welcome opportunity to simply gaze out at the sea or watch the dhows in their rhythmic motion.

Heritage Village [p.125]

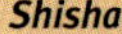

The Heritage Village is a must stop for anyone interested in tracing the dramatic transformation of Abu Dhabi. It offers a glimpse into a way of life and culture that is far removed from the more cosmopolitan and globalised Abu Dhabi we see today.

Shisha [p.18]

The scents emanating from colourful and traditional water pipes is an integral part of the Arab social scene. The best shisha places in town are the cafes around the Breakwater where you can puff away, while taking in beautiful panoramic views of the city.

Shop Till You Drop [p.147]

Keep fresh and cool this summer at one of the many malls. Skim through the Shopping section for detailed descriptions and choose the one that best suits your retail indulgence moods.

Al Ain Oasis [p.122]

This massive oasis is littered with palm plantations and many of the working farms are set up with the ancient falaj irrigation system. A peaceful and idyllic haven, the oasis is a great for a stroll in the cooler months or to escape from the bustling city noise.

Water Babies

Snorkelling, diving, jet skiing – there's lots to do at the beach. Hotels run various in-house activities but also check with tour operators [p.133], or flip to the Activities section [p.177] for independent facilities.

Iranian Souk [p.173]

A trip to the souk is a must for anyone visiting the Middle East, and the Iranian Souk offers visitors a taste of Iran in the heart of Abu Dhabi. Traders dock their boats and unveil a host of goods ranging from spectacular Iranian carpets to more mundane household goods.

Hili Archaeological Garden [p.128]

Archaeology buff or not, you will most certainly appreciate the finds that date back over 4,000 years. The gardens are worth a visit both for adults, who can explore the archaeological heritage of Hili, as well as children, who will be happily entertained in the play area.

National Theatre

The National Theatre hosts some impressive musical extravaganzas with traditional Arab musicians such as oud players. The timetable of events is, however, prone to change on very short notice so be prepared to expect the unexpected.

Dhow Charters [p.184]

A dhow trip is a great chance to gain insight into a long gone, traditional way of life. Discover how the inhabitants of this island made their living prior to the discovery of oil with activities like pearl fishing, now confined to the pages of history.

Island Expedition

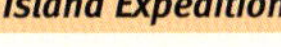

Boating with friends is an ideal way to spend a lazy weekend. If you can get your hands on a boat you can retreat to one of the many secluded islands and spend your time being as active or as lazy as you want. Remember to wear a hat because the sun is usually scorching hot.

Camel Spotting

Camels were once the motorcars of the desert and a key part of the Bedouin lifestyle. Today, they are mostly tourist attractions, providing rides at desert safaris. Camel lovers can head down to the Al Ain Camel Market and buy their very own camel!

Henna

Women can indulge in the traditional custom of adorning hands and feet with henna. Most beauty parlours offer this service and once decorated, you'll come out feeling like an Arab bride. If you don't like it, don't worry, for it washes out in a couple of weeks.

Dhow Building

Pop down to Al Bateen and observe craftsmen going about their daily business of building traditional dhows. You are sure to receive a friendly reception from the craftsmen who are more than willing to share the art of dhow building.

Fish Souk [p.173]

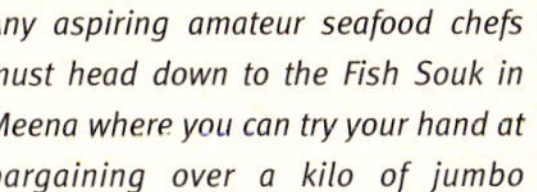

Any aspiring amateur seafood chefs must head down to the Fish Souk in Meena where you can try your hand at bargaining over a kilo of jumbo prawns. For the best purchases get there at the crack of dawn and don't let the smell of raw fish put you off!

Al Ain Museum [p.126]

The opening of the Al Ain Museum in 1971 corresponds with the establishment of the UAE federation. The museum offers you the chance to view photographs of Abu Dhabi before the oil boom that so radically altered the entire social character of this region.

Al Raha Beach

This is the best maintained public beach in Abu Dhabi. For those on a budget and looking to get away from the more confined hotel based beach settings, this is definitely the place to go.

Gold Souk [p.160]

A visit to the Abu Dhabi Gold Souk located in Madinat Zayed is more than just a shopping experience. It's a great opportunity to sample regional jewellery designs, which may be a bit elaborate for your taste, but interesting nevertheless.

Corniche Cruise [p.123]

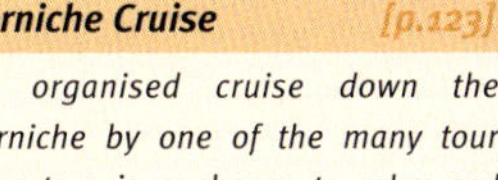

An organised cruise down the Corniche by one of the many tour operators is a chance to relax and sample the best views that Abu Dhabi has to offer. Don't forget your camera, since this really is a great photo opportunity!

Airport Road

The 'spine' of Abu Dhabi runs through the centre of the island from the Al Maqtaa Bridge in the south, to the centre of town in the north. The section that passes through town is extremely busy with high rise apartments on either side, but as you travel away from the city centre, the apartments gradually give way to more suburban, green areas and villas.

Plenty of shops, independent cafes and restaurants line this road, and car dealerships fill most of 15th to 18th streets. Any new arrivals to Abu Dhabi looking for second hand cars are promptly directed to this part of Airport Road.

Al Bateen

On the west side of the island is the area of Al Bateen that houses the InterContinental Hotel with its trendy restaurants, and a few large parks that are popular weekend barbecue spots for Arab families. The leafy feel of Al Bateen, with a number of impressive villas lining the streets, is a welcome relief to the more congested parts of Abu Dhabi.

The Bateen shipyard here is well worth a visit with its smells of freshly cut African and Indian teak emanating from the high piles of wooden planks. Craftsmen use ancient skills to fashion these planks into traditional dhows and racing hulls that can be seen on special occasions during competitions off the Corniche. Little has changed in this age old craft – some of the building methods look positively medieval! The yard offers unique insight into a city that once thrived on maritime resources such as pearl diving and fishing.

Al Meena

If not too busy, the craftsmen will happily share the intricacies of their art. The surroundings are ideal for photography with all the wood and construction amidst sawdust – do ask for permission before clicking the craftsmen.

The yard is open throughout the week except Fridays, the best time to visit being around 17:00.

Al Karama

This green, mainly residential area has numerous villas lining its streets. The Sheikh Khalifa Medical Centre, Central Hospital, Al Jazeirah Hospital and the Kuwaiti and Korean embassies are also located here.

Al Khalidiya

The coast road heading north from the south of the island leads to Al Khalidiya; one of the most sought after residential areas in the capital. The charm of Al Khalidya is in the combination of apartment buildings and large villas located within walking distance of a number of coffee shops. Some of these coffee joints, such as the Mozaic coffee shop, are discreetly tucked away in residential towers. An Abela and Spinneys supermarket service the needs of the population here, with Spinneys attracting the members of the local community who often meet up for breakfast in the supermarket's coffee shop.

The Khalidiya Garden and the Khalidiya Children's Garden provide additional green spaces. These parks are especially popular for picnics and family gatherings during the cooler winter months. Khalidiya is also a short distance from the Inter-Continental and Hilton Hotels and will be very close to the Emirates Palace Hotel, which is set to be completed by the end of 2004.

Al Markaziyah

This centrally located business and shopping area has shops – both local and international – lining the streets, along with numerous restaurants and entertainment venues, such as the Al Mariah and Al Massa Cinemas, and a bowling alley. City hotels and apartments share the streets with embassies, the Al Noor Hospital, Etisalat's headquarters and the Fatouh Al Khair Centre, more commonly known as the Marks and Spencer Centre. (See [p.172] for more details)

Al Meena

Located on the northern tip of the island, east of the Corniche, this warehouse and port district houses the vegetable market, the Animal Souk and the Iranian Souk. The result of recent developments can already be seen with the new Meena Centre that has an Abu Dhabi Co-operative Society, 2XL furniture store, Jarir Bookstore and Cost Less Electronics. Toys R Us and Ace Hardware are also located nearby.

Of interest to many expats is The Club – one of Abu Dhabi's most popular health and sports clubs. With a beach, pool, gym, full sporting facilities, a restaurant, sailing, diving etc, you're bound to find some activity that you fancy! Membership is very reasonable and The Club is particularly attractive to families, with toddlers and children proving a regular fixture around the pool during weekends. However, adults also have the opportunity to get away to the bar or enjoy a fun quiz night, which is held at The Club every Wednesday!

The international Port Zayed is the main port authority in Abu Dhabi and has an active harbour nearby with a small market along the quay. Business here is thriving with interesting odds and ends. Once the day's catch of hammour or fresh lobster has been secured and new traps laid, the local fishermen head to their berths in the fisherman's co-operative area. The sight of 200 traditional wooden dhows and weathered launches at sunset conjures up images of crusty seafarers battling the high seas to bring in their booty of exotic herbs and spices. The boats make great photo opportunities and the best time to view the scene is at dusk when they are gently lit. Get permission however, before you click a crewmember.

Also situated in the dhow harbour is the Al Dhafra Restaurant, a seafood restaurant popular with tourists and locals alike. You can even catch dinner cruises on the Shuja Yacht (see [p.250] for further details) which sails from the harbour along the Corniche every evening. Alternatively, other companies also offer dinner cruises on more traditional old wooden dhow boats.

Al Safarat

Located towards the southern side of the island near Airport Road, this area houses the General Exhibition Centre (GEC) – a purpose built centre hosting international exhibitions. The Grandstand on the main coast road holds military marches for Sheikh Zayed on a regular basis. Most embassies (with the exception of Saudia Arabia, Yemen and Qatar), the Sheikh Zayed Sports Centre, the Sharia Courts and the headquarters for Abu Dhabi International Hotels are based in Al Safarat.

Breakwater

The Breakwater is an area of reclaimed land leading off Abu Dhabi island. The Marina Mall, the Abu Dhabi International Marina Sports Club and the Heritage Village are situated here alongwith various Arabic style restaurants and cafes along the waterfront.

Presently under construction is a new marina and luxury housing development. Also, coming up next to the entrance of the Breakwater is the enormous Emirates Palace Hotel, due for completion by December 2004, when Abu Dhabi is set to host the next GCC Conference.

The Breakwater

Corniche

The Corniche, seen as the heart of Abu Dhabi, is an area of buzzing activity. This stretch of the waterfront is very popular with both Abu Dhabi residents and visitors. On any given night, you can expect to bump into one of over 100 different nationalities taking time out to walk, run, roller blade or cycle along.

Currently, the Corniche is undergoing a process of frantic development that has left certain parts resembling a building site. It has already

undergone the first phase of a Dhs.200 million facelift, designed to enhance its position and add to the beauty of the seafront. The project, including further land reclamation, should be complete by December 2005 (Map Ref 8-A3 to 10-D3).

On the side of the road, you will find a cycle lane and several well equipped play areas for younger children that are shaded by palm trees. Elegant fountains (the most notable being the Volcano Fountain), along with features like the Clock Tower and small folly like rest rooms, dot the roadside. In peak tourist winter months, the carefully manicured lawns bordering the Corniche are ideal for picnics and barbecues.

Towards one end of the Corniche, a road by the Hilton Hotel leads to the Breakwater and the reclaimed area beyond. Marina Mall is located here and future plans include the building of a hotel and luxurious villas. The Breakwater itself is a leisure stretch festooned with brightly lit restaurants and miniature fun fairs where children are happily occupied with the small selection of rides. This leaves you free to pick up a pleasure dhow for a cruise along the Corniche, visit the Heritage Village, admire the tallest flag pole in the world, dine at one of the traditional restaurants or sit in your own majlis and smoke shisha. Most of the outlets here are open at night and the Breakwater also provides spectacular views of the entire length of downtown Abu Dhabi – a photo opportunity that shouldn't be missed.

The newly renovated part of the Corniche is generally referred to as the new Corniche. However, for those new to Abu Dhabi, don't confuse this with the New Corniche, (AKA Eastern Lagoon) which runs along the eastern side of the island.

See Also: *The New Corniche – Parks and Beaches (Exploring).*

Madinat Zayed

On the east side of the island, between Airport Road and Electra Street, lies the Madinat Zayed which holds an enormous shopping centre and Gold Souk of the same name. Located nearby is the central post office along with various government departments such as the Municipality & Town Planning Department, Ministry of Finance & Industry and ADWEA. Both high and low rise apartment buildings, housing numerous businesses (big and small), independent restaurants, dry cleaners etc, dwarf a few odd villas in the area.

Tourist Club Area

Situated on the north east end of the island, at the end of Hamdan and Electra Streets, this very busy area is packed with residential buildings, shops, hotels, and restaurants. It is also home to the Beach Rotana Hotel & Towers, Al Diar Dana Hotel, Emirates Plaza Hotel, Le Meridien Abu Dhabi, International Rotana Inn, Abu Dhabi Mall (with Century Cinemas), Abu Dhabi Marina Yacht Club and the old Abu Dhabi Co-operative Society to name a few. The area is named after the Al Diar Tourist Club – a members club with mostly Arab and family members – offering a beach, pool, gym, park, sporting facilities and food outlets. Of importance to visitors is the City Terminal bus station located across the street from the Beach Rotana Hotel & Towers. Buses depart from this location on a regular basis to the Abu Dhabi International Airport.

The Tourist Club area is certainly a convenient location and is within walking distance to many recreational spots. This proximity has made this area an increasingly popular residential choice among new arrivals, who opt for the many high rise residential buildings located here.

Abu Dhabi Areas – Other

Al Maqtaa

As you move away from the town in the southern part of the island, before reaching Umm Al Nar, you will see the Grand Mosque. The Officers Club and the Al Diar Gulf Hotel & Resort are nearby and conveniently located for those who happen to live on the outskirts and fancy a pint without the journey all the way into town. Further south is the Al Maqtaa Bridge, taking drivers off the island and on the motorways to Al Ain, Dubai and the Abu Dhabi International Airport.

Al Mushrif

Located near Airport Road and Al Karama Street, Al Mushrif is in the centre of the island and yet away from the high rises and heavily constructed areas. Popular landmarks include the Abu Dhabi Golf & Equestrian Centre, the Mushrif Gardens (great for walking the dog), some international schools, most of Abu Dhabi's churches and the Immigration Department.

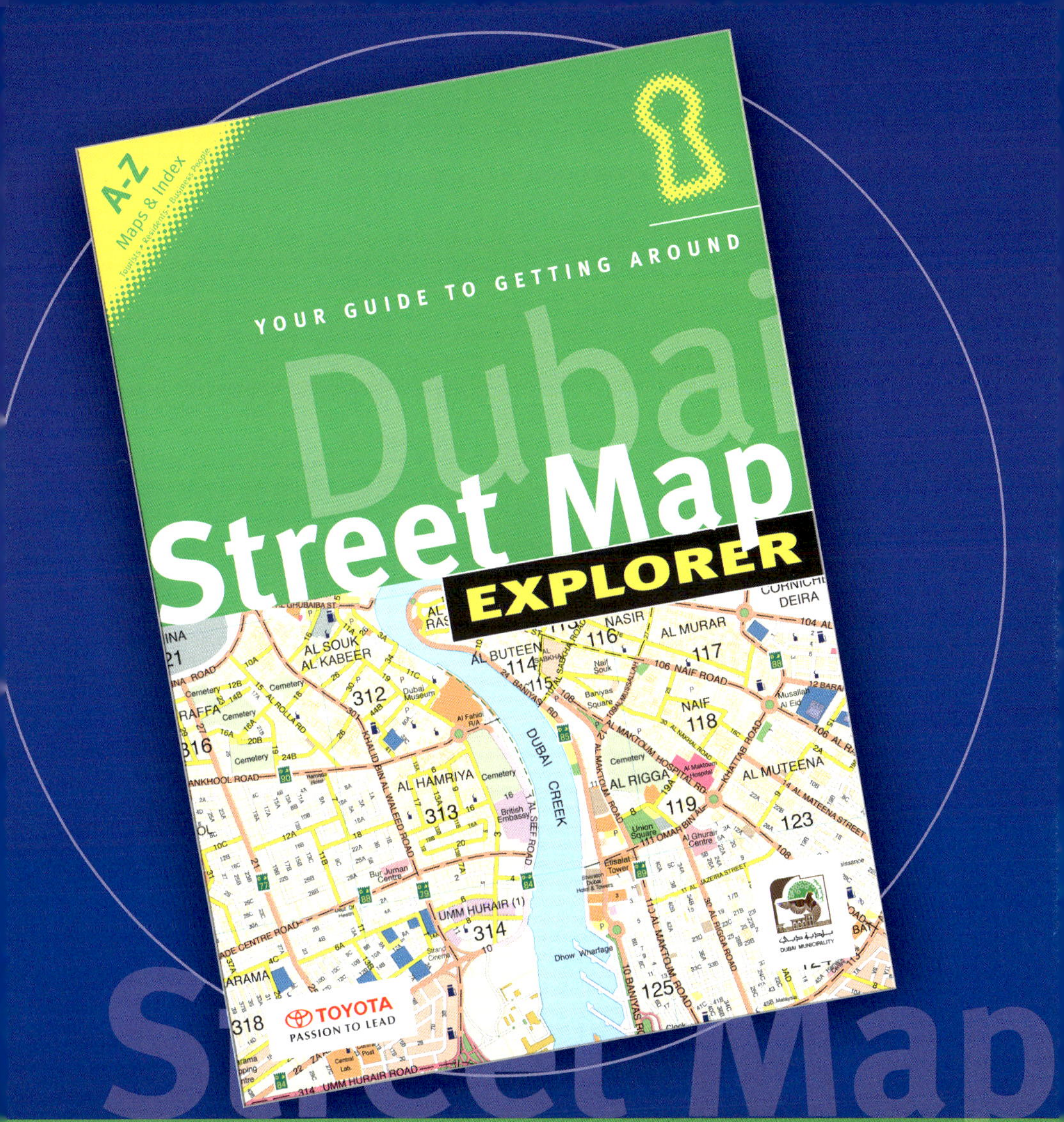

Manasir

Manasir is very popular with Abu Dhabi's expat residents. This green locale has many embassies and various palaces. The area used to house the American embassy, which has now been relocated. For the active reader, take note that this is a great area for cycling and jogging.

The Islands

One of the unique aspects of the emirate of Abu Dhabi is its islands. There are over 200 of them in varying sizes, and the majority are flat, sandy and uninhabited. A popular activity is to go island hopping, or to spend the day on your own private island, exploring, having a barbecue, or simply enjoying the sun and the peace. If you have a private boat, make sure you keep to the dredged channels to avoid running aground. Any boat over 16 ft must have a licence and a radio.

Directly opposite the Corniche is Lulu Island, a large manmade island protected from the sea by a breakwater. Undergoing an exciting transformation, this once barren island has had a massive facelift with thousands of palm trees planted and sand dunes relocated! A variety of buildings, cafes and restaurants have also been constructed. However, at the time of going to print, there was very little information on when it would open to the public.

Sadiyat Island is another island turned into a beach resort. Popular for weekend breaks as well as day trips, it offers a variety of facilities including an entertainment hall, restaurant, chalets for overnight stays, boat mooring facilities and plenty of water sports. The island can be reached from the Abu Dhabi Tourist Club.

Lulu Island

Five kilometres south of Abu Dhabi city is the island of Futaisi, a private island owned by HH Sheikh Hamad Bin Hamdan Al Nahyan. The islanders of this long inhabited island used to supply sweet water and stone for building forts and rulers' houses on Abu Dhabi island. There are still signs of their previous existence such as an ancient mosque, a graveyard and several old wells. There used to be a golf and country club which has now closed down and a leisure destination has been developed in its place with furnished chalets for hire. For just Dhs.50, you can get a motor boat ride to the island. Phone 666 1185 to book a boat.

To the west of Abu Dhabi lies Sir Bani Yas island, owned by HH Sheikh Zayed Bin Sultan Al Nahyan. The President has turned it into a nature reserve with a breeding and conservation programme for indigenous and African animals. However, this island can only be visited through organised groups making prior arrangement.

Other popular islands are Bahraini and Cut Islands, a 40 and 25 minute boat ride away from the Corniche, respectively. You will need to take all supplies with you since there is nothing available there. Flat and sandy Horseshoe Island is home to a number of foxes. Off its shore is Surf Reef – a great spot for windsurfing. Several of these islands have been earmarked for development so access may soon be limited.

Blue Dolphin Company LLC

Location → Htl InterContinental · Bainuna St | 666 9392
Hours → 08:00 - 13:00 16:00 - 19:00
Web/email → www.interconti.com | Map Ref → 10-C1

Blue Dolphin offers two island trips, morning and evening, by traditional dhow on the *Saif, Aldhana* or *Sindbad.*

Cut Island: arrive at a fully equipped island camp, settle in and experience an evening of live music, belly dancing and a traditional barbecue.

Bahraini Island: the sea around this island is too shallow to approach in the dark. However, a visit by day allows you to enjoy a barbecue lunch.

For the more adventurous, Blue Dolphin can drop you at an island for overnight stay. However, this isn't an organised trip and is carried out by special arrangement. Take your own tent, equipment and supplies.

Futaisi Island Resort

Location → Futaisi Island Resort | 666 1185
Hours → 10:30 - 17:30
Web/email → na | Map Ref → na

Discover the wonders of Futaisi Island with this tour. While sightseeing, you will have the opportunity to marvel at the natural flora and fauna, as well as the wildlife – gazelles, ospreys, flamingos, wild rabbits and an interesting variety of birds, who have made the island their habitat. Places of interest include an Arabian fort, an ancient mosque, a graveyard and a mangrove lagoon. Tickets can be bought at the resort for this one hour trip for Dhs.80 per adult and Dhs.15 per child.

Sunshine Tours

Location → Airport Rd | 444 9914
Hours → Timings on request
Web/email → www.adnh.com | Map Ref → 2-B2

Tours to explore the islands around Abu Dhabi by speedboat are offered for half, full day or overnight trips. For overnight trips, tents and sleeping bags are provided. In addition, live entertainment such as band or a belly dancer can be arranged.

Crab hunting and fishing trips are also available and the tour operators will provide all the necessary equipment and meals. On request, they can organise island trips around Abu Dhabi for bigger groups too.

Umm Al Nar

Situated on the outskirts of the city, on the road to Dubai and Al Ain, this area houses the Abu Dhabi Golf Club and large villas. Enthusiastic golfers won't mind the 30 - 40 minute drive to this picturesque course.

Al Ain Areas

Al Ain City

As the birthplace of the ruler of Abu Dhabi and President of the UAE, HH Sheikh Zayed Bin Sultan Al Nahyan, Al Ain occupies a special status and is the second most important town in the Abu Dhabi emirate.

Al Ain lies 148km east of the capital, on the border with Oman. The whole area is known as the Buraimi Oasis and the town actually straddles the border with the Sultanate of Oman. The UAE side is known as Al Ain and the Omani side as Buraimi, named after the oasis. There are 18 fortresses in Al Ain, a testament to the town's importance and its position on the ancient trading routes from Oman to the Arabian Gulf.

The oasis was at the centre of a longstanding territorial dispute between the UAE, Oman and Saudi Arabia; all had a claim to the area as the border had never been properly defined. In the 20th century, the disputes were fuelled by the belief that there might be oil in the region, and in 1952 Saudi Arabia actually occupied part of Buraimi. The dispute was finally settled and in 1966, the border was defined between Oman and Abu Dhabi. However, it was not until 1974 that Saudi Arabia finally dropped its claim to the area.

The oasis is a pleasant stretch of greenery, amidst hostile surroundings and hence Al Ain is often described as the 'Garden City'. Whilst it is not oil rich, it is the most fertile region in the country. Recently, there has been a high profile drive to market Al Ain as a tourist destination with emphasis being placed on Al Ain's unique archeological heritage and historic identity.

In the days before the oil boom, the town was a five day camel ride from Abu Dhabi. Today, it takes about 1½ hours on a modern two lane highway. However, once you're there, watch out for the numerous road humps.

Al Ain Roundabout

The town offers many sightseeing opportunities and, like Abu Dhabi, this section of Local Attractions should be read in conjunction with what the tour operators have to offer.

Al Ain Oasis

Location → Nr Al Ain Museum · Al Mutawaa | na
Hours → na
Web/email → na | Map Ref → 15-B3

This massive oasis is littered with palm plantations, many of which are still working farms. The shady palm trees provide a welcome respite from the heat and noise of the town. At the main entrances into the plantation, picnic tables have been placed for public use. The farms have plenty of examples of falaj, the ancient irrigation system used for centuries to tap into underground wells and to control scarce water resources.

Visitors are welcome to wander around the main part near the Al Ain Museum but it is advisable to stick to the paved areas, which weave between the walled-in trees.

Camel Market

Location → Nr Town Centre | na
Hours → 07:00 - 12:00
Web/email → na | Map Ref → 15-C3

Al Ain's camel market is well known throughout the country and is the last of its kind in the Emirates. The market provides an excellent opportunity to view the 'ships of the desert' up close, and to see and hear the traders discussing the price and merits of their animals. Although the market is open only in the mornings, it is always busy and a great place to enjoy some local colour. An excellent photo opportunity, but be careful where you point your lens and always seek permission first.

Livestock Souk

Location → Nr Al Ain Museum · Zayed Bin Sultan St | na
Hours → 08:00 - 21:00
Web/email → na | Map Ref → 15-C3

Definitely the place to go if you need to pick up a goat or a sheep at a bargain price! Watch the locals arrive in pickups laden with animals and settling in to do some hard bargaining. Arrive early, preferably before 09:00, to soak up the true essence and atmosphere of this large, bustling market. There are people milling around all day in this market which attracts traders from all over the Emirates. Be prepared, however, to be the object of a certain amount of curiosity, and do not be too upset with the rough treatment of the livestock.

Old Prison

Location → Nr Al Ain Museum · Zayed Bin Sultan St | na
Hours → na
Web/email → na | Map Ref → 15-D3

Near the Coffee Pot roundabout, the Old Prison is worth a visit simply for the stunning view of the surrounding town and oasis. The structure is a lone square turret in the centre of a gravel courtyard, surrounded by high walls. Unfortunately, there is no organised system of admittance and the door at the bottom is sometimes padlocked. Hence, admittance is hit and miss.

Buraimi

Visitors to the UAE do not need a visa to enter the Omani side of the Buraimi Oasis. The Omani customs post is about 50 km from the border and visitors will only require an Omani visa only if they wish to travel past this point. If you are driving and decide to enter this part of the oasis, make sure your car insurance covers Oman.

Buraimi Souk is worth a visit for the local atmosphere and colour. On sale is a mix of food and household goods, along with a small selection of souvenir shops selling pottery, woven crafts and silver jewellery. Behind the souk is Al Hilla Fort, which is an interesting starting point to explore the oasis. The other main fort is Al Khandaq Fort, located in Hamasa town in Welayat Buraimi, which is believed to be about 400 years old. Like many of Oman's other forts, it has been extensively restored and although there are no displays, it is enjoyable to wander around and admire the view from the battlements.

Jebel Hafeet

Jabel Hafeet is one of the main highlights of Al Ain. Rising abruptly from the surrounding flat countryside, it offers a stunning view from the top. On a clear day you can see the surrounding wadis, desert plains and oases. In the distance, one can also see the city of Al Ain, situated about 300 metres above sea level. Compared to this city, the height of the mountain at 1,180 metres appears quite dramatic.

The road to the top is well lit most of the way with viewing points and plenty of car parking space. However, the more energetic should try cycling – only an hour or two going up, and 20 minutes coming down! The Mercure Grand Hotel is set in a commanding position with splendid views of the surrounding area, especially from the dining room windows. A visit to the hot springs near the base of the mountain can be coupled with a stay at Ain Al Fayda Resthouse (03 783 8333).

Local Attractions

Camel Racing

Camel racing followed by a freshly cooked campfire breakfast... is there a better way to start the day? For the young and old alike, a morning at the races is a memorable experience. Camels, the owners and their families, the young jockeys, and the visitors, all congregate to create an atmosphere of intense anticipation and excitement at these races.

For visitors, this is an opportunity to see a truly traditional local sport and to visit the 'shops' selling camel paraphernalia (blankets, rugs, beads etc). A winter sport, the races are usually held on Thursday and Friday mornings at the tracks in Abu Dhabi, Al Ain, Dubai, Ras Al Khaimah and Umm Al Quwain. Often, additional races are held on National Day and certain other public holidays. Races start very early (by about 07:30) and are usually over by 08:30, and admission is free.

45 km from Abu Dhabi, on the Al Ain road, is the Al Maqam Camel Race Track. During the cooler months, camel owners from all over the Gulf visit this 10km race track to socialise and compete against each other. Ras Al Khaimah's Digdagga, situated on a plain between the dunes and the mountains about 10 km south of the town, is one of the best racetracks in the country. Beautiful campsites in the big red dunes that overlook the racetrack offer an added attraction.

Camel rides are also available at various heritage sites and within the city of Dubai during the Dubai Shopping Festival. Call the Camel Racing Club (04 342 2208) for details. The local press also has information on dates and times. You could also check with tour operators [p.133] who organise camel rides in the desert, very often at their desert camps.

Corniche Cruises

Blue Dolphin Company LLC

Location → Htl InterContinental · Bainuna St | 666 9392
Hours → 08:00 - 13:00 16:00 - 19:00
Web/email → www.interconti.com | Map Ref → 10-C1

During this hour long cruise, view the spectacular fountain, park areas and multi-coloured skyline of the impressive 8 km long Corniche. Sindbad is a traditional Arabian dhow that departs from near the Al Safina Restaurant on the Breakwater at 17:30 every evening and then every hour, on the hour, for the rest of the evening. However, it is advisable to check sailing times with Blue Dolphin as occasionally the dhow is chartered for private parties. The fare is inclusive of tea, coffee and soft drinks – don't forget your camera!

Prices: *Dhs.10 adults; Dhs.5 children.*

Shuja Yacht

Location → Le Royal Meridien · Al Khalifa St | 695 0539
Hours → 17:30 - 18:30
Web/email → www.lemeridien.com | Map Ref → 8-B2

Check out the sunset on the Shuja Yacht. The route of the cruise is from the jetty, along the Corniche, following the Abu Dhabi skyline. At the Breakwater, guests can view the sun setting over the sea (refer to Shuja Yacht – Boat & Yacht Charters [p.179] for more details).

Shuja Yacht

Sunshine Tours

Location → Airport Rd | 444 9914
Hours → Timings on request
Web/email → www.adnh.com | Map Ref →

The sunset dhow cruise offers an hour long scenic journey along the Corniche, with Arabic coffee and dates served on board. The average price is Dhs.80 per person, including coach transfer if required. Cruises are flexible and can be suited to fit everyone's tastes and budget and can accommodate big and small groups alike.

Falconry Shows

Falconry, the sport of sheikhs, has a deep rooted tradition in the UAE and is practised even today. At one time, the falcons were used to catch wild prey, such as hares, so that the family would not have to kill any of their valuable livestock for meat. Nowadays, Sheikh Zayed has declared Abu Dhabi a conservation zone to protect the depleted wildlife.

However, the keeping of falcons is still popular and it's not unusual to see these beautiful and valuable birds being transported around the Emirates – even at the airport (where of course they fly first class!). In general, it's not possible to watch them being flown, unless personally invited. However, at the Wedding Grounds near the Abu Dhabi Equestrian Club there are sometimes trainers flying their birds during the cooler months. Make sure you ask before taking photographs. In addition, the Heritage/Bedouin Village has falconers demonstrating their art, and on some tours it's possible to see these impressive birds.

Feathers of Arabia

Location → Throughout the UAE | 050 643 0990
Hours → Timings on request
Web/email → na | Map Ref → na

Dan Daman gives falconry displays, showing falcons as well as indigenous birds such as buzzards, kites, owls and eagles. Usually he flies the birds and gives a short talk about the art, after which, visitors can try their hand under close supervision. Demonstrations are often given as part of an Arabian Desert evening.

Dan operates chiefly between 1st October and 31st May. He may, however, display the birds and give lectures during the summer months. He converses in Flemish, German, French and English – so you won't miss a thing. The company also installs falconariums and advises on falcon breeding.

Contact: *(Fax) 06 766 3193*

Fee: *Dhs.1,000 for private booking*

Scenic Flights

Other Options → Flying [p.188]

Currently, there are no companies specifically offering flights for visitors wanting a different perspective of the emirate. However, in the past it has been possible to arrange a charter through some of the tour operators who use either helicopters or fixed wing aircraft from Abu Dhabi Aviation. Trips are generally into the desert and offer incredible views of the huge, endless golden red sand dunes of the Empty Quarter. Cameras aren't allowed for security reasons.

Museums, Heritage & Culture

Museums – City

Other Options → Art [p.150]

Al Maqtaa Fort

Location → Al Maqtaa | na
Hours → na
Web/email → na | Map Ref → 1-C3

Heavily renovated, the Al Maqtaa Fort is one of the very few remaining examples of its kind in the emirate of Abu Dhabi. You can catch the first glimpse of this monument while crossing the Al Maqtaa Bridge as you approach the Abu Dhabi island. The 200 year old fort, standing on the edge of the island, was built to fend off bandits and provides a wonderful contrast to the modern bridge.

Cultural Foundation

Location → Opp New Etisalat · Shk Zayed 1st St | 619 5280
Hours → See timings below
Web/email → www.cultural.org.ae | Map Ref → 9-A1

Sprawling over 14 hectares and located within the famous Old Fort, the Cultural Foundation is the arts centre of the capital and a remarkable monument displaying Abu Dhabi's desire to enrich knowledge, preserve heritage and enhance cultural activities. This simple yet efficient building has grown according to its needs, with a myriad of passages,

arches, courtyards and flowering garden pathways, providing a relaxing atmosphere – an excellent example of Islamic architecture.

The place consists of three buildings, one of which houses the National Archives. It is also home to the National Library and the Institution of Culture & Art. The publishing side of the foundation produces books relating to the UAE, the Middle East and the Islamic world, takes part in book fairs all over the world, and hosts Abu Dhabi's biggest annual book exhibition. Book publishers from Beirut to Cairo compete for space in an event that reflects Abu Dhabi's commitment to the advancement of arts and literature.

For most of the year, except the summer months, the foundation throws open its lecture and exhibition halls to local and international speakers and artists. Programme highlights include visits from international classical musicians, art exhibitions and plays, while embassies regularly hold cultural events and film festivals in the auditorium.

The annual chess festival brings together local, regional and international players. A cinema in the building screens mainly English language films all year round, weaving film festivals into its calendar of events, and offers a good chance to view classic cinema. Be a part of the centre's activities by subscribing to the free monthly guide (ask for your name to be added to the mailing list). After that, entrance to exhibitions and lectures becomes free.

Timings: *08:00 - 14:00 & 17:00 - 21:00; 09:00 - 12:00 & 17:00 - 20:00 Thurs; Closed Fri am*

See Also: *Qasr Al Husn [p.126]; Art Classes[p.208]; Libraries [p.212]; Family Explorer; Cinemas [p.265].*

Cultural Foundation

Heritage Village

Location → Breakwater | **na**
Hours → See timings below
Web/email → na | **Map Ref** → 10-B4

Situated on a 1600 square metre site, the Heritage Village overlooks the Corniche near the Breakwater. It is organised by the Emirates Heritage Club and offers a glimpse into the country's past. Many traditional features of Bedouin life such as the camp fire with coffee pots, goat's hair tent, a well and an irrigation system are all attractively displayed in the open museum creating a true feel of what life must have been like in those days. You can even experience the ancient form of air conditioning in traditional houses built of barasti (dried palm leaves) by standing under the wind tower and feeling a breeze even on the calmest day. There will be plenty of great photo opportunities up close and personal with a camel or even the 'Drinkers of the Wind' – the beautiful Arabian horses in their full ornamental regalia. There are interesting workshops where various craftsmen demonstrate their carpentry, pottery and metal work skills, and women can be seen weaving and spinning.

An air conditioned museum houses a collection of artefacts including jewellery, weapons, coffee pots, diving tools, Holy Qurans and folklore garments. You can buy some of these at a shop for local crafts. After visiting the village you can also sample the typical Arabic cuisine at the beachside restaurant.

Timings: *09:00 - 14:00 & 17:00 - 21:00.*

Entrance: *Adults Dhs.3 and children Dhs.1.*

Heritage/Bedouin Village

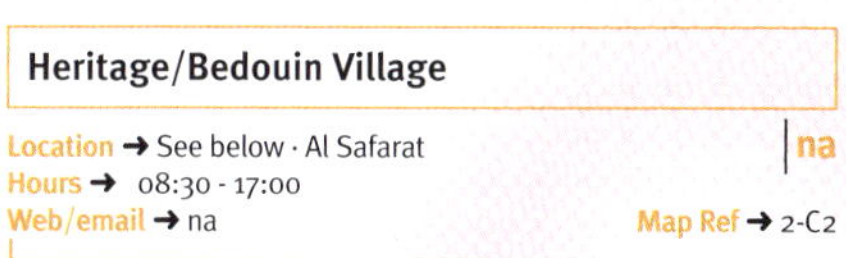

Location → See below · Al Safarat | **na**
Hours → 08:30 - 17:00
Web/email → na | **Map Ref** → 2-C2

This is a must for all visiting VIPs, including Mikhail and Raisa Gorbachev and Lebanese President Hrawi. According to a guide, they all sat beneath the stars on rush mats at the reconstructed Bedouin camp, slugging the strong 'qawah' (Arabic coffee) which is served to all visitors.

Spread across an area the size of two football pitches, the village faithfully replicates the simple nomadic life in Abu Dhabi before the oil boom. Goats' wool summer tents contain original artefacts like swinging cradles and leather drinking pouches. Enthusiastic guides will have

you making rope from date palm husks in no time. There are also superb examples of more permanent structures like the sheikh's mud brick house and traditional mosque. It offers a good chance to marvel at early air conditioning systems, which trapped air using square towers made of jute and wood.

On certain occasions, it's possible to watch traditional agricultural and craft techniques being demonstrated and on Fridays there are falconry demonstrations. For those who want a memento of their stay, the village boasts its own traditional souk where you can buy a range of handicrafts and exotic Arabic perfumes. For thrill seekers there are camel rides around the village costing an additional Dhs.2. Photography is actively encouraged and when you're not posing by a camel, you can go for refreshments available on site. There is sand everywhere, so sensible clothing and shoes are advised.

Entrance: *Free*

Location: *Take Mussafah Road, off the Airport Road and follow signs for the Abu Dhabi International Exhibition Centre. The village is behind the centre.*

Petroleum Exhibition

Location → Nr Commercial Bank · Corniche Rd East | 626 0817
Hours → 07:00 - 14:00
Web/email → na | Map Ref → 8-D3

The Petroleum Exhibition covers Abu Dhabi's phenomenal development from a desert oasis to a thriving cosmopolitan city. Spread across three rooms, there are scale models, photographs and maps which chart the earliest oil exploration in the desert and the Gulf, to the first oil export from Das Island in 1962. Interactive displays like giant drill bits and documentary films (dubbed in English, French and German) give fascinating insight into one of the world's largest oil and gas producers.

Entrance: *Free*

Qasr Al Husn

Location → Khalid Bin Walid | 619 5349
Hours → 07:30 - 13:30; Thu 07:30 - 12:00; Fri closed
Web/email → www.cultural.org.ae | Map Ref → 9-A1

The White Fort or Fort Palace dates back to 1793. It was the official residence of the rulers of Abu Dhabi when they moved from the oasis of Liwa to Abu Dhabi island. Since then, the fort has undergone reconstruction and renovation with major work last done in 1983.

Situated next to the Cultural Foundation, the fort is the oldest building in Abu Dhabi.

Entrance: *Free*

Women's Handicraft Centre

Location → Al Mushrif | 447 6645
Hours → 08:30 - 13:00
Web/email → na | Map Ref → 3-C3

Located on the outskirts of the city, this government sponsored initiative is run by the Abu Dhabi Women's Association as a showcase for local craftswomen. Every item on display is manufactured locally and most are for sale.

The women artists display weaving, handmade souvenirs and traditional artefacts, as well as distinctive Arabian oils, crochet mats, incense and local dress. As you shop you can observe the women going about their work. There is also a small museum showing traditional clothing and artefacts.

Entrance: *Dhs.5*

Museums – Out of City

Other Options → Tours & Sightseeing [p.132]

Al Ain Museum

Location → Sultan Bin Zayed St · Al Muraba R/A | 03 764 1595
Hours → 08:00 - 13:00 15:30 - 17:30
Web/email → www.aam.gov.ae | Map Ref → 15-B3

Opened in 1971, the museum is housed in a low modern structure on the edge of the main Al Ain Oasis. The well laid out presentations illustrate various aspects of life in the Emirates. Of particular interest is the selection of photographs taken in the 1960s of Al Ain, Abu Dhabi and Liwa. This story in pictures reveals just how much the country has changed and developed in such a short space of time.

Other exhibits include Bedouin jewellery, weapons, musical instruments, and a reconstruction of a traditional majlis, which, it appears, is just waiting for guests to arrive before coffee and dates are served! There are extensive displays on archaeology, including many from the nearby Hili Gardens, and a visit here before going to the gardens proves quite informative. The displays from Garn Bint Saud, a site 12 km north of Hili and comprising of more than 40 tombs, take you back to the first millennium BC.

Visitors will also find a reconstruction of everyday life as it was before the arrival of oil revenues. It's interesting to note that the figures are dressed with Omani turbans instead of the traditional headdress of the Gulf Arabs. The area around Buraimi was a source of contention between Abu Dhabi, Oman and Saudi Arabia for many years. For everyone's convenience labelling is in Arabic and English.

The museum shares the same compound as Sultan bin Zayed Fort, or Eastern Fort as it is also known. Built in 1907, it is now open to visitors, although there is little to see beyond the canon in the courtyard.

Entrance: *50 fils*

Timings: *08:00 - 13:00 & 16:30 - 18:30 Sunday - Thursday (from 1st May); 08:00 - 13:00 & 15:30 - 17:30 Sunday - Thursday (from 1st November); 09:00 - 11:30 & 15:30 - 17:30 Friday; closed Saturday.*

Al Ain Museum

Al Ain University Natural History Museum

Location → Al Khubaisi | 03 767 7280
Hours → 07:30 - 16:30
Web/email → www.uaeu.ac.ae | Map Ref → 14-C1

Aimed at those with a serious interest in the flora and fauna of the Emirates, this museum is a small but informative centre run by the university. Photography is allowed with permission from the Department of Geology.

Entrance: *Free.*

Hili Archaeological Garden

Location → Mohammed Bin Khalifa St · Hili | na
Hours → 09:00 - 22:00
Web/email → na | Map Ref → 13-B1

Off the Al Ain - Dubai road, about 10 km outside of Al Ain, is Hili Dig, which is both a public garden and an archaeological site. The archaeological site has remnants of a Bronze Age (2500 - 2000 BC) settlement, which was excavated and restored in 1995. It shows the remains of a round building with several rooms and a well. The site is the source of some of the richest finds in the area, many of which are believed to be over 4,000 years old. If you are keen on archaeology, you will find a visit to Al Ain Museum of more interest, since many of the finds are displayed there.

There are other archaeological structures around the park, but the area is chiefly a garden with plants, fountains and a small play area for children with swings and slides. Near the site is Fossil Valley, which is rich in fossils from thousands of years ago when the area was covered by sea.

Entrance: *Dhs.1.*

See Also: *Hili Fun City & Ice Rink (Activities).*

Jahili Fort & Park

Location → Nr Public Garden · Al Jahili | na
Hours → 09:00 - 22:00
Web/email → na | Map Ref → 15-A3

Jahili Fort is located near the Public Garden and is famous for being the birthplace of Sheikh Zayed, the ruler of Abu Dhabi and President of the UAE. The fort is notable for its main corner turret, which is round with four levels. This large restored structure is set in its own walled park and although visitors can walk around the landscaped gardens, entrance to the main building is not permitted.

Entrance: *Dhs.1.*

Zoo

Al Ain Zoo & Aquarium

Location → Nr Traffic Police · Zoo R/A | 03 782 8188
Hours → Winter 07:00 - 17:00. Summer 07:00 - 18:30
Web/email → na | Map Ref → 17-C2

Al Ain Zoo & Aquarium is one of the best and largest in the Gulf region. The animals are well cared for and enjoy reasonable amounts of space to roam

around in this zoo spread over 400 hectares. The layout may initially seem confusing, but maps available near the entrance should ease your way around the place. Opened in 1969, it's home to a wide variety of both rare and common animals, some indigenous to the Middle East and many from Africa and India. You can find the Arabian oryx and gazelle, as well as kangaroos, hippos, monkeys, big cats, reptiles etc. The zoo also has a large aquarium with sea lions, penguins and fish. A special breeding programme for rare or endangered animals is ongoing.

Entrance: *Adults Dhs.2; children under four years free.*

Timings: *07:00 - 17:30 winter; 08:00 - 17:30 summer. Saturday closed.*

Parks & Beaches

Parks

Other Options → Beaches [p.132]

Abu Dhabi is home to nearly 20 well maintained parks. Most of these are decorated with fountains and equipped with play areas for children. Commitment of the Al Nahyan family to turn the city green is also reflected in many grassy areas around the city that are not organised parks and require no entrance fee, but are often just as popular. During the cooler winter months, all areas (even central reservations) come alive with people organising barbecues and picnics or knocking a ball around.

These parks provide welcome areas of peace and greenery and are for all to enjoy, so treat them with respect and leave them as you would wish to find them. Opening and closing times vary considerably amongst the different parks. There is a standard admission fee of Dhs.1 for adults and free entry for children. During Ramadan, park timings change, generally opening and closing later in the day.

See Also : *Corniche – Local Attractions [p.117]*

Capital Gardens

Al Mushrief Children's Garden

Location → Nr Choueifat School · Airport Rd | na
Hours → 15:00 - 22:00 Fri 15:00 - 21:30
Web/email → na Map Ref → 3-C3

Tucked away from the heart of the city but not too far out, this garden is a pleasant refuge in the capital. Amusement park rides (with varying fees), simple swings, fountains and ample car parking, all can be found in this place popular among the local population. The garden also boasts a cafeteria that is open daily (except Monday) from 17:00 - 21:30. Beware, no video filming is allowed in the park!

Timings: *15:00 - 22:00 Saturday - Thursday; 15:00 - 21:30 Friday. Monday closed for maintenance work. Public holidays 09:00 - 12:00 & 15:00 - 22:00.*

Location: *Mushrief area near the Choueifat School. Driving along Airport Road from the city centre, the entrance to the park is marked opposite the National Theatre.*

Al Nahyan Garden

Location → Beh Sheraton Residence · Khalidiya | na
Hours → 16:30 - 23:00 08:00 - 22:00 Fri
Web/email → na Map Ref → 9-C2

This well maintained and compact park provides another welcome retreat from the bustling city. Its size and layout ensures that your little ones can't get up to too much trouble! Entertainment is limited to simple rides such as swings.

Entrance: *Adults Dhs.1; children free.*

Capital Gardens

Location → Opp City Centre Bldg · Khalifa Bin Zyd St | na
Hours → 14:30 - 22:30 09:00 - 22:00
Web/email → na Map Ref → 8-C2

Located in the middle of the city centre, these immaculately manicured gardens with bougainvillaea walls are a pleasant retreat for the whole family. Each little cove of the garden has a small selection of rides including swings, slides and a merry go round. A large pond in the middle of the lawn erupts into stunning fountain bursts (10 metres high) at certain times taking visitors by

surprise. People have access to refreshments at the vending machines or at an enclosed cafeteria.

Entrance: *Adults Dhs.1; children free.*

Khalidiya Children's Garden

Location → Al Khalidiya St · Khalidiya | na
Hours → 09:00 - 12:00 15:00 - 21:30 15:00 - 22:00 Fri
Web/email → na | Map Ref → 9-E1

This is one of the more popular parks for children. Situated near the Abu Dhabi Women's Higher College of Technology, the garden is somewhat typical of other children's parks in the capital but with a greater number of rides and certainly more variety.

Entrance is restricted to women and children only and the entrance fee is standard, but the costs of the rides vary.

Entrance: *Adults Dhs.1; children free.*

Khalidiya Garden

Location → Al Khaleej Al Arabi St · Khalidiya | 666 1281
Hours →
Web/email → na | Map Ref → 9-D1

This carefully manicured large garden, situated in one of the more affluent parts of Abu Dhabi, takes up a whole block on the junction of 30th Street and the main Khalidiya Road. Although it does not have a cafeteria on its premises, vending machines within the grounds provide light refreshments. A particular favourite with the locals, entrance is restricted to women and children only.

Mosque Gardens

Location → Shk Hamdan St | na
Hours → 15:00 - 23:00 09:00 - late Fri
Web/email → na | Map Ref → 7-E1

Yet another serene retreat in the middle of the city, this garden is pleasantly landscaped with hedgerows. Like most other parks it offers swings and slides for children to play on. It's rarely busy and hence is ideal for families.

Entrance: *Adults Dhs.1; children free.*

New Corniche, The

Location → See below · Corniche | na
Hours →
Web/email → na | Map Ref → 3-A2

This pristine stretch of immaculate lawns, dotted with ornate shelters and large wooden tables, comes alive as families gather for evening picnics. Well lit and clean, it is especially busy on winter nights and during cooler weather.

This is a great location for birdwatching and an ideal fishing spot (the water and mangroves border one side of the park). A word of warning though. If you are new to Abu Dhabi, it is easy to confuse The New Corniche, which is on the eastern side of the island, with the main Corniche in the north. To further complicate matters, the newly renovated part of the main Corniche, near the Hilton Hotel, has also become known as the New Corniche!

Old Airport Garden

Location → Airport Rd | 444 4068
Hours → 06:00 - 22:00
Web/email → na | Map Ref → 2-B1

Quiet, but an ideal place if you want to relax after taking your kids ice skating at the adjacent rink. One side of the park has a number of swings and small, tidy gardens, while the other side is more ornamental with plenty of trees offering shade. However, it is advisable to stay away from the swing side in mornings as it is busy with maintenance workers. If you or the kids are hungry, a KFC outlet is situated right on the edge of the gardens.

Al Ain Ladies Park

Location → Zayed Al Awwal St · Al Muwaiji Area | 03 681 3910
Hours → 15:30 - 22:30 10:00 - 22:30 Fri
Web/email → na | Map Ref → 14-D3

Commonly known as Basra Park, this quiet and attractive garden is for women and children only (boys up to the age of 10 years are also allowed in). Plenty of benches under shady trees allow you to sit and enjoy the peace. Play areas with swings, slides and climbing frames are also there. Abundant greenery attracts a large number of birds in winter.

A small dry wadi with wooden bridges runs through the middle of the park where you can find a small snack bar. Toilet facilities are also available.

Entrance: *Dhs.1 for adults (children under 10 free).*

Public Garden

Location → Zayed Bin Sultan St · Al Mutawaa | 03 765 8122
Hours → 16:00 - 23:00 10:00 - 23:00 Fri
Web/email → na | Map Ref → 15-A3

The main park in the city, the Public Garden is a tranquil and relaxing spot amid the hustle and

bustle of town. Walkways meander under shady trees with patches of grass and carefully tended flowerbeds. Fountains are attractively lit up at night for visitors to enjoy, and play areas for younger children offer see saws, swings and slides. For the older kids, there's a small amusement arcade tucked away by the back entrance.

Around the city, purple road signs in English direct the way to the garden. However, once you are there, all signs are in Arabic.

Entrance: *Dhs.1 (children under 12 yrs free).*

Silmi Garden

Location → Mohammed Bin Khalifa St · Buraimi | na
Hours → 16:00 - 23:00; Fri 10:00 - 23:00
Web/email → na Map Ref → 15-A2

Silmi Garden is a popular spot with locals who come for a stroll in the cool evenings. Like all other parks in Al Ain it is well cared for with plenty of trees, shrubs, flowers, fountains and a play area with swings and slides.

Unfortunately, you have to park on the street and all signs are in Arabic. Even if you're unfamiliar with Arabic, the park is quite easy to locate, especially at night as the walls are lit with multi-coloured lights.

Entrance: *Dhs.1 (children under 11 free).*

Beaches

Other Options → Beach Clubs [p.204]

Since Abu Dhabi City is situated on an island, it is naturally endowed with a number of beaches dotted along the coast, offering stretches of golden sand and turquoise waters. Some places, such as the two mentioned , are organised beach parks that offer extra facilities like changing rooms or a café. You will also find various public beaches that do not require an entrance fee.

Like parks, the beaches too attract more of a crowd during the cooler months (especially at weekends), with people enjoying barbecues or playing cricket or volleyball. Unfortunately, a lot of times visitors leave litter scattered around, which is not too welcoming to other visitors!

However, the up side to public beaches in Abu Dhabi is that, unlike other places in the Emirates, vehicles cannot enter the beaches here, so you won't find people churning up sand as they practise their 4 wheel driving.

Al Dana Ladies Beach

Location → Nr Khalidia Palace Htl · Khalidiya | 665 0129
Hours → See timings below
Web/email → na Map Ref → 10-E4

More than the privacy it is the facilities on site which make it a valuable leisure spot for women in the capital. It has a cafeteria and a recently renovated swimming pool. On Wednesdays, Thursdays and Fridays, the beach is open from 10:00 to dusk (generally around 18:00), and from noon to dusk on other days.

Entrance: *Dhs.10 plus another Dhs.5 if you take your car inside.*

Al Raha Beach

Location → Channel Rd, Abu Dhabi - Dubai Rd · Abu Dhabi | na
Hours → 10:00 - 19:00
Web/email → na Map Ref → 1-A1

Al Raha Beach offers good quality amenities and is the best maintained public beach in Abu Dhabi. Situated on the Abu Dhabi - Dubai Road past the Umm Al Nar roundabout, the beach is divided into two sections. One section is cordoned off for women only, and the other is open to both men and women. Facilities include a cafeteria and there is no entry fee.

Organised Tours

Tours & Sightseeing

Other Options → Weekend Breaks [p.142]

An organised tour can be a great way to discover the UAE, especially if you're only here for a short time, or do not have ready access to a vehicle.

While Abu Dhabi's tourism infrastructure isn't as developed as in the other UAE cities, a growing number of tour companies operate from here. The local companies are complemeted by firms from other emirates who have either set up bases in Abu Dhabi, or arrange to pick up for tours out of Abu Dhabi.

Tours range from a half day city tour to an overnight safari, visiting the desert or mountains and camping in tents. While on a full day, evening or overnight tour, meals are generally provided, the half day city tour will usually see you returning in time for lunch. Check what's included when you book, as sometimes there may be an extra charge

for meals. Generally all tours include soft drinks and water as part of the package.

Most trips require a minimum of four people for the tour to run. Larger companies may take couples or individuals if there's a group already booked that they can join. If you want a tour or car to yourself, you will probably have to pay for four people, even if there are fewer of you.

It's advisable to book three or four days in advance, although in some cases a shorter notice is also enough. A deposit of up to 50% is normal, with the balance payable when you are collected. Cancellation usually means losing your deposit unless appropriate notice is given. This, however, differs from company to company.

On the day of the tour you can be collected from either your hotel, residence or from a common meeting point if you are part of a large group. Tours usually leave on time – no shows do not get a refund, so don't be late! Wear cool, comfortable clothing, and always carry hats and sunglasses. Also wear strong, flat soled shoes when going on desert or mountain tours, in case you're required to go for longer walks. In the desert after sunset, temperatures can drop surprisingly, especially in winter, so it's a good idea to take some warm clothing. Other necessities include sun protection creams and a camera with spare film and batteries.

Tour Operators & Travel Agents

Abdul Jail Travel Agency	622 5225
Abu Dhabi Travel Bureau	633 8700
Advanced Travel & Tourism	634 7900
Al Toofan Travel & Tours	631 3515
Arabian Adventures	633 8111
Emirates Holidays	800 5252
Net Tours	679 4656
OffRoad Emirates	633 3232
Salem Travel Agency	627 4424
Sunshine Tours	444 9914
Thomas Cook Al Rostamani	672 7500
Al Ain Golden Sands Camel Safaris	03 768 8006
Al Mahboob Travel	03 751 5944
Al Rumaithy Travel & Tourism	03 765 6493
Emirates Travel Express	03 765 0777
Gulf Air	03 764 3483
Gulf Travel Express	03 766 6737
Middle East Travel	03 764 1661

Desert safaris are a must for anyone who hasn't experienced dune driving before, including friends and relatives visiting the Emirates. Most companies have excellent safety records, but there is always an element of risk involved when driving off-road. Remember you are the client and if the driver is going too fast for your group, tell him to slow down – there shouldn't be any wheels leaving the ground!

Most companies will take an easier route if there are young children, the elderly or anybody who doesn't want to experience the most extreme dunes. Accidents have happened in the past, but with a good driver you should have total confidence in his driving abilities and you are in for a thrilling ride.

The following descriptions of the main tours are intended only to give an idea of what is most commonly included. Obviously, each tour operator would have their own style, so the content and general quality may differ from one company to another.

Activity Tours

Other Options → Activities [p.177]

In addition to the city and safari tours, some companies offer more specialised activities. From the adrenaline powered buzz of a desert driving course, dune buggy desert safari, mountain biking or hiking, to a rather peaceful canoe tour of Khor Kalba – these tours combine fun and adventure. Note that a basic level of fitness may be required. Refer to the Activities section of the book for other activities that you can enjoy in the emirate.

Tours & Sightseeing

City Tours – In Abu Dhabi

Abu Dhabi Tour

Go sightseeing around the capital on this tour. Visit the Women's Handicraft Centre, Heritage Village, Petroleum Exhibition and Abu Dhabi's famous landmark – the Corniche. (full day)

City Tours – Out of Abu Dhabi

Dubai City Tour

This tour is an overview of the old and new in the city of Dubai. The Gold Souk, the fish market, mosques, abras, Bastakiya windtower houses,

museum and thriving commercial areas with striking modern buildings are some of the usual inclusions. (half day)

Ajman & Sharjah Tour

Ajman is the place to visit if you want to see traditional wooden dhows being built just the way they were hundreds of years ago. Explore and enjoy the museum before driving to the neighbouring emirate of Sharjah where you can visit its numerous famous souks. Finish with a stroll around the restored Bait Al Naboodah house for a glimpse into native life – just as it was before the discovery of oil. (half day)

Al Ain Tour

Known as the 'Garden City', Al Ain was once a vital oasis on the caravan route from the Emirates to Oman. Among many historical sites that can be visited here are one of the first forts to be built by the Al Nahyan family over 175 years ago, and the prehistoric tombs at Hili known to be over 5,000 years old. Other attractions include the Al Ain Museum, camel market, falaj irrigation system, which is still in use, and the quaint souk. (full day)

Ras Al Khaimah Tour

Drive upcountry along what is commonly known as the Pirate Coast, through Ajman and Umm Al Quwain. Explore ancient sites and discover the old town of Ras Al Khaimah and its museum. The return journey passes natural hot springs and date groves at Khatt, via the starkly beautiful Hajar Mountains. (full day)

Mountain Adventures

Shopping Tour

Known as the 'shopping capital of the Middle East', the neighbouring emirate of Dubai is a shopper's paradise. From 'almost designer' clothes at incredibly low prices to electronics, watches or dazzling bolts of cloth in the Textile Souk, everything is available at prices to suit every budget – don't forget to bargain your way through the day! Next, explore the malls; ultra modern and air conditioned, and selling everything you'd expect, plus a lot more. (half day)

See Also: *Bargaining [p.148], Shopping Malls [p.166].*

Safari Tours

Dune Dinners

Late afternoons are ideal for enjoying the thrill of driving over golden sand dunes in a 4 wheel drive vehicle. Departing at around 16:00, the route passes camel farms and fascinating scenery with great photo opportunities. The ride ends at an Arabic campsite where you can enjoy a sumptuous dinner under the calm of a starlit desert night. Return to your drop point at around 22:00. (half day)

East Coast

A journey east to Al Dhaid takes you to a small oasis town known for its fruit and vegetable plantations. Catch glimpses of dramatic mountain gorges before arriving at Dibba and Khor Fakkan on the East Coast. Have a refreshing swim and visit the oldest mosque in the UAE nestling below the ruins of a watchtower. These tours usually include a visit to the Friday Market for a browse through carpets, clay pots and fresh local produce. (full day)

Full Day Safari

This day long tour usually passes traditional Bedouin villages and camel farms in the desert, with a drive through sand dunes of varying colours and heights. Most tours also visit Fossil Rock and the striking Hajar Mountains, the highest mountains in the UAE. A cold buffet lunch may be provided in the mountains before the drive home. (full day)

Hatta Pools Safari

Modern highways, soft undulating sand dunes and a kaleidoscope of colours lead the way to Hatta in the foothills of the Hajar Mountains. Swim in the Hatta Pools and see the hidden waterfall inside a gorge.

The trip generally includes a stop at the Hatta Fort Hotel, where you can relax and enjoy the

swimming pool, landscaped gardens, archery, clay pigeon shooting and a 9 hole golf course. Not every tour has lunch at the hotel; some have it in the mountains, especially in the cooler winter months. (full day)

Mountain Safari

Travelling north along the coast and heading inland at Ras Al Khaimah, the oldest seaport in the region, you enter the spectacular Hajar Mountains at Wadi Bih. Rumble through rugged canyons onto steep winding tracks, past terraced mountainsides and old stone houses at over 1,200 metres above sea level. It leads to Dibba where a highway quickly returns you to Dubai, stopping at Masafi Market on the way. Some tours operate in reverse, starting from Dibba. (full day)

Overnight Safari

This 24 hour tour starts at about 15:00 with a drive through the dunes to a Bedouin style campsite. Dine under the stars, sleep in the fresh air and wake to the smell of freshly brewed coffee. The morning drive heads for the mountains, taking you through spectacular rugged scenery along wadis (dry riverbeds), before stopping for a buffet lunch and then back to Dubai. (overnight).

Out of the City

Out of Abu Dhabi

If you have access to a car, it's worth spending some time exploring places outside the city. To the south of Abu Dhabi is the Liwa Oasis situated on the edge of the infamous Rub Al Khali desert, also known as the Empty Quarter. This region stretches from Oman through the southern UAE into Saudi Arabia. Its golden coloured sand dunes and dramatic desert backdrop, captured in full richness by Wilfred Thesiger in his vivid descriptions, have withstood the test of time. Before you begin exploring this region, it could be well worth getting your hands on a copy of Thesiger's 'Arabian Sands' – a reading of this text will surely enhance your understanding and enjoyment of this region.

North of Abu Dhabi are the six other emirates that form the UAE – Dubai, Sharjah, Ajman, Umm Al Quwain, Fujairah and Ras Al Khaimah. To put the size of Abu Dhabi in perspective, these six emirates cover only 13% of the country's landmass between them!

This section also covers the east coast of the peninsula – a mix of rugged mountains and golden beaches. It is one of the most interesting areas in the country to explore.

For further information on exploring the UAE 'outback', refer to the *Off-Road Explorer (UAE)*, published by Explorer Publishing.

Liwa

About a five hour drive from Abu Dhabi is the Liwa Oasis, one of the largest oases on the Arabian Peninsula. It is also home to the Bani Yas tribe, the ancestors of the current ruling family of Abu Dhabi. Even though a number of small villages cover an area of about 150 kms, its scattered resident communities have made it difficult to find vast tracts of date palms otherwise common in most other settlements in the region. The main attraction of Liwa is the desert with its dramatic red and golden dunes rising to heights of over 300 metres. This area has become increasingly popular for short weekend breaks among visitors to the UAE and Oman as well as Nationals.

See Also: *Wadi & Dune Bashing; Desert Driving – Deserts & Mountains (Exploring).*

Northern Emirates

Further north of Abu Dhabi are the emirates that make up the rest of the country. As you travel north up the West Coast, these are Dubai, Sharjah, Ajman, Umm Al Quwain and Ras Al Khaimah and, on the East Coast, lies Fujairah. They all play an important role in the UAE although none is as large or as powerful as the Abu Dhabi or Dubai emirates.

Ajman

Other Options → **Museums – Out of City [p.132]**

The smallest of the seven emirates is Ajman, the centre of which lies about 160 km from Abu Dhabi. Ajman is not merely a coastal emirate but also has two inland enclaves, one at Masfut on the edge of the Hajar Mountains, and the other at Manama in the interior between Sharjah and Fujairah. Ajman has one of the largest dhow building centres in the UAE, which offers fascinating insight into this traditional skill.

Investment in this small emirate is growing with the opening of the Ajman Kempinsky Hotel & Resort and the popular shopping complex, Ajman City Centre. Outlets here include Carrefour hypermarket, Magic Planet amusement centre, many small shops and a six screen Cinestar cinema complex.

Dubai

Dubai is the second largest and most important of the emirates after Abu Dhabi. Dubai's wealth is founded on trade and although, like Abu Dhabi, it has discovered oil, its natural resources are not as great as those of its southern neighbour.

Originally a small fishing settlement based around a creek, Dubai was taken over by a branch of the Bani Yas tribe from the Liwa oasis in the south in 1830. The Maktoum family led the take over, and descendants of this family still rule the emirate.

This modern city has grown up around a large creek, which makes an excellent starting point for any exploration.

Dubai has a reputation in the Middle East for being a liberal and 'happening' place – it most certainly is the place to come for a good night out! It is also often described as the 'shopping capital of the Middle East' since it will keep a shopaholic with a healthy credit card amused for far longer than a weekend. In recent years Dubai has become a very popular tourist destination and hosts an exciting calendar of sporting events and festivals to encourage this.

South of the city on the road to Abu Dhabi is the largest manmade port in the world: Jebel Ali, and its famous free zone which houses a huge industrial complex. The drive from Abu Dhabi to Dubai can be pretty hair raising with drivers exceeding the speed limit at will, so be pretty vigilant on the road!

Hatta

About 100 km from Dubai and 10 km from the border with Oman, is the town of Hatta. Nestled at the foot of the Hajar Mountains, the town is the site of the oldest fort in the emirate (built in 1790) guarded by several watchtowers on the surrounding hills. The town has a sleepy, relaxed feel about it and beyond the ruins and the Heritage Village, there is little to see or do here. However, past the village and into the mountains are the Hatta Pools, where you can see deep, strangely shaped canyons carved out by rushing floodwater.

As you come to Hatta, left at the fort roundabout on the main Dubai – Omani road, is the Hatta Fort Hotel. This is an ideal weekend destination with various options for food and activities.

On the way to Hatta, just off the main Dubai – Hatta road is the 100+ metres high Big Red sand dune. It's a popular spot for practising dune driving in 4 wheel drives or dune buggies, as well as trying your skill at sand skiing. Alternatively, take a walk to the top (it takes about 20 minutes) for a sense of achievement and a great view. For further information on the area around Hatta, refer to the *Off-Road Explorer (UAE)* by Explorer Publishing.

See Also: *Dune Buggie Riding [p.186]; Sand Boarding [p.198]; Tour Operators [p.133]*

Hatta Heritage Village

Location → Hatta | 04 852 1374
Hours → Sat - Thu 08:00 - 20:00; Fri 14:00 - 20:00
Web/email → na | **Map Ref** → UAE-D3

Hatta Heritage Village is a recreation of a traditional mountain village set in an oasis. Constructed around an old settlement, it encourages visitors to explore the narrow alleyways and learn about the conventional way of life in the mud and barasti houses. A large central

Dubai Creek

fort leads, further up the hill, to the South Tower that overlooks the village. Beyond the children's playground is a falaj, a tranquil oasis of running water and shaded seating areas. A house just opposite the entry to the village displays traditional products and handicrafts.

Ras Al Khaimah

Other Options → **Museums – Out of City [p.132]**

The most northerly of the seven emirates, Ras Al Khaimah (RAK), is one of the most fertile and green areas in the UAE with possibly the best natural scenery of any city in the country. It lies at the foot of the Hajar Mountains, which can be seen rising into the sky just outside the city. Some areas of the town are built on slightly elevated land with a view – rare when compared to other cities in the UAE, which are as flat as the proverbial pancake!

Like all coastal towns in the region, it traditionally relied on a seafaring existence and had an important port for pearling, trading and fishing. It is really two towns; the old town (Ras Al Khaimah proper) and the newer business district across the creek (Al Nakheel). Visit the souk in the old town and the National Museum of Ras Al Khaimah, which is housed in an old fort, a former residence of the Sheikh.

The RAK Free Trade Zone is part of a five year development plan designed to accelerate economic growth in the emirate. A large shopping and leisure complex, known as Manar Mall, provides a one stop shop for everyday needs. Housed within the complex are a Cineplex, family entertainment centre and water sports area.

The town is quiet and relaxed. In fact, it is a good starting point for exploring the surrounding countryside and visiting the ancient sites of Ghalilah and Shimal. Alternatively, visit the hot springs at Khatt or the camel racetrack at Digdagga.

One town in the emirate, Masafi, is home of the country's favourite bottled spring water – the UAE's (far superior) answer to Evian.

RAK is the starting or finishing point of a spectacular trip through the mountains via Wadi Bih to Dibba on the East Coast. It is also the entry point to the Mussandam Peninsula, Oman. Refer to the *Off-Road Explorer (UAE)* for further information on the trip through Wadi Bih, and also for exploring the Mussandam.

See Also: *Wadi & Dune Bashing [p.202].*

Sharjah

Other Options → **Weekend Breaks [p.142]**

Historically, Sharjah was one of the wealthiest towns in the region with settlers earning their livelihood from fishing, pearling and trade, and to a lesser extent, from agriculture and hunting. It is believed that the earliest settlements date back over 5,000 years. Even today Sharjah is a centre for trade and commerce, although Dubai has somewhat overshadowed its importance in this respect. The city grew around the creek or lagoon, which continues to be a prominent landmark in the modern city.

Sharjah is worth a visit, mainly for its various museums. In 1998, UNESCO named this emirate the cultural capital of the Arab world due to its commitment to art, culture, and towards preserving its traditional heritage. Opposite the Sharjah Natural History Museum, on the Al Dhaid road, past Sharjah Airport, a monument has been built to commemorate this award.

Sharjah is also the only emirate with a coastline on both the Arabian Gulf and the Gulf of Oman. A visit from the city of Sharjah to its territory on the East Coast heads through the spectacular Hajar Mountains and takes 1½ - 2 hours (obviously depending on whether you're a speed demon or not). The towns of Dibba, Khor Fakkan and Kalba are all part of Sharjah.

A useful guidebook to refer to for further information on this emirate is *Sharjah The Guide*. For a photographic tour of the stunning architecture of this emirate, pick up *Sharjah's Architectural Splendour*, published by Explorer Publishing.

Sharjah Creek

Sharjah is built around the Khalid Lagoon, commonly known as the Creek, with a walkway around it known as the Sharjah Corniche. The Corniche is a popular spot for a stroll in the cool of the evening, especially with families. Various places for coffee along the way have made it an ideal place to have a leisurely conversation. In the middle of the Creek is a huge fountain, or a jet of water, allegedly the second highest in the world.

From three points on the lagoon, small dhows can be hired for a trip around the Creek to see the lights of the city from the shimmering water. It is also a great photo opportunity during daylight hours. Prices are fixed and it costs Dhs.30 for a 15

minute trip for a party of up to ten, while a tour of the lagoon to the bridge and back takes about 30 minutes and costs Dhs.60.

Majaz Canal

Over the last couple of years, an eighty million dirham project has linked the Khalid Lagoon with the Al Khan Lagoon and the Mamzar Park area via the new 1,000 metre long Majaz Canal.

The aim was to create a 'Little Italy' tourist attraction along the canal, complete with boat rides between the two lagoons. The development is in keeping with the Sharjah Government's desire to develop the tourism industry on a cultural and educational basis. Three bridges have been built over the canal near the Khalid Lagoon, on Al Khan Road, and near Al Khan Lagoon as part of the project.

Al Dhaid

Al Dhaid is a green oasis town on the road from Sharjah to the East Coast. It is the second most important town in the Sharjah emirate and was once a favourite retreat from the deserts and coasts during the scorching summer months. Years ago, an extensive falaj (irrigation system) was built both above and below the ground to irrigate the land. The area is fertile and agricultural produce includes a wide range of fruit and vegetables from strawberries to broccoli and, of course, a large date crop.

On the outskirts of Al Dhaid, shoppers will find roadside stalls selling local pottery, carpets, fruit and vegetables.

During the winter months camel racing is held at the racetrack on the road to Mileiha.

Sharjah New Souk

Location → Nr Corniche · Sharjah | na
Hours → 09:00 - 13:00 16:00 - 22:00
Web/email → na | Map Ref → UAE-C2

Consisting of two low and parallel buildings connected to each other by footbridges, Sharjah New Souk (or Central Souk) is a haven for bargain hunters. The building, intricately decorated and built in an 'Arabian' style, is modern and functional from inside. Consisting of 600 shops, the shops upstairs sell furniture, souvenirs and a fabulous range of carpets from a variety of countries while the shops downstairs sell modern items, such as clothing, small electrical goods, shoes, gold jewellery and toys.

Souk Al Arsah

Location → Nr Bank St · Sharjah | na
Hours → 09:00 - 13:00 16:30 - 21:00
Web/email → na | Map Ref → UAE-C2

This is one of Sharjah's oldest souks, which has been renovated in the style of a traditional market place with shells, coral, African wood and palm leaves. There are about 50 small shops set in a maze of peaceful alleyways, selling traditional silver jewellery, perfumes, spices, coffee pots, wedding chests, and numerous other items, old and new.

Umm Al Quwain

Other Options → Weekend Breaks [p.142]

Lying further north along the coast, between Ajman and Ras Al Khaimah, is the emirate of Umm Al Quwain. The town is based around a large lagoon or creek and has a long seafaring tradition of pearling and fishing. Not much appears to have changed here over the years making the place a showcase of life in the UAE in earlier times. The emirate's six forts and a few old watchtowers still stand proudly around the town. Other than this, there is not much to see or do in the town itself.

However, the lagoon, with its mangroves and birdlife, is a popular weekend spot for boat trips. Since it is sheltered and free of dangerous currents it offers ideal conditions for windsurfing and other water sports. Just north of Umm Al Quwain, the area near the Barracuda Hotel (and grey market liquor store), is a growing fun park area. Dreamland Aqua Park, UAQ Flying Club, UAQ Shooting Club and the opportunity to try karting and paintballing make this the 'activity centre' of the northern emirates. With more resorts and facilities planned, this area can only get better!

UAQ Dreamland Aqua Park

East Coast

Other Options → Weekend Breaks [p.142]

A trip to the east coast of the Emirates is well worth taking, even if you are in the UAE only for a short time. The coast can be reached in 1½ - 2 hours and the drive takes you through the rugged Hajar Mountains and down to the Gulf of Oman. Take the road through the desert to Al Dhaid and Masafi (source of the local bottled water). At Masafi, you can either drive north to Dibba and along the coast to Fujairah and Kalba then back to Masafi, or the other way round.

The mountains and the East Coast are popular for camping, barbecues, weekend breaks and various sporting activities. Snorkelling is excellent even if you're close to the shore and locations such as Snoopy Rock are always popular. Diving is also worthwhile on this coastline with plenty of flora and fauna to be seen on the coral reefs. Check out the *Underwater Explorer (UAE)* published by Explorer Publishing for further information.

Off-roading enthusiasts will find the route to the East Coast, with its various diversions, interesting. Check out the *Off-Road Explorer (UAE)* for further information.

See Also: *Camping [p.30]; Diving [p.185]; Snorkelling [p.200].*

Badiyah

Best known as the site of the oldest mosque in the UAE, Badiyah is roughly located half way down the East Coast, north of Khorfakkan. Officially known as the Al Masjid Al Othmani, the mosque is made from gypsum, stone and mud bricks. It is believed that the mosque was built in the year 20 Hijra in the Islamic calendar, or 640 AD in the Roman calendar, and hence dates back 1,400 years. Recently repaired and whitewashed, this small building is surrounded by a 1½ metre wall. It is still used for prayers so non Muslim visitors will have to be satisfied with photographs from outside. Situated off the coast road, the mosque is built on a low hillside with several ruined watchtowers on the hills behind.

The village of Badiyah itself is one of the oldest settlements on the East Coast and is believed to have been inhabited since 3000 BC.

Bithna

Set in the mountains about 12 km from Fujairah, the village of Bithna is known for its fort and archaeological site. The fort once controlled the main pass through the mountains from east to west and is still very impressive, probably more so than the fort at Fujairah. It can be reached from the Fujairah - Sharjah road where the village of Bithna is signposted. The road to the fort is through the village and wadi.

The archaeological site is known as the Long Chambered Tomb or the T-Shaped Tomb and is said to have been a communal burial site. It was excavated in 1988 and its main period of use is thought to date between 1350 and 300 BC, although the tomb itself is older. Fujairah Museum has a detailed display of the tomb that is worth visiting since the site itself is fenced off and covered against the elements. The tomb can be found by taking a right, and then left turn before the village, near the radio tower.

Dibba

Located at the northernmost point of the East Coast, on the border with the Mussandam, Dibba is made up of three fishing villages. Interestingly, each part comes under a different jurisdiction: Dibba al Hisn is Sharjah, Dibba Muhallab is Fujairah and Dibba Bayah is Oman. However, the unique status has no effect on the relaxed and friendly ambience of this town.

The area is very historical and there are various burial sites throughout the region. Rumour has it that a vast cemetery with over 10,000 headstones can still be seen (although we have yet to hear of anyone actually finding it!). This is the legacy of a great battle fought in 633 AD, when the Muslim armies of Caliph Abu Baker were sent to suppress a local rebellion and to re-conquer the Arabian Peninsula for Islam.

The Hajar Mountains provide a wonderful backdrop to the village, rising in places to over 1,800 metres. Dibba is the starting or finishing point for the stunning drive to the West Coast, through the mountains via Wadi Bih.

Tip: For the journey through Wadi Bih, a 4 wheel drive is pretty essential, since boulders carried by the floods often block the route. So either be prepared to rebuild the road, or to turn back!

See Also: *Khasab Dhow Charters – Dhow Charters [p.184].*

Fujairah

Fujairah often seems to be best known as the youngest of the seven emirates, since it was part of Sharjah until 1952. However, there is a lot more to the only emirate located entirely on the East Coast. A picturesque area, it offers golden beaches bordered by the Gulf of Oman on one side and the

Hajar Mountains on the other. The town is a mix of old and new; worth visiting in particular is the old fort, which is reportedly about 300 years old and overlooks the atmospheric old town.

The surrounding hillsides are dotted with ancient forts and watchtowers, which add an air of mystery and charm. Off the coast, the seas and coral reefs make it a great spot for fishing, diving and water sports. Situated on the migratory route of birds from Africa to Central Asia it is also a good place for bird watching during the spring and autumn migrations.

The emirate has started to actively encourage tourism by opening new hotels and providing even more recreational facilities. Since Fujairah is close to the mountains and many areas of natural beauty, it makes an excellent base from which to explore the countryside and see wadis, forts, waterfalls and even natural hot springs.

The Municipality (09 222 7000) and Fujairah Tourism Bureau (09 223 1436) have come up with an excellent tourism map. It includes great hill shading, roads, graded tracks, 4 wheel drive tracks, a decent co-ordinate system and places of interest. On the reverse side is a brief overview of each place of interest, combined with an overview of the city.

Kalba

If you go driving to the East Coast don't turn back at Fujairah, for just to the south lies the tip of the UAE's Indian Ocean coastline. Here you will find Kalba, part of the emirate of Sharjah, renowned for its mangrove forest and golden beaches. The village is a pretty and modern fishing village that has retained much of its old world charm.

A road through the mountains linking Kalba to Hatta has recently been completed, creating an interesting but longer alternative to returning to Dubai on the Al Dhaid - Sharjah road.

Khor Kalba

South of the village of Kalba is Khor Kalba, set in a beautiful tidal estuary ('khor' is Arabic for creek). This is the northerly most mangrove forest in the world, the oldest in Arabia and considered to be a biological treasure. It is home to a variety of plant, marine and birdlife, not found anywhere else in the UAE. If you are a birdwatcher or nature lover, try to spend a few days in this surprising and beautiful region of Arabia.

For birdwatchers, the area is especially good during the spring and autumn migrations where you will find species including the reef heron and the booted warbler. It is also home to the rare white collared kingfisher, which breeds here and nowhere else in the world. There are believed to be only 55 pairs of these birds still in existence.

A canoe tour by Desert Rangers is an ideal opportunity to reach the heart of the reserve and you can regularly see over a dozen kingfishers on a trip. If you're lucky, you might catch a glimpse of the region's endangered turtles, or a dugong, although sightings are more common when diving rather than from the shore or boat. The mangroves in this area grow due to the mix of saltwater from the sea and freshwater from the mountains, but they are receding due to excessive use of water from inland wells.

Although it has been proposed to make this a fully protected nature reserve, it is still waiting for Federal protection. Nonetheless, it is a unique area so treat it with respect – leave it as you would wish to find it.

See Also: *Desert Rangers – Canoeing [p.180]; Birdwatching Groups [p.209]; Falconry Shows [p.124].*

Khor Kalba Reserve

Khor Fakkan

Khor Fakkan lies at the foot of the Hajar Mountains, halfway down the East Coast between Dibba and Fujairah. It is a popular and charming town, set in a bay and flanked on either side by two headlands, hence its alternative name 'Creek of the Two Jaws'. A favourite weekend spot, it has an attractive corniche (waterfront), beach and a new souk that sells the usual range of the exotic and the ordinary. There are plenty of things to do including fishing, water sports or a trip to Shark Island; alternatively, you can laze in the shade with a fruit juice.

Part of the emirate of Sharjah it has an important modern port. Ships discharging their cargo here can

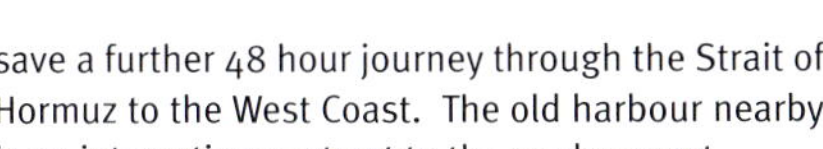

save a further 48 hour journey through the Strait of Hormuz to the West Coast. The old harbour nearby is an interesting contrast to the modern port.

Set in the mountains further inland is the Rifaisa Dam. Local legend has it that when the water is clear, a lost village can be seen at the bottom.

Wahala

This site is inland from Khor Kalba and is notable for a fort, which archaeologists judge to be over 3,000 years old. It is believed that the fort once protected the resources of the mangrove forests for the local population.

Al Hisn Kalba

Location → Kalba, Nr Fujairah · East Coast | 09 277 4442
Hours → 09:00 - 13:00 17:00 - 21:00
Web/email → www.shjmuseum.gov.ae | Map Ref → UAE-E2

Driving along the coast road in Kalba town you will find the restored house of Sheikh Sayed Al Qassimi overlooking the sea. Located at the end of a large grassy expanse, the house has swings and small rides to keep the children entertained. The adults can visit the town museum, housed in Kalba's Al Hisn Fort, just across the road. It includes a limited display of weapons and admission is free.

Note: *Ladies and children only on Wednesdays.*

Sultanate of Oman

Other Options → Weekend Breaks [p.142]

The Sultanate of Oman is a friendly, laid back and very beautiful place to visit, especially after fast paced Abu Dhabi. Visitors are struck by the low rise buildings and colonial style architecture in sharp contrast to the high rise buildings that dominate the Abu Dhabi skyline.

Visitors have two options – either to go east and into Oman proper, or north to visit the Omani enclave known as the Mussandam. Both areas can be visited by either plane or car.

If you are driving into Oman, there are two main border crossing points – at Hatta or through the Buraimi Oasis, near Al Ain. At both places your vehicle may be searched, so it is advisable not to include prohibited items (alcohol etc) in your luggage. The journey from Abu Dhabi to Muscat by car takes 4 - 5 hours and from Al Ain it is about 4 hours. However, crossing the border at the start or end of a public holiday can sometimes be tediously slow with a 1 - 2 hour wait.

Flying to Muscat takes about 45 minutes. Daily flights by Gulf Air, British Airways and Oman Air cost between Dhs.600 - 900 (plus Dhs.250 tax), depending on the season.

The local currency is the Omani Riyal (referred to as RO) which is divided into 1,000 baisa (or baiza). The exchange rate is usually about Dhs.10 = RO.1.

Note that talking on handheld mobile telephones whilst driving is illegal in Oman, as is driving a dirty car (yes, seriously)!

Mussandam

Other Options → Weekend Breaks [p.142]

The Mussandam Peninsula is the Omani enclave to the north of the UAE. This beautiful and pristine region of Arabia has only recently been opened to tourists. The capital, Khasab, is a quaint fishing port largely unchanged by the modern world. This area is of great strategic importance since its coastline gives control of the main navigable stretch of the Strait of Hormuz, with Iran only 45 km across the water at the narrowest point. To the west is the Arabian Gulf and to the east, the Gulf of Oman.

The Hajar Mountains, running through the UAE and the rest of Oman, also dominate this region. The jagged mountain cliffs plunging directly into the sea and the coastline littered with inlets and fjords have earned the place its nickname, 'Norway of the Middle East'. The views along the coast roads are stunning. Inland, the scenery is equally breathtaking and to explore properly a 4 wheel drive and a good head for heights are indispensable! Just metres off the coast are beautiful coral beds with an amazing variety of sea life, including tropical fish, turtles, dolphins (a common sight), sharks occasionally, and on the eastern side, whales.

To reach Mussandam from Abu Dhabi simply follow the coast road north through Ras Al Khaimah. At the roundabout for Shaam, take the exit right and follow the road to the UAE exit post. The Omani entry point is at Tibat and after that follow the road until it runs out. Note that, by car, non GCC nationals can only enter and exit the Mussandam on the Ras Al Khaimah side of the peninsula, not at Dibba on the East Coast. There are UAE and Omani border posts, so the correct visas are required. Alternatively, it is possible to fly to Khasab from Dibba, although it takes longer than driving from Abu Dhabi, and is more expensive.

Refer to the *Off-Road Explorer (UAE)* for further information on this fascinating part of Arabia.

Omani Visas

Visas for Oman are required for most nationalities whether entering by air or road. Different regulations apply depending on your nationality and how long you want to stay in Oman. In general, a visit visa can be obtained on arrival at the airport or on reaching the border crossing for between Dhs.33 - 50. It is a straightforward procedure to apply at the consulate in Abu Dhabi for a visit visa, though this will cost more than just arriving at the border. Alternatively, let your sponsor (hotel, tour operator, Omani company) do the paperwork for you. Certain nationalities in the UAE, on a tourist visa, may obtain an Omani tourist visa (without sponsorship) on arrival at Seeb International Airport for Dhs.60. If you wish to return to the UAE after your visit to Oman, you will need a new visa. If you are a UAE resident, a visa can be obtained on arrival at the border for Dhs.33. British and American citizens with UAE residency may consider applying for a two year multiple entry visa (Dhs.100). If you are travelling to the Mussandam from Ras Al Khaimah to visit the Khasab side, the standard visit visa is needed, either from the consulate or by applying at the border (if you fulfill the criteria).

Note that special clearance is required if you have 'journalist' or 'photographer' as a profession in your passport. Remember that regulations in this part of the world often change virtually overnight, so check details before you leave to avoid disappointment.

Weekend Breaks

Other Options → **Camping [p.30]**

Going away for the weekend is a great way to escape the stress of work and city life. This can either be a 'do it yourself' break within the UAE or going a little farther to Oman. A special deal can also be arranged through travel agents to destinations such as Jordan, the Seychelles or Kish Island.

With distances in the UAE being relatively small, it's easy to be well away from home without having to drive for hours – just checking into a beach hotel minutes from your home will give the feeling of having entered another world! The alternative to staying in a hotel is to camp, a very popular and well established pastime in the Emirates.

For those of us who feel like doing something a little different, just contact the main travel agents in Dubai for any special offers they might have on, say, a trip to Zanzibar, Bahrain or India. These offers are generally available exclusively to GCC residents. The travel agents listed in the table focus on the residents of Abu Dhabi who are looking for good advice, exciting itineraries and holidays that will not cost the earth. One could also find last minute deals on the Internet (ie, www.emirates.com, www.dnata.com or www.arabia.msn.com).

If you decide to stay in a hotel and are booking with them direct, remember that (if asked) they will often give a discount on their 'rack' rate or published price. Quite often, you may stumble upon special promotions, particularly in the quieter summer months when there are some incredible bargains available at five star hotels. The cost of breakfast may or may not be included, so check when you book. Typically, for a weekend in the peak season or for corporate rates, expect a 30% discount off the rack rate. Off peak, the discount can go as high as 60%.

For a list of places to stay, check out the Weekend Break table that lists standard room costs at hotels. However, as explained above, there may be a further discount possible on these rates. Before choosing a destination, you may like to refer to the information on the other emirates under Out of Dubai or the Sultanate of Oman. For more information on the emirate of Dubai, refer to the *Dubai Explorer* by Explorer Publishing. For camping options, see the *Off-Road Explorer (UAE)*, and if you're a fan of the marine world, the *Underwater Explorer (UAE)* summarises 58 top UAE dive sites with suggested dive plans and detailed instructions.

Al Fresco Venues

Weekend Break Summary

United Arab Emirates (+971)

Abu Dhabi	Hotel	Phone	Email	Rate (Dhs.)
Abu Dhabi	Abu Dhabi Hilton	02 681 1900	auhhitw@emirates.net.ae	900 (+16%)
	Beach Rotana	02 644 3000	beach.hotel@rotana.com	275 (B)
	Crowne Plaza	02 621 0000	cpauh@emirates.net.ae	250 (B)
	InterContinental	02 666 6888	abudhabi@interconti.com	790 (16%)
	Le Meridien	02 644 6666	meridien@emirates.net.ae	480 (+16%)
	Millennium	02 626 2700	sales.abudhabi@mill-cop.com	220 (+20%)
	Sheraton Abu Dhabi	02 677 3333	sheraton@emirates.net.ae	750 (+16%)
Al Ain	Al Ain Rotana	03 754 5111	alain.hotel@rotana.com	170 (+6%)
	InterContinental	03 768 6686	alain@interconti.com	600 (+16%)
	Mercure Grand	03 783 8888	mgih@mercure.alain.com	320
Jazira	Al Diar Jazira Beach	02 562 9100	reservations@jaziraresort.com	350 (+16%)
Liwa	Liwa Hotel	02 882 2000	liwahtl@emirates.net.ae	836 (B)
Ajman				
Ajman	Ajman Kempinski	06 745 1555	ajman.kempinski@kemp-aj.com	950
Dubai				
Dubai	Jumeirah Beach	04 348 0000	info@thejumeirahbeachhotel.com	1,600 (+20%)
	One&Only Royal Mirage	04 399 9999	royalmirage@royalmiragedubai.com	1,460 (+20%)
	Ritz-Carlton Dubai, The	04 399 4000	rcdubai@emirates.net.ae	1,290
Hatta	Hatta Fort	04 852 3211	hfh@jaihotels.com	780 (+20%)
Jebel Ali	Jebel Ali Resort	04 883 6000	jagrs@jaihotels.com	1,200 (+20%)
Fujairah				
Fujairah	Al Diar Siji	09 223 2000	sijihotl@emirates.net.ae	650 (15%)
	Fujairah Hilton	09 222 2411	shjhitwres@hilton.com	425 (15%)
Al Aqqah	Le Meridien Al Aqqah	09 244 9000	info@lemeridien-alaqqah.com	900
	Sandy Beach Motel	09 244 5555	sandybm@emirates.net.ae	385 (10%)
Ras Al Khaimah				
Ras Al Khaimah	Al Hamra Fort	07 244 6666	hamfort@emirates.net.ae	700
	Ras Al Khaimah	07 236 2999	rakhotel@emirates.net.ae	250
	RAK Hilton	07 228 8888	ras-al-khaimah@hilton.com	550
Sharjah				
Khor Fakkan	Oceanic Hotel	09 238 5111	oceanic2@emirates.net.ae	575
Umm Al Quwain				
Umm Al Quwain	Flamingo Beach Resort	06 765 1185	fbruaq@hotmail.com	450 (B)

Sultanate of Oman (+968)

	Hotel	Phone	Email	Rate (Dhs.)
Barka	Al Sawadi Resort	+968 895 545	sales@alsawadibeach.com	230 (+17%)
Muscat	Al Bustan Palace	+968 799 666	albustan@interconti.com	1,290 (+17%)
	Chedi Muscat, The	+968 505035	chedimuscat@ghmhotels.com	823 (+17%)
	Crowne Plaza	+968 560 100	cpmct@omantel.net.om	580 (+17%)
	Grand Hyatt Muscat	+968 602 888	hyattmct@omantel.net.om	880 (+17.4%)
	Holiday Inn Muscat	+968 687 123	mcthinn@omantel.net.om	590 (+17%)
	InterContinental	+968 600 500	muscat@interconti.com	700 (+17%)
	Mercure Al Falaj	+968 702 311	accorsales@omanhotels.com	420 (+17%)
	Radisson SAS	+968 685 381	sales@mcdzh.rdsas.com	550 (+17%)
	Sheraton Oman	+968 799 899	sheraton@omantel.net.om	650 (+17%)
Mussandam				
Khasab	Golden Tulip Khasab	+968 830 777	info@goldentulipkhasab.com	459
	Khasab	+968 830 271	khoman@omantel.net.om	340
Nizwa	Falaj Daris	+968 410 500	fdhnizwa@omantel.net.om	295
Salalah	Holiday Inn Salalah	+968 235 333	hinnsll@omantel.netcom	574 (+17%)
	Salalah Hilton Resort	+968 211 234	sllbc@omantel.net.om	660 (+17%)
Sohar	Sohar Beach	+968 841 111	soharhtl@omantel.net.om	350 (+17%)
Sur	Sur Mercure	+968 443 777	reservationssur@omanhotels.com	430 (+17%)

Note Rate = Price in dirhams of one double room; +xx% = plus tax; B = Inclusive of breakfast.
The above prices are peak season rack rates. However, many hotels will offer a discount off the rack rate if asked.

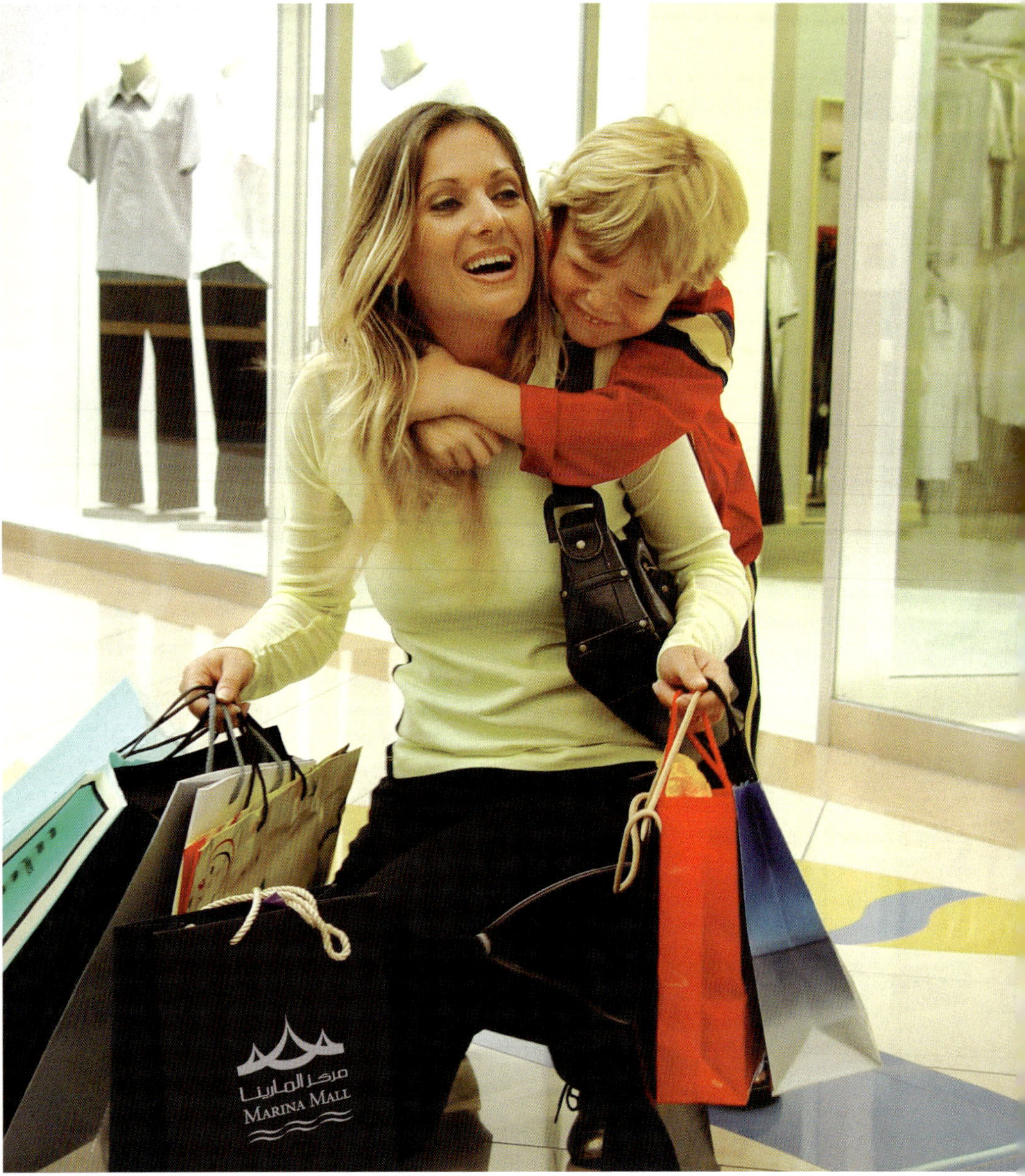

Shopping

EXPLORER

Shopping

Marina Mall

Shopping

Shopping in Abu Dhabi is cultural, entertaining and fun, and a very serious business indeed! However, this does not always translate into bargains galore in every store, leaving visitors often surprised and a little disappointed. Although prices on speciality goods in the region such as carpets, textiles and, of course gold, are extremely competitive, many imported goods are generally similar to any other major city in the world. The key to shopping like a pro is to bargain where possible since prices, especially in the souks, can drop substantially. What this city does afford avid shoppers, however, is choice and innumerable ways to part with their money. Shopping addicts who want to flex their plastic further may enjoy a trip to Dubai, aka the 'Shopping Capital of the Middle East'. For more information, check out Explorer Publishing's *Dubai Explorer*. The following section provides information on all that is relevant for shoppers in Abu Dhabi – what to buy, where to buy it, and a few tips on how to stretch the mighty dirham. Abu Dhabi's glitzy malls, replete with world renowned shops and adequate parking, are covered in detail. The recent past has seen the shopping mall become a social centre for residents and visitors alike. Malls have given birth to a new breed of entertainment, totally equipped with air conditioning, a hotchpotch of nationalities and a vast selection of shops and activities to pass the time. Refer to the coloured boxes for a list of the most popular brand names and where you can buy them. The intrepid shopper will certainly be able to track down some genuine bargains in the shopping malls and various areas of Abu Dhabi, including its souks (worth braving the heat for). Consumers will quickly become aware of the numerous (and endless) promotions and raffles offered by the malls, both big and small, and even the Abu Dhabi International Airport. The majority of these don't even require you to buy a special ticket, but will simply hand them over with your till receipt. Great fun, especially if you win! All international brands including department stores, designer stores and car dealerships are in the UAE on an agency basis, mostly run by a few large National families. Note: Traps for the unwary shopper do exist. Some of the international stores sell items at prices that are far more expensive than in their country of origin and at times, you can even see the original price tags! The price differential can go as high as 30%, so beware.

Refunds & Exchanges

Faulty goods are not usually refunded but can be exchanged at the shop of purchase, so always keep receipts and ask to see the manager if there is a problem. If, however, you have simply changed your mind about a recently purchased item, most retailers are not so obliging. Most will only exchange or give credit notes and very few will refund. You may also find that their policy changes for different items. For any level of success, unwanted items being returned need to be untouched, unworn, unused and in their original packaging. Always check the refund and exchange policy when buying something, and always keep your receipt somewhere safe. You will find that most retailers get hot under the collar if you persist – just let them know that the customer is always right! As a last resort, appeal to their need for ongoing patronage by their customers. Still, if you really think you've been duped, below is some info that might be of help.

Consumer Rights

Unfortunately there are no laws, codes or regulations that protect consumers. In other words, this means the stores can do what they please – something to bear in mind if you are handing over large sums of cash for something you are not quite sure about. There is however an excerpt in the UAE Civil and Commercial Code that states that the customer is entitled to recover the price which has been paid on faulty goods. But unless you are prepared to take the shop to court, a simple exchange will have to suffice. If you are persistent and have a complaint about a purchased item but cannot get any assistance from the shopkeeper, the Emirates Society for Consumer Protection based in Sharjah (06 556 7333) may be able to help you.

Shipping

Shopping is a popular pastime for UAE residents, and even more so for the numerous visitors who come from far and wide to shop their hearts out, especially during the Dubai Shopping Festival. Exporting goods can be a tedious task, but there is certainly no shortage of shipping and cargo agencies that offer good value for money. The best plan of action is to contact an agency directly. You will find plenty of listings under 'shipping' in the

Abu Dhabi Yellow Pages. Most companies operate globally and are quite reliable. For larger items such as furniture, many shippers will happily make room in containers booked by other customers who haven't quite filled them up – and they give good discounts while they're at it. Quotes can vary quite dramatically, but to give an idea, the average cost per kilo to Australia is Dhs.95, to the UK, around Dhs.85, and to North America, Dhs.180. These prices are inclusive of handling and packing charges. You can expect to pay almost double for door to door service, but half if travelling by boat. You also have the option of sending the items by airmail, courier, or sea. For even larger shipments, refer to New Residents [p.47].

How to Pay

In the UAE, you will have no problem exchanging money, withdrawing money or paying for goods. You can easily withdraw cash at ATMs using most cards – check your bank card for logos of international organisations like CIRRUS or PLUS, and look out for cash machines bearing the same logos. Credit cards, too, are widely accepted, the exception being small traders in the souks and local convenience stores. Accepted international credit cards include American Express, Visa, MasterCard and sometimes Diners Club. Discounting the high rates of interest you will have to pay, local banks reward their credit card users with a number of promotions, competitions and discounts. US currency is also widely accepted, even by the ubiquitous local store. Since the dirham is pegged to the US dollar, the exchange rate offered is broadly the same throughout the Emirates. For the astute shopper though, the best bargains are secured by using the local currency. There are numerous money exchange bureaus in all major shopping areas. Being equipped with dirhams will make shopping a whole lot quicker, hassle free, and can potentially translate into some cash discounts for you.

See Also: *New Residents [p.47]*

Bargaining

Other Options → **Souks [p.173]**

Although bargaining is a somewhat alien way of doing business for many, it is a time honoured tradition in this part of the world. Vendors will often drop the price quite substantially for a cash sale, especially in the souks. So, relax, think "something for nothing", and remember to take your time – this can be fun! The key to bargaining is to state what you would be happy to pay for the item, and walk away if you don't get it for that. Always be polite and amiable, and never use rudeness or aggression as bargaining tools. Start with a customary greeting, and know the value of the item in negotiation; you can learn this by scouting around in other shops. Ask the shop assistant how much and when he tells you, look shocked, or at least indifferent. In the souk, a common rule is to initially offer half the quoted price. Once you've negotiated, that's it – it's a verbal contract and you are expected to buy. Remember storekeepers are pros at this and have an instinct for a moment's weakness! However, keep in mind that you don't have to buy if the price is not right. You can always walk away and return later – and very often you'll find that the shop assistant will follow you out of the shop to secure a purchase. The consumer is the one with the power in the bargaining process, so 'use it or lose it'! Away from the souks, bargaining is not common practice, although many stores offer a set discount, claiming that the price shown is 'before discount'. It's always worth asking if you can have money off, especially if you are paying by cash – after all, if you don't ask, you don't get. Even pharmacies have a last price system whereby they will reduce what is shown on the price sticker, normally by ten percent.

What & Where to Buy

Abu Dhabi's stores sell an abundance of goods and you should have few problems finding what you need. The following section covers the main categories of products that can be bought in the city, from carpets and cars to electronics and gold, and where to buy them.

Alcohol

Other Options → **Liquor Licence [p.56]**
On the Town [p.258]

Non-Muslims who are over 21 years of age can purchase alcohol at licensed bars, restaurants, and some clubs for consumption on the premises. However, to buy alcohol for consumption at home requires more than a quick visit to your local supermarket – you'll need to apply for a liquor licence. While it is relatively easy to get your license, there are certain limits – Muslims, for example, are not permitted to apply, and residents who have a liquor licence from another emirate are not permitted to use it in Abu Dhabi. For more information on how to obtain a licence and the

restrictions that apply, see [p.56] in the New Residents section. Once you have your licence, it's easy enough to purchase alcohol from the special stores that are strategically scattered around the city. There is one point to be aware of when buying alcohol using your license – when you get to the checkout, expect to pay 30% more than the marked price. The purchase of liquor attracts a hefty tax here. There are a few 'hole in the wall' stores selling tax free alcohol to unlicensed patrons. These stores are easy to purchase from if you don't mind the trek. The Barracuda Beach Motel next to Dreamland Aqua Park in Umm Al Quwain is one of the most frequented. Similarly, there is another store opposite the Ajman Kempinski, which is quite literally a hole in the wall. Although this sounds like an easy option, you will find the selection not as comprehensive as the licensed outlets scattered throughout the cities. There is also a catch; it is illegal to transport alcohol over the border of an emirate, and in particular, through Sharjah. Police often turn a blind eye to this followed practice, but if you get busted with booze in your car, we told you so! Note that the Abu Dhabi authorities have a strict anti drink driving stance. For further information refer to the booklet 'For Your Safety, be Aware of the Alcoholic Beverages Law' issued by the public relations department of the Abu Dhabi Police. Al Ain has a liquor store in the Al Tawam Hospital (03 767 8948), but this facility can only be used by the hospital staff and is not open to outsiders, even with a valid liquor licence.

Alcohol

African & Eastern Ltd	
Khalidiya	667 6041
Salam St	644 8685
Tourist Club Area	677 1770
Gray & Mackenzie Liquor Shop	
Khalifa St	612 3545
Mussaffah	554 3919
Old Mazda Road	676 5954
Spinneys Liquor	
Hamdan St	677 0577
Khalidiya	681 2356
Najda St	671 7992
Your Shop	
Airport Road	444 9821
Capitol Hotel	677 8370
Al Ain Hilton	03 768 7017

Timings: 10:00 - 14:00 & 17:00 - 21:00; 10:00 - 21:00 Thursdays and Saturdays. Closed Friday.

Arabian Souvenirs

Other Options → Carpets [p.153]

For visitors and residents alike, many items from this part of the world make novel souvenirs, gifts or ornaments for the home. Historically, this was a Bedouin culture and possessions had to be practical and transportable, reflecting the nomadic lifestyle of the indigenous population. Prices and quality of traditional items vary enormously. The souks usually offer the best prices, but there is something to suit all budgets here.

Carpets are a favourite buy. Take your time and see as many choices as possible, build up a rapport with the carpet seller, and haggle, haggle, haggle! Other items with a local theme include the coffeepot and cups (a symbol of Arabic hospitality), prayer beads (that look like worry beads), and wooden knick knacks such as dhows, falconry accoutrement and wooden canes. Genuine traditional items, such as Omani wedding chests, are usually expensive and increasingly difficult to find in the UAE. However, modern 'antiqued' copies are widely available.

Traditional wooden doors are also sought after. These can be used as intended or hung against the wall as a piece of art. Alternatively, it's popular to have them turned into furniture, usually tables with a glass top, so the carving is visible and can be appreciated.

Ancient looking rifles, muzzle loading guns and the functional and decorative 'khanjar' (a short, curved dagger in an elaborately wrought sheath) are also popular buys. However, if you're planning to take any such items back home as gifts or mementos, check first with your airline on procedures or you may just receive a rather hostile welcome from airport security.

Traditional wedding jewellery made of heavy silver and crafted into simply engraved (and extremely heavy) necklaces, bracelets, earrings and rings are coveted forms of historical art, especially as many of the larger pieces make excellent displays when mounted in a glass box frame.

Alternatively, if gold is more to your taste, then you are in the right country – there is an amazing choice of gold jewellery in the Emirates. Abu Dhabi's Iranian Souk [p.166], is well worth a visit, as is the Gold Souk in Dubai. The cost of workmanship is also very competitive, so you can tap the artist in you to create your own designs.

Once valued more highly than gold, the dried resin from the frankincense tree in southern Oman has been traded for centuries, and makes a charming gift, especially when bought with a small wooden chest and charcoal burner to give off its evocative scent. You will probably either love or hate the smell of incense and the heavy local perfumes, but they are great as authentic gifts that exude the culture of the Middle East. Oud is a popular and expensive oil used in many of the perfumes, while myrrh and other sweet smelling mixtures are also sold. Ask to smell some already burning before deciding on your purchase.

Arabian Souvenirs		
Heritage Touch	Marina Mall	681 5615
Gulf Antiques and Carpets Exhibition	Tourist Club Area	645 9956

Shisha or hubbly bubbly pipes are a fun item to have and can be bought along with flavoured tobacco, such as apple, strawberry and grape. Both functional and ornamental ones are available and some stores also sell a protective carrying case – handy if you are taking it into the desert or to the beach.

Where eatables are concerned, look out for delicious Lebanese sweets (usually made from pastry, honey, ground nuts and dates), or fresh dates in the homeland of one of the world's main producers of dates. Iranian caviar too, is widely available and good value for money, as it is sold without import duty or any value added tax.

Arabian Treasures

Finally, there are the usual corny tourist souvenirs of the 'I " Abu Dhabi' variety, fluffy camels, and sand pictures with glass panels that contain the seven different coloured sands of the seven different emirates (it's a wonder there's any sand left in the UAE). However, if you are tired of clichés and looking for a more upmarket and easily transported souvenir, it is worth picking up a good coffee table book such as *Images of Abu Dhabi and the United Arab Emirates*. This artistic photographic book, available in all good bookshops, offers a refreshing and insightful visual perspective on this part of the world.

Art

Other Options → Art Classes [p.208]

While there's nowhere like the Tate Gallery or the Louvre in Abu Dhabi, there are a few art galleries that have interesting exhibitions of art and traditional Arabic artefacts. The Abu Dhabi Cultural Foundation hosts both local and international exhibitions. A free programme of events for the coming month is available from the foundation. The Art Shop and Cornellian Gallery are more souvenir shops than true art galleries but are worth checking out. If you're up for a bit of a drive, it is worth visiting the Sharjah Art Musem (refer to Museums & Heritage for more information).

Art Supplies

Other Options → Art [p.150]

Creative types who like to dabble in arts and crafts can find tools of the trade at the following stores. If you're looking for anything specific, try contacting each individual store first before embarking on a wild goose chase.

Art Supplies		
All Prints	Al Nasr St	633 5853
Jarir Bookstore	Mina Centre	673 3999
Mohammad Al Makhawi Est.	Tourist Club Area	644 3141

Beach Wear

Other Options → Clothes [p.154]

Since many residents spend their weekends either basking by the pool or catching some sporting action on the emirate's fabulous beaches, it is perhaps, not so surprising that people will often

spend as much money on a set of swimming togs as they would on a suit for work!

The specialist beach wear boutiques stock everything from French and Italian designer wear to achingly hip Californian and Australian surfing labels, and generally, prices here are extremely high. Since there is no real 'off' season, these shops tend to have sales and discounts at strange times of the year. So if labels are crucial for your beach wear collection, it's worth asking to be put on a mailing list, thus being first in the queue to snap up the bargains.

The many sports shops in Abu Dhabi also stock a decent range of swimwear, but these veer towards no nonsense styles for competitive swimmers rather than catering to die hard beach babes. For those less bothered about making a fashion statement when they peel off on the beach, head for the department stores in the larger malls.

BHS, Woolworth's, Debenhams and Marks & Spencer all sell a good range of beach wear for women, men and children including all related paraphernalia such as hats and beach bags, all at prices that won't break the bank.

Beach Wear		
Beyond the Beach	The British Club	644 6666
Marks and Spencer	Fatouh Al Khair Centre	621 3646

Books

Other Options → Libraries [p.212]

A reasonable selection of English language books is sold in Abu Dhabi, covering a broad range of subjects from travel or computing to children's books, the latest best sellers, and coffee table books on and about the Emirates. You are unlikely to find as extensive a range of books and bookshops as you would in your home country, although the number and size of outlets is increasing. Most of the larger hotels have small bookshops that offer a limited choice. You will also find that foreign newspapers and magazines, which are flown in regularly, are always much more expensive than at home. To all the males out there who enjoy perusing through racy blokes' mags, be warned – due to censorship laws in the UAE, pictures of semi naked women are always disguised by a giant black pen mark. Worth special mention is the Jarir Bookstore, which claims it's more than just that. This huge store has a wide selection of English and Arabic language books as well as one of the best art and craft supply selections in town. They also stock stationery and office supplies, computers and accessories, school supplies, magazines, party goods, gifts and a very good selection of sensibly priced cards. Another interesting (and cheaper) option is the House of Prose, Abu Dhabi's first and only second hand bookstore. The store offers over 15,000 titles, comprising of a huge selection of fiction, non fiction, science fiction and children's books. They also buy and sell good quality English paperbacks. Abela Superstore, Carrefour, Spinneys and the Co-op supermarkets at Manaseer and the Tourist Club areas also carry a decent selection of books and magazines.

Books		
Al Mutanabbi	Old Airport Rd	634 0319
All Prints	Al Nasr St	633 5853
Book Corner	Marina Mall	681 7662
Books Gallery	Abu Dhabi Mall	644 3869
House of Prose	Liwa Centre	632 9679
Jarir Bookstore	Mina Centre	673 3999
Spinneys	Khalidiya	681 2897
Book Corner	Al Jimi Centre	03 763 0911
University Book House	Nr Clock Tower R/A	03 755 9480

Camera Equipment

Other Options → Electronics & Home Appliances [p.155]

Both amateur and serious photographers will be able to find most of what they need on the shelves in Abu Dhabi. Prices from the agents are usually fixed but quite reasonable, but shop around before you buy, as many famous brands can be found in smaller stores where the price is negotiable. Watch out though for 'parallel imports', UAE agents will not honour the warranty on parallel import items and you may have to send your 'bargain' camera overseas for warranty repairs. Opinion is divided as to whether it's cheaper to buy cameras in the UAE than elsewhere. Due to low import costs, cameras here are less expensive than in the UK for instance, but that doesn't mean that the UAE is the cheapest place in the world; Hong Kong and Singapore are both cheaper, if you know what you are looking for. However, the cheapest price doesn't always make it a bargain. There are several issues to consider before purchasing a camera, and special deals and giveaways, such as free memory cards, camera cases or print vouchers, can add extra value to your purchase. The web is invaluable in researching what is available before you walk into the store. If you are purchasing in Abu Dhabi

to take back home, check out the tax implications of the importing country. It may be that the 'bargain' price, plus the added import tax, is no cheaper (and sometimes more expensive) than the price in your home country. It is also important to get a stamped and dated international warranty otherwise the agent in your home country may not repair any future defects. It's worth noting, for example, that Sony UK refuses to honour warranties on any Sony products bought outside the UK, claiming that they are not an international company. Film is readily available in supermarkets, local shops and hotel foyer shops.

Camera Equipment		
Grand Stores	Abu Dhabi Mall	645 1115
Salam Studio	Abu Dhabi Mall	645 6999
Plug-Ins	Marina Mall	681 5509
Grand Stores	Al Ain Mall	03 751 5551

Cards & Stationery

Other Options → Art Supplies [p.150]
Books [p.152]

Most supermarkets carry an ample supply of greeting cards, wrapping paper and stationery. However, there are a quite a few speciality stores to be found lurking amid the weaving and winding corridors of Abu Dhabi's streets and malls. It is at these places that you will find the best variety in Abu Dhabi, especially for cards, where they offer everything from Christmas and Easter to Mother's Day and Eid cards.

While postcards are a smashing bargain, greeting cards tend to be very expensive, especially those celebrating special occasions or holidays. Locally produced cards are much cheaper, more original, and often better quality – they can be found in most card shops and usually feature local artists' work.

Looking for wrapping paper? THE One and Woolworths have some of the most unique and reasonable selections. Similarly, Ikea sells gift wrapping paraphernalia at a fraction of the price of the more established card and gift wrap stores.

Cards & Stationery		
All Prints	Al Nasr St	633 8572
Book Corner	Marina Mall	681 7662
Carrefour	Marina Mall	681 7100
Gulf Greetings	Tourist Club Area	644 9780
	Fatouh Al Khair Centre	621 5945
	Nr Co-Op, Khalifa St	626 3601
	Abu Dhabi Mall	645 4840
	Marina Mall	681 3338
	Khalidiya	666 1560
THE One	Khalidiya	681 6500
IKEA	Marina Mall	681 2228
Carrefour	Al Jimi Center	03 762 9003
Gulf Greetings	Al Ain Mall	03 751 6540

Carpets

Other Options → Arabian Souvenirs [p.149]
Bargaining [p.148]

Whether you are a regular buyer or just a novice, carpet shopping can be a fascinating experience. In Abu Dhabi, countries of origin for carpets range from Iran and Pakistan to China and Central Asia, and there is a truly exquisite array of designs and colours. However, to ensure that you are buying the genuine article at a good price, it is advisable to learn a bit about carpets before making the final

Persian Carpets

decision. A good place to start if you want to read up on the subject is *Oriental Carpets: A Buyer's Guide*. If possible, visit a number of shops to get a feel for price, quality and traditional designs, as well as the range available. As a very rough guide, the higher the number of knots per square inch, the higher the price and better the quality. Silk is more expensive than wool, and rugs from Iran are generally more valuable than the equivalent from Turkey or Kashmir. Check if it is machine or handmade (handmade ones are never quite perfect and the pile is slightly uneven). Salesmen will happily offer plenty of advice, but don't let that influence your decision too much – your purchase should be based on what you want, at the price you want. Also, don't feel pressured into buying simply because the assistant has just unrolled over thirty carpets for you. Most importantly, do not forget to bargain; it's part of the game and expected in all shops. Prices vary from a few hundred to many thousand dirhams, but are always negotiable. A good starting point to see the wide range available in terms of price and quality is the Carpet Souk at the Port end of Mina Road. Meena Souk (also known as Afghan Souk) is also well stocked. It is advisable to visit the more exclusive shops to compare quality and price. Many hotels house fine quality carpet shops.

Carpets		
Al Radmani Persian Carpets	Al Nasr St	633 1238
Magic Carpets	Zakher Hotel	627 5882
Original Iranian Carpets	30th Street Corniche	681 1156
Persian Carpets	Rotana Mall	681 5900
Red Sea Handmade Carpets	Khalifa St	626 6145

Cars

Other Options ➜ **Buying a Vehicle [p.92]**

New residents are often pleasantly surprised to find that cars here are much cheaper than in their own country, and with competitive interest rates offered by banks and dealers, buying a new car isn't necessarily for an elite few. All the major car manufacturers are represented here and tend to give good discounts towards the end of the year (when next year's model is due in the showroom). Alternatively, the second-hand market is thriving with an abundance of used car dealerships. Airport Road is a good place to start. You'll find everything from barely used Porsches and Ferraris to 4x4s, ideal for some off-roading in the desert. Prices are never final so stand your ground if you're determined to clinch a deal; remember the dealer has paid its previous owner a fraction of the price he's attempting to claim from you. For other good deals, check the newspapers, supermarket notice boards or Websites such as www.valueonwheels.com. It's a good idea to have the vehicle checked out by a reputable garage though, before you take the plunge and buy. For a listing of car showrooms, refer to the New Residents section [p.94].

Clothes

Other Options ➜ **Kids' Items [p.160]**
Tailoring [p.166]

Dedicated followers of fashion will find everything from the priciest designer shops to up-to-the-minute boutiques to pile-it-high-sell-it-cheap bargain basements. Upmarket stores dedicated to designer names are usually found in shopping malls and hotel arcades. Most malls have a good selection of inexpensive quality clothing and there is now an increasing trend towards 'global' stores that sell the same clothing items the world over, turning over their stock every four to six weeks. Handily, they also show

Clothes		
BHS	Hamdan St	621 1242
Blue Marine	Hamdan St	677 0236
Can-Can	Marina Mall	681 4924
Esprit	Abu Dhabi Mall	645 4871
Etam	Abu Dhabi Mall	645 4890
Evans	Nr Emirates Hamdan St	639 2858
Fame	Nr Dana Plaza	665 4300
Giordano	Marina Mall	681 4841
Guess	Abu Dhabi Mall	644 5332
Mango	Abu Dhabi Mall	644 9319
Marks & Spencer	Fatouh Al Khair Centre	621 3646
Miss Sixty	Marina Mall	681 5788
Monsoon	Fatouh Al Khair Centre	621 5069
Next	Abu Dhabi Mall	645 4832
Oasis	Najda St	621 9700
Promod	Marina Mall	681 8050
Rodeo Drive	Khalifa St	626 4800
Sana Fashions	Najda St	677 5667
Splash	Tourist Club area	644 5565
BHS	Nr Jadal R/A, Al Ain	03 755 8988
Evans	Al Ain Mall	03 751 5297
Next	Al Ain Mall	03 751 4872
Splash	Al Ain Mall	03 751 1141

the retail price in each country on the tag, so it's quite satisfying to know that you are paying no more than your friends back home. Mass sales generally take place around August/September and January when stores get rid of the old stock and bring in the new. If you can bear to rummage, discounts of 70% aren't uncommon. Another excellent time for bargains is around the end of Ramadan when the Eid sales begin. For a more comprehensive listing of clothing stores, refer to Main Shopping Malls [p.168].

Computers

Other Options → Electronics & Home Appliances [p.155]

You should have few problems submerging yourself in the latest technology here – whether it's hardware or software, numerous outlets sell up-to-the-minute merchandise. If you are really serious about computers and the latest technology, it's worth driving into Dubai to check out GITEX – the biggest IT exhibition in the Middle East. Each year, usually during October, the exhibition halls at the Dubai World Trade Centre house this exhibition, with every single computer company that you can think of, plus a few others, participating. There's also a GITEX Shopper held at the Airport Expo in Dubai, so when you've cruised the stands and decided what latest gizmo you can't live without, you can pop along and buy it with a good discount. The UAE government, together with the BSA (Business Software Alliance) is clamping down heavily on the sale of pirated software. As a result, most computer shops are reputable and offer the usual international guarantees.

Computers		
Jumbo Electronics	Hamdan St	632 7001
Plug-Ins	Marina Mall	681 5509
Jumbo Electronics	Al Ain Mall	03 751 4705

Electronics & Home Appliances

Other Options → Computers [p.155]

From well known to not-so-instantly-recognisable brands, Abu Dhabi's stores stock a reasonable selection of electronics and home appliances. Prices are often hyped as being lower than in many parts of the world, but check things out before leaving home, especially if you are out to buy a major item. Like most goods, it pays to shop around for the best prices, although shops are generally fairly competitive due to the number of places offering the same, or similar, items. The major players however, are Jumbo Electronics and Plug-Ins. With stores in the main shopping malls of both Abu Dhabi Al Ain, they stock most of the leading brands. Warranties, after sales service, delivery and installation should be finalised before making a purchase. If you intend returning to your home country with an item, make sure the model you buy here will operate there (for example, manufacturers set the sound frequency on televisions differently in different parts of the world, so what works in Abu Dhabi won't necessarily work elsewhere). Alternatively, if you are happy buying second-hand electronics, check out the Classifieds sections of the local daily newspapers, advertising a range of items, often virtually as good as new. It may also be worth going to some of the 'garage' sales that are advertised by people who are usually returning to their home country and are selling off some of their unwanted possessions. You can buy something for nothing from departing expats; they usually sell at ridiculously low prices. Their main priority is often to get rid of everything as quickly as possible, regardless of how much money they lose. Remember, it's a buyer's market, and some great bargains can be found, making these options excellent for people who do not want to part with excessive chunks of their hard earned cash.

Electronics & Home Appliances		
Bango Electronics	Airport Rd	622 5272
Carrefour	Airport Rd	449 4300
	Marina Mall	681 7100
Cost Less	Mina Centre	673 4848
Eros Electricals	Madinat Zayed	633 6432
Geco	Airport Rd	443 6866
Jashanmal	Abu Dhabi Mall	645 6454
Jumbo Electronics	Hamdan St	632 7001
Oasis Ent.	Hamdan St	627 7173
Plug-Ins	Marina Mall	681 5509
Salam Studios	Abu Dhabi Mall	645 6999
Yousaf Habib Al Yousaf	Electra Rd	634 4553
Al Futtaim	Nr. Shk Khalifa St	03 764 1473
Carrefour	Al Jimi Centre	03 762 9003
Jashanmal	Shk Khalifa St	03 751 3151
Jumbo Electronics	Al Ain Mall	03 751 4705
Plug-Ins	Al Ain Mall	03 765 5270

Eyewear

The strength of the sun in the Gulf means that for many people, a good pair of sunglasses is their most important accessory. Consumers will find just about every brand of normal glasses and sunglasses imaginable, from designer names to designer rip offs and much more in between. While prices range from a few dirhams to many hundreds, it is worth buying sunglasses with a good quality lens. Make sure that they give 100% UVA and UVB protection, and are dark enough (and large enough) to protect the eye from the sun's glare. Most of the larger shopping malls have an optician who can make up prescription lenses, offer a good range of glasses and contact lenses, and also give eye tests. These are free of charge in most optical shops, as long as you order your glasses there or specify that the glasses are for driving. However, some places charge Dhs.20 - 50 for the eye test.

Eyewear		
Yateem Optician	Marina Mall	681 8170
Grand Sunglasses	Marina Mall	681 8178
Inter Optic	Abu Dhabi Mall	645 7511
Al Ain Optical	Al Ain Mall	03 751 8600
Grand Stores	Al Ain Mall	03 751 5551

Flowers

Other Options → **Plants & Trees [p.164]**

For special occasions or for that special someone (or as a desperate last minute present), flowers make a beautiful gift. There is a reasonable selection of florists all over the city and these places often sell dried flowers as well as fresh. Excellent flower arrangements can also be bought from supermarkets such as Spinneys and Carrefour. The local florists can throw together superb arrangements at very reasonable prices and their shops are worth a visit even if you don't intend on buying, as their skill and adeptness in flower arranging makes fascinating viewing. If you are looking for florists who deliver internationally as well as locally, refer to the Abu Dhabi Yellow Pages. Interflora signs adorn windows of some local shops that offer international deliveries. Prices vary according to the type of arrangement and flowers you choose, but the minimum order for local delivery is usually Dhs.100 per bouquet.

Flowers

Flowers		
Flower House	Al Nasr	621 1647
Holland Flowers	Hamdan St	632 2636
Oleander	Salam St	677 3131
Green Garden	Khalifa St, Al Ain	03 766 2428

Food

Abu Dhabi has a good range of stores and supermarkets that cater more than adequately to the city's multinational inhabitants. While there may be some speciality foods you cannot buy, most items are available. Prices vary dramatically. Produce is imported from all over the world, and some items are double what they would cost in their country of origin. However, fresh foods, such as fruit and vegetables, can be amazingly cheap, especially if bought from fruit and vegetable marketplaces. There are plenty of 'corner' shops in residential areas, good for a litre of milk and much more. Many accept orders over the phone for local home deliveries, saving you the walk. Popular food shops include the Abu Dhabi Co-operative, which has branches all over the city, and Al Ahlia Prisunic, often simply known as Prisunic. Alternatively, the souks are worth a visit, especially for fruit and vegetables. Carrefour is a huge hypermarket and part of a large French chain. It sells everything from cheap shoes to toothpaste, as well as a good selection of fruit, vegetables, fish and seafood. Other branches of Carrefour can be

found in Ajman, Dubai, Al Ain, Sharjah and Ras Al Khaimah. If you are looking for a certain type of food, there are a number of speciality stores: for American food, try Choithrams, for Asian/Japanese and gourmet delicacies, head for Abela, for British and European, go to Spinneys, and for French, look no further than Carrefour. Although pork is not included on the Arabic menu, the availability of this product is becoming more common. Spinneys has a designated pork section that is quite well stocked.

Food		
Abela Superstore	Khalidiya	667 4675
Al Ahlia Prisunic	Nr Dana Plaza	681 1400
AUH Co-operative Society	Abu Dhabi Mall	645 9777
	Khalifa St	626 4900
Carrefour	Marina Mall	681 7100
	Airport Rd	449 4300
Choithrams	Khalidiya	666 0610
	Shk Zayed 2nd St	676 5355
Emsons	Nr Le Meridien	676 8376
	Najda St	633 8653
Spinneys	Khalidiya	681 2897
	Airport Road	621 2919
Al Ahlia Prisunic	Al Khabeesi, Al Ain	03 763 4111
Choithrams	Main St, Al Ain	03 765 6798
	Al Jimi Centre	03 751 2227

Health Food/Supplements

The health food trend is slowly arriving in Abu Dhabi giving more options to those who take extra care of their diet. Specialist stores and pharmacies selling a range of supplements are popping up on a regular basis.

Larger supermarkets sell an ever increasing (but still limited) range of organic and allergy friendly products as well.

Vitamins, minerals, supplements, organic and health foods are expensive compared to back home and the selection of brands, while improving, is still limited, so bring speciality vitamins and supplements with you if possible.

Health Food/Supplements		
Nutrition Zone	Abu Dhabi Mall	644 4665
Dr Nutrition Centre	Marina Mall	681 2383
Dr Nutrition Centre	Al Ain Mall	03 751 2383

Hardware & DIY

Other Options → Outdoor Goods [p.162]

While it is usually easier to get in 'a man who can' to tackle all those niggling domestic jobs, many still prefer to do it themselves. DIY enthusiasts will find the tools they need to get the job done at hardware stores such as Ace Hardware. Customised paints, glazes, special paint effect materials, electronic tools and hardware materials can all be found here.

Hardware & DIY		
Ace Hardware	Mina Zayed Rd	673 3174
Carrefour	Airport Rd	449 4300
	Marina Mall	681 7100
Carrefour	Al Ain	03 762 9003

Home Furnishings & Accessories

Other Options → Furnishing Accomodation [p.72]

Whether you need kitchenware, bathroom accessories, bed linen, towels, curtain rods, lampshades or furniture, you will find goods to suit every taste and budget. There are some excellent home furnishing stores in Abu Dhabi, but remember that in addition to the stores, many of the supermarkets also sell kitchenware, a selection of linen etc.

A number of expansive stores sell the latest styles in furniture. The larger, well known stores such as THE One, 2XL, Home Centre, Ikea and Homes R Us sell almost everything you need to decorate your home under one roof. Second-hand furniture can often be found through the classified pages in the newspapers or from supermarket noticeboards.

Marina Gulf

Home Furnishings & Accessories		
2XL	Mina Centre	673 0575
Bhs	Hamdan St	621 1242
Cane Craft	Tourist Club Area	678 4505
Carrefour	Marina Mall	681 7100
Eldiar	Khalidiya	666 2522
Gemaco	Airport Rd	633 9100
Grand Stores	Abu Dhabi Mall	645 1115
Home Centre	Najda St	626 2621
Homes 'R' Us	Madinat Zayed	631 2020
Hyssna	Tourist Club Area	673 2796
ID design	Najda St	671 2405
IKEA	Marina Mall	681 2228
Marlin Furniture	Electra Rd	677 4994
Pan Emirates	Airport Rd	621 1030
THE One	Khalidiya	681 6500
Marina Gulf Trading	Al Barsha	04 347 8940

Jewellery, Watches & Gold

Other Options → Souks [p.173]

All tastes in jewellery are catered for here in the Emirates – whether you are looking for gaudy, elegant, cheap, expensive, yellow gold, white gold or glittering stones, you'll find it here in abundant supply. Gold is priced according to the international daily gold rate and available in 18, 21, 22 or 24 carats, in every form imaginable. You can even buy gold ingots of different sizes, either for investment or to melt down and have moulded into your own design. In addition to the weight price, a small charge is added for craftsmanship, which varies according to the intricacy of the design. The standards of workmanship can vary so if you are spending a lot of money, it is worth going to a more reputable store. For adventurous jewellery shoppers, there is plenty to choose from, such as Oman's silver jewellery, Japan's cultured pearls, and India's ethnic creations crafted in rich yellow gold. The new souk at Madinat Zayed on 4th Street has many jewellers including some of the largest jewellery shops in the Gulf. The outlets in these areas cater for all tastes, so have a browse around to see a full variety of Arabic, Indian and European styles. When it comes to watches, the UAE is almost guaranteed to be able to supply whatever you are looking for, at highly competitive prices. You'll get plastic cheapies for no more than a few dirhams, or diamond encrusted designer time pieces coming in at over a hundred thousand dirhams, and everything in between. Check out the souks – not only will you find all the brands you know plus some you don't, but you'll have fun haggling with the colourful shop owners! The Hamdan Centre is a good place to start – you'll find everything from the cheap and tacky to the exquisite and expensive.

Jewellery, Watches & Gold		
Al Manara Jewellery	Abu Dhabi Mall	645 7575
Bvlgari	Abu Dhabi Mall	644 4363
Damas Jewellery	Marina Mall	681 2391
Eastern Jewellery	Khalifa St	676 3958
Khalid Saleh Jewellers	Hamed Centre	632 1012
Khalifa Jewellery	Abu Dhabi Mall	644 0525
Mansour Jewellery	Abu Dhabi Mall	645 8645
Omega	Abu Dhabi Mall	645 6113
Swatch	Abu Dhabi Mall	645 4674
Mont Blanc	Al Ain Mall	751 2211
Rivoli	Al Ain Mall	751 2211

Kids' Items

Other Options → Clothes [p.154]
Family Explorer

No matter what age your kids are, you'll find plenty of shops that sell all those "must have" toys and games. For babies and toddlers, there are loads of outlets selling baby goods, from clothes to cots to car seats. For older kids, the UAE is a great place to buy gadgets and toys like computer games and music makers. Remember, when shopping for kids, keep it age appropriate and put safety before price – even a great bargain should be passed over if you are concerned the toy is of sub standard quality. To get the whole picture on shopping for kids, plus tons of other useful info, check out the *Family Explorer* – it is packed with facts and tips for families with children up to the age of 14 years.

Kids' Items		
Baby Shop	Co-op Complex	644 7739
	Madinat Zayed	634 7012
Early Learning Centre	Marina Mall	681 8868
	Abu Dhabi Mall	645 4766
Tammy	Marina Mall	681 2814
Mothercare	Abu Dhabi Mall	645 4894
Early Learning Centre	Al Ain Mall	03 751 6012
Baby Shop	Al Ain Mall	03 751 1933

Lingerie

Other Options → Clothes [p.154]

Emirati ladies have a reputation for being one of the highest consumers of luxury lingerie in the

world and, as testament to that, almost every mall houses a proliferation of frilly, frighteningly expensive lingerie boutiques. Every designer name in lingerie is healthily represented, so if you're on the lookout for a few decent additions to a bridal trousseau, and money is no object, you'll be in shopping heaven. However, if you veer towards the functional rather than the glamourous, there are several noteworthy alternatives. In the past year or so, lingerie chain La Senza has opened branches in several shopping malls throughout the Emirates, offering a range of underwear and nightwear at affordable prices. Woolworths stocks a great variety of lingerie at excellent value. Marks & Spencer, of course, has a staunch following for its lingerie lines, but expect to pay heavily inflated prices for the privilege of buying the UK's favourite underwear in Abu Dhabi. As long as you don't mind turning up at the cash till with your smalls nestling among the weekly shop, well regarded European lingerie labels are available in many supermarkets.

Lingerie		
La Senza	Marina Mall	681 6230
Cloud Nine	Marina Mall	681 3228
Marks & Spencer	Fatouh Al Khair Centre	621 3646
Triumph	Abu Dhabi Mall	644 0616
Woolworths	Marina Mall	681 0881
La Senza	Al Ain Mall	03 751 8515
Nayomi	Al Ain Mall	03 751 1375

Luggage & Leather

Other Options ➜ Shipping [p.147]

Good leather lasts forever. Imagination and artistry combine in a wide range of fine leather goods, from key rings, gloves or wallets, to handbags, shoes, suitcases etc. Many of the malls have expensive shops selling exclusive designer ranges. However, for more economical choices, the best place is the Hamdan Centre. There are several competitively priced shops selling leather goods and a range of suitcases, from cheap unknown brands to the well known, like Samsonite.

Medicine

Other Options ➜ General Medical Care [p.84]

There's no shortage of pharmacies or chemists in Abu Dhabi – these are indicated on shop signs by what looks like a snake wrapped around a cocktail glass. In the Emirates, you can buy prescription drugs over the counter – if you know exactly what medication you need, this saves the expense and hassle of visiting a doctor, and your friendly pharmacist is always happy to listen to symptoms and suggest a remedy. Remember to check the expiry date of medicine before purchasing it. Most pharmacies also carry a variety of beauty products, baby care items, sunscreens, perfumes etc. Each emirate has at least one pharmacy open 24 hours a day – the location and phone numbers are listed in the daily newspapers. In addition, the Municipality emergency number (Abu Dhabi 677 7929; Al Ain 03 778 8888) gives the names and locations of 24 hour pharmacies, as does the Abu Dhabi Police website (www.adpolice.gov.ae).

Complementary Medicine

Whether you are into aromatherapy or homoeopathy, flower or herbal remedies, you can now find a range of products to suit your needs. Essential oils are available in The Body Shop (Abu Dhabi and Marina Malls) whilst Holland and Barrett (Abu Dhabi Mall) carries both oils and remedies. As exciting as it is to find these products on the shelves in the Emirates, be aware – they are not cheap! It may be preferable to bring a stockpile back with you next time you visit your home country.

Music, DVDs & Videos

Other Options ➜ Music Lessons [p.213]
Musical Instruments [p.162]

Although the selection isn't as large or as up to date as in North America, Asia or Europe, you will find a number of audio and video stores selling the latest releases from all over the world. From famous international bands, Arabic or classical music, to Bollywood and Hollywood releases, Abu Dhabi caters for a variety of styles and tastes. However, CDs, DVDs and videos are only released once they have been screened (and censored, if appropriate) to ensure that they do not offend the country's moral code. Videos are in the PAL format and there are numerous video rental stores around the city – check one out in your area. Recordable CDs, DVDs, audio and videotapes are sold at major grocery stores. Rental prices range from Dhs.4 to Dhs.10 per video and around Dhs.10 (as well as a hefty deposit sometimes) per DVD.

Music, DVDs & Videos		
Abela Video	Khalidiya	666 9962
Carrefour	Marina Mall	681 7100
Virgin Megastore	Abu Dhabi Mall	644 7882

Musical Instruments

Other Options → Music Lessons [p.213]

Whether you are already an accomplished musician, or you have recently decided to explore your musical talents, you may find the selection of musical instrument stores in Abu Dhabi a little disappointing. AKM Music Centre has a decent range (including pianos) – they also sell sheet music. If you can't find what you're looking for, it may be worth a trip to Dubai where you'll find a greater choice.

Musical Instruments		
AKM Music Centre	Behind Crowne Plaza	621 9929
Sonia Electronics	Hamdan St	677 8822

Outdoor Goods

Other Options → Camping [p.180]
Hardware & DIY [p.158]

Aside from the humidity and desert creepy crawlies, the UAE has a fascinating outdoor existence, and off-roading and camping are revered pastimes for many. A weekend away offers a peaceful escape from the hustle and bustle of the city, and there are virtually no limitations on where you can pitch your tent and light your fire. For most people, the lack of heat and humidity make the winter months the best time to go. However, if you choose your location carefully – at altitude or by the sea – the summer months aren't always completely unbearable. To get kitted out with the basics for a night under the stars, or to just have some gear to enjoy a few hours in the great outdoors, check out stores listed below. If you are a particularly avid outdoor enthusiast but can't find the specialised equipment you need here, you'll have to either order it online, or bring it from home.

Outdoor Goods		
Ace Hardware	Mina Zayed Rd	673 3174
Carrefour	Airport Rd	449 4300
	Marina Mall	681 7100
Carrefour	Al Jimi Centre	03 762 9003

Party Accessories

Other Options → Party Organisers [p.258]

Most major supermarkets and stationery stores sell the basic party paraphernalia, and if you go to the more specialised shops, you'll find an even wider range. From cards, balloons, candles, table settings and room decorations to gift wrapping and fancy dress outfits, bouncy castles and entertainers, the choice for both children's and adults' parties is very comprehensive. Gray Mackenzie (612 3545) also offers a free party service. Items should be returned within five days of payment of the deposit – a minimum breakage charge of Dhs.6 per glass will be deducted from the deposit and the balance refunded. A deposit of Dhs.500 will allow you use of 24 pint beer glasses, 24 wineglasses, 2 ice buckets, 2 waiter trays, 3 bar towels and 24 coasters.

Party Accessories		
Balloon Lady, The	Dubai	04 344 1062
Flying Elephant	Shk Zayed Rd, Dubai	04 347 9170

Perfumes & Cosmetics

Other Options → Souks [p.173]

Beauty in the Emirates is big business, and whether the temperature goes up or down, there's always a busy trade in perfumes and cosmetics. Just about every perfume in the world is available here, and new fragrances are for sale almost as soon as they are launched in their country of origin. For a more personalised fragrance, look out for the local perfumeries that are in every shopping area and a vital part of the local grooming ritual. These distinctive fragrances combine a heady mix of aromatic Arabian oils which are individually blended – don't go overboard on application as one dab can last for days.

Local Perfumery

Perfumes & Cosmetics		
Areej	Marina Mall	681 5662
Body Shop	Marina Mall	645 7300
Grand Stores	Abu Dhabi Mall	631 2100
Paris Gallery	Marina Mall	681 3444
Paris Gallery	Al Ain Mall	03 751 1131

Plants & Trees

Other Options → Flowers [p.156]

If you're lucky enough to have a garden, or even a bit of a balcony, it is definitely worth planting a few shrubs, trees or bedding plants in pots, all of which can be found here at reasonable prices. Having a garden full of foliage is great for keeping the sand at bay, and it's surprising how many plants can thrive in such arid conditions, although constant watering is vital. The extra water will add substantially to your water bills, but hiring a gardener will most likely be cheaper than you imagined. Both Khalidiya (Abu Dhabi) and Qattarah (Al Ain) have several nurseries. If you can't be bothered to traipse around in one, try Ikea or Carrefour. All the larger supermarkets stock a good selection of indoor and outdoor plants but expect to pay a few dirhams more for convenience.

Second-Hand Items

Other Options → Books [p.152]
Cars [p.154]

For buying or selling second-hand items, such as furniture, cookers etc, take the time to browse through the Classifieds section of the local newspapers (as well as the Abu Dhabi sections of the Dubai based papers) – you may have to make a lot of phone calls but it's worth it when you bag a great bargain! Alternatively, check out the supermarket notice boards.

Shoes

Other Options → Beach Wear [p.150]
Clothes [p.154]

Whether your penchant is for Doc Martins, flip flops or kitten heeled mules, shoes come in as many shapes and sizes as there are feet. A wide range of styles is available, from high fashion to comfortable casual wear, in a variety of colours, materials and sizes. Training shoes tend to be more reasonably priced here than elsewhere, although addicts may find that their favourite styles are often one season behind.

Shoes		
Aldo	Marina Mall	6814426
Florsheim (Bhs)	Abu Dhabi Mall	645 8400
Italian Shoes	Hamdan Centre	632 3169
K Corner	Abu Dhabi Mall	645 6090
Milano Shoes	Abu Dhabi Mall	645 4836
Nine West	Marina Mall	681 5211
Shoe Mart	Madinat Zayed	634 6461
K Corner	Al Ain Mall	03 751 2245
Shoe Mart	Al Ain Mall	03 7751 3100

Sporting Goods

Abu Dhabi is a great location for a variety of sports, from the more common ones, such as tennis, sailing, golf or football, to more unusual activities like sand skiing. Try the general sports shops listed below for items like squash racquets or sports clothing. You can also find specialist sports shops around the city, and unless yours is an unusual sport in the Emirates or you require a more specialised piece of equipment, you should have little difficulty finding what you require.

Sporting Goods		
Ace Hardware	Mina Zayed Rd	673 3174
London Sports	Hamdan Centre	632 9783
Masaoods	Salam St	050 711 4795
Sportex	Abu Dhabi Mall	644 5551
Sun & Sand Sports	Marina Mall	674 6299
Alpha Sports	Al Ain Mall	03751 9788
Carrefour	Al Jimi Centre	03 762 9003
Gulf Sea Sports	Al Ain	03 765 5391

Sports Shop

Tailoring

Other Options → Clothes [p.154]
Textiles [p.166]

With all the beautiful fabrics available in Abu Dhabi, as well as the proliferation of tailors, it's well worth buying a few yards of material and having items made up to your specification – whether you are after curtains, cushions or clothing, almost anything your mind can conceive is possible! When trying a tailor for the first time, check the quality of work with a single item before you order a whole new wardrobe. Tailors can copy a pattern that you supply, or recreate an original item if you can leave it with them for a few days. Most tailors have a range of pattern books in-house that you can browse through; alternatively check out a bookstore for pattern books. Even pictures from magazines can be used as the basis for a design. The tailor will also advise on how many metres of material are needed (buy a little extra to be on the safe side). Most tailors provide buttons, shoulder pads, cotton and zips etc. Confirm the price (obviously the more complex the pattern, the higher the price) before committing to having it made, and make sure that it includes the cost of the lining, if appropriate. A good tailor should tack it all together so that you can have a trying on session before the final stitching. When it is finished, try it on again. Don't be bashful about asking them to put something right if you are not completely happy. In addition to the numerous tailors, there are specialist embroidery shops catering mainly for the heavily decorated Arabic version of the Western style white wedding dress. Embroidery can create a wonderful effect, especially for a special occasion. However, as embroidery is intricate work, expect to pay a lot more for the finished item.

Choosing a tailor is often based on word of mouth. Most textile shops however, will also recommend some. For our recommended ones, see the Textiles table (below).

Textiles

Other Options → Carpets [p.153]

The shops in the New Souk are a treasure trove of textiles, colours, textures and weaves from all over the world. Shimmering threads adorn thin voile and broderie anglaise, satin and silk tempt, and velvets jostle with peach skin, although good drill cottons are still difficult to find. Serge and wool worsted simply beg to be made into classy gent's suits and taken to colder climes. Shop around as the choice is virtually unlimited and prices are negotiable. Look out for any sales, occurring quite frequently in this area.

Textiles		
Cairo Textiles	New Souk	622 4567
Paris Textiles	New Souk	622 5030
Rivoli Textiles	Hamdan St	679 2996

Places to Shop

The following section covers the three main Abu Dhabi and Al Ain malls plus the numerous additional smaller shopping malls, as well as a variety of souks.

Shopping Malls

The attractive, imaginatively designed, modern shopping malls are one of the highlights of shopping here. They are generally spacious and fully air conditioned, offering a great escape from the often searing heat of the city. Here you will find virtually every kind of store you can imagine, from supermarkets or card shops, to clothes emporiums and specialist perfume shops. However, the popular malls are more than just a place to shop, for in the evenings and especially on the weekends, they are buzzing with activity as people meet, eat, pose and people watch. During festive occasions such as Eid or Ramadan, the larger malls are venues for special events such as dancing or magic shows, often featuring acts from around the world. The malls also feature numerous raffles during these months – the prize for the lucky few is usually a car. Most malls have a food court, offering a range of food options for hungry shoppers, from the ubiquitous hamburger, to Arabic mezze, Italian or Mexican food. Some malls also have children's play areas, arcade games and cinemas, and most have convenient, extensive and free parking. The following are the more popular, larger malls in town.

Shopping Malls – Main

Abu Dhabi Mall

Location → Nr Beach Rotana Hotel · Al Meena | **645 4858**
Hours → 10:00 - 22:00; Fri 15:30 - 22:00
Web/email → www.abudhabimall.com | **Map Ref** → 4-B4

Regarded as one of 'the' places to shop in Abu Dhabi, this four storey mall is also one of the largest in the UAE, housing over 200 retail outlets selling everything the true shopaholic's heart desires. Renowned retail chains such as The Body Shop, Mango, Massimo Dutti, Virgin Mega Store, and Paris Gallery, as well as the huge Co-op hypermarket, vie for the attention of over 26,000 visitors daily. Shopping convenience is paramount here – with 3,000 covered parking spaces, over 15 elevators, restaurants on every floor, a nine screen Cineplex, a huge food court and even a children's theme park, every possible shopper's whim has been covered.

Abu Dhabi Mall by Night

Books, Cards & Gifts
Book Gallery
Carlton Cards
Gulf Greetings

Cinema
Century Cinemas

Clothes
Bhs
Bershka
Betty Barclay
Bossini
Evans
Giordano
Guess
Hang Ten
Kenzo
Levi's
Mango
Massimo Dutti
Mexx
Next
Pierre Cardin
Pull & Bear
Springfield
U2
XOXO

Department Stores
Grand Stores
Jashanmal
Liwa Stores
Salam Studios

Electronics
Axiom Telecom
Bang & Olufsen
Radio Shack
Virgin Megastore

Eyewear
Al Jaber
Yateem

Food
Baskin Robbins
Café Du Roi
Cinnabon
Coffee & More (Internet)
Dunkin' Donuts
Fujiyama (Japanese)
Hardees
Il Firno (Italian)
KFC
McDonald's
Manchow Wok (Chinese)
Pizza Hut
Street Net Café (Internet)
Subway
The Sweet Factory

Home Accessories
Descamps
Frette (White Corner)
Home One
Lifestyle
Zone/Bombay

Hypermarket
Abu Dhabi Co-op

Jewellery & Gold
Alfred Dunhill
Al Futtaim Jewellery
Al Manara Jewellery – Cartier
Bvlgari
Damas
Mont Blanc
Tanagra (Allied)

Kids' Stuff
A 11 Z
La Senza Girl
Mothercare
Premaman

Lingerie
La Senza
Nayomi
Triumph

Music & Videos
Virgin Megastore

Perfumes & Cosmetics
MAC
Paris Gallery
Red Earth
The Body Shop

Services
Al Masood Travel
Dry Cleaning
UAE Exchange

Shoes
Aldo
Ecco
K Corner
Milano
Nine West

Sporting Goods
Mega Sport

Watches
Omega
Rivoli

Al Ain Mall

Location → Al Qwaitat St · Al Ain | 03 766 0333
Hours → Sat - Tue 10:00 - 22:00 (Wed/Thu 23:00); Fri 14:00 - 23:00
Web/email → www.alainmall.org | Map Ref → 15-C3

The Al Ain Mall is a haven for shoppers seeking refuge from the harsh desert heat. Covering three floors, this modern and bright building contains over 100,000 square metres of shopping and entertainment. Offering everything from tailoring to telecom, and several anchor stores such as Spinneys, Home Centre and Paris Gallery, there's more than enough to satisfy even the most hard core shopper. If you're all shopped out, head for the family entertainment area with its 12 lane bowling alley and cinemas – there's even an indoor ice skating rink on the ground floor! Covered parking for 1,000 cars is located on the ground floor.

Al Ain Mall

Books, Cards & Gifts

Gulf Greetings

Cinema

Grand Cineplex

Clothes

Can Can
Etam
Evans
Giordano
Hang Ten
Liz Claiborne
Mexx
Motivi
Naf Naf
Next
Paul Jordan
River Island
Splash
Vid Rio

Department Stores

Grand Stores
Salam Studios & Stores

Electronics

Jumbo Electronics
Phone Station
Plug Ins

Eyewear

Al Ain Optical
Paris Gallery
Yateem Optical

Food

Baskin Robbins
Burger King
Café Du Roi
China Wall
Dubai Mughal Restaurant
Dunkin' Donuts
Gloria Jean's Coffees
Hardees
Jabal Al Quds
KFC
La Cabana Café
Pizza Hut
Sombrero
Starbucks
Sweet.Com

Home Accessories

Design Furniture
Grand Stores
Home Centre
Lifestyle

Jewellery & Gold

Al Mandoos Jewellery
Claires
Mont Blanc
Oriental Stores

Kids' Stuff

Baby Shop
Banati
Chicco & Bambini
Early Learning Centre
Hobby Center
Mothercare
Tweety Kids Saloon

Lingerie

Cloud Nine
Heaven
La Senza
Nayomi
Velvet

Medicine

Al Manara Pharmacy
Dr. Nutrition Center
Herbalos
Lifestyle Nutritionist (Sport One)

Perfumes & Cosmetics

Arabian Oud
Grand Stores
Lifestyle
Mac Cosmetics
Make Up Forever
Nektar
Paris Gallery
Salam Studio & Stores
Yas International Service

Services

Al Ansari Exchange
Class Cleopatra (Women)
Cut R Us (Men)
Dubai Islamic Bank
National Bank of Abu Dhabi
Union National Bank

Shoes

Cesare Paciotti
K Corner
Milano
Mocassino
Shoe Mart

Sporting Goods

Alfa Sports

Watches

Rivoli
Swatch

Marina Mall

Location → Breakwater · Abu Dhabi | 681 8300
Hours → 10:00 - 22:00 Fri 14:00 - 22:00
Web/email → www.marinamall.ae | Map Ref → 10-B4

Situated on the Breakwater, far from the hustle and bustle of the city, this mall offers a breath of fresh (sea) air to its customers! Here you'll find 160 outlets, including many of your favourite shops, such as Woolworths, Plug-Ins, Sun and Sand Sports, Carrefour and Ikea. Restaurants, fast food outlets and coffee shops aplenty offer fuel for weary shoppers. Bargain hunters will love the big sale period, which lasts from 15th January to 28th February. If you ever get bored of shopping (as if!), the nine screen Cinestar complex, Foton World and the musical fountains near the main entrance will keep you entertained.

Marina Mall

Books, Cards & Gifts
Book Corner
Crystal Gallery
Gulf Greetings
Mont Blanc
Scarabee
Tiffany & Co.

Cinema
Cinestar Cinemas

Clothes
Accessorize
Bossini
ELLE
French Connection FCUK
Gap
Gasoline
Giordano
Hang Ten
Levis
Mexx
Miss Sixty
Primavera
Promod
Springfield
Stradivarius
Truworths
Woolworths
Zara

Electronics
Axiom Telecom
Carrefour
Plug-Ins
Radio Shack

Eyewear
Optical Centre
Yateem Optician

Food
Baskin Robbins
Beverly Hills Juice
Burger King
Café Ritazza
Dunkin' Donuts
El Torito
Fuddrukers
Gerard Café
Gloria Jean's Coffees
Hardwalls
Hatem
La Brioche
Lips The Café
London Dairy
Popeye's
Starbucks Coffee
Sweet Factory

Home Accessories
Bayti
Carrefour
Chen One
IKEA
Pier Import

Hypermarket
Carrefour

Jewellery & Gold
Al Futtaim Jewellery
Bvlgari
Damas Jewellery

Kids' Stuff
A 11 Z
B-BUSHH
Early Learning Centre
Kids Land Salon
Ovo

Lingerie
Caresse
Cloud Nine
Girl 2000
La Senza
Nayomi
Silhouettes
Wolford
Women'secret

Medicine
Dr. Nutrition Centre

Perfumes & Cosmetics
Adam & Eve
Areej
Paris Gallery
The Body Shop

Services
Al Ansari Exchange
Smokers' Centre

Shoes
Aldo
Cesare Paciotti
Hush Puppies
Nine West
Via Spiga

Sporting Goods
Alfa Sports
Sun & Sand Sports

Watches
Rivoli
Rolex
Swatch
The Watch House

Shopping Malls – Other

Abu Dhabi Co-operative Society Complex

Location ➜ Nr Le Meridien Htl · Shk Zayed 1st St | 644 0808
Hours ➜ 08:00 - 24:00
Web/email ➜ na | Map Ref ➜ 4-B4

This older shopping centre still buzzes, especially on weekends and evenings! Its main draws are Splash (trendy, inexpensive fashions), Shoe Mart (huge range of shoes), Lifestyle (funky gifts and much more) and Baby Shop. Other small shops include computer suppliers and ladies' fashion outlets.

Al Ain Town Square

Location ➜ Al Khalifa St | 03 766 8830
Hours ➜ 10:00-13:00 17:00-23:30
Web/email ➜ alain2@bhomes.com | Map Ref ➜ na

Located in the heart of the city, Al Ain Town Square is a tranquil spot and a good escape from the noise of bustling urban life. Set on wide terraces and shaded by impressive tents, this outdoor shopping arcade hosts several retail stores and market style shops along with seven restaurants. The musical fountain is a good attraction for the kids. Step in and enjoy a relaxing stroll, a coffee or a meal with the family.

Shopping Malls

Abela Superstore	Khalidiya	667 4675
Abu Dhabi Co-op Society	Shk Zayed 1st St	644 0808
Abu Dhabi Mall	Al Meena	645 4858
Al Ahlia Prisunic	Al Khalidiyah	681 2997
Al Falah Plaza	Al Falah St	642 5800
Al Hana Centre	Corniche Rd West	681 6823
Al Jernain Center	Shk Zayed 1st St	na
Al Muhairy Centre	Shk Zayed 1st St	632 2228
City Centre	Shk Hamdan St	627 7770
Dana Plaza	Shk Zayed 1st St	665 1333
Fotouh Al Khair Ctr	Shk Rashid B Saeed St	621 1133
Hamdan Centre	Shk Hamdan St	na
Khalifa Centre	Tourist Club Area	667 9900
Lamcy Dept. Store	Khalidiya St	621 6755
Liwa Centre	Shk Hamdan St	632 0344
Lulu Centre	Al Salam St	677 9786
Madinat Zayed Shopping & Gold Ctr	East Rd	631 8555
Marina Mall	Breakwater	681 8300
Mina Centre	Al Meena	673 4848
MultiBrand	St. Madinat Zayed	621 9700
Rotana Mall	Shk Zayed 1st St	na
Al Ain Mall	Al Qwaitat St	03 766 0333
Al Ain Town Square	Al Khalifa St	03 766 8830
Al Falah Plaza	Al Khalifa St	03 766 2200
Al Jimi Centre	Al Jimi St	03 763 8883

Al Falah Plaza

Location ➜ Al Falah St | 642 5800
Hours ➜ See timings below
Web/email ➜ na | Map Ref ➜ 5-A3

Situated on Old Passport Road near Habib Bank, this mall is a cheap and cheerful place to stock up on household essentials. Apart from the supermarket on the ground floor, you'll also find a music shop, a pharmacy, a fast food restaurant and a café – and much more!

Timings: *Supermarket 09.00 - 23.30. Stores Sat - Thurs 09:00 - 14:00 & 16:30 - 23:00, Fri 09:00 - 23:30*

Al Hana Shopping Centre

Location ➜ Opp Eldiar · Corniche Rd West | 681 6823
Hours ➜ 07:00 - 24:00
Web/email ➜ na | Map Ref ➜ 9-E2

Fronted by exclusive designer stores, this shopping centre is a haven for the selective shopper. Located opposite the Corniche, it boasts a café on the ground floor with a beautiful waterfront view – an ideal spot to enjoy a refreshing brew when the weather cools.

City Centre

Location ➜ Shk Hamdan St | 627 7770
Hours ➜ 08:00 - 13:00 17:00 - 20:00
Web/email ➜ na | Map Ref ➜ 8-C2

You'll find clothes, sportswear, watches, electronics, music and more at this lively and affordable mall. Unlike the one in Dubai, and with no affiliation, this City Centre is not always packed to the rafters. It does, however, have its own café.

Dana Plaza

Location ➜ Nr Le Meridien Htl · Shk Zayed 1st St | 665 1333
Hours ➜ 10:00 - 13:00 17:00 - 23:30
Web/email ➜ na | Map Ref ➜ 9-C1

Dana Plaza is packed with quality outlets selling everything from cosmetics and stationery to household goods, linen and fashions for the whole

family. For discounts, head for the third floor, or settle down for a coffee break in the café on the ground floor.

Fotouh Al Khair Centre

Location ➔ Shk Rashid B Saeed Al Makt St | **621 1133**
Hours ➔ 10:00 - 22:00
Web/email ➔ fotouhkc@emirates.net.ae | **Map Ref** ➔ 8-E1

Several of the world's favourite brands are jammed into this spacious mall – Marks & Spencer, Wallis, Monsoon, Mango, Nine West and many more. It comes with quirky parking though – Dhs.5 per hour for underground parking, and reserved spaces out front just for ladies and families.

Fotouh Al Khair Centre

Hamdan Centre

Location ➔ Shk Hamdan St | **na**
Hours ➔ 10:00 - 13:30 17:00 - 22:30 Fri 17:00 - 22-30 only
Web/email ➔ na | **Map Ref** ➔ 8-C2

Located in the heart of the city, this vibrant centre is a good place to buy sports equipment, leather, clothing, shoes and touristy knick knacks, all at reasonable prices. It also houses a pharmacy and the Al Massa Cinema complex.

Khalifa Centre

Location ➔ Tourist Club Area | **667 9900**
Hours ➔ 08:30 - 13:30 16:30 - 22:30
Web/email ➔ kcenter@emirates.net.ae | **Map Ref** ➔ 4-B4

This ethnic mall is teeming with craft and souvenir shops selling various treasures of Arabia. You will also find Persian and Baluchi carpets – it's the perfect place to take your out-of-town visitors looking for mementos of their holiday.

Liwa Centre

Location ➔ Shk Hamdan St | **632 0344**
Hours ➔ 09:30 - 13:30 16:30 - 18:30 09:00 - 24:00 Thu
Web/email ➔ na | **Map Ref** ➔ 8-D2

Head to this centre on Sheikh Hamdan Street for jewellery, clothes, makeup, perfume and more – be sure to visit the vibrant food court on the second level, or relax in the coffee shop, which stays open until midnight.

Lulu Centre

Location ➔ Al Salam St | **677 9786**
Hours ➔ 09:00 - 13:00 16:30 - 22:30 16:30 - 22:30 Fri
Web/email ➔ emkegroup@emirates.net.ae | **Map Ref** ➔ 8-A2

This mall sells everything under the sun – from electronics, sportswear and toys, to stationery, clothing, cosmetics and travel accessories – you really can shop 'till you drop! Prices are reasonable too – so what are you waiting for?

Madinat Zayed Shopping Centre & Gold Centre

Location ➔ Nr Main Post Office · East Rd | **631 8555**
Hours ➔ 10:00 - 23:00
Web/email ➔ na | **Map Ref** ➔ 5-A4

Shopaholics will love this mall – it has around 400 outlets selling just about everything. The Madinat Zayed Gold Centre, adjacent to the main mall, glitters with the finest gold, diamond and pearl jewellery. The supervised toddlers' area and the games arcade will keep the kids entertained while you shop.

Mina Centre

Location ➔ Nr Toys R Us · Al Meena | **673 4848**
Hours ➔ 10:00 - 22:00
Web/email ➔ na | **Map Ref** ➔ 7-B4

It's huge, it's new, and it's the place to be if you're looking for modern French furniture (2XL), a good book (Jarir Bookstore) or bargain electrical goods (Cost Less Electronics). It also boasts a huge Co-op, a kiddies' amusement area and even crazy golf.

MultiBrand

Location ➔ Madinat Zayed | **621 9700**
Hours ➔ 10:00 - 22:00 17:00 - 22:00 Fri
Web/email ➔ mbrand@emirates.net.ae | **Map Ref** ➔ 8-B2

This large, open plan store houses well known shops such as Mothercare, Claire's, Next, and Oasis. If your taste in fashion is more USA than UK, you'll find the Liz Claiborne outlet a welcome addition. Alternatively, indulge your shoe fetish at Milano.

Rotana Mall

Location ➜ Nr Al Ahlia Prisunic · Shk Zayed 1st St | na
Hours ➜ 09:00 - 13:00 16:00 - 22:00
Web/email ➜ na Map Ref ➜ 9-D1

A stone's throw from the Abu Dhabi Corniche, this mall is the ideal place to shop for quality furnishings, including carpets and antiques, Arabic pottery and wall hangings. It also has a good range of clothing and footwear, and a branch of The Body Shop.

Souks

Souk is the Arabic word for market or place where any kind of goods are bought or exchanged. Historically, dhows from the Far East, China, Ceylon and India would offload their cargoes, and the goods would be haggled over in the souks adjacent to the docks. Souks were very much a centre for life here, providing a place to meet friends and socialise outside of the family. Over the years the items on sale have diversified dramatically from spices, silks and perfumes to include electronic goods and the latest kitsch consumer trends. Traditionally, the souks were a maze of shady alleyways, with small shops opening on to the paths. Nowadays most of these have been replaced by large, air conditioned centres. Although Abu Dhabi's souks aren't as fascinating as others in the Arab world, such as Fes in Morocco or Mutrah in Oman, they are worth a visit for their bustling atmosphere, eclectic variety of goods, and the traditional way of doing business. Abu Dhabi's main souk area stretches from Sheikh Hamdan Street almost to the Corniche. Some of the souks have porters who will carry your goods and follow you around for a few dirhams (agree on a price though, before they start).

Al Ain Souk

Location ➜ Zayed Bin Sultan St | na
Hours ➜ 09:00 - 22:00
Web/email ➜ na Map Ref ➜ 15-C3

Also known as the Central or Old Souk, the Al Ain Souk is a great place to explore, savour the local atmosphere, and practise your bargaining skills. A mixture of household goods on sale include pots and pans, plastic buckets of every size and colour, and fruit and vegetables – and the prices are good. The souk itself is a rather ramshackle affair but it is certainly different from many of the modern, rather sterile, air conditioned markets that are appearing everywhere.

Fish, Meat & Produce Souk

Location ➜ Btn Al Istigal/Al Nasr St · Al Markaziyah | na
Hours ➜ 07:00 - 14:00 17:00 - 22:00
Web/email ➜ na Map Ref ➜ 8-E2

Follow your nose to this fish, meat and vegetable supermarket, where you can get fresh produce by the kilo at good prices – often lower than in the supermarkets. Early birds will bag the freshest produce! Situated between Al Nasr and Istiglal Streets.

Iranian Souk

Location ➜ Nr Al Meena Carpet Market · Al Meena | na
Hours ➜ 08:00 - 23:00
Web/email ➜ na Map Ref ➜ 7-B4

It may not be air conditioned, but fresh batches of Iranian goods arrive every three days by dhow or barge to this authentic souk, which sells everything from household goods and terracotta urns, to decorative metal, cane and glass items. Photography is prohibited.

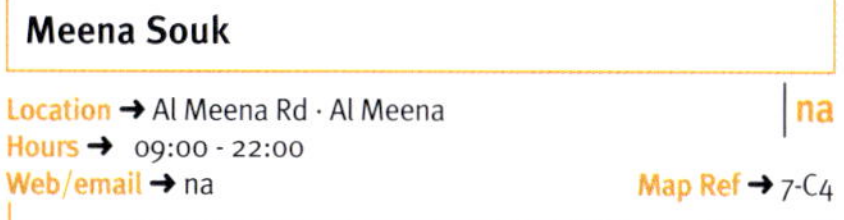

Meena Souk

Location ➜ Al Meena Rd · Al Meena | na
Hours ➜ 09:00 - 22:00
Web/email ➜ na Map Ref ➜ 7-C4

This souk should be on your list if you're looking for carpets, but don't get duped into buying over-priced machine made copies of traditional designs. Also known as the Afghan Souk, it is located on Meena Road near the main port area.

Mwaifa Souk

Location ➜ Nr Jebel R/A, Shk Khalfia B Zayed St · Al Mutarad | na
Hours ➜ 10:00 - 22:00
Web/email ➜ na Map Ref ➜ 14-D3

This modern souk is a long strip of handy shops, including big guns like Choithrams, Shoe Mart and The Body Shop. There is also a bakery, a butcher, a baby shop and a toy shop – and even more outlets can be found across the road!

Activities

EXPLORER

Activities

Activities

Other Options → Exploring [p.113]
Going Out [p.219]

No matter what the season, Abu Dhabi's visitors and residents alike will discover a variety of engaging activities to fulfil almost any interest or hobby, ranging from dramatics to flower arranging; poetry to yoga. Groups catering to different interests are increasing, as are venues for classes and workshops. A word to the wise: calling in or stopping by is often the best way to get accurate information about what's on in a particular venue.

Warm winters provide the perfect environment for outdoor activities. Taking advantage of its position on an island, Abu Dhabi offers many options for seafaring types, from sailing to swimming to snorkelling. In addition, land access rules are relatively relaxed, so it's easy to travel into the mountains or onto remote beaches.

As usual, we welcome your suggestions on any changes and inclusions in this book for next year's edition. If you belong to any club, organisation or group, however small, large, official or unofficial – we'd like to hear from you. Log on to www.Explorer-Publishing.com and pen down your thoughts.

For information on where to buy sports equipment, refer to Sporting Goods [p.164].

Sports

The warm winters in the Emirates provide the perfect environment for athletes and outdoor enthusiasts, but amazingly, even in the hottest months you can find dedicated people enjoying their favourite activity!

Traditional favourites such as tennis, golf, aerobics, and rugby abound, but there are also more radical pursuits such as skydiving, rock climbing, mountain biking and caving. Sometimes word of mouth is the best way to learn about your favourite hobby, so in the event that it's not covered here, ask around.

With the proximity of the Gulf waters, it's no surprise that a large variety in water sports is available, including scuba diving, sailing, surfing, and water skiing. Bear in mind that while the water usually appears tranquil and harmless, there are dangers such as stingrays, jellyfish, and occasional strong currents and riptides. At beach parks, pay attention to the lifeguard's flag, and if you're at one of the unguarded public beaches take greater care.

One of the most popular pastimes is getting out into the wilderness. You too will likely feel the lure of the desert, the dramatic wadis and the uncompromising mountains. If you enjoy camping, hiking, or dune bashing, we suggest you check out the *Off-Road Explorer (UAE)* by Explorer Publishing.

Aerobics

Other Options → Beach, Health & Sports Clubs [p.205]
Dance Classes [p.209]

The Abu Dhabi aerobic scene is a paradise for everyone obsessed with throwing their legs and arms around or pumping some heavy weights to funky music. Crazy... Seriously, you will have a good choice of classes. Check with the club of your choice for timetables and bookings, as they can get crowded. You can either join one of the health clubs, buy a voucher for ten aerobic sessions for about Dhs.200, or turn up as and when you want. Prices per class are between Dhs.20 - 30.

Amusement Centres

Other Options → Amusement Parks [p.178]

Foton World

Location → Marina Mall · Abu Dhabi | 681 5526
Hours → 10:00 - 23:00
Web/email → na | Map Ref → 10-B4

A big range of computer and video games, carousels and other funfair facilities awaits you. Foton World is not a 'learning through playing' centre, but a typical high tech amusement outlet – a good option for keeping your kids busy while you shop.

Cost: *Entry free. Dhs.35 for unlimited number of rides.*

Fun Island

Location → Al Jernain Center · Shk Zayed 1st St | 665 9009
Hours → 10:00 - 22:00; Fri 16:00 - 22:00
Web/email → na | Map Ref → 9-B1

Fun Island caters mostly to kids under five with a large area of soft play facilities: tube slides, ball ponds, hanging ropes and cruiser rollers. Also includes a Lego room and computer games for older children. Birthday party packages are provided.

Entrance: *Dhs.15 per child.*

Fun World

Location → Opp Cultural Foundation · Al Hosn | 632 2255
Hours → 10:00 - 13:30 16:30 - 23:00; Fri 15:00 - 23:00
Web/email → na | Map Ref → 9-A1

Fun World offers computer games that are intended to encourage kids to draw, paint, work out puzzles, thread beads and try their hand at sand art. There's also a soft play area for the youngest generation, a coffee shop and children's hairdresser all on the same floor.

Cost: *Either buy separate tokens or a wristband for Dhs.20, which allows unlimited use of the facilities.*

Gymboree Play & Music

Location → Khalidia Palace Htl · Khalidiya | 665 8882
Hours → 08:00 - 18:00
Web/email → www.gymboree.com | Map Ref → 10-E2

Designed to create educational and fun interaction between parents and their offspring. Depending on age, there are various classes and programmes scheduled – you can even bring babies as young as six months. Theme and birthday parties can be arranged.

Cost: *Dhs.55 for 45 minutes; monthly memberships are also available.*

Kids Play

Location → Toys R Us · Meena Rd | 673 2332
Hours → 10:00 - 22:00
Web/email → na | Map Ref → 7-B4

The centre uses the latest and safest indoor soft play equipment for children under 14 years. The area includes a monorail, a padded play area with whirlpools filled with balls, climbing frames, slides, monkey climb etc.

Entrance: *Dhs.10 (toddlers); Dhs.15 (four years or more).*

Toy Town

Location → Abu Dhabi Mall · Al Meena | 645 5567
Hours → 09:30 - 23:00; Fri 15:00 - 22:00
Web/email → toytown@emirates.net.ae | Map Ref → 4-B4

Spread over 4,000 square metres, this well designed playground transports you to the jungle! Look out for a gigantic spider climbing up the wall and a rubber snake hiding under some stones. Other facilities include a water slide, bumper cars, roller coaster and much more.

Cost: *Between Dhs.2 - 15, depending on the season and time.*

Foton World

Amusement Parks

Other Options → Amusement Centres [p.177]
Water Parks [p.202]

Hili Fun City & Ice Rink

Location → Mohammed Bin Khalifa St · Al Ain | 03 784 5542
Hours → 16:00 - 22:00; Fri 09:00 - 22:00
Web/email → na | Map Ref → 13-B1

The largest amusement park in the Gulf, covering a total area of 86 hectares. Entertainment options include thrilling rides from runaway trains to alien encounters, which can be enjoyed by people of all ages.

Timings: *(Winter) Sun - Wed 16:00 - 22:00; Thu, Fri and public holidays 9:00 - 22:00. (Summer) Sun - Wed 17:00 - 23:00; Thu, Fri and public holidays 9:00 - 23:00. Tue & Wed women and children only. Closed Sat.*

WonderLand Theme & Water Park

Location → Nr Creekside Park · Dubai | 04 324 3222
Hours → 15:00 - 21:00; Thu & Fri 17:00 - 24:00
Web/email → www.wonderlanduae.com | Map Ref → UAE-C2

Experience numerous exhilarating attractions, thrilling rides and games. Facilities include wet and dry rides, go-karting, paintballing, an air conditioned family entertainment centre with a soft play area, video and skill games, bumper cars and food outlets, to name but a few. Refer to the *Dubai Explorer* for more information.

Timings: *Call for details on specified days for ladies, families and schools.*

Archery

There are currently no archery clubs in the Abu Dhabi emirate. However, enthusiasts may wish to visit the small and informal Dubai Archery Group in Dubai (04 344 2591), or the Shooting Club in Ras Al Khaimah (07 236 3622). In addition, the Hatta Fort Hotel has a range and offers classes, both of which are open to hotel residents and visitors. For more information, consult the Sports section of the *Dubai Explorer* by Explorer Publishing.

Hatta Fort Hotel

Location → Hatta Fort Hotel · Hatta | 04 852 3211
Hours → Timings on request
Web/email → www.jebelali-international.com | Map Ref → UAE-D3

The hotel's archery range is 25 metres long and has eight standard target stands. The recurve bow, which is curved forward at the ends and straightens out when the bow is drawn, is suitable for adults and children over the age of ten.

***Cost**: Hotel residents Dhs.10 for 30 mins; visitors Dhs.30 for 30 minutes.*

Badminton

Badminton Club

Location → Club, The · Al Meena | 673 1111
Hours → Wed 19:15 - 23:00
Web/email → www.the-club.com | Map Ref → 7-A2

Players of any standard are welcome to join in the weekly social gathering, although membership of The Club is first required. When the quality and numbers of players permit, league games may be organised against local opposing teams.

Basketball

Al Ain Men's College

Location → Al Ain Men's College · Al Ain | 03 782 0888
Hours → Timings on request
Web/email → na | Map Ref → 17-B2

Teams wishing to play in the AAMC basketball tournament should contact the college for further details. David Jens, the Physical Education Director, can be contacted for information on local basketball, soccer and volleyball teams as well.

Boat & Yacht Charters

Other Options → Corniche Cruises [p.123]

Blue Dolphin Speed Boat Charters

Location → Htl InterContinental · Bainuna St | 666 9392
Hours → Timings on request
Web/email → www.interconti.com | Map Ref → 10-C1

Blue Dolphin has 31 foot Barracuda speedboats, equipped with two 140 hp engines available for charter. Trips cost Dhs.800 for four hours, alternatively the boats can be hired on an hourly basis for Dhs.250 (minimum two hours).

Shuja Yacht

Location → Le Royal Meridien · Al Khalifa St | 695 0539
Hours → 17:30 - 23:00 20:30 - 23:00
Web/email → www.lemeridien.com | Map Ref → 8-B2

The Shuja Yacht is a double decker motor cruiser, available for charter for private individuals or parties. It has a maximum capacity of 140 passengers and is chartered out with experienced crewmembers, including the captain.

***Contact**: Call the above number for individual reservation and 695 0510 for a group (meeting, seminar or private).*

***Rates**: Negotiable, depending on the size of the booking.*

Bowling

Abu Dhabi Tourist Club

Location → Nr Le Meridien Htl · Tourist Club Area | 672 3400
Hours → 08:00 - 24:00
Web/email → adclub@emirates.net.ae | Map Ref → 7-D1

This 12 lane centre is popular with Nationals and expats alike, especially in the evenings and also in the summer months when the heat drives everyone indoors. The layout is simple, with no frills, although soft drinks and snacks are available.

***Cost**: Dhs.7 for one game; Dhs.3 for shoe rental. Take your own socks, or buy them for Dhs.4.*

Khalifa International Bowling Centre

Location → Nr Zayed Sports Complex · Abu Dhabi | 403 4648
Hours → 12:00 - 24:00; Thu 10:00 - 24:00; Fri 14:00 - 24:00
Web/email → na | Map Ref → 2-B1

This state of the art bowling centre boasts 40 lanes and is apparently one of the most modern bowling

alleys in the world. The fee for playing one game is Dhs.7, shoe hire is Dhs.2 and the billiard table costs Dhs.15 for one hour.

Camel Rides

Other Options → Camel Racing [p.123]

Al Ain Golden Sands Camel Safaris

Location → Hilton Al Ain · Al Ain | 03 768 8006
Hours → 09:00 - 13:00 17:30 - 20:00
Web/email → na | Map Ref → 15-D4

For something a bit more adventurous, Al Ain Golden Sands Camel Safaris offers a selection of tours which include camel rides over the dunes of Bida Bint Saud. All the tours include transfers from Al Ain, Arabic coffee and dates.

Camping

Other Options → Desert Driving Courses [p.210]

With the weather rarely anything other than sunny, and some spectacular locations in various parts of the country, the UAE is a great place for camping. The best time to go is between October and April, as in the summer it can get unbearably hot sleeping outside. Choose between the peace and stillness of the desert or camp among the wadis and mountains, next to trickling streams in picturesque oases. Good campsites can be found only short distances from tarmac roads, so a four wheel drive is not necessarily required. Although the UAE has a low rainfall, be very careful in and near wadis during winter, as flash floods can occur.

For most people a basic amount of equipment will suffice. This may include:

- Tent (to avoid creepy crawlies/rare rain showers)
- Lightweight sleeping bag (or light blankets and sheets)
- Thin mattress (or air bed)
- Torches and spare batteries (a head torch is a useful investment)
- Cool box (to avoid food spoiling/keep away from insects)
- Water (always take too much)
- Food and drink
- Camping stove, firewood or BBQ and charcoal (if preferred)
- Matches!
- Insect repellent and antihistamine cream
- First aid kit (including any personal medication)
- Sun protection (hats, sunglasses, sunscreen, long sleeves)
- Jumper/warm clothing for cooler evenings
- Spade
- Toilet rolls
- Rubbish bags (ensure you leave nothing behind)
- Navigation equipment (maps, compass, Global Positioning System or GPS)

For the adventurous with a four wheel drive, there are endless possibilities for camping in remote locations among some of the best scenery in the UAE. The many locations in the Hajar Mountains and the huge sand dunes of Liwa provide very different areas, each requiring some serious off-road driving to reach, but offering the real wilderness camping experience. Campers are lucky in that access to many places is almost unrestricted; take special care, therefore, to respect the environment.

For more information on places to visit, refer to the *Off-Road Explorer (UAE)*.

Desert Camping

Canoeing

Other Options → Kayaking [p.193]

For those interested in getting up close to the marine and bird life of the UAE, or for a slightly different sport that provides access to hidden places, canoeing is an enjoyable and revealing activity.

Areas for good canoeing include Khor Kalba Nature Reserve, the coastal lagoons of Umm Al Quwain, between the new and old towns of Ras Al Khaimah, north of Ras Al Khaimah before Ramsis and through the mangrove covered islands off the north coast of Abu Dhabi. Many of these areas are on their way to becoming protected reserves, so treat them with respect. Some adventurous kayakers occasionally visit the Mussandam in sea touring canoes. Here it is possible to visit secluded bays and view the spectacular rocky coastline, with its fjord like inlets and towering 1,000 metre cliffs.

For further information, check out the Hatta to Kalba route in the *Off-Road Explorer (UAE)*

See Also: *Khor Kalba [p.140].*

Al Jazira Hotel and Resort

Location → Btn Abu Dhabi & Dubai | 562 9100
Hours → Timings on request
Web/email → na | Map Ref → na

One and two man canoes are available, which are ideal for beginners. Anyone from youngsters up (as long as they're big enough to hold the paddles) can try this sport. The resort provides life jackets, paddles and basic instruction.

Rates: *Dhs.30 – 30 minutes; Dhs.60 – 1 hour. Day entry fee – Dhs.50 (adults) and Dhs.30 (children). Different rates for club members, their guests and residents of the hotel.*

Palm Beach Leisure Club

Location → Al Diar Gulf Htl · Al Maqtaa | 441 4777
Hours → 09:00 until sunset
Web/email → www.aldiarhotels.com | Map Ref → 1-D3

A small number of open canoes are available for hire, for paddling around the calm waters off the club's beach, and is suitable for children and adults alike. Canoes are available from 09:00 to sunset.

Costs: *Dhs.40 – 60 minutes; Dhs.20 – 30 minutes. A day entry charge is applicable to all except club members, their guests or residents of the hotel.*

Desert Rangers

Location → Jct 3, Shk Zayed Rd | 04 340 2408
Hours → 08:30 - 14:30 · Dubai
Web/email → www.desertrangers.com | Map Ref → UAE-C2

Desert Rangers offers trips through the mangroves of the unique nature reserve at Khor Kalba on the East Coast in 2 - 3 seat Canadian canoes. Initial instruction is followed by hands on practice to develop skills and confidence.

Cost: *Dhs.300 per person with a guide.*

Caving

Caving here varies from the fairly safe to the extremely dangerous. Some of the best caves are near Al Ain, the Jebel Hafeet area and in the Hajar Mountains just past Buraimi, near the Omani border. The underground passages and caves have spectacular displays of curtains, stalagmites and stalactites, and pretty gypsum flowers. There are no companies offering guided tours; caving is limited to unofficial groups of dedicated cavers.

It is important to understand the dangers of going underground and the precautions that must be taken. Take at least two torches each, and enough spare batteries and bulbs. Other equipment includes several litres of water, a hard hat and long sleeved overall or knee and elbow pads to protect you from sharp rocks, a basic first aid kit and twine to mark less obvious parts of the route. Check the weather forecast to find out about recent rainfalls. Flash floods occur regularly at certain times of the year.

Warning: *No mountain rescue services exist, so anyone venturing into the mountains should be either reasonably experienced or with someone who knows the area. Tell someone where you're going and when you will be back.*

Climbing

Despite the shattered appearance of most of the mountains in the UAE, there is excellent rock climbing in a number of locations, particularly in Ras Al Khaimah, Dibba and Hatta. In addition there are some really good crags around Al Ain/Buraimi and the area near the Oman border, including the infamous 'Wonderwall'. By choosing venues carefully, it's possible to climb year round – even in midsummer with daytime air temperatures approaching 50°C. Most routes are in the higher grades – ranging from (British) Very Severe, up to extreme grades (E5). However, there are some excellent easier routes for new climbers, especially in Wadi Bih and Wadi Kham Shamsi. Many routes, even in the easier grades, are serious propositions with loose rock, poor belays and difficult descents, often by abseil, making them unsuitable for total novices.

Sports climbing is starting to appear, with some areas being bolted where protection would otherwise be impossible. Some of the hardest routes in the country are currently being developed

by serious climbers from Abu Dhabi and Dubai. For further information on climbs around Buraimi and in the Hajar Mountains in Oman refer to the guidebook *Rock Climbing in Oman* by RA McDonald (Apex Publishing 1993, London/Oman).

Pyramids

Location → Wafi City · Dubai | 04 324 0000
Hours → 07:00 - 22:00; Fri 09:00 - 21:00
Web/email → www.pyramidsdubai.com | Map Ref → UAE-C2

This indoor rock climbing wall in Dubai is currently the only one in the Emirates. There's a varied set of walls for climbing routes and bouldering and qualified instructors are available to provide lessons for enthusiasts of all ages and fitness levels.

For more information, consult the Sports section of the *Dubai Explorer*.

Adventurous Climbs

Crazy Golf

Al Diar Gulf Hotel & Resort

Location → Al Diar Gulf Htl · Al Maqtaa | 441 4777
Hours → 09:00 - 22:00
Web/email → www.aldiarhotels.com | Map Ref → 1-D3

A 9 hole obstacle course is available at the Gulf Hotel for all budding Nick Faldos!

Cost: *Dhs.5 for 30 minutes.*

Cricket

Other Options → Sporting Goods [p.164]

With the large numbers of enthusiastic fans from all over the world, especially from India, Pakistan and Sri Lanka, cricket seems to lead even football as the most popular sport in Abu Dhabi! Car parks, rough land and grassy parks all sprout stumps at weekends and evenings, when a mix of ages comes out to play. Many organisations field their own cricket teams for inter company competitions and it's also very popular in schools. Coaching is available.

Major international matches are held regularly in the Emirates, especially at the ground in Sharjah, where it's possible to see some of the world's best teams and to get the chance to cheer your own side on.

Abu Dhabi Cricket Council

Location → Salam Street · Abu Dhabi | na
Hours → 08:00 - 13:30 19:00 - 22:00
Web/email → www.uaecricket.com | Map Ref → 4-C4

The council was established to promote and run cricket affairs in the emirate. There are currently 45 local clubs registered, with over 1,000 players of all nationalities. If you want to play cricket, the council will put you in contact with a suitable club.

Al Ain Cricket Association

Location → Nr Hilton Al Ain · Al Ain | 050 623 1590
Hours → Timings on request
Web/email → atansari@emirates.net.ae | Map Ref → 15-D4

The Association is the oldest cricketing body in the UAE and has been running cricket affairs in Al Ain since April 1989. Currently there are sixteen teams (both seniors and juniors) and over 300 resident players from all nationalities. Coaching is available.

Contact: *Dr Ahmad Tariq Ansari on the above number/email.*

Cycling

Other Options → Mountain Biking [p.195]

Abu Dhabi is not the most bike friendly of places, but if you're willing to brave the traffic, there are plenty of areas to ride. Exploring on two wheels is a great way of getting to know the city.

There are residential areas with fewer cars and some roads have wide footpaths providing traffic free routes. However, riding in traffic requires a lot of care. Drivers underestimate the speed of cyclists and don't allow enough room for them – be especially

careful at junctions and roundabouts. Helmets, although not legally required, are recommended.

Outside the city, the roads are fairly flat until you near the mountains. Jebel Hafeet, the Hatta area and the zone near Masafi down to the coast offer interesting paved roads with better views. The new road from Hatta to Kalba on the East Coast is one of the most scenic routes in the country. Cycling clubs generally ride on weekends, early mornings and evenings.

Darts

Abu Dhabi Darts League

Location → Various locations | na
Hours → Sun 20:30
Web/email → kgbsam180@yahoo.com | Map Ref → na

Darts has been enjoyed in Abu Dhabi for well over 20 years. The action takes place in various hotels, to be enjoyed either as a player or a spectator. All communities are represented in the league and all levels of player are accepted.

Contact: *Chairman Sam Murtada on the above email.*

Dhow Charters

Other Options → Boat & Yacht Charters [p.179]

Large independent groups can try chartering a dhow from the fishermen at Dibba to travel up the coast of the Mussandam. Be prepared to haggle hard – knowing a bit of Arabic will help. Expect to pay about Dhs.2,500 per day for a dhow large enough to take 20 - 25 people.

Since, in theory, you're not entering Oman, visas are not required. It is possible to arrange a stop along the coast for the night, in which case it is recommended that you bring your own camping equipment. Alternatively, you can choose to sleep on board. You will, however, need to take your own food and water, as you will only be provided with ice lockers for storing supplies. Conditions on board are pretty basic and you have limited freedom to plan your own route. Nevertheless, it is a good chance to view the beautiful scenery of the Mussandam, as well as turtles and dolphins, from a traditional dhow. It is also ideal for diving, but hire equipment in advance – you can try the Sandy Beach Motel. Alternatively, spend the days swimming, snorkelling and lazing, or hire a speedboat and explore the coast for an extra Dhs.800 per day.

Al Dhafra

Location → Al Dhafra · Al Meena | 673 2266
Hours → 12:30 - 16:00 19:00 - 24:00
Web/email → www.aldhafra.net | Map Ref → 7-C4

Al Dhafra's dhows accommodate between 10 - 50 people. Trips can be made along the Abu Dhabi Corniche or to nearby islands. Meals or a buffet can be served at an additional cost. There are also daily dinner cruises along the Corniche.

Cost: *Ranges from Dhs.150 - 700 per hour. Daily dinner cruises are Dhs.100 per person.*

Blue Dolphin Dhow Charters

Location → Htl InterContinental Bainuna St | 666 9392
Hours → Timings on request
Web/email → sindbadbd@hotmail.com | Map Ref → 10-C1

Blue Dolphin's three traditional Arabian fishing dhows are all available for charter. Trips can be customised, or you can take your pick from the Island Tours. All dhows are equipped with a buffet, radio, shady deck areas and toilets.

Cost: *Dhs.2,000 - 4,000 for a charter or Dhs.600 - 800 per hour, depending on the size of the yacht.*

Sunshine Tours

Location → Airport Rd | 444 9914
Hours → Timings on request
Web/email → www.adnh.com | Map Ref → 2-B2

Dhow charters are one of the many services offered. Depending on the number of people, the duration of the trip and the menu, all kinds of occasions can be catered for. A great way to celebrate birthdays, staff parties, anniversaries etc.

Sailing Back in Time

A treat for newcomers and visitors alike, a dhow cruise along the Corniche proves a delightful afternoon or evening out. These Arabic boats have changed little over the centuries. A traditional dhow takes months to build but can last for over 100 years. In the past, teak was imported from India and the planks moulded to form the distinctive high bowed vessel. Planks are still secured by locally made wooden nails and the gaps in the wood filled with rolled cotton hammered tightly into place. The boat is then oiled to waterproof it and preserve the wood. Life on board was incredibly basic a hundred years ago, but even modern additions like diesel engines and satellite navigation cannot disguise the harshness of life at sea in these vessels.

Diving

The waters around the UAE are rich in a variety of marine and coral life, and it's possible to dive year round in the warm seas. In addition to exotic fish, such as clownfish and seahorses, one can see spotted eagle rays, moray eels, small sharks, barracuda, stingrays, sea turtles, and much more.

A plethora of diving companies operate in the UAE offering all levels of courses, from introductory dives to instructor level and technical diving, under the different international training organisations, such as CMAS, PADI, NAUI etc.

Many good dive sites are easily accessible from Abu Dhabi, including wreck or deep water dives and reef dives. For shallow dives (8 metres), head to the Old Cement Barge. Deeper dive sites are at Hannan, MS Jazim and MS Lion City. If you would like to explorer further in the UAE, the east and west coasts are rich in dive sites that offer stunning marine life.

In addition, most scuba schools organise trips to the spectacular area north of the UAE known as the Mussandam. Alternatively, from Dibba on the East Coast, boats take divers 5 - 75 km up the coast.

For further information on diving in the UAE and the Mussandam, refer to the *Underwater Explorer (UAE)*.

Abu Dhabi Sub Aqua Club

Location → Club, The · Al Meena | 673 1111
Hours → Timings on request
Web/email → www.the-club.com | Map Ref → 7-A2

This club is affiliated to the British Sub Aqua Club (BSAC), so safety standards are high, and training courses are regularly held for all standards of diver. Dive trip locations include the East Coast and the Mussandam. Membership is open to The Club members only.

Al Jazira Diving Centre

Location → Al Diar Jazira Beach Resort · Jazira | 562 9100
Hours → 09:00 - 18:00
Web/email → na | Map Ref → UAE-B3

Teaching in this centre follows the international standards of recreational diving SS and CMA. On offer are plenty of programmes, from discovery to advanced courses. They also offer a bubble maker course for kids aged 8 - 12 years.

Contact: *Irmgard Mackenbrock, Recreation Manager (050 476 3436).*

Blue Dolphin Company LLC

Location → Htl InterContinental · Bainuna St | 666 9392
Hours → 08:00 - 13:00 16:00 - 19:00
Web/email → www.interconti.com | Map Ref → 10-C1

This company offers a range of PADI dive training, from 'open water' and 'advanced open water diver' to 'rescue diver' and 'divemaster'. Certified divers can take full day dive trips. Classes can be given in Arabic, French or English and all equipment is provided.

Cost: *Dhs.100 (discover diver); Dhs.1,000 (rescue diver) and Dhs.2,000 (divemaster).*

Golden Boats

Location → Nr Cenral Bank Bld · Al Bateen | 666 9119
Hours → See timings below
Web/email → golbomat@emirates.net.ae | Map Ref → 10-C1

Offering diving trips for certified divers and scuba courses for beginners. Courses are available for adults and children aged between 8 - 12 years. A variety in water sports is also offered, including fishing, water skiing, windsurfing and dhow island cruises.

Cost & Timings: *Thu 20:00 - 01:00, Arabic theme night party for Dhs.150. Fri 10:00 - 17:30, family day for Dhs.100 (adults) & Dhs.50 (children).*

Sirenia

Location → Tourist Club Area | 645 4512
Hours → Timings on request
Web/email → veryan@emirates.net.ae | Map Ref → 4-B3

Veryan Pappin, the main PADI master instructor offers dive training from beginner to assistant instructor and a variety of specialities including 'night diving', 'wreck diving', and 'search and recovery diving'. He also undertakes underwater photographic surveys, installation inspections and marine environmental impact assessments.

Contact: *Veryan on the above number or (050 613 4583).*

Dubai

Emirates Diving Association

Location → Al Shindagha · Dubai | 04 393 9390
Hours → Sat & Wed 08:30 - 13:00 17:00 - 21:00
Web/email → www.emiratesdiving.com | Map Ref → UAE-C2

The main aim of this group is to conserve, protect and restore the UAE's marine resources by understanding and promoting the marine environment and environmental diving. Contact them for more information on diving in the UAE.

Fujairah

Sandy Beach Dive Centre

Location → Next to Sandy Beach Htl · Fujairah | 09 244 5050
Hours → 09:30 & 12:00
Web/email → www.sandybm.com | Map Ref → UAE-E2

This dive centre offers a qualified team of dive instructors and support staff. Their famous house reef, Snoopy Island, is alive with hard corals and marine life and is excellent for snorkelling and scuba diving. Trips to Dibba, Khorfakkan and Mussandam are also offered.

Scuba 2000

Location → Al Badiyah Beach · Fujairah | 09 238 8477
Hours → 09:00 - 19:00
Web/email → www.scubauae.com | Map Ref → UAE-E2

This East Coast dive centre is open all year. Snoopy and Sharque islands are two nearby sites that provide excellent diving and snorkelling. The standard courses are available for everyone from beginners to advanced divers. Accommodation is available.

Cost: Dhs.230 (two dives), Dhs.1,500 (open water) and Dhs.800 (advanced).

Scuba International

Location → Fujairah Int Marine Club · Fujairah | 09 222 0060
Hours → 10:00 - 19:00
Web/email → www.scubaInternational.net | Map Ref → UAE-E2

Scuba International offers facilities for both divers and non divers, from recreational dive charters and diver training (PADI, DSAT and TDI), to RYA sanctioned boat handling courses, chamber operating courses, instructor courses and dive vacation bookings.

Note: Scuba International operates a recompression chamber with on call chamber staff that is able to treat any diving emergency 24 hours a day.

7 Seas Divers

Location → Nr Khor Fakkan Souk · Khor Fakkan | 09 238 7400
Hours → 08:00 - 20:00
Web/email → www.7seasdivers.com | Map Ref → UAE-E2

7 Seas Divers offers daily dive trips as well as courses in various languages. The organisation passionately believes in conservation of its fantastic dive sites. It also deals with all professional diving associations such as PADI, CMAS, TDI etc.

Sharjah

Sharjah Wanderers Dive Club

Location → Shj Wanderers · Sharjah | 06 566 2105
Hours → Timings on request
Web/email → www.sharjahwanderers.com | Map Ref → UAE-C2

This diving club is a full member of the British Sub Aqua Club. Clubhouse facilities include a training room, social area, equipment room, compressors, dive gear for hire, two dive boats and on-site pool facilities. Club night is every Tuesday.

Deep Sea Diving

Dune Buggy Riding

Exhilarating and fun, dune buggies are not particularly environmentally sound, but are surprisingly addictive.

Every Friday, the area around the 'Big Red' sand dune on the Dubai – Hatta Road is transformed into a circus arena for off-road lovers. Future Motor Sports, along with about four other companies, rent off-road quad bikes and karts, which are available to drive (without a licence) in fenced off areas. Alternatively, hang around to be entertained by the sight of locals driving their Nissan Patrols on two wheels!

Buggy addicts can also contact tour operators [p.133], since many of them offer the chance to try dune buggies as part of their desert safaris. Remember, if you fall when you go up and over a dune, these things are heavy!

Al Badayer Motorcycles Rental

Location → Hatta Rd · Dubai | 050 636 1787
Hours → 09:00 - 18:00
Web/email → na | Map Ref → UAE-D3

Also called quad bikes, dune buggies are good fun and quite an exciting experience. The establishment has buggies that range in power from 50cc to 250cc. Prices vary from Dhs.80 - 200 per hour. For further details, contact Ahmed Sallam on the above.

Desert Rangers

Location → Dubai Garden Centre · Shk Zayed Rd | 04 340 2408
Hours → 08:30 - 14:30
Web/email → www.desertrangers.com | Map Ref → UAE-C2

Having been given a helmet and a brief talk on safety, you are led to the course to familiarise yourself with the dune buggy. There are single and two seat buggies, allowing up to ten people to be on the course at one time.

Cost: *Half day dune buggy safari – Dhs.350 per person.*

Fishing

Other Options → Boat & Yacht Charters [p.179]

Fishing has become increasingly popular in recent years, and this is one of the reasons why the Government has introduced regulations to protect the fish stocks off the coast of the UAE. Nevertheless, you can still fish if you have the right papers or by chartering a licensed tour guide.

September through to April is the most productive season, although it's still possible to catch sailfish and queenfish in the summer months. Other commonly caught fish include shari, tuna, kingfish, dorado or jacks. The more adventurous with cash to spare may consider deep sea fishing or trawling. Alternatively, the truly competitive may like to enter the annual international fishing competition arranged by the Abu Dhabi International Marine Sports Club (681 5566).

Al Dhafra

Location → Al Meena | 673 2266
Hours → 12:30 - 16:00 19:00 - 24:00
Web/email → www.aldhafra.net | Map Ref → 7-C4

How about a fishing trip with a difference? Al Dhafra has traditional Arabic dhows, which can be chartered. Most clients take their own equipment, since there's only a limited amount on board. Food can be supplied at an additional cost.

Cost: *Starts form Dhs.150 per hour for a 10 people dhow.*

Al Jazira Hotel & Resort

Location → Btn Abu Dhabi & Dubai | 562 9100
Hours → Timings on request
Web/email → na | Map Ref → UAE-B3

Since the waters of the Gulf are full of fascinating marine life, nearly all resorts and hotels provide fishing facilities. Al Jazira is one of the less expensive options, offering fishing trips at either four hours for Dhs.400 or eight hours for Dhs.800.

Beach Rotana Hotel & Towers

Location → Nr Abu Dhabi Mall · Tourist Club Area | 644 3000
Hours → Timings on request
Web/email → www.rotana.com | Map Ref → 4-B3

The hotel's boat is available for hire for fishing or cruising the Gulf. The driver will suggest different locations depending on the season, but with hundreds of small islands just off the coast, good fishing and scenery are guaranteed.

Cost: *Trips, including equipment, cost Dhs.500 (for three hours) for boat hire for a maximum of four people (Dhs.175 per extra hour).*

Blue Dolphin Company LLC

Location → Htl InterContinental · Bainuna St | 666 9392
Hours → 08:00 - 13:00 16:00 - 19:00
Web/email → www.interconti.com | Map Ref → 10-C1

Experience the thrill of the chase from Blue Dolphin's fully equipped Barracuda boats. Instruction is offered for the novice line fisherman – be prepared to catch hammour, barracuda, tuna and sailfish, if you're lucky! Trawling is also available.

Cost: *Dhs.250 per hour (minimum two hours); Dhs.800 for four hours. Includes water and soft drinks.*

Le Meridien Abu Dhabi

Location → Le Meridien · Tourist Club Area | 644 6666
Hours → Various Timings
Web/email → www.lemeridien.com | Map Ref → 7-D1

More or less everything to do with fishing or cruising is offered – fish in the early morning for four hours (Dhs.220 - 275), race among the islands in a speedboat or dream away the hours on the deck of a traditional dhow.

Note: *Island camping costs Dhs.195 per head for a full day, including snacks and BBQ .*

Palms Resort

Location → Sheraton Resort · Corniche Rd | **677 3333**
Hours → 07:30 - 22:30
Web/email → sheraton@emirates.net.ae | **Map Ref** → 8-A3

Expeditions are run from the resort for deep sea fishing, with large catches of hammour, shari, barracuda & kingfish (seasonal) virtually guaranteed. Everything is provided, including refreshments and experienced guides to ensure every trip is a success.

Cost: *Dhs.480 for three hours, plus Dhs.100 per extra hour.*

Timings: *Sunrise trip 06:00 - 09:00; sunset trip 14:00 - 17:00 & 15:00 - 18:00.*

Dubai

Bounty Charters

Location → Various locations | **04 348 3042**
Hours → Timings on request
Web/email → na | **Map Ref** → na

Bounty Charters is a fully equipped 36 ft Yamaha Sea Spirit, captained by an experienced game fisherman from South Africa. Charters can be tailor made, whether you want to try for the challenging sailfish or trawl for the wide variety of fish in the Gulf.

Contact: *Richard Forrester on the above number or (050 552 6067).*

Fujairah

Oceanic Hotel

Location → Beach Rd, Khor Fakkan · East Coast | **09 238 5111**
Hours → 24 hrs
Web/email → www.oceanichotel.com | **Map Ref** → UAE-E2

Round off a visit to the East Coast with a sunset fishing trip to the local fisherman's favourite fishing spot. The catch can be cooked according to your taste by the hotel chef. Equipment supplied.

Cost: *Dhs.600 for maximum five people from*

Timings: *15:00 - 19:00*

Flying

Other Options → Paragliding [p.196]

At present there are no private flying clubs available in the Abu Dhabi or Al Ain area. However, those keen to learn can travel north to learn in Dubai, Umm Al Quwain or Fujairah on the East Coast. A variety of courses and qualifications are offered. Those with a private pilot's licence can contact the Dubai Flying Association (04 351 9691); while at Umm Al Quwain Flying Club (06 768 1447) the brave can not only fly, but can also try skydiving, parachuting or microlighting.

See the Sports section of the *Dubai Explorer* for further details.

Fujairah Aviation Centre

Location → Fujairah Int Airport · Fujairah | **09 222 4747**
Hours → Timings on request
Web/email → www.fujairah-aviation.ae | **Map Ref** → UAE-E2

Facilities include twin and single engine training aircraft, an instrument flight simulator and a repair workshop. Training is offered for the private pilot's licence, commercial pilot's licence, instrument rating and multi-engine rating. Trial lessons and gift vouchers are available.

Costs: *Lessons (per hour) – trial flying Dhs.480; ground training Dhs.50; flight training Dhs.400, flight training for the Cessna 172S Dhs.480, the Cessna 172P Dhs.400 and twin engine Dhs.1,200.*

Umm Al Quwain Aeroclub

Location → Al Ittihad St · UAQ | **06 768 1447**
Hours → Timings on request
Web/email → www.uaqaeroclub.com | **Map Ref** → UAE-C1

This sports aviation club provides opportunities for aviation enthusiasts to fly and train throughout the year at excellent rates. Activities include flying, skydiving, paramotors and helicopter training. The club also offers sightseeing tours by Cessna aircraft.

Cost: *Sightseeing by Cessna – Dhs.300 for 30 minutes; Dhs.50 for 10 minutes. For longer flights, a plane with a pilot – Dhs.600 per hour.*

Location: *16 km along the road from UAQ roundabout heading towards Ras Al Khaimah, before Dreamland Aqua Park and opposite UAQ Shooting Club – just look for the big aeroplane!*

Timings: *08:30 - 17:30 (winter); 09:00 - 19:00 (summer).*

Flying High

Football

Other Options → Sporting Goods [p.189]

Like most places on the planet, you don't have to travel far to have a game of football in the Emirates. On evenings and at weekends, parks, beaches and any open areas seem to attract a game, generally with a mix of nationalities taking part. Even villages in the countryside usually have a group knocking a ball around on the local sand and rock pitch – see if you can join in, or join a more formal club. Fans can watch main international matches on screens at hotel pubs and sports bars throughout the city, while local teams can be viewed at Al Jazeera and Al Wahda stadiums in town.

Abu Dhabi Nomads Club

Location → Various locations · Abu Dhabi | 672 4900
Hours → Timings on request
Web/email → shieldsy18@hotmail.com | Map Ref → 1-D3

Formed by the amalgamation of Abu Dhabi Football Club and Abu Dhabi Strollers to allow expats to continue to play football, the club trains and plays at Al Jazira Sports Club on Monday evenings and they are always looking for good players.

Contact: *Alan Groves, Chairman (698 9246); David Shields, Secretary (050 446 8795).*

Dubai Celts GAA

Location → Dubai Exiles Rugby Club · Al Awir Rd | na
Hours → Sat & Tue 19:00 - 21:00; Summer, Mon only
Web/email → www.dubaicelts.com | Map Ref → na

The club is open to men and women of all nationalities and levels, with Gaelic football and hurling played weekly. The social side is as important as the athletic, and meetings are held in the clubhouse or at Heroes Diner after training sessions.

Contact: *Malachy Mulhall (m_mulhall@dubaicelts.com).*

Golf

The UAE is quite rightly known as *the* golf destination in the Gulf, with excellent year round facilities and many important tournaments being held here. Courses are either fully grassed or brown (sand) courses, or a mixture of the two.

Abu Dhabi is home to a variety of local tournaments held on an annual or monthly basis, such as the regular *Abu Dhabi Duty Free Medal*. While on the international scene in Dubai, the Emirates Golf Club is host to the *Dubai Desert Classic*, which is part of the European PGA (Professional Golf Association) Tour.

On the Green

Abu Dhabi Golf & Equestrian Club

Location → Nr Immigration Office · Al Mushrif | 445 9600
Hours → 06:00 - 22:00
Web/email → www.adec-web.com | Map Ref → 3-D3

This par 70 course boasts what could be the largest par 5 hole in the world. Competitions are held each Friday and the Junior Golf Academy for 8 - 14 year olds currently offers an eight week teaching programme for Dhs.300.

Cost: *Visitors – green fees Dhs.230 (18 holes) Dhs.140 (9 holes); cart hire Dhs.40 (18 holes) Dhs.25 (9 holes); range balls per bucket Dhs.10 (members) Dhs.20 (non members).*

Abu Dhabi Golf Club by Sheraton

Location → Umm Al Nar St · Umm Al Nar | 558 8990
Hours → 06:00 - 24:00
Web/email → www.adgolfsheraton.com | Map Ref → 1-A1

Excellent facilities here include two 18 hole par 72 grass courses, a driving range, putting and pitching greens and a golf academy which holds lessons for juniors as well. Additional facilities include restaurants, pro shop, gym, pool, spa and tennis courts.

Al Ghazal Golf Club

Location → Nr Abu Dhabi Int Airport · Abu Dhabi | 575 8040
Hours → 08:00 - 20:00
Web/email → golfclub@emirates.net.ae | Map Ref → UAE-A4

This purpose built 18 hole sand golf course, driving range, academy and licensed clubhouse is situated two minutes from the capital's airport, and is home to the World Sand Golf Championship. Anyone can play here, including transit passengers with a few hours to kill.

Note: *Airlines arrange free 96 hour passenger transit visas for travellers who want to play golf or use the facilities.*

Rotana Junior Golf League

Location → Golf & Equestrian Club · Al Mushrif | 445 9600
Hours → 06:00 - 22:30
Web/email → na | Map Ref → 3-D3

When it comes to starting golf, the younger the better – kids can learn as members of the golf league from September to April. Tournaments are held on Thursday mornings and pre-tournament coaching sessions are offered on Wednesdays at 16:00 for Dhs.20.

Cost: *Dhs.100 for membership; tournament fees Dhs.30 (3 hole) and Dhs.40 (9 hole).*

Al Ain

Al Ain Golf Club

Location → Nr Hilton Al Ain · Al Niyadat | 03 768 6808
Hours → Timings on request
Web/email → jimross@emirates.net.ae | Map Ref → 15-D4

The Al Ain Golf Club boasts an 18 hole sand course, with browns, a clubhouse and a floodlit driving range. Handicaps gained here are valid internationally. Visitors are welcome with prior notice.

Hilton Al Ain Golf Club

Location → Hilton Al Ain | 03 768 6666
Hours → 08:00 - 22:30
Web/email → www.al-ain.hilton.com | Map Ref → 15-D4

This par 3 course has an average distance of about 80 yards between each hole, and although short in length it can play tough! The course has nearly 30 bunkers and very small quick greens. Open to non members, with lessons available.

Cost: *Starting from Dhs.30 for a half set.*

Dubai

UAE Golf Association

Location → Creek Golf Club · Dubai | 04 295 6440
Hours → 09:00 - 17:00
Web/email → www.ugagolf.com | Map Ref → UAE-C2

Affiliated to the Royal and Ancient Golf Club of St Andrews in the UK, this non profit making organisation is the governing body for amateur golf in the UAE. Its aims are to make golf more accessible in the UAE for everyone.

Hashing

Other Options → Pubs [p.262]

The Hash House Harriers is a worldwide family of social running clubs. It was started in Kuala Lumpur in 1938 and is now the largest running organisation in the world. Hashing consists of following a course laid out by a couple of 'hares'. Running, jogging and walking are acceptable and the courses are varied and often cross country. Hashing is a fun way to keep fit and meet new people, since clubs are invariably very sociable and the running is not competitive.

While it was in Malaysia that the sport first took off, its roots can be traced back to the British cross country sport of 'hare and hounds'. In the 1930s, British servicemen in Malaysia were stationed at the Royal Selonger Club, known as the 'hash house' due to the quality of its food. After a particularly festive weekend, a hare and hound paper chase was suggested, and so the hash began.

Abu Dhabi Island Hash House Harriers

Location → Various locations | 404 8325
Hours → Monday, an hour before sunset
Web/email → www.geocities.com/auh4/index.html | Map Ref → na

If you think you need the drinking capacity of an elephant and the running ability of Sebastian Coe to join a Hash, think again! Sprint, run, walk or hobble; it's up to you to do as much as you like.

Cost: *Dhs.30 (members); Dhs.40 (non members).*

Contact: *Barry on the above number, Chris Lewis (050 667 0887) or Frankie Wilkes (050 616 2694), or log on to the Website.*

Abu Dhabi Mainland Hash House Harriers

Location → Various locations | 665 5893
Hours → Mon 16:30 (winter); 17:30 (summer)
Web/email → na | Map Ref → na

The Mainland Hash (HHH) usually meets off island. This HHH has the reputation of making participants sit on a block of ice! They provide food and beverages in return for a contribution, and entertain participants via a Religious Advisor (RA), hence the ice.

Al Ain Hash House Harriers

Location → Various locations | 050 663 1745
Hours → 17:30 (winter); 18:00 (summer)
Web/email → na | Map Ref → na

Started in 1984, this hash has run over 1000 times with no break, despite rain, lightning and the occasional near hurricane! The runs vary in difficulty. This is a family affair that welcomes people of all ages.

Contact: *Mark Smith on the above number.*

Hiking

Other Options → Climbing [p.181]

Although the area around Abu Dhabi island is fairly flat and uninspiring, a 90 minute drive takes you to very different surroundings, ideal for hiking and far removed from the hectic city. The nearest location is the foothills of the Hajar Mountains. Here the lovely purple mountains and wadis offer peace and tranquillity. The land is heavily shattered and eroded due to the harsh climate, but there are many good trails, ranging from short easy walks to longer, more difficult treks. Once near the mountains – explore! Good areas include anywhere near Al Ain, many places in Wadi Bih, or the mountains near the East Coast. The further off the beaten track you get, the more likely you are to find villages inhabited by folks who live much the same way as they have for centuries gone by.

Be sure to take sensible precautions. Tell someone where you're going and when you should be back, take a map and compass or GPS and stout walking boots. Sunlight is fierce during the day, but at night temperatures can drop surprisingly. Take food, suncream and loads of water. Refer also to the *Off-Road Explorer (UAE)*.

Contacts: *Alistair MacKenzie in Dubai (Alistair@Explorer-Publishing.com); John Gregory in Ras Al Khaimah (050 647 7120).*

Desert Rangers

Location → Jct 3, Shk Zayed Rd · Dubai | 04 340 2408
Hours → 08:30 - 14:30
Web/email → www.desertrangers.com | Map Ref → UAE-C2

This Dubai based company offers hikes in the majestic mountains of the UAE with an experienced guide. A variety of routes can be taken to suit the group's age and level of fitness. For more information, consult the *Dubai Explorer*.

Cost: *Dhs.275 per person.*

Hiking in the Mountains

Hockey

Other Options → Ice Hockey [p.192]

Abu Dhabi Hockey Club

Location → Various locations | 674 4410
Hours → Timings on request
Web/email → na | Map Ref → na

This Club boasts illustrious members who have played for national teams in England, India, Pakistan and Scotland. The club participates in various annual local tournaments, usually fielding men's, women's and mixed teams. They also run a mini hockey league.

Contact: *Manish (050 621 0534).*

Horse Riding

Other Options → Polo [p.196]

Horses are of great significance in this part of the world, both in historical and modern terms, and

despite its size, the UAE has a wealth of equine talent. Recreational riding is extremely well supported, and most stables offer quality horses for hacking in the desert or rides along the beach.

Horse racing is also extremely popular. In March each year, Dubai hosts the world's richest horse race, the US$6 million *Dubai World Cup*, which is one of *the* events on the UAE's social calendar.

Abu Dhabi Equestrian Club

Location → Nr Immigration Office · Al Mushrif | 445 5500
Hours → Timings on request
Web/email → na | Map Ref → 3-D3

Offering horse racing and show jumping grounds, as well as an active riding club with 100 horses suitable for all levels of rider, they also offer comprehensive instruction from beginner to jumping, endurance desert riding and stable management courses.

Cost: *Dhs.50 for one hour.*

Hurling

Dubai Celts GAA

Location → Dubai Exiles Rugby Club · Al Awir Rd · Dubai | na
Hours → Sat & Tue 19:00 - 21:00; Summer, Mon only
Web/email → www.dubaicelts.com | Map Ref → na

Club members meet twice a week on Saturday and Tuesday evening. Ladies' football and camogie are also thriving with many social activities. Players hail from all over and everyone's welcome; whatever your level, you'll receive a warm Irish welcome.

Contact: *For details, log on to the Website.*

Ice Hockey

Abu Dhabi Falcons Ice Hockey

Location → Abu Dhabi Ice Rink · Abu Dhabi | 446 1788
Hours → Timings on request
Web/email → www.abufalcons.com | Map Ref → 2-A1

This organisation is dedicated to the development of youth ice hockey in a fun, safe environment. Teams participate in local tournaments, and the club holds an annual camp with professional Canadian coaches. Boys and girls are welcome.

Contact: *Club President, Vincent Saubestre on the above number.*

Al Ain Youth Ice Hockey Teams

Location → Hili Fun City · Al Ain | 03 705 5561
Hours → Timings on request
Web/email → david.smicer@hct.ac.ae | Map Ref → 13-C1

The Al Ain Youth Ice Hockey Teams comprise four youth teams split according to age. Boys and girls are welcome and team aims are equal ice time for all players in the spirit of fair play. There's also a well established adult league.

Contact: *Team President, David Smicer on the above number or 03 782 1039/050 448 1967.*

Ice Skating

Other Options → Ice Hockey [p.192]

Abu Dhabi Ice Rink

Location → Zayed Sports City | 444 8458
Hours → Timings on request
Web/email → na | Map Ref → 2-B1

Abu Dhabi Ice Rink offers a fun couple of hours to escape the heat. The rink has a variety of other facilities including bumper cars, video games, and a fast food restaurant. Lessons are available for all levels of ability.

Entrance: *Dhs.5 (children under three years free).*

Ice Skating

Hili Fun City & Ice Rink

Location → Mohammed Bin Khalifa St · Al Ain | 03 784 5542
Hours → 16:00 - 22:00 09:00 - 22:00 Fri
Web/email → www.hilton.com | Map Ref → 13-C1

The ice rink is located on the eastern side of the park with a mammoth 60 x 30 metre ice rink seating

3,000 spectators. Besides public skating sessions, there are ice hockey tournaments and ice skating competitions throughout the year.

***Timings**: Sun - Wed 16:00 - 22:00 ; Thu, Fri & public holidays 9:00 - 22:00 (winter). Sun - Wed 17:00 - 23:00; Thu, Fri & public holidays 9:00 - 23:00 (summer). Tue & Wed ladies and children only.*

Jet Skiing

Other Options → Beach Clubs [p.204]

Al Jazira Hotel and Resort

Location → Btn Abu Dhabi & Dubai | 04 562 9100
Hours → Timings on request
Web/email → na | Map Ref → na

If you've not tried it before, think of jet skiing as rather like riding a Harley Davidson, but on water, so it's a bit more exciting. Prices start at Dhs.50 for 15 minutes of adrenaline rush, with speeds of 40km/h possible!

Karting

Other Options → Moto-Cross [p.194]
Dune Buggy Riding [p.186]

Leisure Games Centre

Location → Nr AUH Tourist Club · Tourist Club Area | 679 3330
Hours → See timings below
Web/email → saeed-lgc@hotmail.com | Map Ref → 7-D1

The track includes an electronic circuit timer, two hairpin bends, a U-turn and straights for reaching speeds of up to 50 km/h. Training is provided, targeting different age groups, from 7 – 50 year olds. Karts are fitted with two stroke engines (200cc, 250cc, 390cc).

***Cost**: Dhs.30 for 10 minutes on the track.*

***Timings**: Sat - Tue 09:00 - 12:00 & 17:00 - 24:00; Wed, Thu & Fri 09:00 - 12:00 & 16:00 - 01:00.*

Kayaking

Other Options → Canoeing [p.180]

Beach Hut, The

Location → Sandy Beach Motel · East Coast | 09 244 5050
Hours → 08:00 - 17:30
Web/email → www.sandybm.com | Map Ref → UAE-E2

The Beach Hut offers a variety of water sports equipment. Diving and snorkelling equipment is also available for rent or sale. Alternatively if you just want to paddle out to Snoopy Island to explore, hire a kayak at Dhs.30 an hour.

Kitesurfing

Kitesurfing is a fast growing new sport that's gaining loads of publicity, partly because it's so extreme. It's not windsurfing, it's not wakeboarding, it's not surfing and it's not kite flying, but instead is a fusion of all these disciplines with other influences to create the wildest new water sport for years.

Dubai Kite Club, The

Location → Beh Wollongong University · Dubai | 04 884 5912
Hours → Timings on request
Web/email → www.fatimasport.com | Map Ref → UAE-C2

Along with mountain board kiting, power kiting, display kiting and kite buggys, this club also offers the chance to try kitesurfing – the only downfall is that you have to be fit to even attempt it! Equipment sale and training courses are available.

***Contact**: Fatima Sports on the above number or 050 455 5216.*

Martial Arts

Abu Dhabi Combat Club

Location → AUH Equestrian Club · Al Mushrif | 443 6333
Hours → See below
Web/email → na | Map Ref → 3-D3

Classes offered include freestyle wrestling, judo, brazilian jiu-jitsu and kickboxing. The club also gives training in self defence and unarmed combat classes. They have also organised the world's most prestigious *Submission Wrestling Tournament* for the last six years.

***Timings**: Sat - Wed 17:30 - 18:30 (children); Sat - Wed 19:30 - 21:00 (adults).*

***Cost**: Children Dhs.150 (1 month) - 800 (1 year). Adults Dhs.200 (1 month) - 1,500 (1 year).*

Baroudy's Sports Club

Location → Golden Tower · Corniche | 626 8122
Hours → 09:00 - 21:00
Web/email → tbaroudy@hotmail.com | Map Ref → na

This club teaches taekwondo, which embraces the traditional beliefs of honour, integrity, loyalty and compassion. This art teaches self defence and also improves physical fitness, mental discipline, self

control, concentration and emotional calm. They also run a children's summer camp.

Contact: *Tony Baroudy on the above number or 050 621 4399.*

Emirates Sports Centre

Location → Tourist Club Area | 676 6757
Hours → 09:00 - 13:00 & 16:00 - 21:30
Web/email → na | Map Ref → 8-A1

Sessions in karate and kung fu are available, conducted by experienced instructors, with separate classes for ladies, children and girls. They also arrange for grading sessions and certificates are issued from their international headquarters in Malaysia to successful candidates.

Contact: *Mr Hamid on the above number.*

Cost: *Per week, starting from Dhs.100 (2 lessons) - Dhs.250 (6 lessons).*

Freddie Alfaro Aikido

Location → Hiltonia Beach Club | 050 617 4596
Hours → Timings on request
Web/email → na | Map Ref → 10-C2

Aikido literally means harmony and love with the spirit of the universe. Training is not only designed to defend oneself, but to bring the assailant under control without inflicting injury – Aikido in fact rejects all forms of violence and competition.

Contact: *The above number or 681 2922/692 4218.*

Golden Dragon Kung Fu Institute

Location → Airport Rd · Al Dhafra | 632 5109
Hours → 08:00 - 13:00 16:00 - 22:00; Fri 17.00 - 21:00
Web/email → luhuiming@hotmail.com | Map Ref → 5-C2

The centre focuses on basic Shaolin arts including the Shaolin fist, stick play, knife play, swordplay, spear play and southern fists. A female coach teaches Tai Chi, Shaolin, self defence and varieties of kung fu to ladies and children.

Oriental Karate & Kobudo Club

Location → Tourist Club Area | 677 1611
Hours → Timings on request
Web/email → www.orientalkarate.com | Map Ref → 7-D1

This club offers sessions for all ages and abilities. Lessons are held at various places around Abu Dhabi; call the above number, or the following centres: Madinat Zayed (634 5080), Airport Road (445 7375) and Khalifa Street (622 4182).

Cost: *One month Dhs.100 (classes twice a week).*

UAE Wrestling Association

Location → Various locations | 050 563 3332
Hours → Timings on request
Web/email → www.adcombat.com | Map Ref → na

Previously known as the Abu Dhabi Combat Club [p.193], this association is headed by HE Mohammed bin Thaloob Al Darare. Even though the club now focuses on freestyle wrestling, kickboxing, wrestling judo and Brazilian jiu-jitsu are still offered.

Al Ain

Wadokai Karate Club

Location → Various locations · Al Ain | 050 773 5469
Hours → Timings on request
Web/email → na | Map Ref → na

Wadokai karate places an emphasis on speed and evasion and only light contact is allowed. Any age can train, from six years up and training is built up gradually and carefully. Classes are held throughout the week. Contact Kumari Adikari.

Cost: *Adults – Dhs.20 for members (Dhs.25 for non members); children – Dhs.15 for members (Dhs.20 for non members).*

Mini Golf

Other Options → Golf [p.189]

Hatta Fort Hotel

Location → Hatta Fort Hotel · Hatta | 04 852 3211
Hours → Timings on request
Web/email → www.jebelali-international.com | Map Ref → UAE-D3

The hotel offers a choice of mini golf or a 9 hole cross country fun golf course. Each hole is par 3, ranging from 68 to 173 yards. Golf instruction and lessons are available.

Cost: *Dhs.25 for two people. Dhs.35 per person (9 hole course)*

Entrance: *Dhs.40 (adults) and Dhs.20 (children), redeemable against hotel facilities .*

Moto-Cross

Other Options → Karting [p.193]

Abu Dhabi MX Club

Location → Various locations | 634 5527
Hours → Timings on request
Web/email → na | Map Ref → na

The club organises moto-cross racing and other related informal off-road motorcycling events.

Race classes are organised for all skill levels. Boys and girls are welcome. Beginners can initially borrow a bike, helmet etc, although availability may be limited depending on the day.

Contact: Klaus Schwingenschloegl (050 612 4614).

Cost: Annual fee – Dhs.250 individual; Dhs.350 family.

Motorcycling

Al Ramool Motorcycle Rental

Location → Big Red Dunes Area · Hatta | 050 453 3033
Hours → 07:00 - 18:30
Web/email → na | Map Ref → UAE-D3

Al Ramool rents out LT50, LT80, 125cc, 350cc and 620cc motorcycles. Crash helmets are provided, and prices range from Dhs.20 - 100 for 30 minutes. They offer a variety of tailor made packages– for further details, contact Mohammad Ali Rashed on teh number provided above.

Mountain Biking

Other Options → Cycling [p.182]

Contrary to the initial perception of the Emirates, the interior has a lot to offer outdoor enthusiasts, especially mountain bikers. The 'outback' is rarely visited, but on a mountain bike it's possible to see the most remote places that are inaccessible even by four wheel drive. The best areas are north of Abu Dhabi and are definitely worth the journey, as the variety of rides will satisfy even the most hardcore biker. There's a good range of terrain, from super technical rocky trails in areas like Fili and Siji, to mountain routes like Wadi Bih. The riding is challenging. Be prepared and be sensible – the sun is strong, you will need plenty of water, and it's easy to get lost. Plus falling off on this rocky terrain can be extremely painful!

For further information on mountain biking in the UAE, including details of possible routes, refer to the *Off-Road Explorer (UAE)*.

Biking Frontiers

Location → Various locations | 050 450 9401
Hours → Timings on request
Web/email → www.bikingfrontiers.com | Map Ref → na

So you're a mountain biking fan? If you don't mind thrashing through seriously rocky trails and wadis, and like getting lost once in a while... give Biking Frontiers a call! The group also enjoys camping, hiking and barbecues. Any competent mountain bikers are welcome.

Contact: Paul or Pete via the above Website.

Desert Rangers

Location → Dxb Garden Centre · Shk Zayed Rd | 04 340 2408
Hours → 08:30 - 14:30
Web/email → www.desertrangers.com | Map Ref → UAE-C2

Whether you're a fanatical biker craving challenging terrain or a complete beginner preferring a gentler introduction to the delights of off-road biking, Desert Rangers will determine a suitable route depending on your requirements and group size.

Cost: Dhs.300 per person, inclusive of bike, helmet, guide, pick up, drop off and soft drinks.

Mountain Biking

Mountaineering

Other Options → Climbing [p.181]

The area surrounding Abu Dhabi is mostly flat sandy desert; however, there are regions inland that are a paradise for the more adventurous mountain walker. The northern Ru'us Al Jibal Mountains contain the highest peaks in the area, at over 2,000 metres. To the east, the Hajar Mountains form the border between the UAE and Oman. Trips range from short easy walks leading to spectacular viewpoints, to all day treks over difficult terrain. Many of the routes follow centuries old Bedouin and Shihuh trails and some are still used to access remote settlements. Heat and humidity indicate that walking is best between November and April.

For further information, refer to the *Off-Road Explorer (UAE)*.

***Warning**: No mountain rescue services exist, so trekkers should either be reasonably experienced, or with someone who knows the area. For advice, contact Alistair MacKenzie (Alistair@Explorer-Publishing.com)*

Paintballing

Other Options → Shooting [p.198]

At present there's nowhere in Abu Dhabi to cover friends or relatives in paint! However, addicts can always make the trip north since this fun activity is available in Dubai through Pursuit Games at Wonderlands. For more information see the *Dubai Explorer*.

Pursuit Games

Location → WonderLand · Dubai | 04 324 1222
Hours → Timings on request
Web/email → wonderld@emirates.net.ae | Map Ref → UAE-C2

Great for teenagers and/or adults; get a crowd together and they'll quickly be divided into teams by the experts, who give a thorough safety demonstration before equipping everyone with overalls, 'Darth Vader' type facemasks and special guns equipped with paintballs.

***Cost**: Dhs.70 for a two hour game with 100 paintballs.*

***Contact**: Kaz (050 651 4583).*

Parachuting

At present this exciting sport is not available in the Abu Dhabi emirate. However, those willing to travel can contact Umm Al Quwain Flying Club (06 768 1447) or refer to the *Dubai Explorer*.

Paragliding

Other Options → Flying [p.188]

To attempt paragliding in the UAE you will have to travel to the northern emirates, and visit the Umm Al Quwain Flying Club (06 768 1447), since it is not available in Abu Dhabi. Also refer to the *Dubai Explorer*.

Polo

Other Options → Horse Riding [p.191]

Ghantoot Polo & Racing Club

Location → Shk Zayed Rd · Btn Dubai & Abu Dhabi | 562 9050
Hours → Timings on request
Web/email → na | Map Ref → UAE-B3

The polo season starts in October and continues until the end of April. The calendar is full with regular chukka tournaments and high profile international games. The quality of play and horses is high and spectators are always welcome.

***Location**: Halfway between Dubai and Abu Dhabi, near Al Jazira Hotel and Resort.*

Rally Driving

Emirates Motor Sports Federation

Location → Nr Aviation Club · Dubai | 04 282 7111
Hours → Timings on request
Web/email → www.emsf.ae | Map Ref → UAE-C2

The sanctioning authority for all motor sports and motoring events in the UAE – they organise a variety of events throughout the year; such as the *UAE Rally Championship* and the *Emirates Autocross Championship,* as well as several non competitive events.

Rollerblading

Other Options → Beaches [p.132]

Great fun and great exercise, this sport is for adults and children alike! Look for areas with few people and enough slopes and turns to make it interesting – and to increase your skills and balance. In Abu Dhabi the Corniche and Breakwater make a good long paved area and taking in the view is a bonus (although present construction hampers this somewhat). Another paved area with nice views of the mangroves and gazebos dotting the grass is the

New Corniche on the eastern side of the island. Take care though; it does get busy in the cool of the evenings. Prepare for the inevitable falls with helmets and knee, elbow and wrist pads, just in case!

Rugby

Abu Dhabi Rugby Football Club

Location → Madinat Zayed · Abu Dhabi | 050 662 3069
Hours → Timings on request
Web/email → na | Map Ref → 7-A2

Affiliated to the Arabian Gulf Rugby Football Union, the club currently has over 100 members, and all teams take part in various tournaments. The ladies team were 1999 Gulf League Champions. There are children's sessions as well. All standards of players or non players are welcome.

Contact: *Club Captain, Aubrey Roberts (050 662 3069); Ladies Coach, Clare Shryane (050 626 1661); Riaan Smuts (050 536 3718) for minis and youth.*

Al Ain Amblers Rugby Club

Location → Htl InterContinental · Al Ain | 050 623 0941
Hours → Timings on request
Web/email → na | Map Ref → 15-E4

Formed in early 1981 by expats, the club now consists of all standards of players. Future plans include starting a youth and mini section for children aged 10 - 16.

Contact: *Club Chairman on the above number.*

Dubai Exiles Rugby Club

Location → Nr Dubai Country Club · Al Awir Rd | 04 333 1198
Hours → Timings on request
Web/email → www.dubaiexiles.com | Map Ref → UAE-C2

Training sessions are scheduled throughout the week with the 1st and 2nd XVs meeting on Sundays and Wednesdays, veterans on Tuesdays and Saturdays. There's also training for children (minis) on Mondays and Wednesdays. Matches take place on most Friday afternoons and some Wednesdays.

Note: *Clubhouse facilities are available for hire.*

Running

Other Options → Hashing [p.190]

For over half the year, the weather couldn't be better for running in the Emirates, although even in the summer, despite high temperatures and humidity, you'll find dedicated runners out all over the UAE. In the hottest months, the evenings and early mornings are the best times to run.

Clubs and informal groups meet regularly, with some runs being competitive or training runs, for the events organised throughout the year. Regular, short distance races are held, as well as a variety of biathlons, triathlons and hashes. A favourite competition is the epic Wadi Bih Run. Teams of five run the 70 km from Ras Al Khaimah to Dibba over mountains topping out at over 1,000 metres. Backed by a support vehicle, runners take turns on different stages. A relatively new event is the Dubai Marathon, held in January.

Contact: *Wadi Bih race, John Gregory (050 647 7120).*

Abu Dhabi Striders

Location → Various locations | 050 441 4886
Hours → Wed 18:00
Web/email → na | Map Ref → na

Formed by runners who were looking for fellow enthusiasts, this club's members are from all walks of life with many standards of fitness. Each year, they organise a 10 km half marathon and full marathon as well as various social events.

Contact: *Ash (050 692 8601) or Steve Reay on the above number.*

Al Ain Road Runners

Location → Htl InterContinental · Al Ain | 050 618 3702
Hours → Every Sat, Tue & Wed
Web/email → na | Map Ref → 15-E4

Al Ain Road Runners are generally runners and hashers who want to do a 'bit more'. They have two routes at each training session, one for the jogger of about 5 km and one for the more serious runner. All are welcome.

Sailing

Other Options → Boat & Yacht Charters [p.179]

Sailing is a lovely pastime and one that can easily be indulged in Abu Dhabi. From hotels that charter boats for a one day excursion; to an offshore island or a several week trip, to friends who moor their catamarans at the marina; opportunities to get out on the water abound. Membership of the sailing clubs allows you use of the leisure facilities, to join in the activities, hire sailing and water sports equipment and moor or store your boat (always an extra cost!). Several clubs offer lessons for novices

as well. In addition, many companies avail of this activity by taking employees out on a pleasure cruise or fishing. While the summer months can be scorching, the winter is perfect for setting sail. If you enjoy the sea, you're in the right place!

Abu Dhabi Catamaran Association

Location → Abu Dhabi Corniche | 443 5339
Hours → Timings on request
Web/email → na | Map Ref → na

This small but keen sailing club caters to the multi-hull boat sailor in Abu Dhabi. They offer advice to prospective owners, access to spare parts, tools, and lots of friendly 'know how'. Membership fees are reasonable and new members are always welcome.

Contact: *Commodore Kingsley Ashford-Brown on the above number.*

Abu Dhabi Sailing Club

Location → Club, The · Al Meena | 673 1111
Hours → Timings on request
Web/email → www.the-club.com | Map Ref → 7-A2

A fleet of Kestrels and Lasers are assigned to members who qualify as helms, who are also then responsible for maintenance and seaworthiness. Instruction can be arranged for beginners, leading through to certification. Membership open only to members of The Club.

Cost: *Annual membership of the sub-section is Dhs.950.*

Contact: *Carol Milne (621 7394).*

Sand Boarding/Skiing

The big dunes at Liwa are a wonderful place to try this exciting and unusual sport. Feel the 'rush' of the wind as you take a slow, jerky ride down the sandy slopes. It's a quick sport to learn and it doesn't hurt when you fall.

The boards are usually standard snowboards, but as the sand is quite hard on them, they often can't be used for anything else afterwards. Some sports stores sell 'sand boards', which are cheaper and more basic snowboards. As an alternative for children, a plastic sledge is enough to provide a lot of fun.

All the major tour companies offer tours and give basic instruction on how to stay up, surf and fall properly. This can be available either as part of another tour or as a dedicated sand boarding tour. A half day sand boarding tour costs Dhs.175 - 200.

Shooting

Other Options → Paintballing [p.196]

At present there are no shooting clubs in Abu Dhabi for expats to join, so your best bet is to head north to Dubai, Ras Al Khaimah or Umm Al Quwain for some target practice.

Hatta Fort Hotel

Location → Hatta Fort Hotel · Hatta | 04 852 3211
Hours → Timings on request
Web/email → www.jebelali-international.com | Map Ref → UAE-D3

Clay pigeon shooting is one of the many activities offered at the hotel. More frequently visited as an overnight retreat, they have a variety of sports, plus the added attraction of superb food and beverage facilities, including a Friday barbie for Dhs.85 net.

Entrance: *Dhs.40 (adults), Dhs.20 (children), redeemable against hotel facilities.*

Cost: *Dhs.95 for 25 shots. Day visitors on Fridays and public holidays.*

Jebel Ali Shooting Club

Location → Nr Jebel Ali Golf Resert & Spa | 04 883 6555
Hours → 13:00 - 22:00
Web/email → www.jebelali-international.com | Map Ref → UAE-B3

Shooting is done in clay on five different floodlit ranges from Skeet to Ball Trap, American Trap, Olympic Trap and Sporting, as well as on the indoor 25 metre computerised pistol range. Instructors are available for lessons in either pistol or clay shooting.

Cost: *Clay shooting Dhs.100 (non members) & Dhs.75 (member); Pistol shooting Dhs.75 (non members) & Dhs.50 (members).*

Ras Al Khaimah Shooting Club

Location → Al Dehes · Nr RAK Airport | 07 236 3622
Hours → 15:00 - 20:00
Web/email → na | Map Ref → UAE-D1

This club welcomes anyone interested in learning to shoot any type of gun, from 9mm pistols to shotguns and long rifles. There are a variety of ranges, from the indoor 50 metre rifle range to the outdoor 200 metre rifle range.

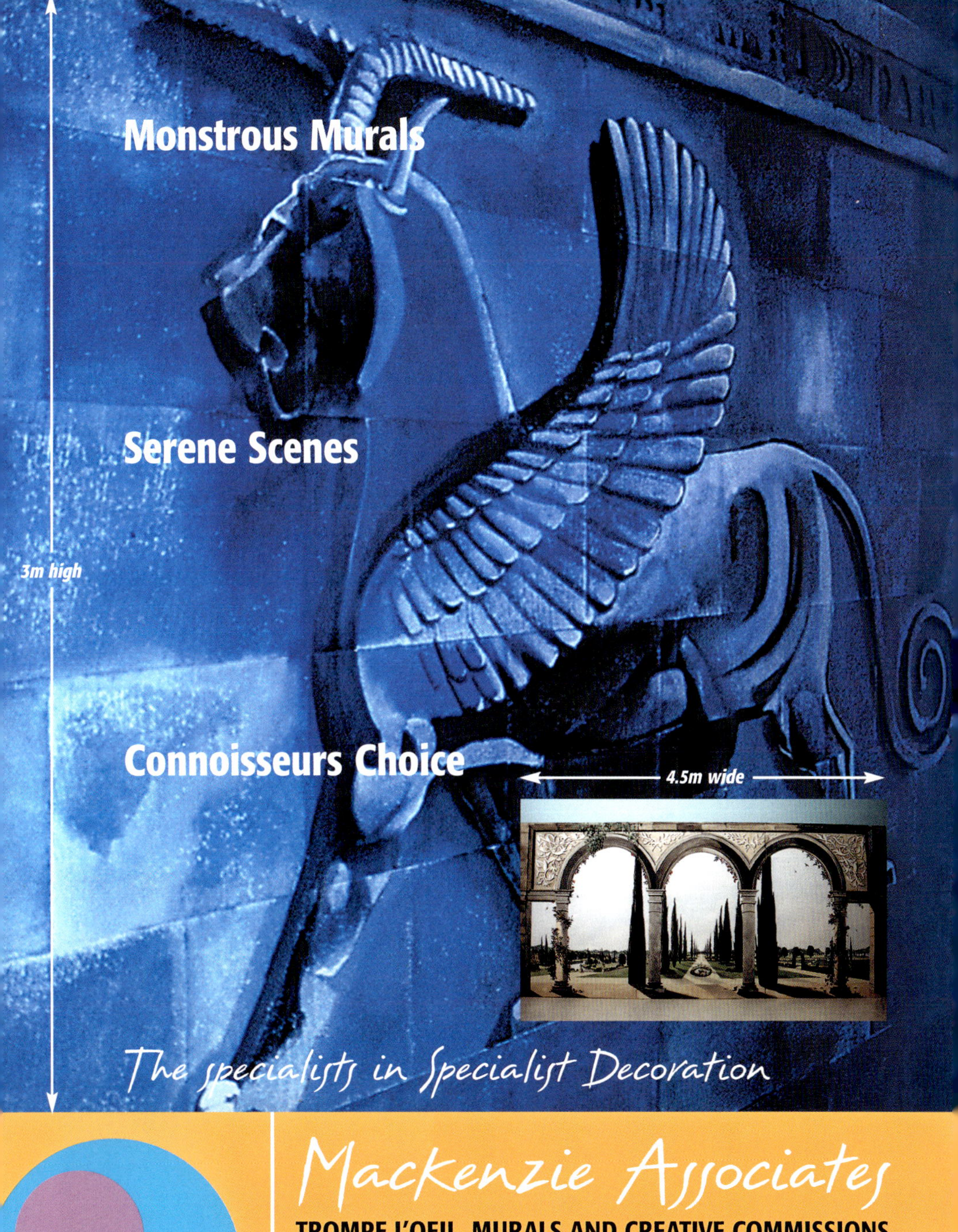
Monstrous Murals
Serene Scenes
3m high
Connoisseurs Choice
4.5m wide
The specialists in Specialist Decoration

Skydiving

Umm Al Quwain Aeroclub

Location → Al Ittihad St · Umm Al Quwain | 06 768 1447
Hours → Timings on request
Web/email → www.uaqaeroclub.com | Map Ref → UAE-C1

In addition to flying, paramotors and microlights, this club operates as a skydive school and boogie centre. You can train for your international parachute licence; enjoy an eight level AFF (Accelerated Free Fall) or try a tandem jump with an instructor.

See Also: *Flying [p.188]*

Snooker

Abu Dhabi Snooker Centre

Location → Sedar Bld · Khalidiya | 633 3300
Hours → 09:00 - 24:00; Fri 15:00 - 24:00
Web/email → mmgroup@emirates.net.ae | Map Ref → 9-A1

This was the first snooker hall in Abu Dhabi and is currently open to anyone wishing to play, although a membership scheme may eventually come into operation. There are eight full sized BBL Monarch tables imported from the UK. Pre-booking is advisable.

Cost: *Dhs.25 for one hour.*

Al Ain

Shooters

Location → Htl InterContinental · Al Ain | 03 768 6686
Hours → 18:00 - 01:00
Web/email → na | Map Ref → 15-E4

Home to four pool tables and a snooker table and available to all who want to brush up on their skills. The club aims to be closely associated with other pool and snooker clubs around the country. Refreshments and snacks are available.

Snorkelling

Other Options → Diving [p.185]

A mask and snorkel is a great way to see the varied underwater life of the Gulf or the East Coast, where it is especially good. On the Gulf of Oman coast, popular places include Snoopy Island, near the Sandy Beach Motel, Dibba. There are also good spots further north, such as the beach north of Dibba village, where the coast is rocky and there's coral close to the shore. For somewhere closer to home, the sea off Jumeira Beach in Dubai has a fair amount of marine life. Most hotels or dive centres rent equipment; snorkel, mask and fins. Costs vary greatly, so shop around.

Check out the *Underwater Explorer (UAE)* for further information on where and how to go snorkelling in the UAE.

Blue Dolphin Company LLC

Location → Htl InterContinental · Bainuna St | 666 9392
Hours → 08:00 - 13:00 16:00 - 19:00
Web/email → www.interconti.com | Map Ref → 10-C1

Snorkel equipment can be hired for Dhs.50 per set for 24 hours. Alternatively, for Dhs.500 the company will take about five people to an interesting snorkelling area, such as off Ras Al Ghurb Island. Timings available on request.

Fujairah

Beach Hut, The

Location → Sandy Beach Motel · Fujairah | 09 244 5050
Hours → 08:00 - 17:30
Web/email → www.sandybm.com | Map Ref → UAE-E2

For those who want an exhilarating snorkelling experience, this East Coast venue is the only way to go. Snoopy Island is just off their private beach and is an excellent site to enjoy the underwater world.

Cost: *Equipment rental Dhs.50 per day.*

Underwater Life

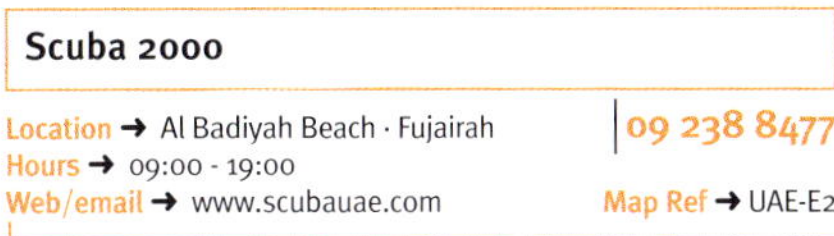

Scuba 2000

Location → Al Badiyah Beach · Fujairah | 09 238 8477
Hours → 09:00 - 19:00
Web/email → www.scubauae.com | Map Ref → UAE-E2

This East Coast centre offers snorkelling, either directly from the beach or with a boat ride, usually to Snoopy and Sharque Islands. Snorkelling trips cost Dhs.90 inclusive of boat ride, fins, mask, snorkel and boots. Additional water sports facilities are also available.

Oceanic Hotel

Location → Beach Rd · Khor Fakkan | 09 238 5111
Hours → 09:00 - 17:00
Web/email → www.oceanichotel.com | Map Ref → UAE-E2

The hotel offers boat rides to Sharque Island and provides snorkelling gear for Dhs.60. All prices apply to hotel residents.

Entrance: *Dhs.45 (adults) & Dhs.25 (children)*

Squash

Other Options → Beach, Health & Sports Clubs [p.204]

Courts are for hire mainly through the hotel sports clubs and private clubs. The squash league provides the best opportunities for competitive playing and meeting new players.

Abu Dhabi Squash League

Location → Various locations | 622 4292
Hours → Wed 18:30
Web/email → na | Map Ref → na

Run under the auspices of the Abu Dhabi Squash Rackets Association, the league has been going for over 25 years. Several tournaments are run throughout the year. There's no age eligibility, but a reasonable level of play is required.

Cost: *Annual fee Dhs.1,000 per team.*

Contact: *Chairman Medhat Al Hammami on the above number.*

Swimming

Other Options → Beach, Health & Sports Clubs [p.204]

Abu Dhabi's location on the Arabian Gulf means easy access to water that's relatively clean and a pleasant temperature for most of the year. During the three hottest months of the summer, the water near the beach is often hotter than a bath!

Most hotels have swimming pools that are open for use by the public for a day entrance fee. This charge varies, but ranges from Dhs.50 - 60 weekdays and Dhs.75 - 100 at weekends. Swimming lessons are available. The pools are usually cooled for the summer months.

Swimming off the beaches is possible, whether it's a public beach, beach club or park. Remember to be modest in your choice of costume and, on the East Coast of the UAE, keep an eye out for jellyfish.

Warning: *When swimming in the sea, do not underestimate the strength of the tides and currents. Even on the safest looking beaches, rip tides have been known to carry people out to sea.*

Table Tennis

Other Options → Beach, Health & Sports Clubs [p.204]

Please refer to the list of beach, health and sports clubs. Most offer at least one table tennis table.

Tennis

Other Options → Beach, Health & Sports Clubs [p.204]

Tennis is well provided for in Abu Dhabi, with courts available for use by the public in hotels or in private organisations solely for their members. Many courts have floodlighting to allow play in the evenings – the coolest time of the day, and about the only time you'll want to play outside in the summer. Prices for hiring courts vary between Dhs.25 - 50 weekdays, but you may be charged as much as Dhs.100 on weekends. Group or individual coaching is widely available.

For those interested in professional tennis, Dubai has firmly established itself on the international tennis circuit with the US$1,000,000 *Dubai Duty Free Tennis Open*, held in the middle of February each year at Dubai Tennis Stadium. For further information, check out the *Dubai Explorer*.

Dubai Tennis Academy

Location → American University · Dubai | 04 397 5828
Hours → Timings on request
Web/email → na | Map Ref → UAE-C2

The Academy offers professional coaching year round for aspiring players of all ages and abilities. They organise international tennis

clinics to tie in with major tournaments on the pro tennis circuit. Their full time adult and junior programmes include private lessons, group clinics and competitions.

Triathlon

There are a fair number of triathlon enthusiasts in the Emirates. Through the winter season, from about October to April, there's quite a busy calendar of triathlons, biathlons and aquathons held in Abu Dhabi and Dubai.

Abu Dhabi Triathlon Club

Location → Various locations | 050 311 5346
Hours → Timings on request
Web/email → www.geocities.com/abudhabitri | Map Ref → na

Formed in late 2000 for a simple reason; to encourage people to get together for training, racing, and socializing. The club is pretty informal, and as such as no 'president' etc. Members are kept up to date via Yahoo Groups.

Wadi & Dune Bashing

Other Options → Camping [p.180]

With vast areas of rarely visited wilderness to explore, wadi and dune bashing are among the most popular pastimes in the UAE. The wadis, the mountains, the desert and the African 'savannah like' plains offer a variety of challenging driving.

Dune or desert driving is possibly the toughest challenge and a lot of fun, while in the wadis the driving is relatively straightforward. If you're going off-road, it's always advisable to travel with at least two vehicles. If anything goes wrong, you'll be glad for an extra pair of hands or a tow. If you are trying desert driving for the first time, go with an experienced person, since driving on sand requires very different skills to other surfaces. Caution should be the watchword.

One point about the word 'bashing' – while a popular term for this form of entertainment, it can be misleading. Most, if not all, of your journey should be on existing tracks to protect the environment from further damage. For more information, refer to the *Off-Road Explorer (UAE)*.

Tour companies offer a range of desert and mountain safaris. See Tour Operators [p.133].

Four wheel drives can be hired from most car hire companies. See Car Rental Agencies [p.92].

OffRoad Emirates

Location → Nr BHS Bld · Shk Hamdan St | 633 3232
Hours → 08:00 - 13:00 16:00 - 19:00
Web/email → www.offroademirates.com | Map Ref → 8-A1

Specializing in tours through the desert regions of Abu Dhabi, as well as trips into Oman and Sir Bani Yas Island. Trips are well suited for individuals and small groups who share a sense of adventure and respect culture, nature and history.

Contact: *George Duncan on the number above.*

Wakeboarding

Other Options → Beaches [p.132]

Al Jazira Hotel and Resort

Location → Btn Abu Dhabi & Dubai · Jazira | 562 9100
Hours → Timings on request
Web/email → na | Map Ref → UAE-B3

The Al Jazira Resort, with its secluded bay, is a great spot to learn this sport without looking like a complete loser. Once you've figured the basics out, addiction might follow. Ten minutes, including a driver, costs around Dhs.50.

Water Parks

Other Options → Amusement Parks [p.178]

At present, Abu Dhabi doesn't have a water park; however, a family trip to Dreamland Aqua Park in Umm Al Quwain is worthwhile, and is excellent value for money. Wild Wadi in Dubai is another attractive option. For further information on water parks, refer to the *Dubai Explorer*.

Water Park

Dubai

SplashLand

Location → WonderLand · Dubai | 04 324 1222
Hours → See below
Web/email → www.wonderlanduae.com | Map Ref → UAE-C2

SplashLand is part of the WonderLand Theme & Water Park experience. Try any of the nine water rides, sunbathe poolside or eat at one of the restaurants. Lockers and changing rooms are available. See entry under Water Parks [p.202] also.

Timings: Change seasonally, so call to confirm.

Wild Wadi Water Park

Location → Umm Suqeim · Dubai | 04 348 4444
Hours → See timings below
Web/email → www.wildwadi.com | Map Ref → UAE-C2

Dubai's Wild Wadi, based around the adventures of Juha, Sinbad's mythical friend, offers a variety of water rides, from the relaxing to the downright thrilling. For the young and young at heart, this stunning park offers a day of unforgettable fun.

Timings: Open from 11:00 daily but closing times vary. Check before you head there.

Umm Al Quwain

Dreamland Aqua Park

Location → North on RAK Rd · Umm Al Quwain | 06 768 1888
Hours → 10:00 - 20:00
Web/email → www.dreamlanduae.com | Map Ref → UAE-C1

Dreamland Aqua Park brings you the excitement of four million gallons of fresh water, over 60 acres of grounds and 25 aquatic and non aquatic attractions. It is one of the largest aqua parks in the world.

Entrance: Dhs.40 (adults); Dhs.20 (children).

Timings: Vary according to season. Fri & public holidays for families, season pass holders and pre-booked groups only.

Water Skiing

Other Options → Beach Clubs [p.204]

Al Jazira Hotel and Resort

Location → Btn Abu Dhabi & Dubai · Jazira | 562 9100
Hours → Timings on request
Web/email → na | Map Ref → UAE-B3

Fascinated by the thought of doing dazzling acrobatics on water, but don't want to be seen attempting it at your club? Drive up to Al Jazira for the perfect opportunity to escape and learn how to ride the water professionally. Coaching is available.

Cost: Dhs.50 for 10 minutes. Six coaching sessions, Dhs.400.

Well Being

Long term visitors or residents will find that although the choice of activities in Abu Dhabi is not huge, the range is continuously changing and growing. The following section covers a variety of pleasurable and interesting activities for your leisure time, from educational classes and the environment to language schools or the performing arts, such as music and dance, and much more in between. There's also a comprehensive review of the beach and health clubs that the emirate has to offer. Most of these are operated by the hotels, which often act as the focus for activities and events in the city. Whatever your leisure pleasure, there's a good chance someone in town is willing to provide it.

Beauty & Hair Salons

Other Options → Beauty Training [p.208]

Beauty is big business in the UAE. Women here take their grooming seriously and often sport impeccable hair and makeup. The aesthetic and approach can vary among the many cultures residing in Abu Dhabi; and it can be fun to explore the range of styles and services.

Many salons offer a variety of treatments, from European facials to Morrocan steam baths; from full body waxing to bridal hair and makeup. Nail bars are also starting to spring up in Abu Dhabi. Some provide extra services; all are nice places for a relaxing afternoon with the girls.

One local tradition you might want to try out is henna design. Elaborate and delicate patterns are painted on the hands and feet. These are used especially to mark special occasions such as weddings, but don't worry too much, they fade after a few weeks.

As can be expected, the quality and range of treatments vary greatly, so trial and error or word of mouth is probably the best way to find a good salon.

Health Spas

Other Options → Beach, Health & Sports Clubs [p.204]

Health Spa & Leisure Club

Location → Le Meridien · Tourist Club Area | 697 4254
Hours → 09:00 - 22:00
Web/email → spa@meridien-abudhabi.co.ae | Map Ref → 7-D1

The ultimate in stress relief and personal pampering! Treatments include sessions in the aquamedic pool, massages, facials, seaweed wraps, Turkish baths as well as more medicinal treatments, such as 'pressotherapy' for lymphatic drainage.

Massage

Other Options → Beach, Health & Sports Clubs [p.204]

Probably the ultimate way to pamper and unwind is by having a massage. Whether it's a regular weekly treat or to get over a particularly trying time at work, it's sure to relax and soothe. Massage is an area where the multicultural nature of the city comes into play, and you can try an assortment of different types of massage. Available currently are Thai, Swedish, and Ayurvedic massage, which are on offer at various hotels, health clubs and salons in Abu Dhabi. Prices and standards vary, so shop around until you find someone that suits you. The cost for a full body massage ranges from Dhs.100 - 220 for one hour of heaven.

Meditation & Reiki

Reiki and meditation are excellent for creating a sense of calm and well being. While meditation can be performed at home with only basic knowledge, reiki is a healing technique based on the belief that energy can be channelled into the patient by means of touch.

Translated as 'universal life force energy', reiki can, like meditation, emotionally cleanse, physically invigorate and leave you more focused.

Beach, Health & Sports Clubs

Relaxation junkies and fitness fanatics should have no problem finding facilities that suit them from among Abu Dhabi's excellent range of beach, health, golf and sports clubs. Neighbourhood gyms also exist for those who prefer things basic.

Built on an island, there are few good public beaches in the capital. There are some wide stretches of sand in the northwest corner of the island, but they lack facilities. Al Raha Beach is a large public beach with facilities, but it is out of the way, being just over the bridge. Many people, therefore, choose to join one of the beach clubs to swim, play sports, sunbathe and enjoy excellent food and drink in relative peace and quiet.

Most places offer membership schemes. Before becoming a member, have a good look around at what's on offer. Most of the clubs allow day entry to non members for a fee. At weekends, many have a Friday brunch or barbecue and the price includes use of the leisure facilities as well as food. They are popular with families and can get quite busy.

Refer to the Club Facilities Table [p.206] for club details, including rates and facilities.

Beach Clubs

Other Options → Beaches [p.132]

Abu Dhabi Marina 'The Yacht Club'

Location → Tourist Club Area | 644 0300
Hours → Timings on request
Web/email → www.abudhabimarina.com | Map Ref → 4-B4

This club, with its gym, squash, and tennis courts, has its own private beach and marina. Surrounded by small waterfalls, sunloungers and an Arabic tent, it's easy to relax by the large swimming pool. A children's area is also available.

***Entrance**: Dhs.50; peak times Dhs.100.*

Abu Dhabi Tourist Club

Location → Nr Le Meridien Htl · Tourist Club Area | 672 3400
Hours → 08:00 - 24:00
Web/email → adclub@emirates.net.ae | Map Ref → 7-D1

This club offers a range of activities for all ages. From water sports and children's play areas to a bowling alley, marina facilities, badminton, tennis, martial arts, library, food outlets and an Internet café, the club is a virtual hive of activity.

Club, The

Location → Club, The · Al Meena | 673 1111
Hours → 08:00 - 01:00; Fri 08:00 - 24:00
Web/email → www.the-club.com | Map Ref → 7-A2

Reasonable prices, a wide range of facilities, entertainment and activities and a friendly

atmosphere are the hallmarks of The Club. Membership is by application and access restricted to members and their guests.

Palm Beach Leisure Club

Location → Al Diar Gulf Htl · Al Maqtaa | 441 4777
Hours → 9:00 until sunset
Web/email → www.aldiarhotels.com | Map Ref → 1-D3

Family orientated with large grassy grounds interspersed with palms, this leisure club is ideal for those living in the outer areas of the city. The swimming pool and beach are delightful, and there's a gym and a play area for younger children, plus plenty of acitivites on offer. Call for details.

Palms Resort

Location → Sheraton Resort · Corniche Rd East | 677 3333
Hours → 07:30 - 22:30
Web/email → sheraton.abudhabi@sheraton.com | Map Ref → 8-A3

One of the older and more established beach resorts in Abu Dhabi offering a gym, swimming pool, children's pool, play area and activity club. Activities include sailing, windsurfing, water skiing, catamaran, fishing, island and sightseeing cruises, banana rides, tennis and squash.

Sadiyat Island Beach Resthouse

Location → Tourist Club · Tourist Club Area | 672 3400
Hours → Timings on request
Web/email → na | Map Ref → 7-D1

Managed by the Abu Dhabi Tourist Club, this resort is a short boat ride away from the capital. A variety of water sports and games are on offer. Chalets provide overnight accommodation, while the restaurant offers international cuisine.

Al Diar Jazira Beach Resort

Location → Al Diar Jazira Htl · Jazira | 562 9100
Hours → 09:00 - 18:00; Thu & Fri 09:00 - 19:00
Web/email → jazbeach@emirates.net.ae | Map Ref → UAE-B3

Want to get out of Abu Dhabi for a while? This resort has enough to entertain the whole family, including a beach, water sports centre, health club, pool and golf. There's also a beach party on Fridays with free camel rides.

Sports Clubs

Abu Dhabi Ladies Club

Location → Nr Ladies Beach · Al Ras Al Akhdar | 666 2228
Hours → Timings on request
Web/email → na | Map Ref → 10-E4

This opulent club provides a unique concept in entertainment, sports, fitness and leisure exclusively for ladies and children. Besides the usual fitness facilities, the Club offers children's activities, a library, computers, arts and crafts classes, and the famous Cleopatra's Spa.

Cost: *Dhs.1500 (3 month), Dhs.2,500 (6 months) & Dhs.3,500 (1 year).*

Expand Your Horizons

While outdoor and physical activities are well represented in Abu Dhabi, there are other leisure time pursuits available to stimulate the intellect

Health Club

Club Membership Rates & Facilities

Club Name	Location	Area	Map	Tel. no.
Beach Clubs & Spas				
Abu Dhabi Marina & Yacht Club	Nr Le Meridien Hotel	Tourist Club Area	7-D1	644 0300
Abu Dhabi Tourist Club	Nr Le Meridien Hotel	Tourist Club Area	7-D1	672 3400
Beach Club, Rotana*	Nr Le Meridien Htl, Tourist Club Area	Tourist Club Area	7-D1	644 3000
Beach Club, The, Khalidia	Khalidia Palace Hotel	Al Ras Al Akhdar	10-E2	666 2470
Club, The*	Al Meena Port	Al Meena	7-A2	673 1111
Health Spa and Leisure Club	Le Meridien Hotel	Tourist Club Area	7-D1	697 4254
Hiltonia Beach & Sports Club	Hilton Abu Dhabi	Corniche Rd West	10-C2	681 1900
Palm Beach Leisure Club	Al Diar Gulf Hotel & Resort	Al Maqtaa	1-D3	441 4777
Palms Resort	Sheraton Abu Dhabi Resort & Towers	Corniche Rd	8-A3	677 3333
Jazira				
Al Diar Jazira Beach Resort	Between Dubai & Abu Dhabi Road	Jazira	na	562 9100
Health Clubs				
Abu Dhabi Health & Fitness Club	Abu Dhabi Golf & Equestrian Club	Al Mushrif	3-D3	445 9600
Abu Dhabi Ladies Club	Nr Khalidia Palace Hotel	Al Ras Al Akhdar	10-E4	6662228
Abu Dhabi Health Club	Al Ain Palace Hotel	Corniche Rd	8-B3	679 4777
Falcon Health Club	Abu Dhabi Tourist Club	Tourist Club Area	7-D1	672 3400
Inter-Fitness, Abu Dhabi	Hotel InterContinental	Al Khalidya	10-C1	666 6888
Le Club Health & Fitness	Millennium Hotel	Shk Khalifa St	7-B2	626 2700
Powerfit Executive Fitness Centre	Crowne Plaza	Shk Hamdan St	7-C1	621 0000
Sands Hotel Fitness Club	Sands Hotel	Shk Zayed 2nd St	7-C1	633 5335
Skyline Health Club*	Hilton Baynunah Tower	Corniche Rd	9-A2	632 7777
Viking Health Club*	Sheraton Residence, Abu Dhabi	Shk Zayed 1st St	9-B1	666 6220
Al Ain				
Bodylines*	Al Ain Rotana Hotel	Shk Zayed Rd	15-A3	754 5111
Hiltonia Resort & Aquatic Club*	Hilton Al Ain	Al Niyadat	15-D4	768 6666
Inter-Fitness, Al Ain*	Hotel InterContinental	Al Niyadat	15-D4	768 6686

*Weekend prices are subject to change.

State of the Art Fitness Equipment

Annual Membership Rates					Gym						Activity				Relaxation				
Male	Female	Couple	Family	Non Members (daily)	Treadmills	Exercise Bikes	Step Machines	Rowing Machines	Free Weights	Resistance Machines	Tennis Courts	Swimming Pool	Squash Courts	Aerobics/Dance Exercise	Massage	Sauna	Jacuzzi	Plunge Pool	Steam Room
3,500	2,500	3,500	4,000+	50	1	1	1	–	✔	2	3	2	2	–	–	–	–	–	–
On req	On req	On req	On req	–	6	5	3	2	✔	10	6	2	–	–	✔	✔	✔	–	✔
3,800	2,500	5,000	6,600	35	✔	✔	✔	✔	✔	✔	3	2	2	✔	✔	✔	✔	–	✔
3,800	2,800	5,000	800	35	9	2	2	1	✔	8	1	3	–	✔	✔	✔	✔	–	✔
On req	On req	–	On req	–	8	6	3	3	✔	10	4	1	2	✔	✔	✔	✔	✔	✔
8,000	6,000	10,000	10,000	90	5	4	2	2	✔	16	2	2	2	✔	✔	✔	✔	✔	✔
6,400	4,700	9,300	10,400	100	8	6	2	3	✔	4	2	2	1	✔	✔	✔	✔	✔	✔
4,000	3,000	7,000	7,000	80	5	3	2	2	✔	30	4	1	2	✔	✔	✔	✔	✔	✔
8,500	4,900	10,500	10,500	100	8	4	2	2	✔	25	2	3	2	✔	✔	✔	✔	✔	–
1,500	1,500	2,000	2,500	100	1	2	1	1	✔	–	2	2	1	–	✔	✔	✔	–	✔
4,000	3,000	4,500	6000	100	7	10	6	2	✔	6	4	2	2	✔	✔	✔	✔	✔	✔
–	3,500	–	7,000	–	5	3	2	2	✔	11	2	2	–	✔	✔	✔	✔	–	✔
2,400	1,800	–	3,400	50	4	6	2	1	✔	15	–	✔	2	✔	✔	✔	✔	✔	✔
2,000	2,000	–	–	30	6	5	3	2	✔	10	6	1	–	✔	✔	✔	✔	–	✔
14,000	13,000	9,500	11,000	50	9	6	3	2	✔	13	4	1	1	✔	✔	✔	✔	✔	✔
3,000	2,500	5,000	–	60	2	3	1	–	✔	1	–	1	–	–	✔	✔	✔	–	✔
3,499	2,499	4,099	5,099	60	5	6	2	1	✔	17	–	✔	–	–	✔	✔	✔	✔	✔
1,500	1,200	1,500	2,200	30	–	–	–	–	✔	–	–	–	–	–	–	–	–	–	–
On req	On req	On req	2,800	35	3	2	1	1	✔	9	–	1	–	✔	✔	✔	–	–	✔
2,500	2,000	3,500	4,000	30	3	3	1	–	✔	8	–	1	–	–	✔	✔	–	–	✔
2,750	1,800	3,250	On Req	80	3	2	1	1	✔	15	2	2	2	✔	✔	✔	✔	–	✔
2,300	2,300	2,800	3,000	35	5	6	5	2	✔	1	4	3	1	✔	✔	✔	✔	–	✔
3,000	2,500	3,500	4,000	70	5	4	2	2	✔	1	4	3	2	✔	✔	✔	✔	✔	✔

Luxurious Pools

or the artist in you. These range from classes in singing and musical instruments to sculpture, languages, and Arabic calligraphy. There are also special interest groups focusing on hobbies as diverse as film making, poetry, quilting and cookery. Ask around and check local newspapers and magazines for the latest information. Schedules are not always available in advance, so often your best bet is to visit a gallery or cultural organisation to get up to date news. You can also check notice boards at health clubs and supermarkets; at times local groups or clubs place flyers there.

Delma Corner (of the Cultural Foundation)

Location → Opp New Etisalat · Shk Zayed 1st St | 619 5313
Hours → 08:30 - 14:00 17:00 - 21:00
Web/email → www.cultural.org.ae | Map Ref → 9-A1

Inside the Cultural Foundation, there is a relaxed meeting point for artists in all mediums, from music to art to filmmaking and poetry. There are 16 groups devoted to these varied pursuits. In addition, exhibitions are staged – a vital cultural niche in the capital.

Art Classes

Other Options → Art Supplies [p.150]

Art Movies

Location → Various locations · Abu Dhabi | na
Hours → Timings on request
Web/email → artmoviesabudhabi@hotmail.com | Map Ref → na

The fourth season of Art Movies, a celebration of European films, is due to open in October 2004. This organization screens movies, which, as their slogan proclaims, are 'Beyond Hollywood and Bollywood'. Contact the email address above for more information.

Craft Corner

Location → Lulu Refreshments Bld · Airport Rd | 622 2563
Hours → Timings on request
Web/email → CCAbuDhabi@aol.com | Map Ref → 8-E2

Craft Corner offers a variety of quality craft supplies at affordable prices. They also offer craft classes in a relaxing environment where everyone receives individual attention. Classes change monthly so make sure to request a calendar.

Cultural Foundation

Location → Opp New Etisalat · Shk Zayed 1st St | 619 5357
Hours → 10:00 - 12:00 18:00 - 20:00
Web/email → www.cultural.org.ae | Map Ref → 9-A1

The Cultural Foundation has a thriving and popular art workshop, which attracts both adults and children. Classes include silk painting, watercolours, oils, ceramics, sculpture, Arabic calligraphy etc. Some of the finished art produced by students is featured at exhibitions.

Hemisphere Design Studio & Gallery

Location → Nxt to Russian Embassy · Khalifa St | 676 8614
Hours → Timings on request
Web/email → hemispheredesign@hotmail.com | Map Ref → 8-A2

This gallery offers a new concept in art & design services, stocking a wide range of original artwork, as well as offering classes, workshops and courses in a variety of arts and crafts activities. The goal is to promote local artists.

Ladies Art Group, The

Location → Cultural Foundation · Shk Zayed 1st St | 619 5313
Hours → Saturday morning
Web/email → na | Map Ref → 9-A1

This group, ranging from complete beginners to trained experts, meets once a week to paint. Workshops are occasionally organised for introducing new mediums or techniques. Anyone is welcome to join regardless of their level of ability.

Contact: *Delma Corner at the Cultural Foundation.*

Beauty Training

Other Options → Beauty & Hair Salons [p.203]

Cleopatra & Steiner Beauty Training Centre

Location → Wafi Residence · Dubai | 04 324 0250
Hours → 08:30 - 20:00
Web/email → www.cleopatrasteiner.com | Map Ref → UAE-C2

This is the Middle East's first internationally endorsed beauty and holistic training centre, offering a wide variety of topics. The centre provides opportunities for beginners or those pursuing their hobby, as well as those wishing to build on existing qualifications.

Birdwatching

Other Options → Environmental Groups [p.210]

As a destination for birdwatchers, Abu Dhabi's reputation has grown over the years. The increasing lushness of the area attracts ever more birds, many of which are not easily found in Europe or the Middle East. Over 80 species breed locally, while over 400 have been recorded on their migration between Africa and Central Asia. Species spotted include the Socotra Cormorant, Chestnut bellied Sandgrouse, Crab Plover, and Saunders' Little Tern.

Several good areas for birdwatching in Abu Dhabi are the eastern lagoon on the New Corniche, the port area, Mushrif Palace Gardens and around the Abu Dhabi Equestrian Club. Resident ornithologists are extremely active and assist visitors during individually tailored tours. For information on these, contact Birdwatching Tours (050 650 3398).

Other excellent places for birding around the Emirates include the mangrove swamps in Umm al Quwain and Khor Kalba – the only place in the world where you can spot the white collared kingfisher. Desert Rangers do arrange canoe tours to the mangroves.

Birdwatching Enthusiasts

Bridge

Al Ain Bridge Club

Location → Htl InterContinental · Al Ain | 03 768 6686
Hours → Mon 20:00
Web/email → carl.haigh@hct.ac.ae | Map Ref → 15-E4

The club holds weekly duplicate sessions in a relaxed, congenial atmosphere. Beginners are welcome, although to take part in the duplicate session, you should be able to cope with basic bidding and play. They may hold beginners lessons if there is sufficient interest.

Contact: *Carl Haigh (050 743 0133).*

Chess

Abu Dhabi Chess & Culture Club

Location → Behind Islamic Bank · Madinat Zayed | 633 1110
Hours → 17:00 - 23:00
Web/email → www.abudhabichess.com | Map Ref → 7-D1

Abu Dhabi Chess & Culture Club was opened in 1979 and has since participated in many activities locally and internationally. The club has sponsored numerous competitions and enrols members of all ages, who now total about 800. All are welcome.

Dance Classes

Other Options → Music Lessons [p.213]

Sociable, great fun and excellent exercise for all ages and levels of ability, dance has a universal appeal that breaks down barriers and inhibitions (sometimes)!

In addition to the following organisations that are dedicated to dance, some health clubs, restaurants and bars hold weekly sessions in flamenco, salsa, samba, jazz dance, ballroom, and so on. Salsa in particular is becoming quite popular, and bars such as The LAB at the Beach Rotana Hotel and Tequilana at the Hilton have regular nights dedicated to salsa lessons and Latin music. In addition, some health clubs offer dance based aerobic classes that are good fun and surprisingly energetic. Others offer bellydancing classes for those who want to learn more about the regional culture through dance.

American Arabian Gulf Squares

Location → Various locations | 445 2490
Hours → Timings on request
Web/email → na | Map Ref → na

Originally from America, square dancing has spread all over the world. The steps are easy to learn, it's excellent exercise and it's enjoyable! For information on timings and classes, call Denise Smith on the above number.

Tap Dancing

Location ➜ Corniche Social Club · Abu Dhabi | 642 1777
Hours ➜ Timings on request
Web/email ➜ na | Map Ref ➜ 8-A3

If your children want to tap dance over the parquet floor like Fred Astaire, then these classes are for them. The teacher, Louisa al Rumaithi, instructs children and adults from age four upwards. Lessons last 30 or 45 minutes, depending on age.

Cost: Dhs.25 per session.

Desert Driving Courses

Other Options ➜ Camping [p.180]

For those who would like to master the art of manoeuvring a four wheel drive vehicle over rolling sand dunes, several organisations offer a full day course accompanied by professional drivers. Both individual and group tuition per vehicle is available. Picnic lunch and soft drinks may be included. Participants are expected to bring their own four wheel drive, alternatively you can hire a vehicle at an additional cost. Expect to pay around Dhs.200 - 300 for the day, depending on the programme.

Desert Rangers

Location ➜ Dubai Garden Centre · Shk Zayed Rd | 04 340 2408
Hours ➜ 08:30 - 14:30
Web/email ➜ www.desertrangers.com | Map Ref ➜ UAE-C2

Offering lessons on learning how to handle a car in the desert – from the basics of venturing off-road, negotiating easy dunes and how to avoid getting stuck – to the more advanced, with guided drives to more challenging areas of the desert.

Note: Courses are available for individuals or groups and can be combined with barbecues and other activities.

Jeep UAE Off-Road Driving Academy

Location ➜ Various locations · Dubai emirate | 04 285 0455
Hours ➜ Timings on request
Web/email ➜ na | Map Ref ➜ na

Jeep owners wanting to discover the 'do anything, go anywhere' nature of their vehicle can take a specialised full-day driving course. You'll learn the full range of your Jeep's capabilities in a controlled desert environment.

Cost: Dhs.280 for 2 persons. New Jeep customers are offered this course free.

Dog Training

Dog Training Classes

Location ➜ Various locations | 04 347 2592
Hours ➜ Timings on request
Web/email ➜ na | Map Ref ➜ na

Man's best friend having behaviour problems? Training can change an impossible dog into a wonderful family companion. Training for deaf dogs is also provided.

Contact: Anne on the above number or 050 655 8925.

Drama Groups

Abu Dhabi Dramatic Society (ADDS)

Location ➜ Club, The · Al Meena | 673 1111
Hours ➜ Timings on request
Web/email ➜ www.the-club.com | Map Ref ➜ 7-A2

You must be a member of The Club to join ADDS, an enthusiastic group of individuals from all walks of life. If you don't fancy being centre stage, there is always plenty to do behind the scenes! Performances take place throughout the year.

Environmental Groups

Over the last few years, environmental issues have gradually become more important in the UAE. There are increasing numbers of glass and plastic recycling points around the city, most notably outside Spinneys supermarkets. The Khaleej Times sponsors bins for collecting newspapers for recycling; these are easily spotted at a variety of locations, but mainly outside shopping centres. In addition, the government is taking action with school educational programmes and general awareness campaigns, plus the development of conservation areas such as Sir Bani Yas Island and, on the East Coast, Khor Kalba Nature Reserve. However, there is still much work to be done to persuade the average person to be more active environmentally.

If you want to get involved, contact one of the environmental groups operating in the Emirates. These range from the Emirates Environmental Group to Feline Friends. They always need volunteers and funds. Go on, do your bit!

Abu Dhabi Emirates Natural History Group

Location → Various locations | 050 611 8846
Hours → Timings on request
Web/email → www.arabianwildlife.com/main.htm Map Ref → na

The group meets on the first and third Tuesday of every month for an evening lecture on any aspect of natural history, from astronomy or archaeology to botany or zoology. They also meet regularly for outdoor excursions.

Cost: *Dhs.100 for membership.*

Contact: *Steve James on the number above.*

Feline Friends

Location → Various locations | 673 2696
Hours → 19:30 last Tue of the month
Web/email → felinefriendsuae.com Map Ref → na

This non profit organisation of volunteers aims to care for sick and injured street cats and kittens, rescue abandoned cats and foster them until permanent homes can be found; control the local street cat population humanely by sterilisation and encourage responsible animal ownership and care.

Al Ain Emirates Natural History Group

Location → Htl InterContinental · Al Ain | 050 533 0579
Hours → Tue 19:30
Web/email → enhg.4t.com/index.html Map Ref → 15-E4

Interested in the environment and natural history? Come to the meetings on the second and fourth Tuesday of every month – talks include topics as varied as UAE medicinal plants, Bedouin food, or the Mussandam. Field trips are organised every weekend.

Cost: *Annual membership Dhs.80 (family) & Dhs.50 (individuals); Dhs.10 per meeting (non members).*

Contact: *Brien Holmes on the above number.*

Emirates Environmental Group

Location → Crown Plaza Htl · Dubai | 04 331 8100
Hours → 09:00 - 18:00; Thu 09:00 - 14:00
Web/email → www.eeg-uae.org Map Ref → UAE -C2

A voluntary, non governmental organisation devoted to protecting the environment through education, action programmes and community involvement. Membership includes individuals, corporate members and schools. They publish a free bilingual, biannual newsletter, with a circulation of 20,000, plus a monthly newsletter for all members.

Cost: *Annual fees Dhs.50 (adults) and Dhs.10 - 25 (students).*

K9 Friends

Location → Various locations · Dubai | 04 347 4611
Hours → Sat - Thu 09:00 - 13:00
Web/email → www.k9friends.com Map Ref → na

K9 Friends has many aims, including the provision of a re-homing service for stray and abandoned dogs; promoting responsible dog ownership and encouraging a neutering programme to help control the population of stray dogs. Volunteers and foster homes are always needed.

Gardening

Other Options → Plants & Trees [p.164]

Flower & Garden Group

Location → Various locations | 445 6622
Hours → Timings on request
Web/email → na Map Ref → na

Aimed at creating environmental awareness and promoting individual gardening in the Gulf by planting seeds, flowering plants and trees. General meetings are held once a month, and there are also various workshops and field trips, as well as exhibits by floral artists.

Contact: *Call 621 7781 or 050 622 3701.*

Language Schools

Alliance Française

Location → Choithram Building · Khalidiya | 666 6232
Hours → 09:00 - 13:00 16:00 - 20:30; Thu 09:00 - 13:30
Web/email → www.chez.com/alliancead Map Ref → 8-C2

The Abu Dhabi branch of the Alliance Française was established in 1974, and aims to widen access to the French language and culture to encourage education, cultural exchange and friendly dialogue between countries. In addition to language courses, the centre provides information on France.

American Language Center

Location → Opp Hamdan Centre · Shk Hamdan St | 627 2779
Hours → 08:00 - 13:00 17:00 - 21:00 Thu 09:00 - 13:00
Web/email → alc@emirates.net.ae Map Ref → 8-C2

The center runs various English courses each month. Courses include TOEFL preparation and all levels of general or specialised English teaching. There are separate classes for ladies, with classes

tailor-made to suit student requirements. They also run a summer school for children.

Berlitz

Location → Opp Burger King · Khalidiya | 667 2287
Hours → 08:00 - 21:00
Web/email → berlitz@emirates.net.ae | Map Ref → 9-D1

For more than a century, Berlitz has been operating worldwide and the 'Berlitz method' has helped more than 41 million people acquire a new language. The Abu Dhabi branch offers a variety of courses that can be customised to fit specific requirements.

British Council

Location → Al Nasr St · Khalidiya | 665 9300
Hours → 08:30 - 13:30 16:30 - 19:00
Web/email → www.britishcouncil.org/uae | Map Ref → 8-B2

The British Council promotes cultural, scientific, technological and educational co-operation between the UK and other countries. It operates a range of English and Arabic language courses. In addition, the British Council promotes cultural events, exhibitions, performances, talks and workshops

Circolo Italiano Culturale E Ricreativo – CICER

Location → Italian Embassy · Al Manasir | 050 415 9047
Hours → Timings on request
Web/email → www.cicer-abudhabi.com | Map Ref → na

Working closely with the Italian Embassy, the association also offers a variety of services including the use of a small Italian library and video library for members. Other benefits include special discounts from several outlets in town.

Contact: *Loredana Frizzi on 050 792 9740 or the above number.*

ELS Language Center

Location → Al Khalidiyah | 666 9225
Hours → 08:30 - 13:30 16:30 - 19:30
Web/email → www.els.com | Map Ref → 9-D1

Their intensive English programme focuses on practical English, featuring grammar, conversation, reading and writing, and gives access to the multimedia lab – courses are open to all. ELS also provides educational counselling to assist individuals who are considering studying abroad.

Int'l English Inst for Language Studies

Location → Opp Bus Station, Defence St | 642 2407
Hours → 09:00 - 13:00 17:00 - 21:00
Web/email → na | Map Ref → 3-B4

The Institute offers a range of language courses to suit all requirements and levels of ability, including English, French, Spanish, Italian and German. Separate classes are available for children over seven years old and for ladies.

ELS Language Center, Al Ain

Location → Hamdan B Zayed St · Al Jimi Khabisi | 03 762 3468
Hours → 08:30 - 13:30 16:00 - 21:30; Thu 09:00 - 13:00
Web/email → www.ELS.com | Map Ref → 12-E4

For information on this school, see the entry under ELS Language Center, Abu Dhabi [p.212].

Libraries

Other Options → Books [p.152]

Alliance Française

Location → Choithram Building · Khalidiya | 666 6232
Hours → 09:00 - 13:00 16:00 - 20:30; Thu 09:00 - 13:30
Web/email → www.chez.com/alliancead | Map Ref → 8-C2

The Alliance Française has a multimedia library comprising more than 12,000 books, 2,500 videos, hundreds of CD ROMs and CDs and a selection of French periodicals. Everybody can use the library, although a membership fee is required if you want to check out material.

Club, The

Location → Club, The · Al Meena | 673 1111
Hours → See timings below
Web/email → www.the-club.com | Map Ref → 7-A2

Members can enjoy an excellent selection of fiction and non fiction titles in the well stocked library at The Club. A CD ROM section, Internet access and a DVD library are also featured here.

Timings: *Sat, Sun, Tue & Wed 10:00 - 19:00; Mon 11:00 - 21:00; Thu 10:00 - 18:00; Fri closed.*

National Library

Location ➜ Cultural Foundation · Shk Zayed 1st St | 633 6483
Hours ➜ See timings below
Web/email ➜ www.cultural.org.ae | Map Ref ➜ 9-A1

The National Library is responsible for collecting, keeping and organising all national literary information. The library was built to hold a staggering two million titles. The library also has an Internet section, which can be used for a moderate fee.

***Timings**: 08:00 - 14:00 & 17:00 - 22:00; Thu 09:00 - 12:00 & 17:00 - 20:00; Fri 17:00 - 20:00.*

Daly Community Library

Location ➜ St Andrews Centre · Al Mushrif | 446 4752
Hours ➜ See timings below
Web/email ➜ na | Map Ref ➜ 3-C3

Daly Community Library, opened in 1978, has nearly 7,000 books, covering fiction and non fiction for adults and children. Books are ordered from the UK and new publications, including best sellers, are added regularly. This subscription library is open to all.

***Cost**: Annual subscription Dhs.100 plus Dhs.75 initial joining fee (adults); Dhs.50 plus Dhs.40 initial joining fee (children).*

***Timings**: Wed 12:00 - 14:00 & 17:00 - 18:30; Thu 11:00 - 13:30; Sun 15:30 - 19:30.*

Music Lessons

Other Options ➜ Dance Classes [p.209]

Beethoven Institute of Music

Location ➜ Al Nasr St | 632 7588
Hours ➜ Timings on request
Web/email ➜ na | Map Ref ➜ 8-E2

Started in 1984, this was one of the first music institutes in the UAE. On offer are lessons on the piano, organ, guitar and drums. Children can start as young as six and summer courses are also held.

***Contact**: Call the above number or 633 9195.*

Royal Music Academy

Location ➜ Nr Eldorado Cinema · Elektra Street | 674 8070
Hours ➜ 09:00 - 12:00 16:00 - 21:00
Web/email ➜ vinsylauh@hotmail.com | Map Ref ➜ 8-B1

At the Academy, instruments include the guitar, drums, violin, piano and keyboards, while watercolour, pencil drawing and dance classes are also offered. The academy also conducts summer camps for children; activities include swimming, ice skating, arts and crafts, painting and camping.

Nature Reserves

Sir Bani Yas Island

Location ➜ From Meena Zayed Port · Abu Dhabi | na
Hours ➜ na
Web/email ➜ na | Map Ref ➜ 7-A4

This private island was established as a breeding and conservation reserve for indigenous UAE fauna and other desert animals. Visitors are allowed, but only on a prearranged basis in organised groups such as societies or school parties. Overnight stays are also arranged.

***Location**: 9 km off Jebel Dhanna headland, 170 km west of Abu Dhabi.*

***Contact**: Environment and Wildlife Management (EWM) or PO Box 77, Abu Dhabi.*

Gazelles at Sir Bani Yas Island

Pottery

Other Options ➜ Cafe Ceramique [p.252]

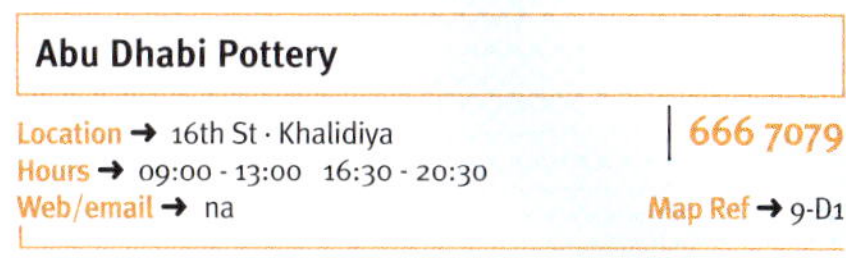

Abu Dhabi Pottery

Location ➜ 16th St · Khalidiya | 666 7079
Hours ➜ 09:00 - 13:00 16:30 - 20:30
Web/email ➜ na | Map Ref ➜ 9-D1

For those fascinated by clay, pottery classes are available for adults and children aged five and up. Try hand building and wheel techniques. Everything is done under the supervision of friendly staff, except the glazing since toxic materials are involved.

***Cost**: Dhs.35 per session (plus clay and firing fees); Dhs.240 per month (four sessions).*

Singing Lessons

Other Options → Music Lessons [p.213]

Abu Dhabi Choral Group

Location → St Andrew's Church · Al Mushrif | 681 2340
Hours → Tue 20:00
Web/email → na | Map Ref → 3-C3

This community choir is open to anyone interested in singing. They are all amateurs and at present have 73 members. It's a non profit making organisation and when possible, once production expenses are covered, a donation is made to a charity.

Contact: *Marcia Jeiroudi on the above number.*

Social Groups

A new resident will be looking for ways to meet like minded people, form friendships, and have some help in navigating a new culture. Depending on your temperament and interests, a social group might be just the thing. With its cosmopolitan population, it's not surprising that Abu Dhabi has a large number of social and cultural groups. These are sometimes linked to an embassy or business group. However, if your particular interest or background is not covered, now's the perfect opportunity to challenge your organisational skills and start something new – there'll always be someone out there who'll join in! Refer also to the New Residents/Business section [p.48].

Abu Dhabi Ladies

Location → Sands Hotel · Shk Zayed 2nd St | 050 446 0516
Hours → Wed 10:00 - 12:00
Web/email → na | Map Ref → 8-C1

Abu Dhabi Ladies offers a range of social activities and support to expat women of all ages and nationalities. They meet every Wednesday for a coffee morning, and there's always someone to lend an ear or give advice to new arrivals.

Cost: *Annual subscription Dhs.40.*

Contact: *Sue Brown on 050 313 3602 or the above number.*

Abu Dhabi Mums

Location → Various locations · Abu Dhabi | 050 492 9738
Hours → Timings on request
Web/email → www.abudhabimums.ae | Map Ref → na

Abu Dhabi Mums is a social group for mums with pre-school children. The group provides informal support and activities for both parents and children. It is open to anyone who is expecting or has children up to the age of five years.

Contact: *Revi on the above number.*

American University of Beirut Alumni Assoc.

Location → TNT Bld · Khalifa Bin Zyd St | 679 5633
Hours → Timings on request
Web/email → www.aubalumni.org | Map Ref → na

The Abu Dhabi branch of the Association organises events such as concerts, lectures, days out, 'Layali Ramadan', fundraising dinners and the Alumni Spring Ball. The group currently has more than 700 graduate members. To join, or for information, call the above number.

American Women's Network

Location → Various locations | 681 7060
Hours → See timings below
Web/email → na | Map Ref → na

The goal of this informal group of women is to offer an informative, warm and welcoming atmosphere to newcomers and help connect them to local resources and interests. Although primarily for Americans, they also welcome women with links to America.

Contact: *Lizabeth McKillop or Sharon Moynihan (634 8417).*

Club des Femmes Francophones

Location → Novotel Centre Htl · Shk Hamdan St | 633 3555
Hours → Sat & Tue 11:00 - 13:00
Web/email → novoad@emirates. | Map Ref → 8-D2

The objective of the apolitical and non religious association is the exchange of different cultures and traditions among all French speaking ladies. There are also many regular activities throughout the year, such as bowling, silk painting, yoga, badminton, bridge and scrabble.

Royal Society of St George, The

Location → Various locations | 445 6403
Hours → Timings on request
Web/email → rssg-auh.cjb.net | Map Ref → na

This society holds events on a regular basis, including formal dinners and a New Years' Eve Ball. Other events include car treasure hunts, quizzes, Ramadan curry night etc. Proceeds raised at events are distributed to UK charities each year.

Membership: *Open to all English families; associate membership for anyone supporting the society's objectives.*

Contact: *For further information, log on to the Website.*

South African Group Abu Dhabi, The

Location → Various locations | 445 4034
Hours → Timings on request
Web/email → www.sagroupuae.com | Map Ref → na

Catering to South Africans in Abu Dhabi and Al Ain, this group organises various events for the community, including dinners, dances, barbecues and desert trips. The Afrikaans Christian Children's Group meets at the Evangelical Church at 19:00 every Monday evening.

Contact: *050 612 9643 or the above number.*

St Andrews Society of Abu Dhabi

Location → St Andrews Centre · Al Mushrif | 050 443 5175
Hours → Timings on request
Web/email → na | Map Ref → 3-C3

This group of expat Scots, joined by more than a few 'foreigners', enjoys getting together for social gatherings and Scottish cultural activities including the Burns' Supper in January. Write to the society at PO Box 59451, Abu Dhabi for more information.

Cost: *Dhs.50 per year, everyone welcome.*

St David's Society

Location → Various locations | 677 9751
Hours → Timings on request
Web/email → www.st.davidsabudhabi.org | Map Ref → na

The youngest of the British tribal societies, formed by some enthusiastic Welsh expats, with a current membership of over 120. A regular newsletter keeps members informed of monthly events, such as quiz evenings, dhow trips, weekend breaks or social gatherings.

Contact: *President, Peter Stevens (050 614 5191) or Vice President, Peter Rhydderch (050 622 1832).*

Cost: *Dhs.50 per person (annual fee), not exceeding Dhs.100 per family.*

Al Ain

Al Ain Irish Society

Location → Various locations | 050 663 2721
Hours → Timings on request
Web/email → na | Map Ref → na

The society is active with a number of events including the annual Irish Ball. Irish dancing classes are taught and in past years there have been Gaelic language classes for children. Membership is open to anyone with an interest in Irish culture.

Contact: *President Jerome McCormack on the above number.*

Al Ain St George's Society

Location → Various locations | na
Hours → Timings on request
Web/email → rasalala@emirates.net.ae | Map Ref → na

The Society was founded in November 1996 by Annie Lawton and Sue Aiken. All those interested in English culture; the English way of life, or even just in meeting new faces, can contact Sue on the above email for further information.

American University of Beirut Alumni Assoc.

Location → Al Ain St · Al Ain | 03 767 7444
Hours → Timings on request
Web/email → www.aubalumni.org | Map Ref → na

More information on this Al Ain based Alumni Association can be obtained by contacting Antoinette Yzbeck on the above number. Alternatively, there is an Abu Dhabi based Alumni Association. For more details see [p.214].

Wine Tasting

African & Eastern (N.E.) Ltd

Location → Al Khazna Tower · Bani Yas St | 631 2300
Hours → 09:30 - 13:00 16:00 - 20:00; Fri closed
Web/email → timothy@africaneastern.ae | Map Ref → na

African & Eastern arrange occasional tastings on an ad hoc basis. To take part you will need a liquor licence. Call Timothy Broughton on the above number if you would like to add your name to the database for the next event.

Gray MacKenzie Liquor Shop

Location → Opp Le Meridien Htl · Al Khalifa St | 627 3131
Hours → Timings on request
Web/email → na | Map Ref → na

Gray MacKenzie arranges occasional tastings on an ad hoc basis. To take part you will need a liquor licence. Call the customer service line on the above number or 612 3545 for further details.

Le MERIDIEN
ABU DHAB

Going Out

EXPLORER

Going Out

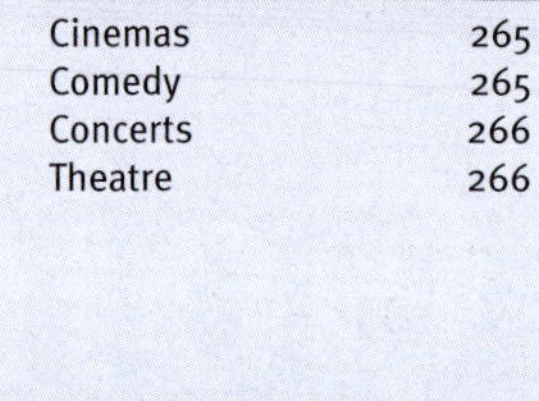

Eating Out in Abu Dhabi

Going Out

If you're going out and about in Abu Dhabi, you will come across a surprising variety of places to go and things to do. It may not be quite the buzzing city found in other parts of the world, but it is rapidly developing and getting busier. At present, Abu Dhabi offers adequate choices that will keep even the most ardent socialite happy.

The following section has been divided into two; the city's numerous restaurants are listed under Eating Out [p.219], while cafés, bars, pubs, nightclubs and any 'cultural' entertainment, such as theatre, cinema and comedy clubs, are listed under On the Town [p.258].

Eating Out

Cosmopolitan and bustling, Abu Dhabi has an excellent and ever increasing variety of restaurants. From Moroccan to Mexican, Indian to Italian and everything in between, there really is something to suit every palate and budget. Most places open early in the evening at around 19:00, but generally aren't busy until about 21:00. In addition to dining out, dining in with a takeaway is also very popular to the extent that you may wonder if anyone in Abu Dhabi even knows how to cook!

Most of Abu Dhabi's popular restaurants are in hotels and these are pretty much the only outlets that can serve alcohol with your meal (if you want alcoholic beverages, check the Alcohol Available icon in individual reviews). However, there are quite a number of unlicensed independent restaurants throughout town, which are superb and so, shouldn't be ignored. The food in some of these places could pleasantly surpass your expectations.

Options are diverse, from a choice of Emirati food in an authentic, ancient village setting, to seafood on a traditional floating dhow or a more upmarket yacht.

Quite a few restaurants specialise in more than one style of cuisine; for instance, an Indian restaurant may also serve Thai and Chinese food. In addition, many places promote theme nights with different types of cuisine or ingredients, such as Italian or seafood, allowing you to sample some truly international cuisine. This way, the choice of what you can eat dramatically increases. Many restaurants have weekly buffet nights where you can eat (and often drink) as much as you like for an all inclusive price providing good value for money.

Drinks

Although Abu Dhabi is among the more liberal states in the GCC, alcohol is only available in licensed restaurants and bars that are situated within hotels as well as in a select few non hotel outlets (such as golf clubs and some government owned establishments).

The mark up can often be considerable – it's not unknown for a Dhs.20 bottle of indifferent wine to be charged at Dhs.80 plus. A bottle of house water can also be outrageously marked up, especially for premium brands. Imported water can be charged at up to Dhs.25 a bottle, and if you object to this, we suggest you send it back and ask for local bottled water (but not tap water). A standard one litre bottle usually costs Dhs.1 in a supermarket and is in no way inferior to imported brands. In fact, the UAE is probably the only country in the world where water is more expensive than petrol!

See Also: *Alcohol [p.148]*

Hygiene

Outlets are regularly checked by the Abu Dhabi Municipality for hygiene. They are strict on warning places to improve and, when necessary, even closing them down. So you can rest assured when you're at the 'tatty' little shawarma shop by the side of the road or a small independent restaurant. It is absolutely safe to eat there and you're unlikely to get food poisoning. Indeed, you'll probably have an excellent cheap and atmospheric meal.

Tipping

There is usually a 15 - 16% service charge on top of the basic bill. These taxes are incorporated into the customer's bill but often indicated with a '++' denoting an addition to the price. At some restaurants, these taxes are included in the price, but even then, this information will be indicated somewhere on the menu. It is still unclear as to whether the latter charge is actually passed on to staff or withheld for poor service but, when in doubt, give the servers a break. Following the standard tipping rule of 10% will not be out of line, but appreciated instead.

Explorer Top Picks

Not sure what's hot and what's not in the city? Don't make your dining experience a 'hit and miss' with a random option. Guarantee yourself a fabulous time with a choice from our discerning top picks.

Alfresco

Restaurant	Page
Bayview	235
Prego's	241
Sevilo's	241
Top Deck Bar	261
Vasco's	238

American

Restaurant	Page
Rock Bottom Café	224
49er's The Gold Rush	223
Heroes Diner	223

Arabic Experience

Restaurant	Page
Al Areesh	230
Al Falah	250
Al Khayam	246
Al Mawwal	226
Lebanese Flower	227

Business Dinners

Restaurant	Page
Al Fanar	235
Al Mawwal	226
Bonsai	242
Club Restaurant, The	235
Flavours	233
Vasco's	238

Cheap Chow

Restaurant	Page
Al Aris	224
Caravan	233
Foodlands	233
La Brioche	254
Nihal Restaurant	234

Deliciously Unpretentious

Restaurant	Page
Bam Bu!	228
Haveli	234
La Brasserie	232
La Brioche	254
Zyara Café	255

Family Oriented

Restaurant	Page
Al Falah	250
Alamo, The	249
Bayview	235
Chili's	249
Las Palmas Complex	227

Fusion

Restaurant	Page
90 Degrees	232
Flavours	233

French

Restaurant	Page
Le Bistrot	232
Le Beaujolais	232
La Brasserie	232

Indian

Restaurant	Page
Kwality	234
Foodlands	233
Maharaja	234
Tanjore	235
Haveli	234
India Palace	234

Italian

Restaurant	Page
La Mamma	240
Peppino	241
Prego's	241
Casa Romana	240
Ciro's Pomodoro	240
Amalfi	240
Pappagallo	241

Japanese

Restaurant	Page
Benihana	242
Bonsai	242
Soba	242
Zen	242

Live Music

Restaurant	Page
Tequilana Discotheque	264
Cave De Rois	264
Colosseum	264

Mediterranean

Restaurant	Page
Gardinia	243
Chequers	243
La Terrazza	243

Merry Zoos

Restaurant	Page
a.m.p.m	261
Colosseum	264
Gardinia	243
Paco's	241
Rock Bottom Café	224

Mexican

Restaurant	Page
El Sombrero	244
El Torito	244

Posh

Restaurant	Page
Benihana	242
Cloud Nine - Cigar & Bottle Club	260
Crystal Cigar & Champange Bar	260
Flavours	233
Rodeo Grill	249

Romantic

Restaurant	Page
Al Fanar	235
Cloud Nine – Cigar & Bottle Club	260
Club Restaurant, The	235
Le Bistrot	232
Trader Vic's	246

Smokin'!

Restaurant	Page
Cloud Nine – Cigar & Bottle Club	260
El Sombrero	244
Harvesters Pub	263
Jazz Bar & Dining	261
L'Auberge	227

Steakhouses

Restaurant	Page
Rodeo Grill	249
Rainbow Steakhouse	248

Sunsets

Restaurant	Page
Bayview	235
La Brioche	254
Las Palmas Complex	227
Top Deck Bar	261
Vasco's	238

Tex Mex

Restaurant	Page
Chili's	249
Alamo, The	249
Ranch, The	249

Thai

Restaurant	Page
Royal Orchid	250
Talay	250

Trendy/Terminally Hip

Restaurant	Page
a.m.p.m	261
Ciro's Pomodoro	240
Idioms	254
Six Degrees Café	255
Zyara Café	255

Veggie

Restaurant	Page
90 Degrees	232
Bayview	235
Chili's	249
Foodlands	233
Kwality	234
La Mamma	240
Royal Orchid	250

Wine Cellars

Restaurant	Page
Chequers	243
Flavours	233
Prego's	241
Rodeo Grill	249
Vasco's	238

Area Top Picks

Feeling lazy? Want to tumble out of bed and roll into a nearby joint? Just choose your area from the list below and relish in the listed dining and drinking options in the vicinity.

Independent Reviews

We undertake independent reviews of all restaurants and bars that are included in this book. All the outlets mentioned have been visited by our food reporters and the views expressed are our own. The aim is to give a clear, realistic and as far as possible, unbiased view (that we are permitted to print) However, if we have unknowingly led you astray, please do let us know. We appreciate all feedback, positive, negative and otherwise. Please log on to www.Explorer-Publishing.com and share your views. Your comments are never ignored.

Ratings

Rating restaurants is always a highly subjective business. We ask our reviewers to summarise their experiences (see the bottom of each entry) in terms of Food, Service, Venue and Value. They are also asked to compare the restaurant with other venues in the category and same price range. In other words, you may notice that a local café has the same summary rating as a premium gourmet restaurant. This is not to say that they are equal. It's just a way of gauging the standard of restaurants that are similarly styled and priced. We hope this will help you make informed choices regardless of your taste or budget.

Each rating is out of five – one orange dot means poor, two and a half means acceptable and five means fab:

Food ●●●◐○ Serv ●◐○○○ Venue ●●●●● Value ●●●●○

Venues scheduled to open after publication receive 'na' ratings:

Food – na Service – na Venue – na Value – na

Restaurant Listing Structure

With over 150 specially selected outlets in this guidebook, the choice can seem daunting. Listed alphabetically by region, then country or commonly known style of cuisine, this section hopes to add to your dining experience by giving as much information as possible on the individual outlets. For an 'at a glance' clarification of this listing, refer to the index at the beginning of this section.

As with all good, simple rules, there are exceptions. Restaurants in the international category usually serve up such a variety in food that it is impossible to pin them down to one section. For example, a restaurant that specializes in seafood cooked in various styles will be found in the Seafood section, while a Thai restaurant that cooks a lot of fish, Thai style, will still be listed under Thai. Make sense? We hope so...

Where a restaurant specializes in more than one type of cuisine, the review appears under the main category.

In order to avoid any confusion in restaurant listings, any non English names retain their prefix (Al, El, La and Le) in their alphabetical placement, while English names are listed by actual titles, ignoring prefixes such as 'The'. Bon appetit!

Privilege Cards

The table below shows a list of privilege or discount cards for use at various establishments. These cards are basically offered to encourage you to return as often as possible. Generally, they can be used at a number of restaurants, and most offer incredible discounts and other added benefits, making them excellent value for money.

Privilege Cards

Hotel / Company	Includes	Phone	Cost
Hilton Hotels	All Hilton Hotels worldwide except the USA and Canada	681 7883	795
Rotana Hotels	Beach Rotana Hotel & Towers, Al Maha Rotana Suites, Al Rawda Suites, International Rotana Inn	678 0255	630 – 895
Sands Hotel	Sands Premier Club	633 5335	550
	La Piazza Restaurant (30 lunches)	633 6335	1150
Sheraton	Abu Dhabi: Sheraton Resort & Towers, Sheraton Suites Dubai: Sheraton Jumeirah, Sheraton Creekside, Sheraton Deira	677 0149	595
Hilton Hotels	All Hilton Hotels worldwide except the USA and Canada	03 768 6666	795

Icons – Quick Reference

For an explanation of the various symbols or icons listed against the individual reviews, refer to the Quick Reference Explorer Icons table below.

The prices indicated are calculated as the cost of a starter, main course and dessert for one person. This includes any relevant taxes, but excludes the cost of drinks. Another good cost indication is the restaurant location (whether or not it is situated inside a hotel), type of cuisine, whether the outlet is licensed etc. The Dhs.150 icon indicates that an average meal should cost anywhere between Dhs.125 to Dhs.175, ie Dhs.150 ± 25.

Quick Reference Explorer Icons

 Explorer Recommended

 Average price ± Dhs.25 (3 courses per person, including tax & service)

 NO Credit Cards Accepted

 Live Band

 Alcohol Available

 Have a Happy Hour

 Will Deliver

 Kids Welcome

 Reservations Recommended

 Dress Smartly

 Outside Terrace

 Vegetarian Dishes

Vegetarian Food

Vegetarians may be pleasantly surprised by the range and variety of veggie cuisine that can be found in restaurants in Abu Dhabi. Although the main course of Arabic food is dominated by meat, the staggering range of meze (which are often vegetarian) and the general affection for fresh vegetables should offer enough variety to satisfy even the most ravenous herbivore.

Nowadays, most outlets offer at least one or two veggie dishes. However, if you want a little more variety, choices include the numerous Indian vegetarian restaurants catering to the large number of Indians who are vegetarian by religion. These offer diverse styles of cooking and a range of tasty dishes – for vegetarians, this option is hard to beat. Other highlights include loads of excellent Italian, Mexican, Far Eastern and International restaurants all over the city.

A word of warning: if you are a strict veggie, confirm that your meal is completely meat free. Some restaurants cook their vegetarian selection with animal fat or on the same grill as the meat dishes.

Restaurants

American

Other options → Steakhouses [p.248]

49er's The Gold Rush

Location → Al Diar Dana Hotel · Al Meena | 645 8000
Hours → 12:00 - 02:30 Thu & Fri 12:00 - 03:30
Web/email → www.sfcgroup.com | Map Ref → 4-B4

Centrally situated, this popular venue is generally always packed, so get there early to enjoy an entire evening of entertainment. The rich timber finishes reflect a traditional ranch type atmosphere, and the food is delicious with steaks that melt in your mouth. Service cannot be faulted, and with live music and a great venue for quite a reasonable price, you can't go too wrong. Check out the various theme nights for added spice. PDG

Food ●●●●○ Serv ●●●●○ Venue ●●●●○ Value ●●●○○

Heroes Diner

Location → Crowne Plaza · Shk Hamdan Bin Mohd. St | 621 0000
Hours → 12:00 - 01:00
Web/email → www.abu-dhabi.crowneplaza.com | Map Ref → 8-C1

Arguably the city's best sports bar, Heroes is nearly always heaving with frenzied fans that come to watch the game in the company of similarly sports mad folk. The familiar pub fare is tasty and portions are generous. Thankfully the table service is friendly and surprisingly efficient, so there is no need to wrestle your way through the crowds just to get to the bar. Regular events such as Ladies Night, Quiz Night and Dance Night pack even more punters in. GW

Food ●●●●○ Serv ●●●◐○ Venue ●●●◐○ Value ●●●◐○

Rock Bottom Café

Location → Al Diar Capitol Hotel · Al Meena St | 677 7655
Hours → 12:00 - 16:30 19:00 - 03:30
Web/email → www.rockbottomcafe.com
Map Ref → 7-E2

Named after the Wall Street crash, this vibrant American diner has a somewhat split personality – go early in the evening to enjoy a quiet dinner, or hang around until later when the live music starts and the pace becomes frenetic. The menu features succulent steaks, sizzling seafood, and innovative salads, as well as a range of lighter snacks. Quality food and value for money are distinct characteristics. The daily happy hour extends until 21:00. APB

Food ●●●●● Serv ●●●◐○ Venue ●●●●○ Value ●●●●◐

Americas

Lumping together Central, North and South America may seem strange, but there is method to the madness. Generally speaking, this cuisine is especially good for meat lovers. Many of the steakhouses and American joints, for example, offer prime quality meat especially flown in from the States to be cooked to your preference. Desserts vary widely in this category, but often the old favourites like Mississippi mud pie, apple pie or chocolate cake with lashings of ice-cream can be found somewhere on the menu – to the delight of those who like to finish with a dish that is sweet, filling and calorie laden. In general, this is hearty fare with the emphasis on portion size: steaks, ribs and burgers in such restaurants usually make dainty eaters cringe with disbelief. Often main courses in this category come with chips, but most restaurants will offer alternatives, such as baked potato or salad, if you show some concern for your arteries.

Moving south, the cuisine is still meat based – in particular, Argentinean cooking is noted for serving high quality steaks, but Caribbean dishes show a little more familiarity with fruit, vegetables and chicken. The hotter and spicier Mexican and Tex-Mex cooking usually has a wider choice for vegetarians. Some of the options include refried beans, guacamole, salsa, nachos (small, hard tortillas topped with melted cheese, peppers and chilli), fajitas (a soft tortilla, wrapped around sizzling vegetables and cheese or meat) and enchiladas (a tortilla filled with meat or cheese and served under a rich sauce), plus some great salads. Great if you have the appetite of a bear, but be careful if you like to have room for dessert.

Arabic/Lebanese

Other options → Dinner Cruises [p.250]

Al Aris Restaurant & Grill

Location → Al Salam St · Opp Abu Dhabi Com Bank | 645 5503
Hours → 07:00 - 01:00
Web/email → na
Map Ref → 8-A1

Al Aris is one of the many clean and cheerful Arabic/Lebanese restaurants, conveniently located on Salam Street. Mainly Arabic and Lebanese cuisine (not excluding the ever popular shawarma) is served by efficient and cheerful staff making this an ideal spot for a quick meal or takeaway. The fruit juices are incredibly fresh. Seating is available outside as well as inside with a family room on the upper level. Prices are sinfully reasonable and free home delivery is available. CC

Food ●●●○○ Serv ●●●◐○ Venue ●●○○○ Value ●●●●◐

Al Atlal

Location → Sands Hotel · Shk Zayed 2nd St | 633 5335
Hours → 20:00 - 02:30
Web/email → www.sands-hotel.com
Map Ref → 8-C1

Centrally located, Al Atlal is within easy reach of all, and especially popular with the locals. Authentic Lebanese food is served in a cosy Lebanese atmosphere complemented with very loud and

Al Atlal

American | Arabic/Lebanese

Going Out

SANDS HOTEL Abu-Dhabi فندق ساندز ابوظبي

The best value ★★★★★ hotel in Abu Dhabi

Al Diar Hotels & Resorts فنادق ومنتجعات الديار

P.O.Box 32430, Abu Dhabi, U.A.E./Tel: 02 6335335 / Fax: 02 6335766
E-mail: sandshot@emirates.net.ae / www.sands-hotel.com

CHEQUERS WINE BAR

Gift Voucher

Dhs.100

SANDS HOTEL Abu-Dhabi فندق ساندز ابوظبي
The best value ★★★★★ hotel in Abu Dhabi

Al Diar Hotels & Resorts فنادق ومنتجعات الديار

Reservation essential: 02 6335335. This voucher is not during special events and promotions.

Offer valid till 31st October 2004.
Valid only for 2 persons or more.

THE HARVESTERS PUB

Gift Voucher

25% Discount

Offer valid till 31st October 2004.
Valid only for 2 persons or more.

SANDS HOTEL Abu-Dhabi فندق ساندز ابوظبي
The best value ★★★★★ hotel in Abu Dhabi

Al Diar Hotels & Resorts فنادق ومنتجعات الديار

Reservation essential: 02 6335335. This voucher is not during special events and promotions.

Offer valid till 31st October 2004.
Valid only for 2 persons or more.

---

la Piazza

Gift Voucher

Dhs.50

Offer valid till 31st October 2004.
Valid only for 2 persons or more.

SANDS HOTEL Abu-Dhabi فندق ساندز ابوظبي
The best value ★★★★★ hotel in Abu Dhabi

Al Diar Hotels & Resorts فنادق ومنتجعات الديار

Reservation essential: 02 6335335. This voucher is not during special events and promotions.

Offer valid till 31st October 2004.
Valid only for 2 persons or more.

AL ATLAL
LEBANESE RESTAURANT

Gift Voucher

Dhs.100

Offer valid till 31st October 2004.
Valid only for 2 persons or more.

SANDS HOTEL Abu-Dhabi فندق ساندز ابوظبي
The best value ★★★★★ hotel in Abu Dhabi

Al Diar Hotels & Resorts فنادق ومنتجعات الديار

Reservation essential: 02 6335335. This voucher is not during special events and promotions.
Applicable only to Main Course.

Offer valid till 31st October 2004.
Valid only for 2 persons or more.

IMPERIAL CHINESE

Gift Voucher

Dhs.50

Offer valid till 31st October 2004.
Valid only for 2 persons or more.

SANDS HOTEL Abu-Dhabi فندق ساندز ابوظبي
The best value ★★★★★ hotel in Abu Dhabi

Al Diar Hotels & Resorts فنادق ومنتجعات الديار

Reservation essential: 02 6335335. This voucher is not during special events and promotions.
Applicable only to Main Course.

Offer valid till 31st October 2004.
Valid only for 2 persons or more.

lively music and belly dancing. A set menu includes an expansive meze and grilled mixed kebabs, plus many more dishes to satiate the hungry diner. Overall, service meets requirements and the place is a reasonably priced offering of food and lively entertainment for a hungry soul. KG

Food●●●○○Serv●●●○○Venue●●●○○Value●●●○○

Al Birkeh

Location → Le Meridien · Al Meena | 644 0666
Hours → 12:00 - 15:30 20:00 - 02:30
Web/email → www.lemeridien-abudhabi.com | Map Ref → 7-D1

   100

Widely touted as one of the best Arabic restaurants in town, this established venue serves traditional Middle Eastern fare in a festive setting, complete with live music and a belly dancer. Start your culinary journey with a selection of hot and cold meze before moving on to your main course of grilled meat or fish (and lots of it!). For the gastronomically brave only, the menu includes some exotic dishes such as raw liver, washed down with the strong aniseed drink 'Arak'. JR

Food●●●●○Serv●●●○○Venue●●●○○Value●●●○○

Al Dana

Location → Htl InterContinental · Bainuna St | 667 3098
Hours → 12:00 - 16:00 20:00 - 02:30
Web/email → www.intercontinental.com | Map Ref → 10-C1

  150

For a classic Lebanese evening, head straight to Al Dana. The food is top quality and the service, genuinely friendly and attentive. A set menu satisfies most requirements, and consists of a great selection of hot and cold mezes; the meats too, are grilled to perfection. But wait for eleven o'clock, when an impressive live show makes this experience a well rounded 'Lebanese package'. With a commensurately good atmosphere, it is wise to book on weekends for a decent table. MFW

Food●●●●○Serv●●●●○Venue●●●●○Value●●●●○

Al Mawal

Location → Hilton Abu Dhabi · Corniche Rd West | 681 2773
Hours → 12:30 - 15:30 20:00 - 02:00
Web/email → Mawal@emirates.net.ae | Map Ref → 10-C2

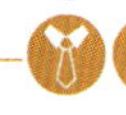    100

Walk over a bridge with a river flowing underneath, through lush foliage and under a grapevine, and experience classic Lebanese hospitality. After showing you to your table, welcoming and attentive staff swiftly serve you with complimentary baskets of fresh vegetables, bread, olives and more, and the exhaustive menu covers even the most exclusive dishes. Live entertainment comprising of a band, a belly dancer and a singer completes the experience. Although a bit pricey, this restaurant is worth every dirham. MM

Food●●●●○Serv●●●●○Venue●●●●○Value●●●●○

> **Go Arabic**
>
> *A common mistake is to categorise Arabic food into one general category. Break this myth and sample the different delights, from Lebanese and Moroccan to the local Emirati flavours.*

Al Mawal

Al Qasr Restaurant & Grill

Location → Opp Beach Rotana Htl · Al Meena | 644 9933
Hours → 10:00 - 24:00
Web/email → www.aplace2eat.com | Map Ref → 4-B4

  100

With floor to ceiling windows, this quiet restaurant unveils a view of the City Terminal in the southeastern part of Abu Dhabi city. Tender appetisers of stuffed vine leaves and well balanced moutabel pave the way for main courses of hammour and average mixed grill. Lunch offers an incredibly astounding selection of 99 dishes including Middle Eastern rice, curries and other specialities with service staff that are capable and eager to please. EDMM

Food●●●○○Serv●●●○○Venue●●○○○Value●●●○○

Argila

Location → Khalidia Palace Htl · Al Ras Al Akhdar | 666 2470
Hours → 18:00 - 02:00
Web/email → www.khalidiapalacehotel.co.ae | Map Ref → 10-E2

If you fancy Lebanese/Arabic cuisine and fresh fruit juices, this is the place to be. Distinctly Middle Eastern fare is served in a friendly no fuss manner and you can choose your setting; by the water, further back in the garden, indoors in the large Arabic tent, or in the more private family rooms. Also, true to its name, shisha is available. Just order your favourite hubbly bubbly and enjoy a puff after dinner amidst relaxed environs. GW

Food ●●◐○○ Serv ●●●○○ Venue ●●◐○○ Value ●●●◐○

Hidden Rock

Location → Mercure Grand Hotel · Al Ain | 03 783 8888
Hours → 19:00 - 22:00
Web/email → www.mercure.com | Map Ref → 17-B4

Location is everything (or so estate agents say) and the half hour drive up Jebel Hafeet mountain for a spectacular view and temperatures 6 - 8 degrees cooler make Al Khayma well worth the trip. Sit on the terrace at night to get a dramatic sense of place: sample a standard Arabic buffet until 22:00 and carry on with a shisha until 02:00, while taking in a 180 degree vista of the Al Ain lights twinkling below. Currently undergoing a summer refit for wind proofing. JS

Food ●●●◐○ Serv ●●●●○ Venue ●●●●◐ Value ●●●◐○

L'Auberge

Location → Nr Corniche Residence Htl | 627 3070
Hours → 12:00 - 16:00 19:00 - 24:00
Web/email → na | Map Ref → 8-C2

Although L'Auberge may have slipped down somewhat on the list of top Arabic restaurants in the city, its prime location in the heart of the business district ensures a bustling lunchtime trade. The menu covers a wide range of Lebanese specialities and European fare, and the Friday brunch is very popular. The venue is modern and spacious, albeit fairly plain, but the waiters are all friendly and very helpful. Prices veer a little towards the higher side. MM

Food ●●●○○ Serv ●●●○○ Venue ●●○○○ Value ●●○○○

Las Palmas Complex

Location → Layali Zman · Corniche Rd East | 627 4555
Hours → 09:00 - 24:00
Web/email → na | Map Ref → 8-D3

Access to this once sprawling complex has become less convenient since work began on the Corniche redevelopment programme but it is still a great family venue worth visiting. It incorporates Café Lafayette, open for coffee, snacks and shisha, Layali Zaman and the Beach Castle restaurant. A live band plays Arabic music on Wednesdays and Thursdays, and there is a popular Friday brunch for only Dhs.55. Takeaways and outside catering are available, as is a useful valet parking service. CC

Food ●●◐○○ Serv ●●●○○ Venue ●●●○○ Value ●●●○○

Lebanese Flower

Location → Nr Choithrams · Khalidiya | 665 8700
Hours → 07:00 - 02:00
Web/email → na | Map Ref → 9-B1

The sidewalk location of this popular Lebanese restaurant can result in a few parking difficulties, with cars lining up outside to collect takeaway orders. Once inside the brightly lit, comfortable interior however, you'll find a range of high quality grilled meats and fish accompanied by freshly baked Arabic bread from the nearby bakery. A selection of Middle Eastern curries and meat dishes is available at lunchtime. Service is super efficient – the slightest nod of your head will bring a bevy of enthusiastic waiters to your table. RH

Food ●●●◐○ Serv ●●●◐○ Venue ●●◐○○ Value ●●●◐○

Marroush

Location → Corniche Rd East | 621 4434
Hours → 11:00 - 01:00
Web/email → na | Map Ref → 8-E3

The multitude of cars lined up outside this Lebanese street café is the first thing to catch your attention – and given the somewhat grimy décor, it is not surprising that this bevy of drive by customers chooses to take their food away. However, the standard Lebanese dishes on the menu are delicious and freshly grilled, and there is the usual range of decadent fruit cocktails piled high with syrup, nuts and cream.

Recommended as a cost effective venue for light meals and takeaways. MMI

Food Serv Venue Value

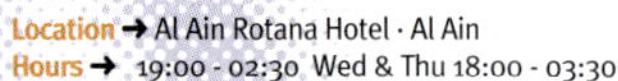

Min Zaman

Location → Al Ain Rotana Hotel · Al Ain | 03 754 5111
Hours → 19:00 - 02:30 Wed & Thu 18:00 - 03:30
Web/email → www.rotana.com | Map Ref → 15-A3

Once you manage to find this restaurant in the depths of the Rotana hotel (ask for directions at reception), you are in for a superb evening of regional food and entertainment that is well worth a second visit. Hot and cold meze head the menu, followed by the usual grilled meats and fish, and desserts and shisha – which you'll enjoy against an entertaining backdrop of live music, singing and belly dancing. Min Zaman gets pretty crowded on Thursday nights, so reservations are recommended. AP

Food Serv Venue Value

Shamyat

Location → Nr Regency Htl · Al Salam St | 671 2600
Hours → 09:00 - 24:00
Web/email → www.shamyat.com | Map Ref → 8-B2

Shamyat serves up authentic Arabic cuisine, and although you won't find any surprises on the menu, the food is fresh and tasty – do not leave without trying the bread prepared on the premises by a traditional bread maker. This venue tends to get frantically busy on some days, but an abundance of greenery and trickling water fountains help keep the ambience calm and relaxing. Shamyat is definitely a recommended pit stop for your next out of town visitors. KU

Food Serv Venue Value

Chinese

Other options → Far Eastern [p.231]

Bam Bu!

Location → Marina & Yacht Club · Al Meena | 645 6373
Hours → 12:00 - 15:00 19:00 - 24:00
Web/email → na | Map Ref → 4-B4

Whether out for a romantic dinner or a celebration with all your friends, you can't go wrong with Bam Bu; a little slice of the Orient with an enchanting view of the yachts at the Marina. The set menu (Dhs.99, including unlimited selected beverages) is a good choice for the uninitiated – just sit back and relax while a constant stream of freshly prepared delicacies are brought to your table. Speciality dishes such as lobster or Peking duck are charged for accordingly. EF

Food Serv Venue Value

Imperial Chinese Restaurant

Location → Sands Hotel · Shk Zayed 2nd St | 633 5335
Hours → 12:00 - 15:30 19:00 - 24:00
Web/email → www.aldiarhotels.com | Map Ref → 8-C1

A huge gold Buddha presides over the entrance to this regal Chinese venue, and the extravagant theme is continued both in the interior design and the menu. Here you'll have the opportunity to try a range of authentic and tasty Chinese dishes, washed down with Chinese wine and beer. The staff, attired in traditional dress, are polite and eager to please, although take care when ordering, as mix ups may occur if you are not specific. CC

Food Serv Venue Value

Oasis Chinese Restaurant

Location → Opp AUH Dental Clinic · Madinat Zayed | 635 1545
Hours → 12:30 - 15:30 18:00 - 24:00
Web/email → na | Map Ref → 5-B4

With its gaudy décor (think giant red lanterns, plastic flowers and artificial plants), Oasis is not where you'd stop for an evening of sophistication, but it does offer cheap and cheerful Chinese chow that is popular with families. The vast menu (over 250 offerings!) can make the head spin, but the photographs of the more traditional plated meals will ease the pressure somewhat. Home delivery available. MM

Food Serv Venue Value

Panda Panda Chinese Restaurant

Location → Nr Jashanmal · Ist Istiglal St | 633 9300
Hours → 12:30 - 16:00 19:00 - 24:00
Web/email → panda@emirates.net.ae | Map Ref → 8-E2

This contemporary eatery mixes modern and traditional oriental influences – the result is a convivial venue serving wholesome Chinese food in a

family friendly setting. The extensive menu caters equally well to vegetarians, seafood lovers and carnivores, with the Hot and Sour Soup and the Schezuan Beef both heartily recommended. Service is quick, attentive and enthusiastic, which might displease you if you're in the mood to linger over your food. If the prices seem high at first, remember that portions are usually generous enough to feed two. APB

Food ●●●○○ Serv ●●●●○ Venue ●●●●● Value ●●●●○

Restaurant China

Location → Novotel Centre Hotel | 632 5661
Hours → 12:00 - 15:30 19:00 - 23:30
Web/email → novoad@emirates.net.ae | Map Ref → 8-D2

100

This restaurant has been dishing up yummy Chinese cuisine to its satisfied customers for 22 years now, and it's still going strong. The food and service are both of consistently high standards, with the Peking duck and Kung Pao prawns worthy of a special mention here. The authentic décor and directional lighting enhance the warm, welcoming ambience – all in all this is a highly recommended venue, and proof that sometimes the oldies are indeed the goodies. DMM

Food ●●●●○ Serv ●●●●○ Venue ●●●○○ Value ●●●●○

Ro-Ro

Location → Khalidia Palace Htl · Khalidiya | 666 3936
Hours → 12:00 - 15:30 18:00 - 23:30
Web/email → www.khalidiapalacehotel.co.ae | Map Ref → 10-E2

100

It could be said that the quality of the food at Ro-Ro is not the city's best, but the prices are very reasonable and as long as you choose your dishes wisely, you can end up enjoying a respectable Chinese dinner for next to nothing. The restaurant is licensed, and although the drinks range is limited, once again the bargain prices have to be applauded. The service is friendly and helpful, and the clean, comfortable interior is pleasant enough. GW

Food ●●○○○ Serv ●●●●○ Venue ●●○○○ Value ●●○○○

Royal Noodle House

Location → Al Meena St | 677 7010
Hours → 12:00 - 16:00 19:00 - 24:00
Web/email → na | Map Ref → 7-E2

100

As with most venues falling into the 'Noodle Bar' genre, dining here is designed to be swift and effortless. Tick your choices off on the menu sheet, hand it to the waiter and your order should arrive shortly afterwards. This particular venue serves an adequate variety of noodle based, fish and meat dishes, including soups and stir fries. Mahogany panelling dominates the décor, making this a slightly more elegant contender in this category. EDMM

Food ●●○○○ Serv ●●●●○ Venue ●●●●○ Value ●●○○○

Emirati

Other options → Arabic/Lebanese [p.224]

Al Areesh

Location → Al Dhafra · Al Meena | 673 2266
Hours → 12:00 - 16:00 19:00 - 23:00
Web/email → www.aldhafra.net | Map Ref → 7-C4

100

For an authentic Arabian experience, look no further. At Al Areesh, guests are instantly welcomed and assisted in choosing from a buffet comprising an attractive selection of seafood, chicken and meat. Food at this restaurant is extremely fresh and plentiful. A healthy choice of 'local' and traditional starters and desserts can be washed down with freshly made cocktails that are highly recommended. Families with young children are well catered for and private 'majlis style' rooms accommodate the larger groups. This is definitely a hidden gem. CM

Food ●●●●○ Serv ●●●○○ Venue ●●●●○ Value ●●●●○

Al Kasser Tourism Complex

Location → Breakwater · Al Ras Al Akhdar | 681 6211
Hours → 17:00 - 02:00
Web/email → na | Map Ref → 10-B4

50

Ideally located in the Heritage Village, this traditional café should be on top of your list of places to take out of town visitors. Where else can you stand under a wind tower to test the earliest form of air conditioning? While you sip on fresh fruit cocktails, you can marvel at the contrast between the authentic artefacts of a bygone age and the glistening, ultra modern city across the turquoise waters of the Corniche. The menu features typical Arabic fare, with a buffet in the evenings. MM

Food ●●○○○ Serv ●●●○○ Venue ●●●●○ Value ●●●●○

Al Safina Dhow Restaurant

Location → Breakwater · Al Ras Al Akhdar | **681 6085**
Hours → 11:00 - 15:30 18:30 - 22:00
Web/email → na | **Map Ref** → 10-A4

100

The Al Safina Dhow, owned by Sheikh Zayed, was once used for sailing. Now permanently moored just off the Breakwater, its purpose is to serve as the venue for a very popular restaurant attracting both residents and tourists. The a la carte menu offers a selection of Gulf specialties such as shrimps, hammour, chicken and lamb, and service is always pleasant and attentive. After dinner, move to the upper deck, which unveils magnificent views of the Corniche and the truly impressive Abu Dhabi skyline. CC

Food ●●●●○ Serv ●●●◐○ Venue ●●●●○ Value ●●●◐○

Far Eastern

Other options → Japanese [p.242]

Jade

Location → Al Diar Mina Hotel · Al Salam St | **677 8415**
Hours → 13:00 - 01:00 Fri 18:00 - 24:00
Web/email → www.aldiarhotels.com | **Map Ref** → 8-A2

Enter the stark minimalism of the Jade interior for a lighter, healthier twist on Far Eastern cuisine – think Fusion rather than authentic Japanese or Chinese. The appetizers, including chicken dumplings, sushi and sashimi, are good value for money and are light enough to pave the way for a main course dish such as black bean noodles or teriyaki smoked salmon. The small selection of conventional wines should steer you towards the Japanese sake, served hot or cold. CP

Food ●●●○○ Serv ●●●◐○ Venue ●●◐○○ Value ●●◐○○

Wok, The

Location → Crowne Plaza · Shk Hamdan Bin Mohd. St | **621 0000**
Hours → 19:00 - 23:00
Web/email → www.abu-dhabi.crowneplaza.com | **Map Ref** → 8-C1

The Wok peddles its own reputation for offering good value for money, and it's true – you really can get an above average 'meal deal for a steal' here. After you've scanned through the a la carte menu, the fun begins and the food, all expertly and freshly prepared, starts to arrive at your table

Far Eastern

For lovers of light, generally healthy food with an emphasis on steamed or stir-fried cooking methods, Far Eastern cuisine is an excellent option either for dining out or takeaway. Seafood and vegetables dominate the menu, but the staples are rice and noodles, with dishes enhanced by the use of delicate and fragrant herbs and spices like ginger and lemon grass, and coconut milk. The food can be spicy, but generally less so than a fiery, denture melting Vindaloo curry.

The décor of Thai, Malaysian and Polynesian restaurants often reflects a stereotypically exotic view of the Far East, with bamboo, beach huts and 'demure' oriental waitresses. Sometimes this combines to create a tasteful, relaxing and classy ambience, and sometimes it doesn't quite make it. With the exception of Chinese outlets, Far Eastern restaurants are generally located in hotels in more upmarket surroundings, with prices that match. Japanese restaurants generally offer a choice of seating options, from teppanyaki tables where the entertainment is provided by the chefs as they juggle, dice and slice, to private tatami rooms. Any way you like it, the standard of Japanese food in Abu Dhabi is high, but, again, with prices to match.

Abu Dhabi also has a great number of Chinese restaurants, and standards vary greatly from monosodium glutamate-laden, taste killing dishes to light and delicious cuisine. Many of the independents (ie, those not linked to a hotel or club) offer good value for money, with large portions of quality food. As with Indian outlets, many Chinese restaurants offer tasty takeaway and home delivery, giving Abu Dhabi residents even less incentive to learn how to use their wok.

The Wok, Abu Dhabi

in a steady flow. Beer, water and a selection of wines are all included for Dhs.99. Understandably popular with large and small groups, The Wok fills up quickly, so book in advance. MM

Food ●●●●○ Serv ●●●●○ Venue ●●●◐○ Value ●●●●●

Wok, The

Location → Htl InterContinental · Al Ain | 03 768 6686
Hours → 12:30 - 15:00 19:30 - 23:00
Web/email → www.interconti.com | Map Ref → 15-E4

 100

Staff members here are proud of their food, service and reputation, and with good reason – The Wok is one of the better restaurants serving Far Eastern cuisine in the area. Set in the landscaped grounds of the hotel, the ambience here is quiet and relaxed, thanks to the tranquil garden views, the soft background music and the stylish décor. The Wok is popular and reservations are essential, particularly for the outstanding seafood buffet on Sunday nights. SW

Food ●●●●○ Serv ●●●●○ Venue ●●●●○ Value ●●●◐○

French

La Brasserie

Location → Le Meridien · Al Meena | 645 5566
Hours → 12:00 - 16:00 18:00 - 24:00
Web/email → www.lemeridien-abudhabi.com | Map Ref → 7-D1

100

This established eatery, overlooking Le Meridien's lively Culinary Village, serves a good selection of French regional cuisine, whether you opt for the varied buffet or choose from the extensive a la carte menu. The seafood buffet on Monday nights is popular, as is the Friday brunch. When the weather is cooler, the terrace is a wonderful place for an evening of laid back alfresco dining. CP

Food ●●●●○ Serv ●●●◐○ Venue ●●●○○ Value ●●●◐○

Le Beaujolais

Location → Novotel Centre Hotel | 633 3555
Hours → 12:00 - 24:00
Web/email → novoad@emirates.net.ae | Map Ref → 8-D2

100

With its red checked tablecloths and French speaking, glass clinking clientele, Le Beaujolais virtually transports you out of Abu Dhabi to a charming little bistro in Paris. The menu offers a choice of seafood and meat dishes, rounded off perfectly with a dessert selection including favourites such as crackly crusted crème brulee and individual cheese plates. A daily set menu is also available. The service, headed by a friendly maitre'd, is welcoming and attentive, but never obtrusive. ECF

Food ●●●◐○ Serv ●●●◐○ Venue ●●●◐○ Value ●●●◐○

Le Bistrot

Location → Le Meridien · Al Meena | 644 9830
Hours → 12:30 - 15:30 19:00 - 23:30
Web/email → www.lemeridien-abudhabi.com | Map Ref → 7-D1

  150

Connoisseurs of fine wines and elegant French cuisine will enjoy a superb culinary experience at Le Bistro in Le Meridien's central garden. In cooler months, the terrace offers a great opportunity to watch the world go by while feasting on some top quality fare. The menu is a little limited and vegetarians will be miserable, but fans of simple fish and meat dishes prepared in a classic French style will be more than happy. Cheap it ain't, but then you get what you pay for. JR

Food ●●●●○ Serv ●●●◐○ Venue ●●●◐○ Value ●●●●○

Le Rabelais

Location → Novotel Centre Hotel | 633 3555
Hours → Call for timings
Web/email → novoad@emirates.net.ae | Map Ref → 8-D2

Currently undergoing renovations, Le Rabelais is being transformed into a cosier, 40 seat restaurant with new décor and a revised a la carte menu. RP

Food – na Serv – na Venue – na Value – na

Fusion

Other options → International [p.235]

90 Degrees

Location → Htl InterContinental · Bainuna St | 693 5214
Hours → 12:00 - 15:30 19:00 - 24:00
Web/email → www.intercontinental.com | Map Ref → 10-C1

French, Italian, Spanish and Moroccan dishes each compose 90 degrees of an intercontinental circle, promising perfection. Genial servers and skilled musicians complement a handsomely spare setting.

Whether you choose to dine indoors or out on the terrace overlooking the marina, allow plenty of time to peruse the menu. The eclectic range of Mediterranean cuisine is diverse enough to be a conversation piece in itself! Watch out for the prices though, which can be off compass by several degrees. AP

Food ●●◐○○ Serv ●●●◐○ Venue ●●●●◐ Value ●●○○○

Flavours

Location → Sheraton Abu Dhabi · Corniche Rd East | 677 3333
Hours → 12:00 - 16:00 19:00 - 23:30
Web/email → www.sheraton.com | Map Ref → 8-A3

This modern and imaginative fusion restaurant serves a variety of very well presented food from an extensive menu. A sushi bar and a well stocked wine cellar further cater to a broader palate. Clean airy lines form the interior of the restaurant and an open plan kitchen manned by competent chefs complements the ambience. Cheerful and unobtrusively attentive staff serve while you dine away, and soft tunes emanating from a talented pianist complete the experience. CC

Food ●●●●○ Serv ●●●●○ Venue ●●●●◐ Value ●●●◐○

German

Brauhaus

Location → Beach Rotana · Al Meena | 644 3000
Hours → 12:30 - 23:30
Web/email → fb.beach@rotana.com | Map Ref → 4-D3

This German beerhall style venue, with its wooden trestle tables and mahogany wall panelling, is great for a relaxed night out with a group of beer drinking friends. Although the menu offers a selection of fish and chicken dishes, the specialties of the house are definitely pork, veal, wurst, sauerkraut and mash, chased down with large clay mugs of lager. The outdoor terrace is a welcome escape from the congested bar atmosphere inside, but can get also crowded during the cooler months. DMM

Brauhaus

Food ●●●◐○ Serv ●●●◐○ Venue ●●●◐○ Value ●●◐○○

Indian

Caravan

Location → Al Hamed Centre · Shk Zayed 2nd St | 639 3370
Hours → 12:30 - 16:30 18:30 - 23:30
Web/email → caravan@emirates.net.ae | Map Ref → 8-D1

For a cheap, "no frills" Asian meal, Caravan certainly delivers the goods. The menu offers a tasty selection of Chinese, Indian and Thai cuisine, and the evening buffet (incredible value for money at Dhs.39) includes soups, salads, a selection of main courses and desserts. The service is remarkably friendly and helpful given that this is a low cost venue. A home delivery service is available. KMC

Food ●◐○○○ Serv ●●◐○○ Venue ●◐○○○ Value ●●●◐○

Casa Goa

Location → Zakher Hotel · Umm Al Nar St | 627 7701
Hours → 12:00 - 15:30 19:30 - 01:00
Web/email → zakhotel@emirates.net.ae | Map Ref → 8-B2

Casa Goa may appear a bit rough round the edges upon first glance, but if you're a spicy food lover, you'll find a range of curries here that will set your lips on fire. A warning to the uninitiated – south Indian cuisine is far spicier than the milder northern dishes (think Vindaloo rather than Korma). If you're the kind of person that eats raw chillies for fun, you'll love it. Fortunately, this venue is licensed, so you can douse the flames with a frosty beer. JR

Food ●●◐○○ Serv ●●●◐○ Venue ◐○○○○ Value ●◐○○○

Foodlands

Location → Opp Al Manhal Palace · Airport Rd | 633 0099
Hours → 12:00 - 15:30 18:30 - 24:30
Web/email → na | Map Ref → 8-E1

Recently opened at its new location on Airport Road, Foodlands is the place to go for a reasonably

Going Out | German | Indian

priced family meal. There are two separate areas, depending on whether you are dining or just fancy a quick snack – both offer tasty Indian, Chinese, Arabic and Continental cuisine, served with a smile. Parking can be a problem, so prevent road rage on busy nights by taking a taxi. Future plans include opening for breakfast and a new snack menu. DPJP

Food ●●●●○ Serv ●●●●○ Venue ●●●●○ Value ●●●●◐

Haveli

Location → Nr New Etisalat Bld · Airport Rd | 632 1448
Hours → 12:00 - 16:00 19:00 - 24:00
Web/email → na
Map Ref → 9-B1

   50

This uncomplicated restaurant delivers the expected – hearty Indian fare, warm service and rock bottom prices. They do a range of chicken and lamb kebabs prepared in the tandoori oven, as well as a surprising variety of tasty curries, ranging from mild to fiery. Traditional South Indian Thalis offer the chance to sample a number of curries and desserts, for less than Dhs.20. DML

Food ●●●◐○ Serv ●●●●○ Venue ●●●○○ Value ●●●●○

India Palace

Location → Opp ADNOC FOD HQ · Al Salam St | 644 8777
Hours → 12:00 - 16:00 19:00 - 24:30
Web/email → sfcroup.com
Map Ref → 4-C4

100

This unassuming restaurant features an extensive menu and is generally busy at lunchtimes and evenings, with a 'mixed bag' of diners. The flavoursome and authentic dishes are generously portioned and offer good value for your dirham. The food is tasty and as can be expected, certain dishes are pretty fiery. Those with more delicate palates can request milder versions of their favourites. Quick, courteous waiters will patiently guide you through the menu if you are not an expert on North Indian Cuisine. EDMM

Food ●●●●○ Serv ●●●◐○ Venue ●●◐○○ Value ●●●●○

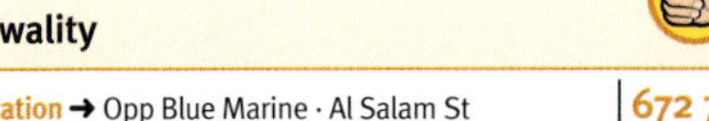

Kwality

Location → Opp Blue Marine · Al Salam St | 672 7337
Hours → 12:00 - 15:00 19:00 - 24:00
Web/email → na
Map Ref → 8-A2

  50

If you like authentic Indian food at a very reasonable price, then Kwality is one of the best options in town. From North Indian Tandoori dishes to Goan curries, Kwality offers the diner a wonderful tour through Indian cuisine. Watch the chefs in the open kitchen prepare succulent kebabs and hot, fluffy naans, while you whet your appetite with peppery poppadoms and spicy chutneys. The food, service, and welcoming atmosphere make this one of the 'must do' Indian restaurants in the capital. DML

Food ●●●●◐ Serv ●●●●◐ Venue ●●●●○ Value ●●●●○

Maharaja

Location → Le Meridien · Al Meena | 644 6666
Hours → 12:30 - 15:30 19:00 - 24:00
Web/email → www.lemeridien-abudhabi.com
Map Ref → 7-D1

There's certainly no shortage of excellent Indian food in the capital, but this venue provides a five star setting and impeccable service to go with it. The décor is carefully thought out, from the crisp table linen to the interesting knick knacks on the walls. The food is tasty and expertly prepared, and although the bias is towards northern cuisine, the chef often creates dishes from other regions. The Thursday buffet gives the chance to sample a bit of everything at a reasonable price. ECF

Food ●●●◐○ Serv ●●●●◐ Venue ●●●●○ Value ●●●◐○

Nihal Restaurant

Location → Nr Sands Htl · Shk Zayed 2nd St | 631 8088
Hours → 12:00 - 15:00 18:30 - 24:00
Web/email → nihal88@emirates.net.ae
Map Ref → 8-C1

This established Indian restaurant offers great curries at rock bottom prices, and the menu is extensive enough to tickle just about anyone's fancy. The fragrant spices of the subcontinent are all expertly blended into tasty traditional dishes, served up with the usual relishes, yoghurts and chutneys. If Indian food is not your favourite, there are also various Chinese dishes on offer. Nihal does a bustling takeaway trade, as well as a well reputed outside catering service. Cheap chow at its best. CP

Food ●●●○○ Serv ●●●◐○ Venue ●●◐○○ Value ●●●●○

DUI

Drinking and driving is illegal in Abu Dhabi, and although it's tempting to jump in the car after just one beer - don't! You may find yourself locked up for a couple of months. Be responsible when it comes to drinking and driving. Remember that you're in a Muslim country and must adhere to the rules here.

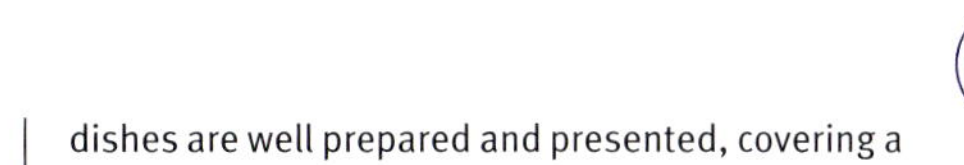

Tanjore

Location → Htl InterContinental · Al Ain | **03 768 6686**
Hours → 12:30 - 15:00 19:00 - 23:00
Web/email → www.interconti.com | **Map Ref** → 15-E4

Tanjore is a wonderful introduction to the tastes of India. Essentially a curry lover's dream, the restaurant's menu is still varied enough to please and appease the most demanding of tastes. The menu provides crystal clear dish descriptions with helpful guidance on what's hot, hotter, healthy and vegetarian – a bonus for the Indian cuisine novice. A rich atmosphere and surroundings complement the delicious and tantalising flavours, and the service is all one would expect of a five star hotel. AP

Food Serv Venue Value

International

Other options → **Seafood [p.248]**

Al Fanar

Location → Le Royal Meridien · Shk Khalifa Bin Zyd St | **674 2020**
Hours → 12:30 - 15:30 19:30 - 23:00
Web/email → www.lemeridien.com | **Map Ref** → 8-B2

Abu Dhabi's only revolving restaurant provides stunning views of the city and sumptuous food in a beautiful setting. Made from the finest of ingredients, the food is cooked to perfection and exquisitely presented. Impeccable service and a great wine list only add to a perfect evening. If in the mood to splurge, whether on a business lunch or a romantic dinner, Al Fanar is the ideal choice. But keep your valuables well away from the windowsill; they've been known to revolve well away from your table! KU

Food Serv Venue Value

Arabesque

Location → Htl InterContinental · Al Ain | **03 768 6686**
Hours → 12:30 - 15:30 19:30 - 22:30
Web/email → www.interconti.com | **Map Ref** → 15-E4

This top hotel buffet comes at a very affordable price. Served in spacious attractive surroundings by polite and unobtrusive staff, the meal includes salads that are fresh and varied, and plenty of alternatives to the ubiquitous Lebanese meze. Hot dishes are well prepared and presented, covering a wide range of tastes and geographic backgrounds. Where lunch is spiced up with a live cooking centre featuring a cuisine of the day, evenings include a small set menu that complements the buffet. And the desserts are definitely worth the drive. AP

Food Serv Venue Value

Bayview

Location → Beach Rotana · Al Meena | **644 3000**
Hours → 08:00 - 23:00
Web/email → fb.beach@rotana.com | **Map Ref** → 4-B3

If alfresco dining beneath huge beach brollies, sipping cocktails and watching the sunset on a cool evening sounds appealing, then head on down to this venue situated in the rather plush sports complex of the Beach Rotana Hotel. An abundance of freshly prepared salads, mains and desserts awaits you, and there is also a fine selection of drinks. The food, although pricey, is tasty, healthy and well presented, but the service could use a bit of fine tuning. CC

Food Serv Venue Value

Club Restaurant, The

Location → Club, The · Al Meena | **673 1111**
Hours → 19:00 - 00:30
Web/email → www.the-club.com | **Map Ref** → 7-A2

This dinner only venue features an impressive entrance area complete with fireplace constructed of stone and wine bottles, which leads you to the softly lit, Roman style interior – the perfect setting for a romantic evening. With theme nights through the week, except for Fridays and Saturdays, The Club Restaurant offers a superb choice of different cuisines, each as tasty as the next. The service is attentive and the prices reasonable. Strangely (for these parts), mobile phones are not allowed into the restaurant. Reservations required. MM

Food Serv Venue Value

Cote Jardin

Location → Novotel Centre Hotel | **633 3555**
Hours → Call for timings
Web/email → novoad@emirates.net.ae | **Map Ref** → 8-D2

Cote Jardin (ex Trattoria Pizzeria Del Centro), undergoing renovation at the time of print,

Indian | International

Going Out

promises to be a bright and enjoyable all day restaurant with a calm atmosphere and friendly service. Chef Alain Denis is waiting in the wings to bring you his take on some of the world's favourite international dishes. RP

Food – na Serv – na Venue – na Value – na

Flavours

Location → Hilton Al Ain · Al Ain | 03 768 6666
Hours → 12:00 - 15:00 19:00 - 23:00
Web/email → www.hilton.com Map Ref → 15-D4

While perhaps not high on the list of romantic venues, the bright ambience of Flavours is pleasant enough and offers a satisfactory dining experience for business meetings and family groups. Eat your way around the world with themed buffets on most nights of the week. Friday brunches here should strike a chord with frazzled parents – pack the kids off to play at the Kids' Club and enjoy a complimentary glass of bubbly in peace. JS

Food Serv Venue Value

Garden, The

Location → Crowne Plaza · Shk Hamdan Bin Mohd. St | 621 0000
Hours → 12:00 - 16:00 19:00 - 23:00
Web/email → www.abu-dhabi.crowneplaza.com Map Ref → 8-C1

Indulge the nature lover within you in this faux alfresco 'garden' venue, decorated with an abundance of plants and complete with waterfall. Daily theme nights cover the cuisines of the world – every evening you'll find an impressive buffet laid out, designed to confuse and delight your taste buds. House beverages are included in the price on most nights. On Fridays, the Mighty Brunch is a family affair, with truckloads of tasty food and plenty of entertainment for the kids. CC

Food Serv Venue Value

Seafood Night at The Garden

L'Opera Brasserie

Location → Le Royal Meridien · Shk Khalifa Bin Zyd St | 674 2020
Hours → 12:30 - 15:30 19:30 - 22:30
Web/email → www.lemeridien.com Map Ref → 8-B2

With its pleasing décor and prime spot off the lobby of this newly renovated hotel, L'Opera makes an appealing venue for light meals, snacks and coffee. There is a small international buffet offering a mix of cuisines from around the world, and the a la carte menu also offers a moderate selection of breakfasts, starters, and fish or meat dishes. The adjacent terrace offers the option of alfresco dining. EDMM

Food Serv Venue Value

La Veranda

Location → Sheraton Residence · Khalidiya | 666 6220
Hours → 12:30 - 15:30 19:00 - 23:00
Web/email → www.sheraton.com Map Ref → 9-B1

The first thing that strikes you about La Veranda is the majestic, Renaissance décor – all gleaming marble tiles, wrought iron detail and Victorian chandeliers. Sadly, this does not translate into a warm, charming ambience – there is a noticeable lack of background music, paintings, lamps or even plants. The international buffet offers standard Euro Mediterranean cuisine with a few Arabic dishes alongside; alternatively there is an a la carte option. The service is friendly and super efficient. MH

Food Serv Venue Value

Le Belvedere

Location → Mercure Grand Hotel · Al Ain | 03 783 8888
Hours → 12:30 - 15:00 19:00 - 22:30
Web/email → www.mercure.alain Map Ref → 17-B4

Perched atop Jebel Hafeet, Le Belvedere has a wonderful (yet restricted) view over the city of Al Ain. Serving both buffet and a la carte meals, this restaurant offers a variety of international cuisine

with a distinct Mediterranean influence. The Friday seafood buffet is a speciality and well worth the drive to the top of the mountain. But perhaps the best way to experience Le Belvedere is to book in for a night at the hotel, and enjoy the full package. GW

Food Serv Venue Value

NRG Sports Café

Location → Le Meridien · Al Meena | **644 6666**
Hours → 16:00 - 02:30
Web/email → www.lemeridien-abudhabi.com | **Map Ref** → 7-D1

  100

Armchair athletes will love this sports café, with its multitude of TV screens, reasonably priced snacks and a happy hour that lasts until 21:00. Cleverly decorated with sports paraphernalia with an arena ambience and open kitchen pumping out fast and furious fusion food, NRG is as good a spot as any to catch your favourite game live on TV. You can try out your best sporty spice moves on the dance floor or, better still, keep your eyes glued to the score line. APB

Food Serv Venue Value

NRG Sports Café

Palm, The

Location → Al Diar Capitol Hotel · Al Meena St | **678 7700**
Hours → 12:30 - 15:30 19:00 - 23:00
Web/email → adcaphtl@emirates.net.ae | **Map Ref** → 7-E2

 100

Ideal for families, The Palm offers a reasonably priced buffet; packed with fresh, tasty salads, hot meals and desserts. The simple décor is clean and welcoming, and large glass windows allow an abundance of light into the cheerful dining area. With friendly, efficient staff, plenty of parking and the no fuss buffet, The Palm is also perfect for in and out business lunches. PDG

Food Serv Venue Value

Vasco's

Location → Hiltonia Beach Club · Corniche Rd West | **692 4328**
Hours → 12:00 - 15:00 19:00 - 23:00
Web/email → na | **Map Ref** → 10-C2

      150

Vasco's is a contemporary, fine dining venue offering a fusion of European, Arabic and Asian cuisines. Food is prepared to a very high standard, imaginatively presented, and served to your table by friendly and knowledgeable waiters. As this is one of the more popular restaurants in the capital, reservations are essential for lunch and dinner. In winter, the patio offers a pleasant, alfresco setting and lovely views. Recommended. AR

Food Serv Venue Value

Vasco's

Eat Out Speak Out

www.EatOutSpeakOut.com

Explorer Publishing is quite proud to be a bit of a 'people's publisher'. We understand your hangovers, your need for excitement, your boredom thresholds and your desire to be heard, and we're always striving to make our publications as interactive with our loyal readership as possible. In the past, our Food Correspondent's telephone has been ringing constantly with people wanting to add their two pennies' worth to the reviews in our guidebooks.

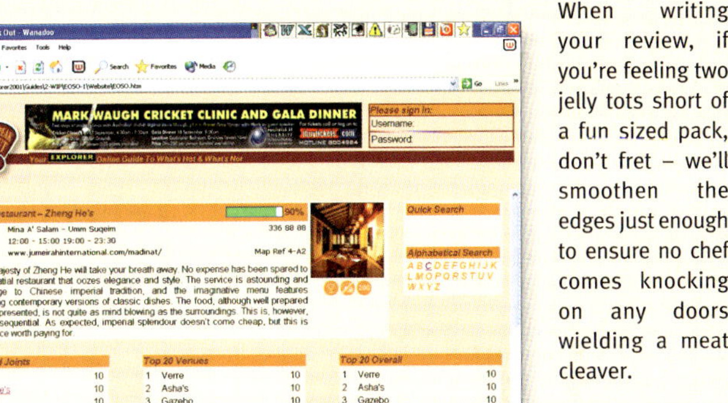

Hence, our most ingenious solution for a satisfied diner, accurate food reporting and lower decibels in the work place, is **EAT OUT SPEAK OUT**.

This Website provides the opportunity to pen down all of your comments, frustrations, tips and tantrums about specific dining experiences at any of the restaurants listed in our guide. Not only will we publish your thoughts online, we'll also pass on your review (anonymously, of course) to the outlet concerned and take your views into consideration for next year's edition of our guidebook.

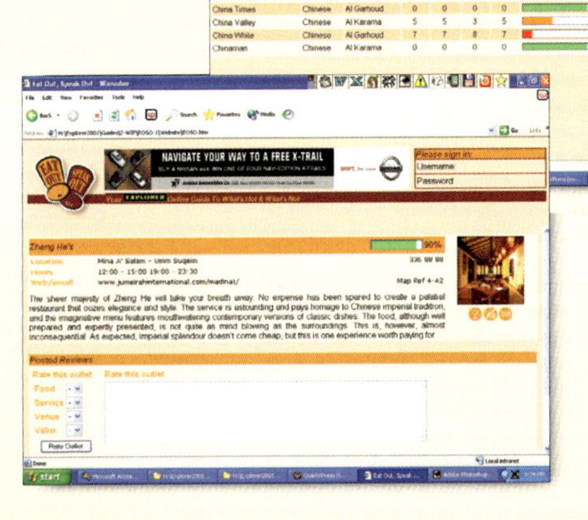

Now that you know what it's all about, we will restrain you no longer...

Once logged on to **www.EatOutSpeakOut.com**, select the restaurant you wish to review by typing in the outlet name. Alternatively, you can search for your restaurant alphabetically, by cuisine or area/location.

Once you've found the object of your wrath or praise, simply scroll through people's previously penned prose and then enter your own. Don't forget to put in those all important ratings too.

When writing your review, if you're feeling two jelly tots short of a fun sized pack, don't fret – we'll smoothen the edges just enough to ensure no chef comes knocking on any doors wielding a meat cleaver.

Once you've got it all off your chest, relax and read what everyone else has to say about your favourite joint. See the restaurant rated by 'Venue' and also skim through the 'Best Overall' category.

Come on, lets hear what you have to say to improve, or reward the service here!

Italian

Other options → Mediterranean [p.243]

Amalfi

Location → Le Royal Meridien · Shk Khalifa Bin Zyd St | 674 2020
Hours → 12:00 - 15:45 19:30 - 23:30
Web/email → www.lemeridien.com | Map Ref → 8-B2

   150

Resurrected from the ashes of its predecessor, the new Amalfi at Le Royal Meridien offers patrons an elegant dining experience. Calamata olives, tapenade and chopped fresh tomato with hints of garlic remain on the table throughout as you down delectable dishes of humble minestrone and mussel mariniere. Served in cleverly designed angular crockery, the tarragon hammour fillet with mussels and creamy tomato sauce meat lasagne are just the tip of the yummy iceberg, served by a confident yet hushed staff. A dining experience not to be rushed. EDMM

Food ●●●●○ Serv ●●●◐○ Venue ●●●●○ Value ●●●◐○

Casa Romana

Location → Hilton Al Ain · Al Ain | 03 768 6666
Hours → 12:00 - 15:00 19:00 - 23:00
Web/email → www.hilton.com | Map Ref → 15-D4

  50

Viva Italia! The well known Casa Romana, overlooking the bustling lobby of the hotel, has an extensive menu of authentic Italian dishes, all generously portioned and delicious. Expect to find all your Italian favourites here, including pizza, pasta and a rather tasty seafood risotto. The décor evokes the feel of a rustic country terrace, although the sometimes frenzied activity of the lobby can be a distraction. AP

Food ●●●◐○ Serv ●●●●○ Venue ●●◐○○ Value ●●●◐○

Ciro's Pomodoro

Location → Al Diar Capitol Hotel · Al Meena St | 672 7357
Hours → 19:00 - 03:00
Web/email → adcaphtl@emirates.net.ae | Map Ref → 7-E2

100

If you just can't resist a charming Italian, then this unique, trendy venue is perfect for you. The menu covers all the classics like pastas, salads, pizzas and grilled dishes, and the numerous pictures of celebrities visiting Ciro's around the world will keep you entertained while you wait for your meal to arrive. The food is delectable, the service friendly and attentive, and a live band is there most days to serenade you through your meal. Superb. MMI

Food ●●●●○ Serv ●●●◐○ Venue ●●◐○○ Value ●●●◐○

La Mamma

Location → Sheraton Abu Dhabi · Corniche Rd East | 677 3333
Hours → 12:00 - 15:30 19:00 - 24:00
Web/email → www.sheraton.com | Map Ref → 8-A3

  100

Linger over a hearty Italian meal at La Mamma, which offers a wide selection of pizzas, pasta, and meat and fish dishes in a relaxed setting. Start with the antipasti buffet, with its tantalising and generous spread. La Mamma doesn't quite hit the mark with its more 'gourmet' main courses, but if you stick to the simpler dishes, it's well worth a visit. DML

Food ●●●●○ Serv ●●●○○ Venue ●●●●○ Value ●●●●○

La Piazza

Location → Sands Hotel · Shk Zayed 2nd St | 633 5335
Hours → 12:00 - 15:30 19:00 - 23:30
Web/email → www.sands-hotel.com | Map Ref → 8-C1

  100

Not cluttered with the usual décor and refreshingly free of traditional clichés, La Piazza is a quiet respite from the usual Abu Dhabi scramble for both residents and hotel patrons alike. The menu stays true to its Italian theme with a good selection of authentic starters, main dishes and desserts that are all enjoyable, good value and well presented.

La Piazza

The alternative is a buffet, which seems to be the most popular choice with patrons. PDG

Food Serv Venue Value

Pappagallo

Location → Le Meridien · Al Meena | 644 6666
Hours → 12:30 - 15:30 19:00 - 24:00
Web/email → www.lemeridien-abudhabi.com Map Ref → 7-D1

50

Pappagallo is like a little slice of Tuscany right in the heart of the Le Meridien Culinary Village. The menu caters to most tastes, offering all the usual favourites of Italian cuisine, such as pastas and pizzas, as well as a wonderful antipasto buffet. Whether you dine alfresco or indoors, the food is good, the atmosphere pleasant, and the service satisfactory. TAP

Food Serv Venue Value

Peppino

Location → Grand Continental Htl · Umm Al Nar St | 626 2200
Hours → 12:00 - 15:00 19:00 - 23:30
Web/email → grndconh@emirates.net.ae Map Ref → 8-B2

Peppino's has been around for a long time, and although this shows in the décor, the food is still good. While it offers a decent spread of standard Italian fare, Peppino's is most famous for its pizzas, featuring a thin, crispy crust and interesting toppings. The wine list is respectable and, like the food, is fairly priced. The service here is good, but they also offer takeaways and home delivery, if you prefer. KU

Food Serv Venue Value

Pizzeria Italiana

Location → Al Diar Gulf Htl · Al Maqtaa | 441 4777
Hours → 11:00 - 22:30
Web/email → adglfhtl@emirates.net.ae Map Ref → 1-D3

A warm welcome awaits you at this appealing Italian café. The interior is simple and rustic, with crisp, fresh linen draped over wooden tables, and the outside terrace is good for alfresco dining. Salads, pizza and pasta dominate the menu, although there are a few interesting additions as well. Both the food and the wine are very reasonably priced. APB

Food Serv Venue Value

Portofino

Location → Marina & Yacht Club · Al Meena | 644 0300
Hours → 12:00 - 15:00 19:00 - 23:30
Web/email → www.abudhabimarina.com Map Ref → 4-B4

Portofino's probably won't win any awards for food quality, but the menu offers satisfactorily prepared Italian classics like pizza, pasta and tiramisu. On the plus side, the portions are generous and the prices are reasonable. The main draw card here though, is the pleasant location overlooking the pool, which lends itself to relaxed outdoor dining in the winter months. Shisha pipes are available, if desired. CC

Food Serv Venue Value

Prego's

Location → Beach Rotana · Al Meena | 644 3000
Hours → 12:00 - 15:30 19:00 - 23:30
Web/email → fb.beach@rotana.com Map Ref → 4-B3

Tucked away in the corner of this busy hotel, Prego's boasts an enchanting setting with its large, airy interior and superb terrace overlooking the beach. The food is wonderful – aside from the variety available at the pizza bar, the menu has a selection of both classic and innovative pasta dishes, main courses and desserts. Pizzas are prepared in an authentic wood fired oven. Prego's is family friendly, but the comfortable spaces between tables make this a good choice for an intimate dinner too. PD

Food Serv Venue Value

Sevilo's

Location → Millennium Hotel · Shk Khalifa Bin Zyd St | 626 2700
Hours → 12:00 - 15:00 19:00 - 23:30
Web/email → www.milleniumhotels.com Map Ref → 8-B2

The cooler months are the best time to make use of the poolside terrace at this venue, complete with stunning views of the city and gardens. The varied, yet uncomplicated menu delivers classic Italian cuisine, which is freshly prepared and generally of a high standard. Sevilo's is a pleasant, intimate eatery and delivers a trifecta of high points – good food, pleasant setting and great service – to ensure you'll have an enjoyable evening. KMC

Food Serv Venue Value

Japanese

Other options → Far Eastern [p.231]

Benihana

Location → Beach Rotana · Al Meena | 644 3000
Hours → 12:00 - 15:00 19:00 - 23:00
Web/email → fb.beach@rotana.com Map Ref → 4-B3

The gracious, contemporary Japanese cuisine, the minimalist décor and the crowd pleasing teppanyaki chefs make this venue a 'must do' on the Abu Dhabi restaurant circuit. The menu includes the usual soups, salads and desserts, but if it's Japanese you're after then don't miss out on the sushi and of course the teppanyaki, prepared at live cooking stations by entertaining chefs. Prices may seem high at first, but for a feast of melt in your mouth treats, it's good value. APB

Food ●●●●● Serv ●●●●● Venue ●●●●● Value ●●●●◐

Bonsai

Location → Health & Fitness Club · Al Mushrif | 443 4807
Hours → 12:00 - 23:00 Fri 13:00 - 22:00
Web/email → www.adhfc.com Map Ref → 3-D3

It's always a good sign when a Japanese restaurant is frequented by lots of Japanese customers – Bonsai is a great venue for business and relaxed dining. Subdued décor and soft lighting complement the subtle flavours of Japanese classics such as sushi, sashimi, tempura and teriyaki dishes, and the restaurant also boasts a tepanyaki bar and three tatimi rooms. Even the service is traditionally Japanese – quiet, efficient and reserved. Bonsai is highly recommended for moderately priced, authentic fare in a comfortable, peaceful atmosphere. MMI

Food ●●●●○ Serv ●●●○○ Venue ●●●●○ Value ●●●◐○

Soba

Location → Le Royal Meridien · Shk Khalifa Bin Zyd St | 674 2020
Hours → 19:00 - 24:00; Fri closed
Web/email → www.lemeridien.com Map Ref → 8-B2

Trendy and contemporary without trying too hard, soba is a welcome addition to the Abu Dhabi restaurant scene – an evening spent here is generally a wonderful experience from start to finish. The menu features sushi, sashimi, tempura and noodle dishes from various Asian countries, such as pad Thai and Singaporean noodles. Food is fresh, flavourful and cooked to perfection. Highly recommended for top class Asian Cuisine in beautiful surroundings. ECF

Food ●●●●● Serv ●●●●○ Venue ●●●●◐ Value ●●●●◐

Zen

Location → Al Ain Palace Hotel · Corniche Rd East | 679 4777
Hours → 12:00 - 15:00 19:00 - 24:00
Web/email → www.alainpalacehotel.com Map Ref → 8-B3

While the minimalist décor is a touch on the drab side, and the high pitched, xylophonic zinging of the background music is clanging at times, Zen has a string of satisfied customers, including many from the Japanese expat community. The secret of this success is simple: the food is authentic, delicious and fresh. Whether you choose the sophisticated sushi, or the light hearted live cooking of the teppanyaki bar, you'll be impressed by the simplicity and subtlety of the flavours. TAP

Food ●●●●○ Serv ●●●◐○ Venue ●●●◐○ Value ●●●○○

> **Valet it**
>
> *Still single because you're always late for your date? In Abu Dhabi, finding a parking space is a time wasting exercise. If you're dining at a restaurant in a hotel, don't stress for a spot. Boldly drive your beaten up bandwagon to the main entrance, and hand over your keys to a valet. Just make sure he does work for the hotel... or you'll be walking home.*

Sushi Platter

Korean

Other options → Far Eastern [p.231]

Arirang

Location → Khalidia Palace Htl · Al Ras Al Akhdar | 665 0563
Hours → 12:00 - 15:00 19:00 - 23:00
Web/email → www.khalidiapalacehotel.co.ae Map Ref → 10-E2

100

This no frills restaurant serves Japanese cuisine, and is also the only Korean choice in town. Remember though, that if you order from the Korean menu, all your food will brought at the same time. Most of the dishes are served barbecued with oriental spices to give it a unique flavour. Plus, the retro setting with dark wooden booths and shoji screens makes the entire dining experience distinctly different and well worth a visit. EF

Food ●●◐○○ Serv ●●●●○ Venue ●●◐○○ Value ●●●◐○

Mediterranean

Other options → Italian [p.240]

Chequers

Location → Sands Hotel · Shk Zayed 2nd St | 633 5335
Hours → 19:00 - 24:00
Web/email → www.sands-hotel.com Map Ref → 8-C1

150

This modern, intimate venue is a pleasing choice if you fancy a cosy meal accompanied by good wine and a spot of live music. The service is attentive and the meals beautifully presented, but if you are a particularly picky diner, you may find the food itself a little bland. However, thanks to the excellent wine list, the singer and her sidekick on the baby grand piano, your evening at Chequer's will be a largely enjoyable one. CP

Food ●●◐○○ Serv ●●●◐○ Venue ●●●◐○ Value ●●●○○

Gardinia

Location → Al Ain Rotana Htl · Al Ain | 03 751 5111
Hours → 12:30 - 15:30 19:30 - 23:30
Web/email → www.rotana.com Map Ref → 15-A3

100

Live piano music fills the air while a carved ice swan presides over an array of fresh seafood laid out in a wooden dhow – welcome to Gardinia. This venue is popular throughout the week and reservations are a necessity. Seafood lovers won't know where to start but the seafood chowder is recommended and the red snapper will not disappoint. The service can be slow, but the antics of your culturally diverse fellow diners provide ample entertainment while you wait. JS

Food ●●●●○ Serv ●●●◐○ Venue ●●●●○ Value ●●●◐○

La Terrazza

Location → Hilton Abu Dhabi · Corniche Rd West | 681 1900
Hours → 12:00 - 15:00 19:00 - 23:00
Web/email → www.hilton.com Map Ref → 10-C2

100

La Terrazza serves up a buffet of Arabic/Mediterranean food and hosts theme nights several times a week. If you're a non smoker, the location of the buffet right in the middle of the smoking section may bother you, but the food is pleasant enough. This is a typical 'hotel lobby' restaurant, which ably serves the needs of hotel guests or business meetings over lunch, but it's not really a place to go out of your way for. EF

Food ●◐○○○ Serv ●●●●○ Venue ●◐○○○ Value ●◐○○○

> **Dress Up**
>
> *Abu Dhabi seems to have an unspoken (smart) dress code on the social scene. You could, perhaps, get away with shorts in some of the pubs and hotels. However, it is recommended that you check out the dress code beforehand (particularly for nightclubs) in order to avoid the embarrassment of being refused entry and your pals aren't. (Also a good test of friendship!)*

La Terrazza

Mexican

Other options → Tex Mex [p.249]

El Sombrero

Location → Sheraton Abu Dhabi · Corniche Rd East | 677 3333
Hours → 12:00 - 16:00 19:00 - 01:00
Web/email → www.sheraton.com
Map Ref → 8-A3

El Sombrero comes highly recommended, whether you're out for a relaxed dinner for two or a raucous night with your amigos. Fascinating Mexican artefacts and well thought out décor set the scene, while the food and the service both score highly. This lively venue is good on any night of the week – in particular, check out the theme nights on Tuesdays and Wednesdays. PDG

Hidden Charges

When the bill arrives, subtly check out the dreaded small print (slyly lurking at the bottom of the bill) that says 'INCLUSIVE +15% +5%'. Be careful what you touch, as you may find that even the most innocent eye contact with a nut bowl can result in surplus charges.

Food ●●●●○ Serv ●●●●○ Venue ●●●●● Value ●●●◐○

El Torito

Location → Htl InterContinental · Bainuna St | 667 1760
Hours → 12:00 - 02:00
Web/email → eltorito@emirates.net.ae
Map Ref → 10-C1

With the best (and largest!) margaritas in town and traditional Tex-Mex fare, El Torito makes for a great night out. The lively Colombian quartet puts on a fine show while you tuck into generous portions of sizzling fajitas, enchiladas and burritos. Daily happy hour: 17:00 - 19:00. CC

Food ●●●●● Serv ●●●●● Venue ●●●●○ Value ●●●◐○

Mongolian

Other options → Far Eastern [p.231]

Coconut Bay

Location → Hiltonia Beach Club · Corniche Rd West | 681 1900
Hours → 10:30 - 18:45
Web/email → na
Map Ref → 10-C2

The a la carte menu at Coconut Bay is impressive, but during the cooler months the Mongolian barbeque on Friday evenings is a hands down winner. On other days, the extensive selection of sandwiches and the original salads make this a great place to recharge after a hard day's relaxing on the beach – the setting is ideal for a casual dinner and a few sundowners. Kids are welcome and there is a special menu for hungry little tummies. DML

Food ●●●●○ Serv ●●●●○ Venue ●●●●● Value ●●●●○

Moroccan

Other Options → Arabic/Lebanese [p.224]

Marakesh

Location → Millennium Hotel · Shk Khalifa Bin Zyd St | 626 2700
Hours → 19:00 - 02:00
Web/email → www.milleniumhotels.com
Map Ref → 8-B2

Despite the elaborate décor, Marakesh has a fairly casual ambience which suits business and leisure diners alike. Exotic and delectable Moroccan food (with more than a hint of Lebanese influence) is served in generous portions and delivered to your table by a bevy of highly efficient waiters. A live band adds atmosphere, and later in the evening an eye poppingly beautiful belly dancer makes a dramatic appearance. The air conditioning is rather frosty, so go prepared! Marakesh is open for dinner only, and closed on Fridays. CC

Food ●●●◐○ Serv ●●●●● Venue ●●●●● Value ●●●◐○

Nepalese

Curry House

Location → Nr Janata Bank · Shk Zayed 2nd St | 632 8860
Hours → 11:00 - 15:00 18:00 - 24:00
Web/email → na
Map Ref → 8-D1

Take your tastebuds on a culinary journey to Nepal at this unpretentious restaurant (formerly Kathmandu). The traditional Nepalese menu includes vegetable dishes, soups and curries, as well as a variety of momos (Nepalese dumplings) accompanied by a spicy sauce. The naan bread, served fresh and hot, is particularly memorable. Indian and Chinese specialities are also available. This venue is a bit classier than your local thali joint, and comes highly recommended for a tasty, inexpensive meal. ECF

Food ●●●○○ Serv ●●●○○ Venue ●●○○○ Value ●●●●○

Persian

Other Options → Arabic/Lebanese [p.224]

Al Khayam

Location → Hilton Al Ain · Al Ain | 03 768 6666
Hours → 12:00 - 15:00 19:00 - 23:00
Web/email → www.hilton.com | Map Ref → 15-D4

 100

At Al Khayam, you are sure to be presented with delicious meals cooked to near perfection. An extensive and varied wine list caters for all tastes and complements an array of Iranian grills, kebabs and other Middle Eastern delights. Fresh bread and tangy salads add to the other dining pleasures and table service is attentive – always prompt and cheerful. In fact, the attractive authentic Persian surroundings alone justify a reservation. GW

Food ●●●●◐ Serv ●●●◐○ Venue ●●●◐○ Value ●●●○○

Polynesian

Other Options → Chinese [p.228]

Trader Vic's

Location → Al Ain Rotana Hotel · Al Ain | 03 754 5111
Hours → 11:30 - 15:30 19:30 - 23:30
Web/email → www.rotana.com | Map Ref → 15-A3

 100

Forget the desert and spend an evening in tropical island mode at this popular Polynesian venue, where the décor is so authentic you'll swear you can actually feel the occasional sultry sea breeze. The menu forgoes authentic Polynesian food, preferring instead to satisfy the cosmopolitan clientele with a delicious and diverse range of international dishes. The wine list is extensive, albeit somewhat overshadowed by the impressive list of cocktails, some of which are so potent they should carry a health warning! AP

Food ●●●●○ Serv ●●●◐○ Venue ●●●●○ Value ●●●◐○

Trader Vic's

Location → Beach Rotana · Al Meena | 644 3000
Hours → 12:30 - 15:00 19:30 - 23:30
Web/email → fb.beach@rotana.com | Map Ref → 4-B3

 150

Whether for business or pleasure, Trader Vic's is one of the longstanding favourite restaurants in Abu Dhabi. The consistent quality of the food, the

Middle Eastern

There is no one distinct Middle Eastern or Arabic cuisine, but it is instead a blend of many styles of cooking from the region. Thus, an Arabic meal will usually include a mix of dishes from countries as far afield as Morocco or Egypt to Lebanon and Iran. However, in Abu Dhabi, modern Arabic cuisine almost invariably means Lebanese food. Typical ingredients include beef, lamb, chicken, rice, nuts (mainly pistachios), dates, yoghurt and a range of seafood and spices. The cuisine is excellent for meat eaters and vegetarians alike.

A popular starter is a selection of dishes known as 'mezze' (meze or mezzeh), which is often a meal in its own right. It is a variety of appetisers served with flat bread, a green salad and 'radioactive' pickles. Dishes can include 'humous' (ground chickpeas, oil and garlic), 'tabouleh' (parsley and cracked wheat salad, with tomato), 'fatoush' (lettuce, tomatoes and grilled Arabic bread) and 'fattayer' (small, usually hot, pastries filled with spinach or cottage cheese).

Charcoal grilling is a popular cooking method, and traditionally dishes are cooked with many spices including ginger, nutmeg and cinnamon. An authentic local dish is 'khouzi' (whole lamb, wrapped in banana leaves, buried in the sand and roasted, then served on a bed of rice mixed with nuts), which is most often available at Ramadan for the evening meal at the end of the day's fast ('Iftar'). It would also have been served at the 'mansaf'; the traditional, formal Bedouin dinner, where various dishes were placed on the floor in the centre of a ring of seated guests.

Other typical dishes include 'kibbeh' (deep-fried balls of mince, pine nuts and bulgar (cracked wheat), and a variety of kebabs. Seafood is widely available, and local varieties of fish include hammour (a type of grouper), chanad (mackerel), beyah (mullet) and wahar, which are often grilled over hot coals or baked in an oven.

Meals end with Lebanese sweets, which are delicious, but very sweet. The most widely known is 'baklava' (filo pastry layered with honey and nuts) and 'umm Ali' (mother of Ali in English), which is a rich, creamy dessert with layers of milk, bread, raisins and nuts - an exotic bread and butter pudding.

attentive staff and the relaxed tropical ambience keep people coming back (except maybe those on a tight budget). Try one of their world famous cocktails as you peruse the exciting menu – it's always difficult making the final choice from the tantalising French Polynesian dishes! A discreet trio provides entertainment without disrupting conversation. HG

Happy Hour: *Daily 17:30 - 19.30*

Food ●●●●○ Serv ●●●◐○ Venue ●●●●◐ Value ●●●●○

Trader Vic's

Waka Taua Terrace

Location → Le Meridien · Al Meena | 644 6666
Hours → 17:00 - 24:00
Web/email → www.lemeridien-abudhabi.com | Map Ref → 7-D1

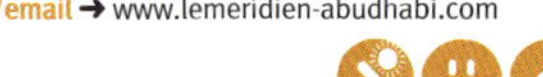

With an idyllic setting on the water's edge, the Waka Taua is popular with the 'sundowner set'. You might find it difficult to track down a menu here, although a limited range of light snacks (along the lines of chicken satay, buffalo wings and nachos) is available to help you curb the munchies. Ideally, this is the place where you'd stop for a few cocktails before heading off for a meal elsewhere. A live band entertains in the evenings. APB

Food ●●◐○○ Serv ●●◐○○ Venue ●●●◐○ Value ●●●○○

Seafood

Other Options → Dinner Cruises [p.250]

Fishmarket, The

Location → Htl InterContinental · Bainuna St | 666 6888
Hours → 12:30 - 15:00 19:30 - 23:00
Web/email → www.intercontinental.com | Map Ref → 10-C1

Shop for your supper at this established seafood restaurant – hand pick your ingredients from the freshest local produce at the 'market stall', ably assisted by friendly and knowledgeable staff, and then sit back and relax while your selection is whisked off to the kitchen and transformed into a delectable feast. The ambience is warm and pleasing, and the cooking style leans towards the Far Eastern and Thai cuisines. Food is charged according to weight, and is of exceptional quality. CP

Food ●●●●○ Serv ●●●●○ Venue ●●●○○ Value ●●◐○○

Spanish

Other Options → Tapas Bars [p.262]

Teplancha

Location → Htl InterContinental · Bainuna St | 666 6888
Hours → 18:00 - 24:00
Web/email → www.intercontinental.com | Map Ref → 10-C1

The unlikely mixture of Japanese teppanyaki and northern Spanish tapas seems to work just fine at this unpretentious venue overlooking the marina – the food here is unfussy and very, very tasty. Round up a few friends, order a selection of starter sized portions of chicken, meat or vegetarian finger foods and tuck in – it's an evening of Mediterranean magic under the stars. CM

Food ●●●●○ Serv ●●●○○ Venue ●●●◐○ Value ●●●◐○

Steakhouses

Other Options → American [p.223]

Rainbow Steak House

Location → Nr BHS Bld · Shk Hamdan Bin Mohd. St | 633 3434
Hours → 12:30 - 16:00 18:30 - 24:00
Web/email → www.rainbowauh.com | Map Ref → 8-C1

The quiet, friendly surroundings of the Steak House have recently been refurbished and this venue is definitely worth a visit. As the name suggests, steaks are a speciality here – there is a good range and all are cooked to perfection. They also do a good selection of seafood, and Chinese, Indian and continental cuisine. Lunch and dinner buffets are available daily at unbelievably low prices (Dhs.35 for lunch and Dhs.40 for dinner), yet the friendly, efficient service remains uncompromised. J

Food ●●●●○ Serv ●●●◐○ Venue ●●●◐○ Value ●●●●○

Rodeo Grill

Location → Beach Rotana · Al Meena | 644 3000
Hours → 12:00 - 15:30 19:00 - 23:30
Web/email → fb.beach@rotana.com **Map Ref** → 4-B3

200

Enter the hallowed 'gentlemen's club' atmosphere of this premium steakhouse and you won't regret it – the food is of particularly high quality, the venue is sublime and the service faultless. Steak lovers will be especially pleased by the first class selection of Angus, Australian, Tenderloin, Ribeye and Bison steaks, which are handpicked according to weight and cooked to perfection. A range of seafood and poultry alternatives is also available. If you have any room left, don't you dare leave without trying the chocolate soufflé – culinary nirvana! CC

Food Serv Venue Value

Tex Mex

Other Options → **American [p.223]**

Alamo, The

Location → Marina & Yacht Club · Al Meena | 644 0300
Hours → 12:00 - 15:00 19:00 - 24:00; Fri 11:00 - 15:00
Web/email → www.abudhabimarina.com **Map Ref** → 4-B4

100

Places for Pork

Remember that you are in a Muslim country. Nevertheless, all you pork freaks out there curbing your fetish, know that, although rare, you can still find pork on the menu. Understandably, the local, independent outlets are unlikely to serve any, but hotel restaurants are more accommodating to the cause. The bacon butty lives on.

The Alamo, with its cantina style atmosphere and typical Alamo memorabilia, is renowned for its frozen margaritas, succulent spare ribs, sizzling fajitas and Friday brunch. An 'All You Can Eat' menu inclusive of unlimited house beverages, is available Friday through Tuesday from 19:00 - 23:00 – a fabulous deal! Furthermore, friendly and polite service staff and an entertaining Latino band complete the ingredients for a perfect 'casual night out' venue. CC

Food Serv Venue Value

Chili's

Location → Grand Al Mariah Complex · Umm Al Nar St | 671 6300
Hours → 11:00 - 24:00
Web/email → www.chillis.com **Map Ref** → 8-B2

100

It's not just the food that will attract you to Chili's – although the enticing Tex-Mex menu, brimming with juicy steaks, spicy chicken and lots of cheese and refried beans, is certainly good enough reason to go. But the super helpful service, family friendly atmosphere and the small touches like bottomless soft drinks, will keep you coming back. Prices may seem high for a casual family restaurant, but the quality is superb. 'Guilt free' menu options will please the health conscious. Parking can be a challenge! APB

Food Serv Venue Value

Chili's

Ranch, The

Location → Al Diar Gulf Htl · Al Maqtaa | 441 4777
Hours → 12:00 - 24:00
Web/email → adglfhtl@emirates.net.ae **Map Ref** → 1-D3

100

The Ranch menu offers a good selection of steaks, burgers and Tex-Mex favourites, but the starters and desserts are on the mediocre side, so you're better off forgoing them for the excellent main dishes. The venue is lively and crowded, which can dilute the service efforts of the staff at times, although there is a particularly talented live band to entertain you while you try and catch the attention of your waiter. KMC

Food Serv Venue Value

Thai

Other Options → Chinese [p.228]

Royal Orchid, The

Location → Al Salam St · Al Markaziyah | 644 4400
Hours → 11:30 - 15:30 19:00 - 24:00
Web/email → n/a | Map Ref → 8-A1

For a 'cheap chow' venue, the Royal Orchid has a few surprisingly classy touches – linen napkins, scented hot flannels to clean your hands with and fresh orchids in abundance – a far cry from the old tissue box and plastic flowers seen in similar independent eateries! The menu covers Chinese, Thai and Mongolian cuisines, which you can order hot, spicy or mild according to your taste. The food is outstanding and the prices are low – no wonder it has acquired such a bevy of devoted clientele. MM

Food ●●●●○ Serv ●●●●○ Venue ●●●◐○ Value ●●●●◐

Talay

Location → Le Meridien · Al Meena | 644 6666
Hours → 12:00 - 15:00 19:00 - 24:00
Web/email → www.lemeridien-abudhabi.com | Map Ref → 7-D1

This Thai restaurant is a wonderful place to sip on a cocktail while watching the evening sky fade over a quiet beach – a great tonic for frazzled nerves at the end of a long day! Choose from the fresh display of seafood (live lobster included), and have it prepared to your personal tastes. Alternatively, the a la carte menu offers a good range of starters, seafood, meat, rice and noodle dishes, all flavoured to suit western palates. Typically Thai service is attentive but not intrusive. MM

Food ●●●●○ Serv ●●●●○ Venue ●●●○○ Value ●●●●◐○

Turkish

Other Options → Arabic/Lebanese [p.224]

Istanbul

Location → Le Meridien · Al Meena | 644 6666
Hours → 19:00 - 24:00
Web/email → www.lemeridien-abudhabi.com | Map Ref → 7-D1

While lacking the authenticity of a true Turkish eatery, Istanbul still makes for an interesting dining experience for those looking for something other than 'the run of the mill'. During cooler months the impressive outdoor terrace offers a more soulful alternative to the somewhat cavernous interior, which lacks atmosphere despite being well decorated. Amongst the menu offerings, the meze starter stands out, and for the main event you should definitely try one of the hearty meat stews. MFW

Food ●●●○○ Serv ●●○○○ Venue ●●●●○ Value ●●○○○

Dinner Cruises

Other Options → Boat & Yacht Charters [p.179]

Al Falah

Location → Al Dhafra · Al Meena | 673 2266
Hours → 20:30 - 22:30
Web/email → www.aldhafra.net | Map Ref → 7-C4

This traditional dhow offers daily dinner cruises in a tranquil setting as it floats along the picturesque Corniche. The upper deck boasts a majlis and the lower air conditioned deck can seat approximately fifty people. A sumptuous menu includes lavish Arabic fare which can be tailored to individual preferences. As you dine, the ethnic charm of the dhow and the serenity of the placid Arabian waters will ensure an unforgettable evening. The dhow can also be hired for private functions. CC

Food ●●●◐○ Serv ●●●○○ Venue ●●●●○ Value ●●●○○

Shuja Yacht

Location → Le Royal Meridien · Shk Khalifa Bin Zyd St | 695 0539
Hours → See timings below
Web/email → www.lemeridien.com | Map Ref → 8-B2

An evening cruise on the luxurious yacht Shuja transforms the city from the usual concrete jungle (when seen at eye level) into a magnificent Manhattan skyline from the water! The themed hot and cold buffet changes each evening, but offers excellent Italian, Arabic, seafood and Mediterranean dishes, plus delicious desserts – dinner more than compensates for the somewhat dubious pre-dinner cocktails. The yacht is available for private functions, so call ahead to check that it's sailing. Sensibly, the Shuja is closed during summer. CC

Hours: *Sunset cruise 17:30 - 18:30, Dhs.45 net (welcome drink only); dinner cruise 20:30 - 23:00, Dhs.130 +17% (seafood buffet); Friday lunch cruise, 13:30 - 15:30*

Food ●●●●○ Serv ●●●◐○ Venue ●●●●○ Value ●◐○○○

Cafés & Coffee Shops

Abu Dhabi is a great city for those who love café culture – take a break from work or shopping, relax with a cup of tea, a cake and the newspaper, or simply enjoy a good gossip session with friends.

All styles of cafés exist around the city. Some border on being a restaurant serving excellent cuisine, from cake to a full blown, three course meal. Others have a more coffee shop approach with cake, coffee, a few sandwiches and even scones.

The following section encompasses cafés, coffee shops, ice-cream parlours, Internet and shisha cafés.

Al Finjan Tea Lounge

Location → Le Meridien · Al Meena | 644 6666
Hours → 08:00 - 22:30
Web/email → www.lemeridien-abudhabi.com | **Map Ref** → 7-D1

100

Situated in the lobby, and overlooking the garden and fish pond, the Al Finjan Tea Lounge is a perfect haven for serenity seekers. A limited menu comprises snacks, main meals and afternoon teas. Try and avoid the average main meal and skip right to desserts and pastries, which are delectable and well worth the wait and price. Service is friendly if a bit slow and the calm and peaceful atmosphere is worth a quick visit for light refreshments.

Food ●●●○○ Serv ●●◐○○ Venue ●●●●○ Value ●●●○○

Art Cauldron

Location → Opp Navy Gates · Al Falah St | 644 4309
Hours → 11:30 - 16:00 18:30 - 01:00
Web/email → na | **Map Ref** → 4-C3

50

Escape from the normal pretensions of other city eateries to this funky and comfortable little café. Eclectic décor, simple furniture and friendly service create the perfect ambience for hanging out with friends or just sipping leisurely on your cappuccino as time passes by. The (slightly pricey) menu offers salads, pizzas, calzones and sandwiches – all made with fresh ingredients and perfectly accompanied by a good selection of coffees. The bruschettas, with fresh tomatoes, garlic and pesto, are particularly recommended. TAP

Food ●●●◐○ Serv ●●●◐○ Venue ●●●●◐ Value ●●●○○

Cafe Ceramique Abu Dhabi

Location → Nr Choithrams, 26th St · Khalidiya | 666 4412
Hours → 08:00 - 24:00
Web/email → www.café-ceramique.com | **Map Ref** → 9-C1

The novelty factor is high at Café Ceramique, with its trendy layout, 'naked' ceramics and arty magazines – definitely a good place to go if you want to develop your inner artist! While you work on creating your next masterpiece, you can munch on a variety of light meals and snacks. Although the service could be more attentive and the availability of menu items is sometimes low, the food is innovatively presented and tasty. A popular venue for children's parties. APB

Food ●●●○○ Serv ●○○○○ Venue ●●●◐○ Value ●●●○○

Café de la Paix

Location → Fotouh Al Khair Centre · Airport Rd | 621 3900
Hours → 09:00 - 22:30
Web/email → na | **Map Ref** → 8-E1

50

This popular French café is a welcome haven for those worn out from a hard morning's shopping at Marks & Spencer. Indulge in a bit of people watching from the outside seating area while you sip on your coffee. The freshly baked patisserie are hard to resist! The food menu has a French twist and includes fresh salads, crepes and sandwiches, as well as heartier fare such as the Chicken Kiev (highly recommended). VM

Special Offer: *Daily three course meal for Dhs.50*

Food ●●●●○ Serv ●●●●○ Venue ●●●●○ Value ●●●●○

Cafe Firenze

Location → Nr British Council · Al Nasr St | 666 0955
Hours → 07:00 - 24:00
Web/email → na | **Map Ref** → 9-B2

Café Firenze is a good place to linger with a nice hot cuppa while flipping through the glossy magazines on hand or catching up with friends. The lunch and dinner menus offer standard café fare such as sandwiches, salads and pizzas. Pastries include opera cake, tiramisu, and éclairs, all freshly baked off-site and delivered daily. While not a gustatory marvel, Firenze is justly popular as one of the few non chain, independent western style cafes in the capital. ECF

Food ●●●○○ Serv ●●◐○○ Venue ●●●●○ Value ●●◐○○

Cappuccino's Lobby

Location → Crowne Plaza · Shk Hamdan Bin Mohd. St | 621 0000
Hours → 07:00 - 23:00
Web/email → www.abu-dhabi.crowneplaza.com Map Ref → 8-C1

Cappuccino's is a quiet and informal café, with comfy sofas and coffee tables in contemporary shades of gold and teal. Service is prompt and friendly. A selection of sandwiches, pizzas, main meals and salads is available, although prices are on the higher side. The food is not overly exciting, although portions are generous, and the quiche is particularly good. This is an ideal place for a relaxing tea or coffee and a mouth watering cake or pastry. J

Food ●●◐○○ Serv ●●●◐○ Venue ●●●◐○ Value ●●◐○○

Citrus

Location → Millennium Hotel · Shk Khalifa Bin Zyd St | 626 2700
Hours → 12:00 - 15:30 19:00 - 23:00
Web/email → www.milleniumhotels.com Map Ref → 8-B2

Business lunchers and people watchers will enjoy this refreshingly elegant café located in the hotel foyer. The buffet and a la carte menus are both packed with delicious, fresh food, and the buffet in particular is very good value for money. For an evening out, the extensive wine list and soft music provide the perfect accompaniment to your meal. The curry night on Thursdays, priced at Dhs.70 including drinks, is a crowd puller. GW

Food ●●●●○ Serv ●●●●○ Venue ●●●●○ Value ●●●●○

Dilmah T-Bar

Location → Club, The · Al Meena | 673 1111
Hours → 10:00 - 20:00
Web/email → www.t-series.dilmah.com Map Ref → 7-A2

T-Bar, situated in the lobby of the Club's Health Complex, is a haven for tea connoisseurs, with an exhaustive selection of teas to choose from and deep, comfy sofas to sink into while you sip on your favourite cuppa. If you tire of watching the hard bodies stride in and out of the gym (as if!), you can watch TV or read the various newspapers and magazines provided. Each cup of tea is accompanied by a mouthwatering homemade cookie, all for Dhs.4. MM

Food ●●●○○ Serv ●●●○○ Venue ●●●○○ Value ●●●○○

Downtown Café

Location → Sheraton Residence · Shk Zayed 1st St | 666 6220
Hours → 06:00 - 23:00
Web/email → www.sheraton.com Map Ref → 9-B1

The managers at the helm of this newcomer to Abu Dhabi's café scene are keen to make a good impression and attract regular clientele – hence the great food, superb service and excellent value for money. International menus (both buffet and a la carte) offer a variety of meals with an unmistakable Arabic and Mediterranean influence. GW

Food ●●●●○ Serv ●●●●○ Venue ●●●◐○ Value ●●●●◐

Gerard Patisserie

Location → Marina Mall · Breakwater | 681 4642
Hours → 08:00 - 14:00 18:00 - 24:00
Web/email → www.marinamall.ae Map Ref → 10-B4

Located at the top of the escalators in this busy mall, Gerard's is a great venue for people watching and a quick cuppa in between shopping. The simple menu offers light meals such as sandwiches and salads, and of course there is a good selection of pastries and beverages, both hot and cold. The service is friendly and efficient. PDG

Food ●●●○○ Serv ●●●●● Venue ●●◐○○ Value ●●◐○○

Havana Cafe

Location → Al Ras Al Akhdar · Breakwater | 681 0044
Hours → 09:00 - 00:45
Web/email → www.havanagroup.co.ae Map Ref → 10-B4

Situated in one of the finest locations in Abu Dhabi, the Havana Café has stunning views that encourage relaxed alfresco dining during the cooler months. The international menu has something for everyone, and while breakfasts and lunches are fairly quiet affairs, Havana transforms into a vibrant dinner venue as the sun goes down. The service is courteous, and a 'shisha man' in traditional costume selling shisha pipes is an added attraction. KMC

Food ●●●○○ Serv ●●●◐○ Venue ●●●●○ Value ●●●◐○

Maatouk Healthy Heart Café

Location → Health & Fitness Club · Al Mushrif | **443 6333**
Hours → 09:00 - 22:00
Web/email → www.adhfc.com | **Map Ref** → 3-D3

100

Set in a one time royal residence, which now houses the Abu Dhabi Health and Fitness Club, the Moatouk Healthy Heart Café provides wholesome fare which is perfect for before or after a workout. The predominantly European menu boasts a range of lean cuisine such as nutritious salads, pasta and steaks. Various coffees and herbal teas are also available for the less hungry. The service is friendly and efficient, and the prices are reasonable. VMI

Food ●●●◐○ Serv ●●●◐○ Venue ●●●○○ Value ●●●◐○

Hut, The

Location → Shk Khalifa Bin Zyd St · Al Ain | **03 751 6526**
Hours → 08:00 - 01:00
Web/email → na | **Map Ref** → 14-D3

50

If you long for the charm of the cafés of Europe, this charming little venue is passable enough to keep you going until your next holiday. It offers an oasis of calm on the bustling Khalifa Street, with its warmly decorated interior and gentle ambience. Recommended for breakfasts and all day snacks, the food is consistently pleasant and servings are generous. This reliability, plus a friendly, helpful staff, make The Hut a perennial favourite on the Al Ain café scene. AP

Food ●●●○○ Serv ●●●◐○ Venue ●●●●○ Value ●●●○○

Idioms

Location → Corniche Rd West · Khalidiya | **681 0808**
Hours → 09:00 - 24:00
Web/email → na | **Map Ref** → 9-D2

100

This trendy yet unpretentious 'new kid on the block' has an interesting menu, friendly staff and a good location (near the Corniche in Khalidiya). Standard menu items such as salads, sandwiches and burgers jostle for your attention against some rather tasty pastas and main dishes. You simply must try the signature espresso cocktails served in shot glasses – a 'Sweet Swiss' or a 'Sweet Afro' adds a unique finish to a pleasant dining experience. CC

Food ●●●●○ Serv ●●●●◐ Venue ●●●◐○ Value ●●●●○

La Brioche

Location → Marina Mall · Breakwater | **681 5531**
Hours → 09:00 - 24:00
Web/email → www.marinamall.ae | **Map Ref** → 10-B4

100

Whether you need to make a quick pit stop in between shopping, or meet up with friends for a coffee and a chat, this charming bistro on the ground floor of the Marina Mall is worth a visit. The extensive, reasonably priced menu serves the usual coffee shop fare of croissants, sandwiches, pizzas and soups, but also has a selection of sweet and savoury crepes, some interesting fruit cocktails and several speciality hot drinks. Take aways and outside catering also available. CC

Food ●●●●○ Serv ●●●●◐ Venue ●●●◐○ Value ●●●●○

Le Boulanger

Location → BHS Bld · Shk Hamdan Bin Mohd. St | **631 8115**
Hours → 07:00 - 24:00
Web/email → tenchi@emirates.net.ae | **Map Ref** → 8-C2

50

This busy French café in the heart of the city is a great place to enjoy a European style breakfast, good coffee and a browse through the daily newspapers from around the world. The menu is extensive, featuring tasty food in generous quantities – the daily set menu is good value at Dhs.30. This venue incorporates a bakery counter selling the freshest breads, croissants, tarts and cakes, which can be eaten on the premises or taken home to enjoy later (or both!). KU

Food ●●●◐○ Serv ●●●◐○ Venue ●●●◐○ Value ●●●◐○

Le Boulanger

Palm Court

Location → Le Royal Meridien · Shk Khalifa Bin Zyd St | 674 2020
Hours → 07:00 - 24:00
Web/email → www.lemeridien.com
Map Ref → 8-B2

Spend a few peaceful hours at this welcoming lounge in the Le Royal Meridien, where the full afternoon tea (English or French) is excellent value for Dhs.58. This timeless tradition is perfectly executed here, with dainty finger sandwiches and plump scones served on fine bone china, while you gaze out over the gardens and the pianist plays softly in the background. Upgrade to the Royal traditional tea (Dhs.99) which includes a glass of chilled champagne. CP

Food ●●●●◐ Serv ●●●●○ Venue ●●●●◐ Value ●●●◐○

Riviera

Location → Al Meena | 676 6615
Hours → 12:00 - 24:00
Web/email → na
Map Ref → 4-B4

This bright and airy café mixes a relaxed Mediterranean setting with typical Lebanese cuisine. The tasty meze and freshly grilled dishes are recommended, and accompanied perfectly by piping hot Arabic bread, which is baked on the premises. You'll even find a few European specialities on the menu, just in case Lebanese food doesn't tickle your fancy. The only area that could use a bit of a makeover is the service, which doesn't seem to fall into the 'speed and a smile' category. MMI

Food ●●◐○○ Serv ●●○○○ Venue ●●●○○ Value ●●●○○

Sheherazade

Location → Al Diar Gulf Htl · Al Maqtaa | 441 4777
Hours → 06:00 - 23:00
Web/email → adglfhtl@emirates.net.ae
Map Ref → 1-D3

This licensed restaurant offers both buffet and a la carte fare, featuring dishes that are varied and tastily prepared. The accompanying wine list, while extensive, is a little on the pricey side, but the sensible price of a beer or house wine by the glass will keep punters happy. This is a pleasant venue for a pleasant meal. GW

Food ●●●●○ Serv ●●●◐○ Venue ●●●◐○ Value ●●●◐○

Six Degrees Café

Location → Al Salam St · Al Meena | 644 4224
Hours → 09:00 - 02:00
Web/email → na
Map Ref → 4-B3

With big squashy armchairs and a wide variety of shisha flavours to choose from, Six Degrees is a pleasant place for lunch and a spot of Internet browsing with a game of pool thrown in for good measure. The menu sticks to old favourites such as burgers, sandwiches, soups and salads with a good selection of fresh fruit cocktails. With major sporting events shown on the big screen, the café is very popular with young people of various nationalities. JR

Food ●●●○○ Serv ●●◐○○ Venue ●●◐○○ Value ●●●●◐

Vienna Plaza

Location → Hilton Abu Dhabi · Corniche Rd West | 692 4171
Hours → 08:00 - 23:00
Web/email → www.hilton.com
Map Ref → 10-C2

This bright, airy café, in a secluded enclave on the ground floor of the Hilton hotel, is a welcome refuge from the frantic pace of city life. Whether you pop in for morning coffee or afternoon tea, the fine range of hot or cold beverages, creamy cakes and fresh pastries will have you relaxed and refreshed in no time! A small terrace is available, although the chaotic traffic on the Corniche Road may spoil your alfresco plans for a peaceful cappuccino. FDMM

Food ●●●○○ Serv ●●●◐○ Venue ●●●●○ Value ●●●○○

Zyara Café

Location → Nr Hilton Residence · Corniche Rd east | 627 5006
Hours → 08:30 - 24:00
Web/email → n/a
Map Ref → 10-C2

Zyara in Arabic means 'visit' and this trendy, library lounge type café definitely deserves one. The café's glass frontage offers a good view of the busy traffic on the Corniche, and the laid back interior, with its rustic, Victorian style, is an ideal meeting place for friends and business acquaintances alike. The quality and presentation of the food is excellent, although this does come at a price, and the service is friendly and attentive. Incidentally, leave your plastic at home – payment is on a cash only basis. CC

Food ●●●●● Serv ●●●●○ Venue ●●●●○ Value ●●◐○○

Internet Cafés

If you want to surf the Web, visit a chat room, email friends, play the latest game but want to be more sociable about it, or when you do not have your own facilities for being online, Internet cafés are a perfect choice. Over the last few years, these cafés have become a common feature throughout Abu Dhabi. The mix of coffee, cake and technology has proved an irresistible draw, and this particular niche will doubtless continue to expand.

As always, the facilities, ambience, prices and clientele vary considerably, so poke your head through the door and then make your decision. Prices are typically around Dhs.15 - 20 per hour. Happy surfing!

Shisha Cafés

Shisha cafés are common throughout the Middle East, offering relaxing surroundings and the chance to smoke a shisha pipe (aka Hubbly Bubbly or Narghile) with a variety of aromatic flavours. These cafés are traditionally the retreat of local men who meet to play backgammon and gossip with friends, but over the years have gained popularity with locals and visitors alike, especially in the cooler winter evenings. Most outlets offer a basic menu, generally Arabic cuisine and a few international options, plus coffees, teas and fruit juices.

Just choose your flavour of shisha and sit back – this is what life is all about! Prices are typically around Dhs.15 - 25 and flavours range from strawberry to mint, cappuccino, rose, apple, mixed fruit... the list is endless.

Shisha

There are numerous places around Abu Dhabi where you can indulge. Your best plan of action for finding a place is to first decide if you'd like to go a bit more upscale, or if you'd prefer a more authentic experience. For the upscale option, go to the Al Mawal at the Abu Dhabi Hilton or head to the Breakwater and you'll find the Havana Café as well as a row of Arabic restaurants serving shisha. Take in the view of the sparkling city lights as you relax with friends, shisha pipe in hand. For something a little more downscale but with character nevertheless, wander along any of the interior blocks between the main thoroughfares in town and you'll come across numerous local, back alley shisha spots. Sit yourself down with the locals and observe the action on the streets.

During Ramadan, most five star hotels have a shisha tent set up. This experience is one not to be missed as these tents become cultural melting pots with a great mix of nationalities enjoying the fragrant aromas of shisha tobacco as they nibble on tasty Arabic meze.

In Al Ain, the Heritage Village is recommended for an 'authentic' local shisha experience while the Hiltonia Club at the Hilton Al Ain and Al Naswer at the Hotel InterContinental are relatively good options. For an added treat, head to Min Zaman at the Al Ain Rotana Hotel and appreciate some belly dancing as you puff away. Other spots worth checking out are Al Dihleese (Al Ain Public Gardens), Dot com (Khalifa Street), La Marquise (Al Ain Mall), Al Nakheel (Al Ain Oasis) and Ya Leil Ya (Ain Al Jimi Mall).

If you get 'hooked' (pun intended) and would like to purchase your own shisha, try the Carrefour hypermarket for a good range. They offer a variety of pipes and some basic tobacco flavours. You can then puff away on your pipe while sitting in the middle of a desert around a campfire and watching the stars – a very satisfying experience indeed!

Food on the Go

Bakeries

In addition to bread, bakeries here offer a wonderful range of pastries, biscuits and Lebanese sweets. Arabic eatables include 'borek' (flat pastries, baked or fried with spinach or cheese) and 'manoushi' (hot bread, doubled over and served plain or filled with meat, cheese or 'zatar' (thyme seeds). Biscuits are often filled with ground dates. All are delicious and must be tried at least once.

Foodcourts

Most shopping malls have a food court as part of their facilities, and it's usually a dedicated level. Food courts are a particular favourite among tired shoppers looking to rest their aching feet after an intense shopping spree. The meals and snacks are reasonably priced, and promptly served from numerous outlets. You will find that most of the fast food hamburger chains have outlets here, and the range of cuisine otherwise, is quite multicultural and diverse.

Popular with all ages and nationalities, the variety of food provides something for every palate; even the fussiest of eaters should find their nibble of choice. The casual and relaxed environment is ideal for families and the young 'uns as most food courts house a play area that keeps the children more than occupied and very happy!

Fruit Juices Etc.

Fresh juices are widely available, either from shawarma stands or juice shops. They are delicious, healthy and cheap, and made on the spot from fresh fruits such as orange, mango, banana, kiwi, strawberry, cantaloupe melon, water melon, grapefruit and pineapple (if you can't decide, go for the mixed fruit cocktail).

Yoghurt is also a popular drink, often served with nuts, and the local milk is called 'laban' (a heavy, salty buttermilk that doesn't go well in tea or coffee). Arabic mint tea is available but probably not drunk as widely here as it is in other parts of the Arab world. However, Arabic coffee (thick, heavy and strong) is extremely popular and will have you buzzing on a caffeine high for days!

Shawarma

Throughout the city, you will find sidewalk stands selling 'shawarma' (made from rolled pita bread filled with lamb or chicken that is carved from a rotating spit) and salad. Costing about Dhs.3 each, this is not only an inexpensive option but also well worth trying as an excellent alternative fast food to the usual hamburger. Shawarma stands usually sell other dishes too, such as 'foul' (a paste made from fava beans) and 'falafel' (or ta'amiya), small savoury balls of deep fried beans. And talk about value for money, for just Dhs.11, you can buy a whole grilled chicken, salad and hummus!

While most shawarma stands offer virtually the same thing, slight differences make some stand out from the rest. People are often adamant that their particular favourite serves, for example, the best falafel in town. These stands are often the first place you eat when you come to the UAE. However, look around – every restaurant has its own way of doing things and you might find that the best place is, surprisingly, the smallest, most low key restaurant you happened upon by chance.

Friday Brunch

An integral part of life in the capital, the famous Friday brunch is a perfect event for a lazy start or end to the weekend, especially once the hot weather arrives. Popular with all sections of the community, it provides Thursday night's revellers with a gentle awakening and some much needed nourishment. For families, brunch is a pleasant way to spend the earlier part of the day, especially since many venues organise a variety of fun activities for kids, allowing parents to fill themselves with fine food and drink, and to simply relax.

Different brunches appeal to different crowds; some have fantastic buffets, others are in spectacular surroundings, while still others offer amazing prices for all you can eat.

Parties at Home

Caterers

A popular and easy way to have a party, organise a business lunch or celebrate a special occasion is to have in-house catering, which allows you to relax and enjoy yourself, and leaves you free to focus on anything but the cooking! Numerous outlets offer this service, so decide on the type of food you want – Indian, Chinese, Italian, Lebanese, finger food etc, and check with your favourite restaurant or café if they do outside catering. Alternatively, most of the larger hotels have an outside catering department, usually capable of extravagant five star functions.

Specialist companies also provide a variety of services at very reasonable prices. For in-house catering, the venue doesn't always have to be your home – how about arranging a catered party in the

desert? Caterers can provide everything, from food, crockery, napkins, tables, chairs and even waiters, doormen and a clearing up service afterwards. Costs vary according to the number of people, dishes and level of service etc, required.

For a list of hotel numbers, check out the hotel table in General Information [p.1]. For restaurant and café names, flip though the Going Out section of the book. You can also refer to the catering section of telephone books, especially the Hawk Business Pages or the Yellow Pages (www.yellowpages.co.ae).

In-House Catering	
Abu Dhabi Airport Catering & Services Est	575 7321
Four Catering & Service	677 7307
Ramia Catering & Foodstuff Est	552 1262

Party Organisers

Other Options → Party Accessories [p.162]

Flying Elephant

Location → Jct 3, Shk Zayed Rd · Dubai | 04 347 9170
Hours → Timings on request
Web/email → www.flyingelephantuae.com | Map Ref → UAE-C2

After nearly seven years in operation, the Flying Elephant team know how to throw a humdinger of a party. These are the folks you should be chatting to for event planning advice, whether you are having an intimate party for a handful of friends in your garden, or a special occasion celebration of galactic proportions. From the decorations and music to the lighting and entertainment, they will advise, plan and execute right down to the very last detail.

Food – na Serv – na Venue – na Value – na

On the Town

You will soon discover that Abu Dhabi has a surprising variety of places to go and things to do. The city may not have the quantity of outlets of a big city like New York, but there's plenty to keep even the most ardent socialite happy! The following section includes the cultural entertainment that is on offer, such as theatre and comedy clubs, cinemas, cafés, bars, pubs and nightclubs.

To complement the bars and nightclubs, refer also to the information in Eating Out [p.219]. Many restaurants have a very good bar as well as a dance floor, which kicks in towards midnight. However, since they are usually reviewed only once, they will be listed in the restaurant section.

In Abu Dhabi, people tend to go out late, usually not before 21:00. Even on weeknights, kick off is surprisingly late and people seem to forget, after

Friday Brunch

Restaurant	Location	Phone	Buffet	A La Carte	Breakfast	Lunch	Kid Friendly	Alcohol	Outside Terrace	Cost		Timings
										Adult	Child	
Alamo	Abu Dhabi Marina Club	644 0300	Y	N	Y	Y	Y	Y	N	65	35	11:00-15:00
Al Fanar	Le Royal Meridien	674 2020	Y	N	Y	Y	Y	Y	N	99	45	12:30-15:30
Café Firenze	Al Nasr Street	666 0955	N	N	Y	Y	N	N	Y	25	-	07:00-13:00
Le Boulanger	Shk Hamdan Bin Mohd St	631 8115	Y	N	Y	Y	Y	N	N	25	12.50	08:30-15:00
City Cafe	Al Maha Rotana	610 6666	Y	Y	Y	Y	Y	N	N	55	25	11:30-15:30
Flavours	Sheraton Resort & Towers	677 3333	Y	N	Y	Y	Y	Y	N	95	47.50	12:00-16:00
La Brasserie	Le Meridien Hotel	644 6666	Y	N	Y	Y	Y	Y	Y	79	39.50	12:30-16:30
La Piazza	Sands Hotel	633 5335	Y	Y	Y	Y	Y	Y	N	75	37.5	12:00-15:30
P.J. O'Reillys	Le Royal Meridien	674 2020	Y	N	Y	Y	Y	Y	Y	55	27.5	12:00-15:30
Restaurant, The	The Club	673 1111	Y	N	Y	Y	Y	Y	Y	40	20	12:00-16:00
Rosebuds	Beach Rotana Hotel	644 3000	Y	N	Y	Y	Y	Y	Y	95	55	12:00-15:30
The Garden, Level 9	Crowne Plaza	621 0000	Y	N	Y	Y	Y	Y	N	90	45	1230-1530
Gardinia	Al Ain Rotana	03 754 5111	Y	N	Y	Y	Y	Y	Y	80	40	12:30-16:00
Hiltonia Clubhouse	Hilton Al Ain	03 768 6666	Y	Y	Y	Y	Y	Y	Y	45	25	1200-1530

about the tenth drink, that they really ought to be at work the next day. If you're venturing out to Arabic nightclubs or restaurants before 23:00, you're likely to find them almost deserted.

Wednesday and Thursday, being the start of most peoples' weekend, are obviously busy but you will also find that during the week many bars and restaurants offer promotions and special nights to attract customers, thus creating a lively atmosphere. Particularly popular is Ladies Night, which is the busiest night of the week for some places (refer to the table on p[262]). Women are given tokens at the door that offer free drinks – the number varies from one to an endless supply, and it may be limited to certain types of drink. This ploy certainly seems to attract male customers too. With men outnumbering women in Abu Dhabi (by two to one), women for once, can take full advantage in this unbalanced world.

In this section, you will find the main places that have Ladies Nights at some point during the week.

Generally, cafés and restaurants close between 23:00 and 01:00, and most bars and nightclubs split between those who close 'early' at 01:00 and those who stay open 'late' until 02:00 or 03:00. Few are open all night.

Refer to the Eating Out section [p.219] for more information, such as the alcohol laws.

Night out at the Hilton Jazz Bar

Bars

Abu Dhabi has a decent number of bars of various different styles. Most are located in hotels and, while many bars come and go, the more popular ones are always busy.

The city's more upmarket locations range from terminally hip cocktail lounges to jazz, cigar and champagne bars. All provide salubrious surroundings for those opulent and self indulgent moments.

For more details on when and where to go for a drink in Abu Dhabi, refer to the start of the section On the Town [p.258]. For information on the individual bars, read on...

Door Policy

Abu Dhabi is a relaxed place when going out, and the easygoing atmosphere means there are few restrictions or problems getting into places. Understandably, anyone who is drunk or rowdy may find their entry refused. Sometimes the 'Members Only' sign on the entrance needs a bit of explaining. Membership is usually introduced to control the clientele frequenting the establishment, but is often only enforced during busy periods. At quieter times, non members may have no problem getting in, even if unaccompanied by a member. Basically, the management uses the rule to disallow entry if they don't like the look of you or your group, and they will point to their sign and say 'Sorry'. Large groups (especially all males), single men and certain nationalities are normally the target. You can avoid the inconvenience and the embarrassment, by breaking the group up or by going in a mixed gender group.

Dress Code

Most bars sport a reasonably relaxed attitude towards their customers' dress sense. Some places, however, insist on no shorts, jeans or sandals, while others require at least a shirt with a collar. Most nightspots do not permit the national dress and nightclubs generally have a dressier approach – dress to impress.

Specials

Many places have occasional promotions with different themes and offers. These run alongside special nights, such as Ladies Night, and are usually held on a weekly basis. You can find out which promotions are coming up from the weekly

and monthly entertainment publications, as well as directly from the venues concerned. Special nights, such as the popular quiz nights are mainly promoted in a bar or pub, and many attract quite a following. Delightfully, the prizes are often very good.

Beach/Waterfront Bars

L.A.B. – Lounge at the Beach Bar

Location → Beach Rotana · Al Meena | 644 3000
Hours → 17:00 - 03:00
Web/email → fb.beach@rotana.com | **Map Ref** → 4-B3

100

Before ten, this is a sophisticated meeting place for those who want to chat. Arrive later if you'd rather party in a cross between a futuristic, all flashing nightspot and an Ibiza rave. In contrast to the loud but attractively lit bar area, the spacious terrace overlooking the beach is relaxed and welcoming.

Not the cheapest drinking hole in town but certainly a stylish venue with potential for a good time. Don't be deceived by the refreshing taste of the cocktails (from Dhs.20 - 25), they're strong! HG

Venue ●●●●○ Value ●●●○○

L.A.B – Lounge at the Beach Bar

Cigar Bars

Cloud Nine – Cigar & Bottle Club

Location → Sheraton Abu Dhabi · Corniche Rd East | 677 3333
Hours → 17:00 - 02:00
Web/email → www.starwood.com | **Map Ref** → 8-A3

If a refined evening of cognac, caviar and the finest cigars appeals to you, Cloud Nine is where you should be – from the first puff on your hand picked Cohiba, Monte Cristo or Bolivar (delivered to you on a silver platter) to the last bit of beluga passing your lips, this luxurious venue exudes a pleasing mix of old boys' charm and trendy sophistication. Service is pleasant and discreet, and a live pianist adds further elegance to a classy (if a bit smokey) evening out. CC

Happy Hour: *17:00 - 20:00*

Venue ●●●●○ Value ●◐○○○

Crystal Cigar & Champagne Bar

Location → Millennium Hotel · Shk Khalifa Bin Zyd St | 626 2700
Hours → 15:00 - 02:00
Web/email → www.milleniumhotels.com | **Map Ref** → 8-B2

Experience the tranquil ambience of this champagne and cigar bar, where elegantly understated décor combines perfectly with an excellent range of champagne and Cuban cigars. The masterful bar manager will help you select the perfect smoke while you sit back and relax in surroundings of polished wood, leather and subdued lighting – the tinkling tunes played by the in-house classical jazz pianist make the perfect accompaniment. If all this sophistication leaves you feeling peckish, a small range of snacks is available. KMC

Venue ●●●●● Value ●●●◐○

Cocktail Lounges

Balcony Bar, The

Location → Hilton Abu Dhabi · Corniche Rd West | 681 1900
Hours → 18:00 - 24:00
Web/email → www.hilton.com | **Map Ref** → 10-C2

Inject a little sophistication into your evening with a pre-dinner drink or a nightcap at this

stylish bar on the balcony of the Pearl restaurant. The drinks menu is impressive – hard tack, soft drinks and everything in between, but if you're going posh, there's no shortage of champagne here. Feeling peckish? You can even order crudités, canapés and caviar. Very civilised, dahlings! EF

Venue ●●●●○ Value ●●●●○

General Bars

a.m.p.m.

Location → Htl InterContinental · Bainuna St | **666 6888**
Hours → 18:00 - 03:30 Wed 21:00 - 03:30
Web/email → www.intercontinental.com | **Map Ref** → 10-C1

This sophisticated, classy and very trendy bar with its spacious setting is ideal for all. Food varies from delicious pizzas and traditional burgers to finger food favourites to share. A wide choice of tempting desserts and creative cocktails are also on offer. All are well presented, value for money, and served with a welcoming smile. Soak up the atmosphere with a range of fun 'theme nights' to suit your mood and dance into the early hours with disco favourites from the guest DJs. CM

> **Ramadan Timings**
>
> *During Ramadan, opening and closing times of restaurants change considerably. Be sure to call and check before landing somewhere, only to find all the lights off and nobody home. Many nightclubs remain open, but the dance floor is closed off... so you'll just have to save those jiggy jiggy moves for a later date!*

Happy Hour: *18:00 - 21:00 daily*

Venue ●●●●◐ Value ●●●●◐

Opus Bar

Location → Le Meridien · Al Meena | **644 6666**
Hours → 12:30 - 24:30
Web/email → www.lemeridien-abudhabi.com | **Map Ref** → 7-D1

This elegant bar is the kind of place you might take your boss for an after work drink – with its comfy chairs and civilised noise levels, you'll be able to discreetly demand that promotion without having to shout over the music! The food is the usual pub fare (think Arabic meze, chicken fingers, burgers and sandwiches), and it is served up in a slightly more refined setting than your usual local watering hole. JR

Venue ●●●○○ Value ●●●●●

Paco's

Location → Hilton Al Ain · Al Ain | **03 768 6666**
Hours → 12:00 - 15:00 20:00 - 24:00
Web/email → www.hilton.com | **Map Ref** → 15-D4

The times may be a-changin', but not at Paco's. Popular because it is exactly the same now as it was when it opened in 1991, this British watering hole is a tonic for the homesick expat's soul. After a steaming plate of bangers and mash, a rather excellent pint of Guinness (hard to come by in these parts), and a spot of footie on the big screen TV, you'll almost forget you are miles away from home. JS

Happy Hour: *12:00 - 20:00 daily*

Venue ●●●◐○ Value ●●●●○

Top Deck Bar

Location → Club, The · Al Meena | **673 1111**
Hours → 12:00 - 22:00
Web/email → www.the-club.com | **Map Ref** → 7-A2

Sail away to this marine themed bar, situated within the Abu Dhabi Sailing Club. The 19 step climb to reach the Top Deck may leave you a bit puffed, but is worth it for the views over the waterfront. The wood decked terrace with its wooden furniture and retractable sunshade is in ship shape, and the indoor bar continues the sailing motif, replete with trophies and ship ornaments. With its good food and beautiful setting, this regular hang out for sailing club members exceeds expectations. MM

Venue ●●●●○ Value ●●●●○

Jazz Bars

Jazz Bar

Location → Hilton Abu Dhabi · Corniche Rd West | **681 1900**
Hours → 19:00 - 01:00
Web/email → www.hilton.com | **Map Ref** → 10-C2

For a relaxed evening of jazz, champagne and good food in a stylish setting, the Jazz Bar is worth a visit. Each dish on the extensive menu

is available in two sizes – 'down beat' for the not so hungry, and 'main melody' for the ravenous. Special dietary needs can be met on request. As can be expected in any good bar, the wine list and drinks selection are impressive. The popular band 'Southern Glow' keeps the rhythm alive and attracts a crowd, especially on weekends.

Food Serv Venue Value

Sports Bars

Other Options → Activities [p.177]

Hiltonia Sports Bar

Location → Hilton Al Ain · Al Ain | **03 768 6666**
Hours → 11:00 - 21:45
Web/email → www.hilton.com | **Map Ref** → 15-D4

Frequented by sporty types and families, this venue is ideal for a drop of liquid refreshment either by the pool or inside under the big TV screen. Bar snacks dominate the menu, although there is a leaning towards healthy cuisine. The venue itself is bright and casual and makes a great pit stop after a round of golf, a game of tennis or a gym workout. On Fridays there is a reasonably priced buffet lunch.

Venue Value

Ladies Night

49er's The Gold Rush	Tues/Wed/Sat
Bravo Tapas Bar	Fri/Sat
Cave des Rois, Al Ain	Tues/Wed
Gauloises Club	Sun
Harvesters Pub	Tues
Hemingways	Tues/Wed/Sun
Heroes Diner	Tues
Illusions	Sat/Mon
L.A.B. Lounge at the Beach	Tues
Mood Indigo	Sun
NRG Sports Café	Wed
P.J. O'Reilly's	Tues
Paco's, Al Ain	Sun/Wed
Rock Bottom	Tues
Rockwell	Wed/Sat
Scorpio	Mon/Fri
Tavern	Wed
Tequilana Disco	Sun

Tapas Bars

Other Options → Spanish [p.248]

Bravo Tapas Bar

Location → Sheraton Abu Dhabi · Corniche Rd East | **677 3333**
Hours → 17:00 - 01:00
Web/email → www.sheraton.com | **Map Ref** → 8-A3

Although this venue lacks the authentic ambience of a true Spanish tapas bar, the tapas themselves are reasonably priced and make good bar munchies to share with a few friends. Bravo is as good a place as any for a quick drink after work or as a rendezvous point before heading out for a night on the town.

Venue Value

Pubs

Pubs in Abu Dhabi generally look quite close to the real thing – enough to transport you from the brown desert to the green, green grass of home. Some of these pubs (the English ones especially) are very well established and were among the first modern places for socialising in Abu Dhabi. Popular with all nationalities, a good number of pubs manage very successfully to recreate the warm, fuzzy atmosphere of a typical hostelry. Thousands of miles from their proper location, these places have become genuine locales for many people, offering just what they've always done – good beer, tasty food, good crack and a chilled hangout.

Captain's Arms

Location → Le Meridien · Al Meena | **644 6666**
Hours → 12:00 - 01:30
Web/email → www.lemeridien-abudhabi.com | **Map Ref** → 7-D1

Overlooking the gardens and located in the Village Courtyard, this tavern, with its cosy interior and upbeat, outdoor terrace, offers the ambience of a traditional British Pub. The daily happy hour (17:00 - 20:00), nightly entertainment and food and drink specials bring in the crowds. Food portions are generous and satisfying, although you won't find many culinary surprises here. The service could be

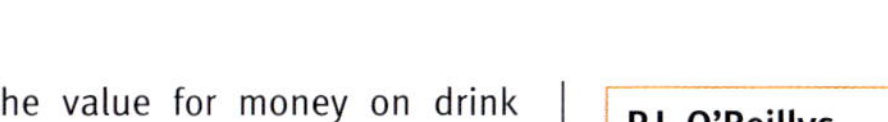

better, but it is the value for money on drink specials that gives this place its appeal. J

Venue ●●●●○ Value ●●●●○

Harvester's Pub

Location → Sands Hotel · Shk Zayed 2nd St | 633 5335
Hours → 12:00 - 01:30
Web/email → www.sands-hotel.com **Map Ref** → 8-C1

This smoky basement bar is the epitome of a 'working man's club', with live entertainment and four busy dartboards. Accordingly, the menu offers traditional English 'cuisine', like all day breakfast, bangers and mash, and even chip butties. This lively bar is usually heaving with a predominantly male expat crowd, no doubt recalling fond memories of their local pubs back home. Great for a boys' night out. APB

Venue ●●◐○○ Value ●●●◐○

Horse & Jockey Pub

Location → Htl InterContinental · Al Ain | 03 768 6686
Hours → 12:00 - 24:00
Web/email → www.interconti.com **Map Ref** → 15-E4

This unpretentious little watering hole, frequented by thirsty expats, offers a menu of standard English pub grub such as fish and chips, curries and sandwiches. The Friday brunch is reasonable, both in terms of food quality and price. Monthly promotions and theme nights, as well as a weekly quiz night, karaoke and bingo, draw regular crowds. The large TV screen will interest you if you're a sports fan, or you can escape to the quiet haven of the terrace outside. AP

Venue ●●●○○ Value ●●●○○

Mood Indigo

Location → Novotel Hotel · Shk Hamdan Bin Mohd. St | 633 3555
Hours → Call for timings
Web/email → novoad@emirates.net.ae **Map Ref** → 8-D2

Having become a little dark and dingy, Mood Indigo is currently undergoing a bit of a makeover. The new bar will be very different and a bit more sophisticated, with its colonial furnishings and live music courtesy of the resident pianist. Seating has been increased to 82, and up to 20 people can sit at the very long, custom made bar. RP

Venue n/a Value n/a

P.J. O'Reillys

Location → Le Royal Meridien · Shk Khalifa Bin Zyd St | 695 0515
Hours → 12:00 - 15:30 18:00 - 22:30
Web/email → www.lemeridien.com **Map Ref** → 8-B2

Known affectionately as PJ's, this welcoming Irish pub is home to a throng of happy punters all through the week. As you would expect, the décor is as Irish as it comes; but the menu offers a more diverse international selection of dishes. Happy hour runs from 12:00 to 20:00 daily, and even longer on Fridays, making this a favourite meeting point to catch up with friends, share a few stories, tell a joke or two, and mingle with the friendly crowd. GW

Venue ●●●○○ Value ●●●○○

Tavern

Location → Sheraton Abu Dhabi · Corniche Rd East | 677 3333
Hours → 12:00 - 01:00
Web/email → www.sheraton.com **Map Ref** → 8-A3

The Tavern may not epitomise sophisticated dining, but they do cracking roast dinners which will please those in need of some 'morning after' carbo-loading. The no frills approach, comfortable dining area and the limited yet familiar menu, create a relaxed, functional atmosphere with no pretension. Early birds get the armchairs, so get there as close to noon as possible. M-W

Venue ●●●○○ Value ●●◐○○

Quiz Nights

Ally Pally	Tuesday
Harvester's	Sunday
Heroes Diner	Monday
Horse & Jockey Pub Al Ain	Sunday
Mood Indigo	Tuesday
Pacos, Al Ain	Saturday
The Club Bar	Wednesday

Nightclubs

Packed with all nationalities, Abu Dhabi's nightclubs are busy from about 23:00 till the wee hours. The city has a reasonable number of dedicated nightclubs as well as numerous other venues that have schizophrenic personalities (bars or restaurants earlier in the evening, and later turning into a hip joint where you can cut

loose and shake your thang!) If you want to indulge in some authentic clubbing, head to the neighbouring emirate of Dubai, which is quite famous for frequent visits by international DJs and special nights by various event organisers.

Crystal Clear...

Isn't it annoying when you ask for a bottle of mineral water and are cleverly served the most expensive one on the menu?! Be aware, the imported brands may be much dearer but the Emirati water is just as good. Don't be shy – specify! Or pay the price.

Additionally, since you're in the Middle East, do not overlook the option of Arabic nightclubs. This is your chance to sample diverse Arabic cuisine and enjoy a night of traditional Arabic entertainment, usually with a belly dancer, a live band and a singer. These venues start buzzing very late in the evening, so they may still be empty during normal packed hours at other nightspots – a classic reflection on the Arabic way of starting late and finishing, well... later.

For information on door policy and dress code, refer to Bars [p.259].

Cave De Rois

Location → Zayed Bin Sultan St · Al Ain | 03 754 5111
Hours → 21:00 - 03:30
Web/email → www.rotana.com | Map Ref → 15-A3

  50

Located in the depths of the Rotana, this lively dive redeems the lethargic nightclub scene in Al Ain somewhat. With slick live music from the Philippino band and a rousing floorshow, the 'Cave of Kings' has what it takes to get even the shyest toes tapping. The freshest tunes, courtesy of the resident DJ, lure an eclectic mix of all ages and nationalities onto the dance floor. The club is spacious, with plenty of comfortable seating, prompt bar service and reasonably priced cocktails. JS

Theme Nights: *Dance Night (Saturday); Karaoke (Sunday); Nurses' Night (Monday); Ladies' Night (Tuesday & Wednesday); Party Night (Thursday); Hotelier Night (Friday).*

Happy Hour: *21:00 – 00:00, Friday to Monday*

Venue ●●●◐○ Value ●●●○○

Colosseum

Location → Marina & Yacht Club · Al Meena | 644 0300
Hours → 21:00 - 03:30
Web/email → www.abudhabimarina.com | Map Ref → 4-B4

   50

Visit this Roman style nightclub any night of the week and rub shoulders with the young and hip on the snug, yet pumping, dance floor. The latest RnB and pop fusion beats, belted out by capable DJs, make this multi-cultural venue one of the city's favourite hotspots. As an added bonus, drinks are reasonably priced and ladies get in free! APB

Venue ●●●◐○ Value ●●●○○

Gauloises Club

Location → Le Meridien · Al Meena | 644 6666
Hours → 21:00 - 02:30
Web/email → www.lemeridien-abudhabi.com | Map Ref → 7-D1

Gauloises may be a nightclub that is a little past its peak, but its prime location seems to keep it hopping along. The dance floor is vastly under used, thanks in part to the rather lacklustre DJ and his out of date tunes. On the plus side, the club hosts salsa classes and various theme nights. MMI

Venue ●●○○○ Value ●●○○○

Tequilana Discotheque

Location → Hilton Abu Dhabi · Corniche Rd West | 681 1900
Hours → 22:00 - 02:00
Web/email → www.hilton.com | Map Ref → 10-C2

Transport yourself to a tropical beach, dotted with thatched huts and palm trees glistening under a starry night sky at this cleverly decorated, upmarket discotheque inside the Hemingways complex. The resident DJ gets the crowd jumping with a mix of fresh sounds, and if you're an exhibitionist at heart then the semi-private karaoke

Tequilana Discotheque

room is where you'll find like minded souls. Regular promotions and salsa nights twice a week bring in the crowds.

Airline Crew Promotion: *50% discount every night*

Ladies Night: *Unlimited free margaritas from 23:00 – 02:00 on Mondays*

Salsa Nights: *Sundays and Wednesdays*

Venue ●●●●○ Value ●●●◐○

Entertainment

Cinemas

A trip to the cinema is one of the most popular forms of entertainment in the Emirates and movie buffs here are relatively well catered for, although showings are generally limited to the latest Arabic, Asian or Hollywood films. At present, there are five cinemas in Abu Dhabi and two in Al Ain showing English language films, with another few showing Indian and Arabic films.

Most of the newer cinemas are multi-screen mega sites, while the older cinemas tend to be larger, with fewer screens and a traditional, crowded cinema atmosphere.

For movie times, check the daily newspapers as well as 'Entertainment Plus', the weekly magazine of Gulf News that comes out every Wednesday.

Movie release dates vary considerably with new Western films reaching the UAE from anywhere between four weeks to a year after release in the United States. New movies are released every Wednesday. Films often don't hang around for too long, so if there's something you really want to see, don't delay too much or it will be gone!

The air conditioners inside are on super high and cinema halls tend to become very cold, so make sure you take a sweater. On weekends, there are extra shows at midnight or 01:00 – check the press for details. Tickets can be reserved, but usually have to be collected an hour before the show and sales are cash only. However, with so many screens around now, you will often find cinemas half empty, except for the first couple of days after the release of an eagerly awaited blockbuster.

Cinema

Comedy

The regular comedy scene in Abu Dhabi is, unfortunately, quite limited. However, there are regular visits from the Laughter Factory and the British Airways Playhouse as well as the occasional comical theatre production or one off event.

Cinemas

Name	Tel No.	Map Ref	Location	Language	Price
Al Massa Cineplex	633 3000	8-C2	Hamdan Centre	English	25-30
Century Cinemas	645 8988	4-B4	Abu Dhabi Mall	English	30
CineStar	681 8484	10-B4	Marina Mall	English	30
Cultural Foundation	621 5300	9-A1	Sh. Zayed 1st Street	English	5
Eldorado	676 3555	8-B1	Sh. Zayed 2st Street	Malayalam	15-20
Grand Al Mariah	678 5000	8-B2	Umm Al Nar Street	English	25-30
National Cinema	671 1700	8-B1	Umm Al Nar Street	Hindi	20
Al Massa	03 754 4447	15-A3	Near Rotana Hotel	Arabic, English	25-30
Club Cinema	03 722 2255	17-A4	Near Oasis Hospital	Hindi, Malayalam	15-20
Grand Cineplex	03 751 1228	15-C3	Al Ain Mall	English	20-25

Comedy shows tend to be aimed at the British population, so other nationalities may not find the sense of humour as funny as the Brits in the audience do.

Events are often promoted only a short time before they actually take place, so keep your ears to the ground for what's coming up.

Laughter Factory, The

Location → Crowne Plaza · Shk Hamdan Bin Mohd. St | **621 0000**
Hours → Call for timings
Web/email → www.abu-dhabi.crowneplaza.com **Map Ref** → 8-C1

Based on a concept that has been tremendously successful in the UK, America and Hong Kong, this comedy club provides acts by both established and up and coming comedians. The artists, imported straight from the UK comedy scene, are carefully selected to entertain the mainly expat audiences in this region. The winning formula of three distinct comedy styles performed in one evening caters to a wide range of comic tastes. Shows are usually held bi-monthly, except during the summer months.

Concerts

In Abu Dhabi, there is no regular calendar of events for music lovers, although recent years have seen a decided increase in happenings in the music scene. Still, at different times of the year (mainly in winter), international sporting events, concerts and festivals feature international artistes, bands and classical musicians. Ticket prices are around the same as they are in Dubai, and a bit higher than what you would expect to pay elsewhere.

Visits by international bands are not very frequent but they do happen, so keep your ear to the ground. Club events, such as Ministry of Sound Nights have also taken place in Abu Dhabi and in the past year, the Abu Dhabi Music Foundation has hosted several cultural events. Moreover, the everpopular Jazz Festival in November and Latino Festival in March (organised by Chillout Productions – 04 391 1196) are two annual events that are not to be missed.

Promoters usually have no long term programmes and details are only available about a month in advance. So for details of events, check the daily press or monthly magazines, and listen out for announcements and advertisements on Emirates 1 and 2 FM as well as the northern radio stations, Channel 4 FM and Dubai FM. Tickets go on sale at the venues and through other outlets, such as Virgin Megastore. Tickets for some concerts can also be purchased online at www.ibuytickets.com or www.itptickets.com.

If you're experiencing live music deficiency and suffer from severe withdrawal symptoms, hop across to neighbouring Dubai where there is a lot more going on. Again, check the press and radio for details.

Theatre

The theatre scene in Abu Dhabi is rather limited with fans relying chiefly on touring companies and the occasional amateur dramatics performance. One regular highlight is the British Airways Playhouse, which tours the world.

The amateur theatre, namely the Abu Dhabi Drama Society, always welcomes new members either on stage or behind the scenes. There is also the occasional murder mystery dinner where you are encouraged to display your thespian skills by being part of the performance.

British Airways Playhouse

Location → Htl InterContinental · Bainuna St | **666 6888**
Hours → Call for timings
Web/email → www.intercontinental.com **Map Ref** → 10-C1

Renowned for providing regular theatre and comedy evenings for nearly two decades, the British Airways Playhouse is a favourite among theatregoers and was the first dinner theatre to be staged in the Emirates. The Playhouse stages four seasons every year. Shows are rehearsed, produced and cast in London and in the past have starred some pretty well known names, such as Leslie Phillips, Patrick McNee, Alfred Marks, Dora Bryan and John Inman. Events are not regular; call for details on upcoming ones.

Food – na Serv – na Venue – na Value – na

British Airways Playhouse

Location → Htl InterContinental · Al Ain | **03 768 6686**
Hours → Call for timings
Web/email → www.interconti.com **Map Ref** → 15-E4

For information, refer to British Airways Playhouse (Abu Dhabi) above]. Events are not regular; call for details on upcoming ones.

Food – na Serv – na Venue – na Value – na

CENTURY CINEMAS
THE ULTIMATE CINEMA EXPERIENCE

believe...

Maps

EXPLORER

Maps

Map Legend

Corniche Hospital	Embassies / Hospitals
Al Meena	Areas / Roundabouts
Crowne Plaza	Hotels
Bowling City	Activities
City Centre	Shopping/Souks
National Cinema	Cafés/Cinemas
Clock Tower	Important Landmarks
Etisalat	Business
Wadi Tawia	Exploring

Map pages 1-3 are at a scale of 1:25,000 (1cm = 250m)
Map pages 4-10 are at a scale of 1:10,000 (1cm = 100m)
Map pages 12-15 are at a scale of 1:25,000 (1cm = 250m)
Map pages 11,16-17 are at a scale of 1:50,000 (1cm = 500m)

User's Guide

To further assist you in locating your destination, we have superimposed additional information, such as main roads, roundabouts and landmarks on the maps. Many places listed throughout the guidebook also have a map reference alongside, so you know precisely where you need to go (or what you need to tell the taxi driver).

To make it easy to find places and give better visualization, the maps have all been orientated parallel to the coastline of the Corniche, which runs along the northwest side of the island (not north orientated). While the overview map on this page is at a scale of approximately 1:130,000 (1cm = 1.3km), all other maps range from 1:10,000 (1cm = 100m) to 1:48,000 (1cm = 480m).

Technical Info - Satellite Images

The maps in this section are based on rectified QuickBird satellite imagery taken in 2003.

The QuickBird satellite was launched in October 2001 and is operated by DigitalGlobe™, a private company based in Colorado (USA). Today, DigitalGlobe's QuickBird satellite provides the highest resolution (61 cm), largest swath width and largest onboard storage of any currently available or planned commercial satellite.

MAPS geosystems are the Digital Globe master resellers for the Middle East, West, Central and East Africa. They also provide a wide range of mapping services and systems. For more information, visit www.digitalglobe.com (QuickBird) and www.maps-geosystems.com (mapping services) or contact MAPS geosystems on 06 572 5411.

Abu Dhabi Zones, Sectors & Streets

Abu Dhabi Island is split into two zones using New Airport Road (Sheikh Rashid Bin Saeed Al Maktoum Street) as the dividing line. The area to the east is zone 1 (east) and the area to the west is zone 2 (west). The zones are further divided into numbered square sectors which are bordered by the main streets (creating a road network that is based on a grid system).

All streets (main and secondary) that are parallel to New Airport Road are given even numbers with the numbers increasing as they move away from New Airport Road towards either coast. Those streets that are parallel to the Corniche (ie, at right angles to New Airport Road) are given odd numbers, which increase as you move away from the Corniche. At the main street intersections, blue road signs show the zone and sector names while at secondary streets, green road signs are used. And just to confuse matters, many roads have more than one name! Listed in the index are the main roads with their official or map name, their common name, their street number and their position in relation to New Airport Road or the Corniche.

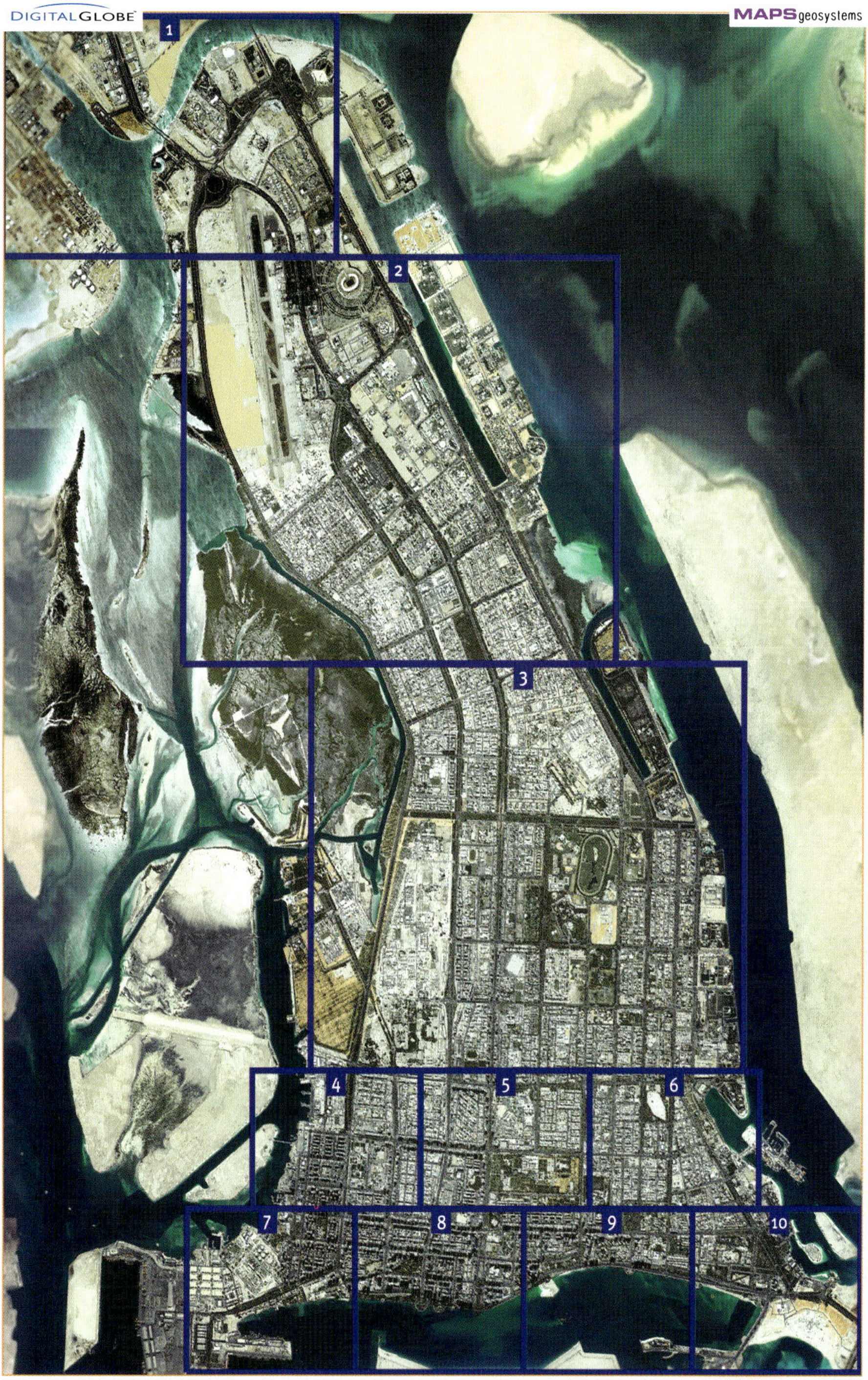

DIGITALGLOBE

MAPSgeosystems

1

2

3

4

5

6

7

8

9

10

Abu Dhabi & Northern Emirates

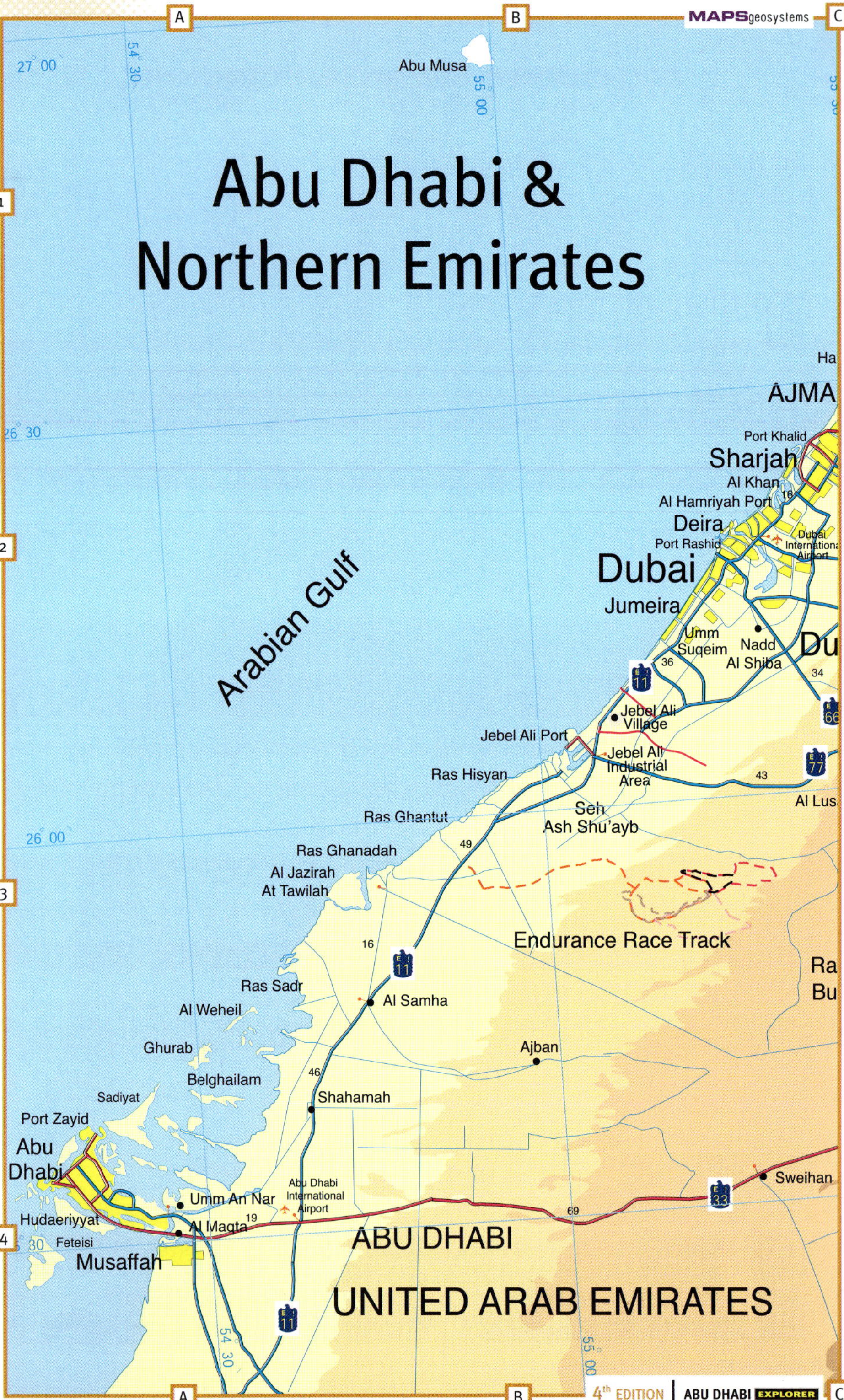

MAPSgeosystems

Imagery courtesy of *MAPS geosystems* – Master Reseller for *Digital Globe*

Abu Musa
Arabian Gulf
AJMA
Port Khalid
Sharjah
Al Khan
Al Hamriyah Port
Deira
Port Rashid
Dubai International Airport
Dubai
Jumeira
Umm Suqeim
Nadd Al Shiba
Jebel Ali Village
Jebel Ali Port
Jebel Ali Industrial Area
Ras Hisyan
Al Lus
Ras Ghantut
Seh Ash Shu'ayb
Ras Ghanadah
Al Jazirah At Tawilah
Endurance Race Track
Ras Sadr
Al Weheil
Al Samha
Ghurab
Ajban
Belghailam
Shahamah
Sadiyat
Port Zayid
Abu Dhabi
Umm An Nar
Abu Dhabi International Airport
Sweihan
Hudaeriyyat
Al Maqta
Feteisi
Musaffah
ABU DHABI
UNITED ARAB EMIRATES

UAE

Maps

DIGITALGLOBE
Musandam (Sultanate of Oman)
Gulf of Oman
Ras Al Khaimah
RAS AL KHAIMAH
Umm Al Qaiwain
AJMAN
Sharjah
Fujairah
Madha (Sultanate of Oman)
SULTANATE OF OMAN
Al Buraymi
Al Ain
Khor Fakkan
Kalba
Dibba
Hatta
This map is not an authority on international boundaries
Copyright © 2000 by Dubai Municipality

Community & Street Index

The following is a list of the main streets in Abu Dhabi, which are referenced on map pages 1 - 10. Many roads are longer than one grid reference, in which case the main grid references have been given.

Street	Map Ref
Airport Rd	1-D4; 2-C2; 3-C1
Al Falah St	4-D3; 5-A3
Al Istiqlal St	8-E2
Al Ittihad St	8-E1/E2/E3
Al Karamah St	3-C3; 5-D2
Al Khaleej Al Arabi St	3-D4; 6-B3; 9-D1
Al Maktoum St	5-B3/B4; 8-E1
Al Manhal St	5-C3/D3/6-A3/B3
Al Meena Rd	7-B3/C3/D3/E2
Al Nahyan St	3-D4; 5-E1
Al Nasr St	8-E2; 9-A2/B2
Al Saada St	3-B2/C2
Al Salam St	3-A4; 4-C3/C4; 8-A1/A2
Al Sharqi St	8-C1
Bainunah St	6-C2/D3/D4; 10-C1/C2
Bani Yas St (Najda)	4-E1/E2/E3/E4; 8-B1
Bateen St	5-D1; 6-B1
Coast Rd	1-E3; 2-D2; 3-D1
Corniche Rd (East)	8-B3/D3
Corniche Rd (West)	9-a2/C2/E2; 10-A2/B2
Defence Rd	see Haza'a Bin Zayed St (East)
Defence St	3-B4/C4
Delma St	3-D4
East Rd	3-B3/5-A1/A2/A3/A4/8-C1
Eastern Ring Rd	1-D3; 2-A3; 3-A1
Electra St/Rd	see Shk Zayed Second St (East)
Eleventh St	see Bateen St (West)
Eleventh St	see Haza'a Bin Zayed St (East)
Eleventh St	see Sudan St (Middle – West)
Fifteenth St	see Mohammed Bin Khalifa St (West)
Fifth St	see Shk Hamdan Bin Mohammed St (East)
First St	see Corniche Rd (East)
First St	see Corniche Rd (West)
First St	see The Corniche
Hamdan St	see Shk Hamdan Bin Mohd. St (East)
Haza'a Bin Zayed St	4-D1/E1; 5-A1/B1

Street	Map Ref
Juwazat St	see Al Manhal St (West)
Khalid Bin Waleed St	9-A2
Khalidiyah St	9-E1/E2
Khalidyah St	see Shk Zayed First St (West)
Khalifa Bin Shakhbout St	3-D3; 6-A2/A3
Khalifa Bin Zayed St	8-A1; 8-B2/B3
Khalifa St	see Al Istiklal St (East)
Khubeirah St	10-B2/C2
King Khalid Bin Abdel Aziz St	3-D3; 5-E3/ E4; 9-C1/C2
Liwa St	8-D2/D3
Lulu St	8-C2/C3
Mohammed Bin Khalifa St	3-C3/C3/D3
New Airport Rd (Muroor Rd)	2-B3/C3; 3-B1/ B2/B3/B4
Nineteenth St	see Al Saada St (East)
Nineteenth St	see Saeed Bin Tahnoun St (West)
Ninth St	see Al Falah St (East)
Ninth St	see Al Manhal St (West)
Old Passport Rd	see Al Falah St (East)
Port Rd	7-B3/C3/D3/E2; 8-A2
Saeed Bin Tahnoon Street	3-C2/D2/E2
Seventh St	see Shk Zayed First St (West)
Seventh St	see Shk Zayed Second St (East)
Shk Hamdan Bin Mohd. St	7-E1; 8-B1/B2
Shk Rashid Bin Saeed	3-C2/C3/C4;
Shk Zayed the First St	8-E1; 9-C1; 10-A1
Shk Zayed the Second St	7-E1; 8-A1/B1/C1/D1
Sultan Bin Zayed St	3-E3; 6-C2; 9-E1/E2
The Corniche	see Corniche Rd (East)
Third St	see Al Istiklal St (East)
Third St	see... Khalifa St
Third St	see Khalifa Bin Zayed St (West)
Thirteenth St	see Delma St (West)
Thirteenth St	see Defence St (East)
Umm Al Nar Street	8-B1/B2/B3

Future Developments

Scheduled for completion in early 2007, the Abu Dhabi Third Crossing or Sheikh Zayed Bridge will add to the Al Maqtaa and (Al) Mussafah Bridge. This Dhs.635 million project will cross the Al Maqtaa channel and link Abu Dhabi city to Dubai and the Northern Emirates.

Streetwise

Fellow cartographers beware! The hot gossip circulating town is that street names in Abu Dhabi will be changed in the near future. Whether this change will be drastic or not is yet to be confirmed. Watch this space!

A
B
C
MAPSgeosystems
Abu Dhabi Golf Club by Sheraton
Al Ain
1
Dubai
Umm Al Nar
Channel St
2
Car Showrooms
3
Under Construction
4
2
Imagery courtesy of MAPS geosystems – Master Reseller for Digital Globe

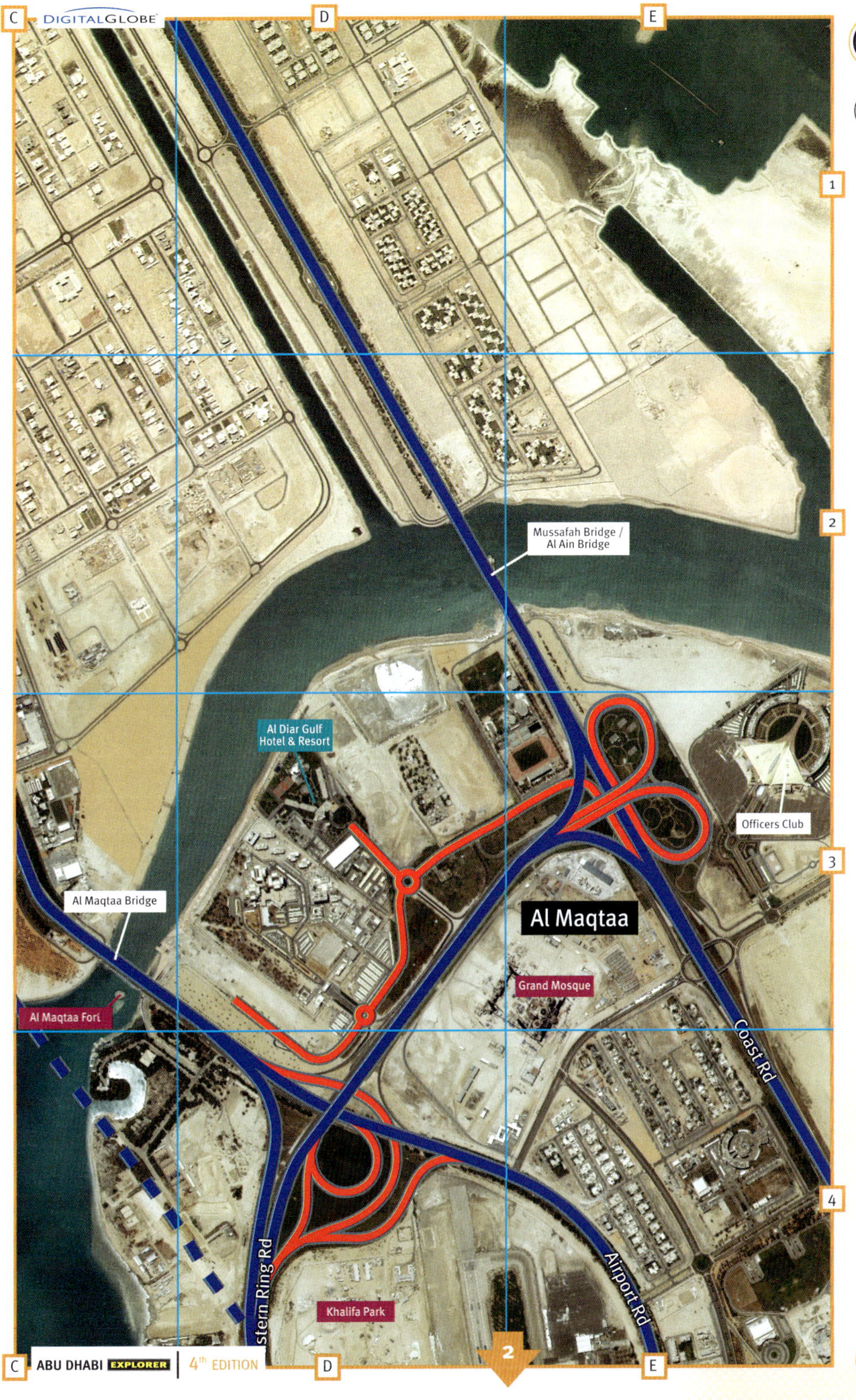
DigitalGlobe
Mussafah Bridge / Al Ain Bridge
Al Diar Gulf Hotel & Resort
Officers Club
Al Maqtaa Bridge
Al Maqtaa
Grand Mosque
Al Maqtaa Fort
Coast Rd
Airport Rd
stern Ring Rd
Khalifa Park
2
Maps
1

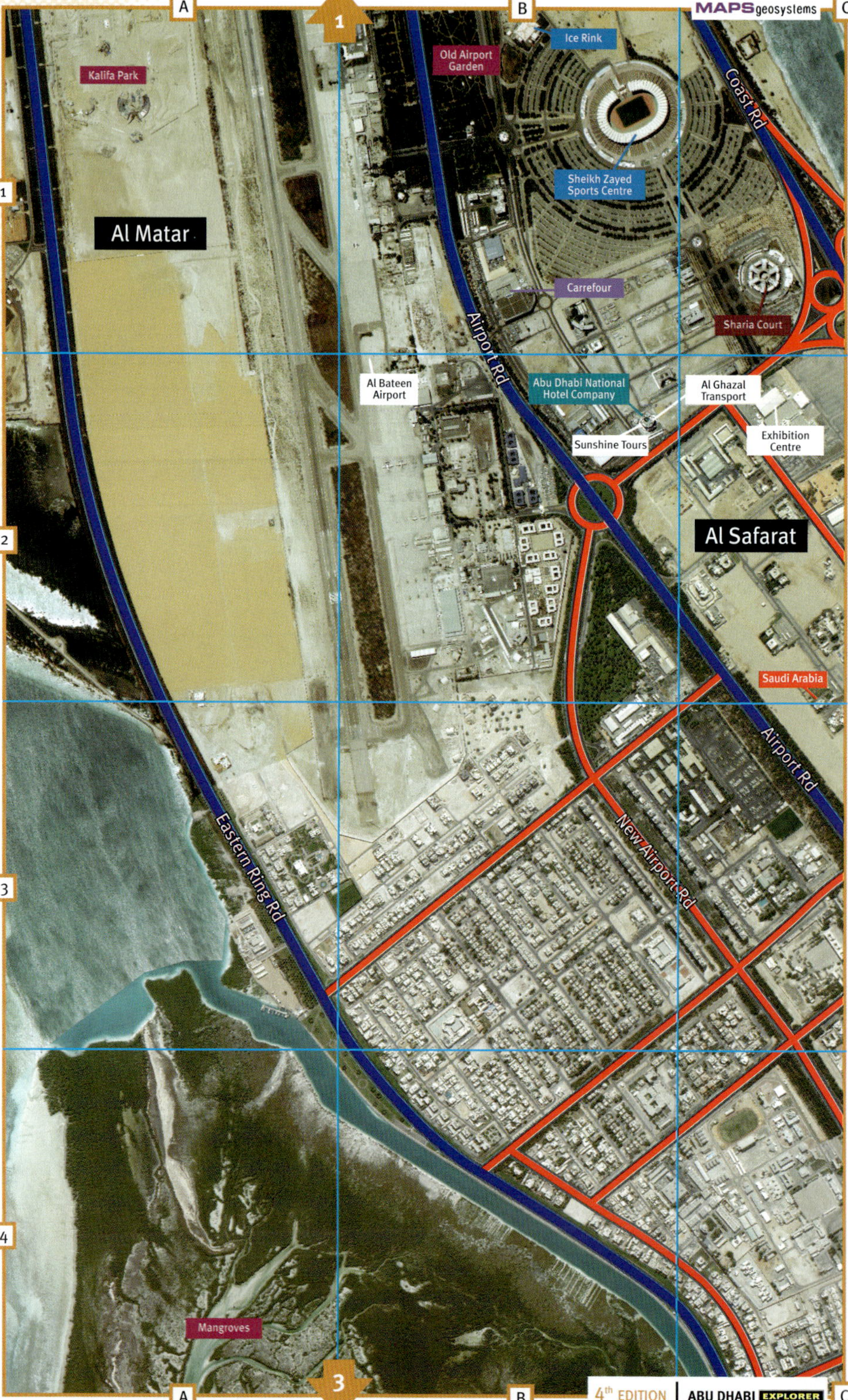

MAPSgeosystems

Kalifa Park

Old Airport Garden

Ice Rink

Coast Rd

Sheikh Zayed Sports Centre

Al Matar

Carrefour

Sharia Court

Airport Rd

Al Bateen Airport

Abu Dhabi National Hotel Company

Al Ghazal Transport

Exhibition Centre

Sunshine Tours

Al Safarat

Saudi Arabia

Airport Rd

New Airport Rd

Eastern Ring Rd

Mangroves

A B C

1 2 3 4

Imagery courtesy of *MAPS geosystems* – Master Reseller for *Digital Globe*

2 Maps

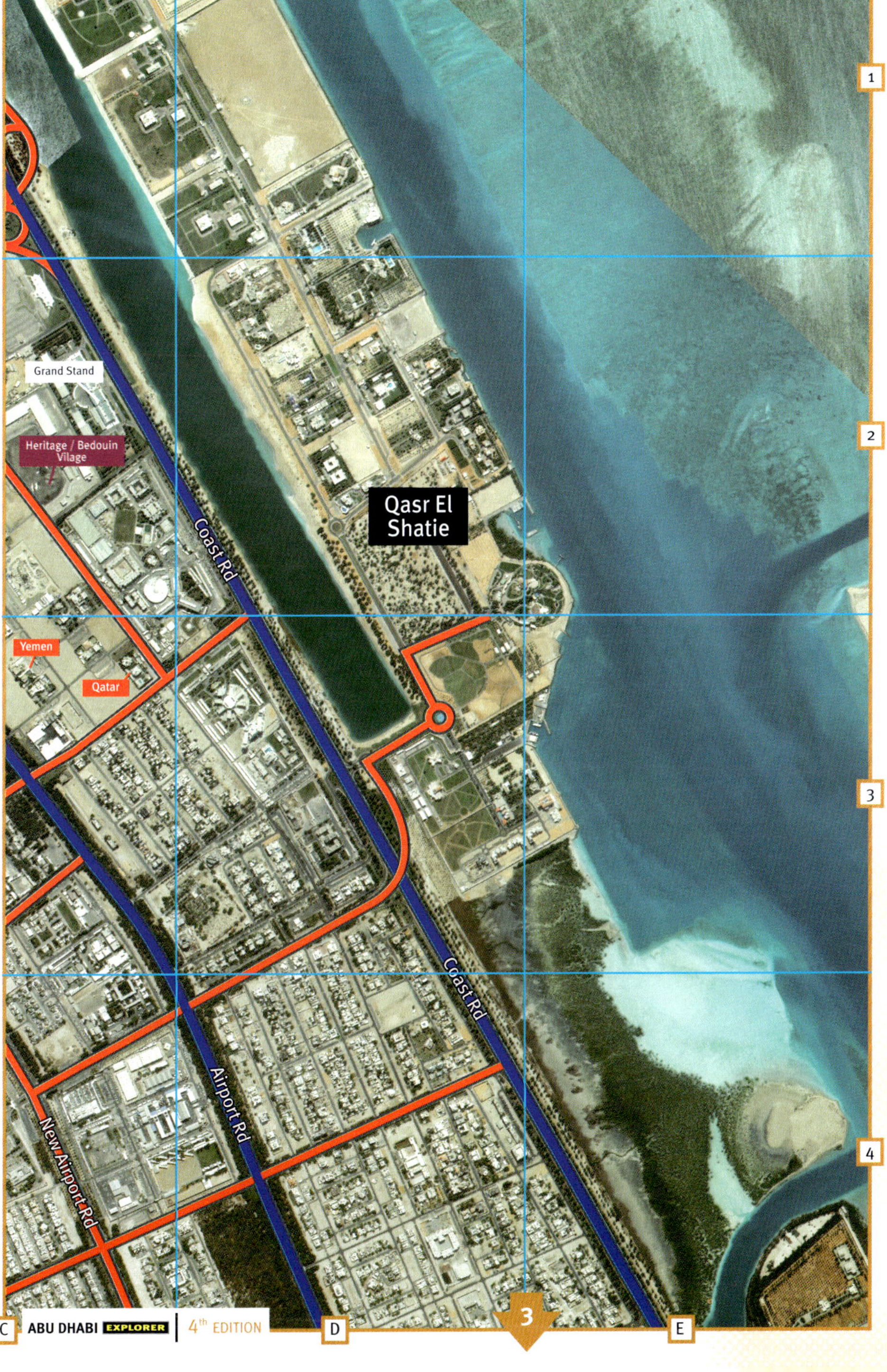
DIGITALGLOBE
C
D
E
1
Grand Stand
Heritage / Bedouin Village
Qasr El Shatie
Coast Rd
Yemen
Qatar
Coast Rd
Airport Rd
New Airport Rd
1
2
3
4
3
C
D
E

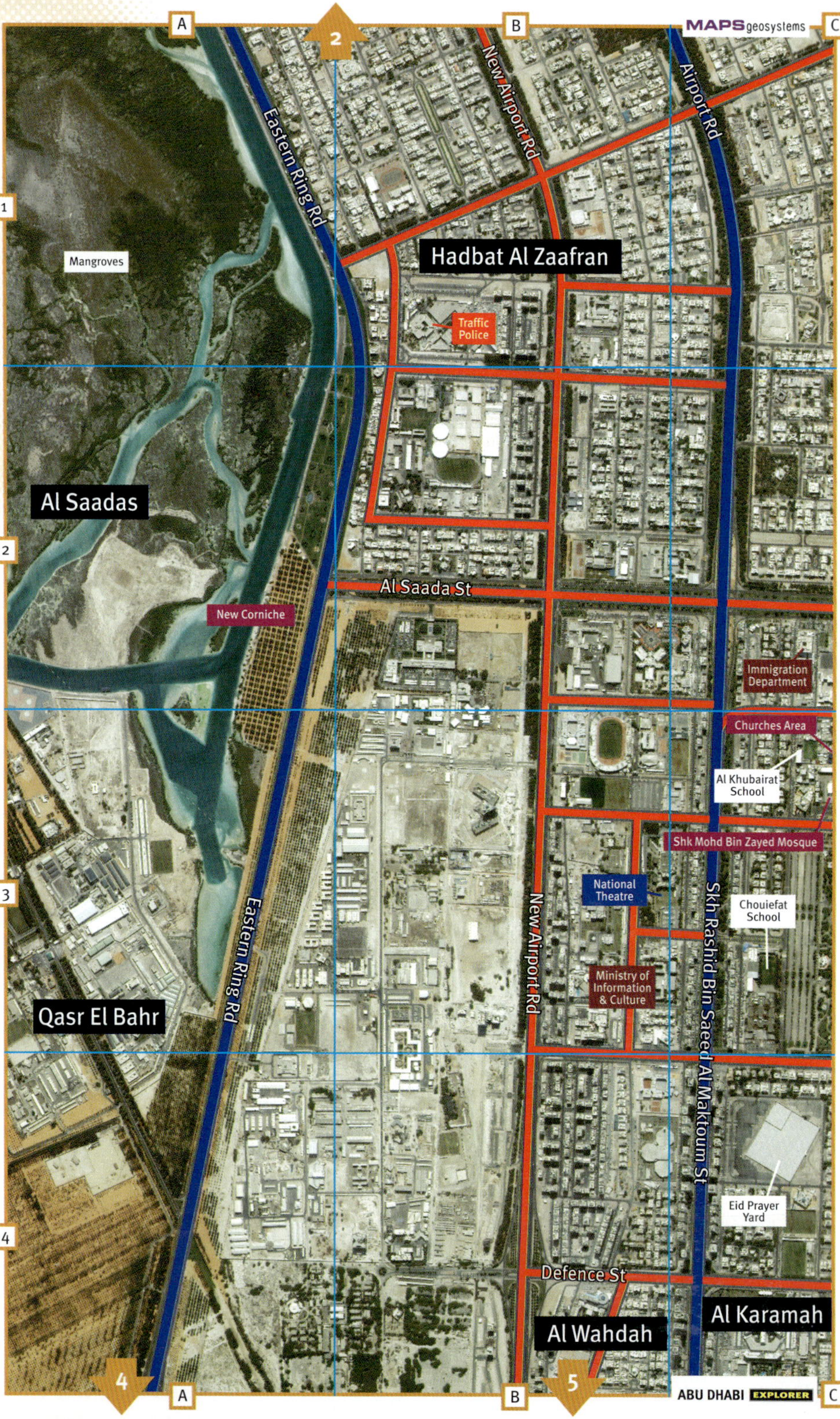

MAPS geosystems

A B C

2

1

2

3

4

Hadbat Al Zaafran

Mangroves

Traffic Police

Al Saadas

Eastern Ring Rd

New Airport Rd

Airport Rd

Al Saada St

New Corniche

Immigration Department

Churches Area

Al Khubairat School

Shk Mohd Bin Zayed Mosque

National Theatre

Chouiefat School

Ministry of Information & Culture

Skh Rashid Bin Saeed Al Maktoum St

Qasr El Bahr

Eid Prayer Yard

Defence St

Al Wahdah

Al Karamah

4

5

A B C

3

Maps

DigitalGlobe
C
D
E
2
1
2
3
4
5
6
Qasr El Shatie
Coast Rd
Al Mushrif
Saeed Bin Tahnoon St
Khalifa Bin Shakhbout St
Sultan Bin Zayed St
Oman
Korea
Abu Dhabi Health & Fitness Club
Race Track
Abu Dhabi Golf & Equestrian Club
Al Karamah St
Al Mushrif Childrens Garden
Mohammed Bin Khalifa St
Al Bateen
Al Nahyan St
Gulf Diagnostic Centre
Ministry of State
Delma St
Al Rowdah
ABU DHABI EXPLORER

3

Maps

Imagery courtesy of *MAPS geosystems* – Master Reseller for *Digital Globe*

DIGITALGLOBE
C
D
E
3
1
2
3
4
5
5
8
Haza'a Bin Zayed St
Al Dhafrah
Bani Yas St
Finland
School Area
Water & Electricity HQ
Emirates Computers
Al Falah St
Municipality & Town Planning Department
Ministry of Finance & Industry
Madinat Zayed
Al Futtaim Motors
Al Salam St
Abu Dhabi New Primary School
Bani Yas St
Etisalat
Ninth St
Bahrain
A & E
ADNOC-FOD

4
Maps

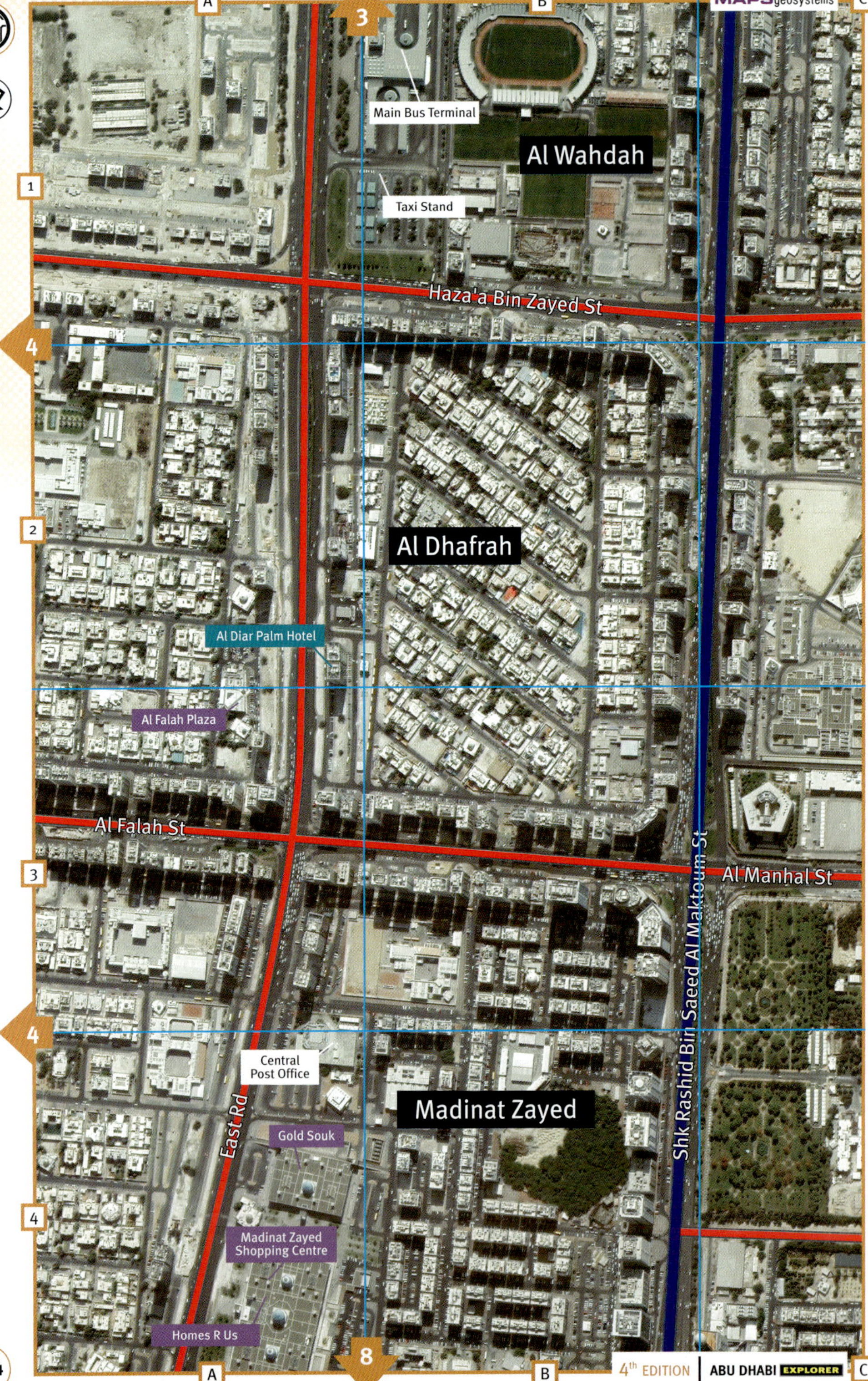
MAPSgeosystems
Main Bus Terminal
Al Wahdah
Taxi Stand
Haza'a Bin Zayed St
Al Dhafrah
Al Diar Palm Hotel
Al Falah Plaza
Al Falah St
Al Manhal St
Shk Rashid Bin Saeed Al Maktoum St
Central Post Office
Madinat Zayed
East Rd
Gold Souk
Madinat Zayed Shopping Centre
Homes R Us
A
B
C
1
2
3
4
3
4
4
8
Imagery courtesy of MAPS geosystems – Master Reseller for Digital Globe

DIGITALGLOBE
C
D
E
3
China
Jordan
Greece
Al Karamah
Al Rowdah
Al Karamah St
Al Nahyan St
1
USA
Kuwait
Korea
Dar Al Shifa Hospital
Bateen St
6
AUH Co-operative Society
Al Jazeera Hospital
King Khalid Bin Abdel Aziz Saeed St
Sheikh Khalifa Medical Centre
2
Al Manhal
Central Hospital
3
Al Manhal St
6
Al Manhal
4
9

5

Maps

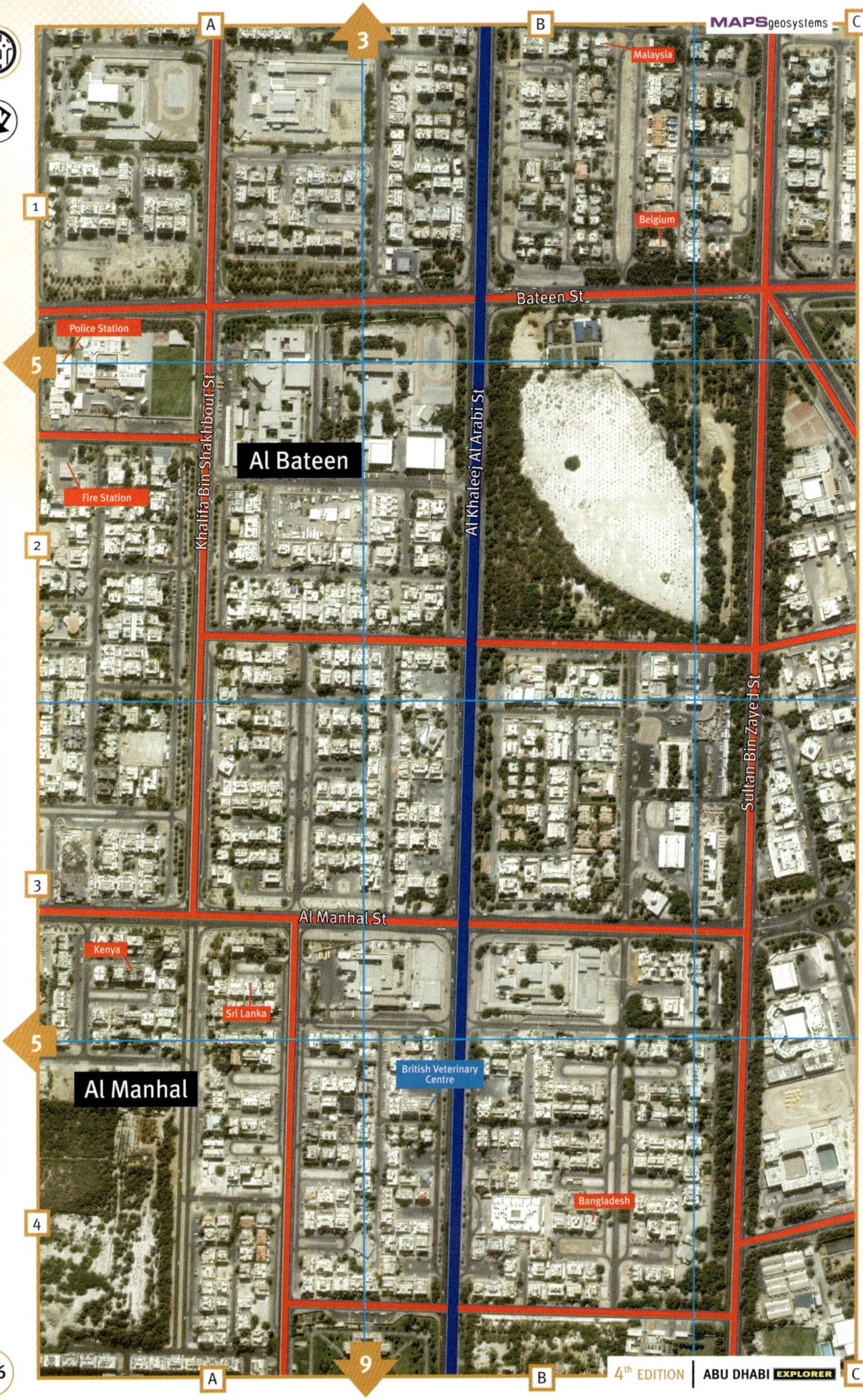

Imagery courtesy of MAPS geosystems – Master Reseller for *Digital Globe*

A B C

1 2 3 4

3

5

9

Malaysia

Belgium

Bateen St

Police Station

Fire Station

Al Bateen

Khalifa Bin Shakhbout St

Al Khaleej Al Arabi St

Sultan Bin Zayed St

Al Manhal St

Kenya

Sri Lanka

Al Manhal

British Veterinary Centre

Bangladesh

DIGITALGLOBE
C
D
E
3
1
2
3
4
Bainunah St
Bateen Dhow Shipyard
Abu Dhabi Woman's Association
Al Bateen
Ministry of Planning
Ministry of Public Works
Ministry of Agriculture & Fisheries
10

MAPSgeosystems
Imagery courtesy of MAPS geosystems – Master Reseller for Digital Globe
A
B
C
1
2
3
4
The Club
Water & Electricity Club
Al Meena
Slaughterhouse & Livestock Market
Fire Station
Port Rd
Customs Department
Port Zayed
Fish Market
Al Meena Vegetable Market
Meena Souk
2xL / Abu Dhabi Co-op / Jazeira Bookstore
Meena Centre
Iranian Souk / Afghan Bazaar
Kids Play / Toys 'R' Us / Ace Hardware

7
Maps

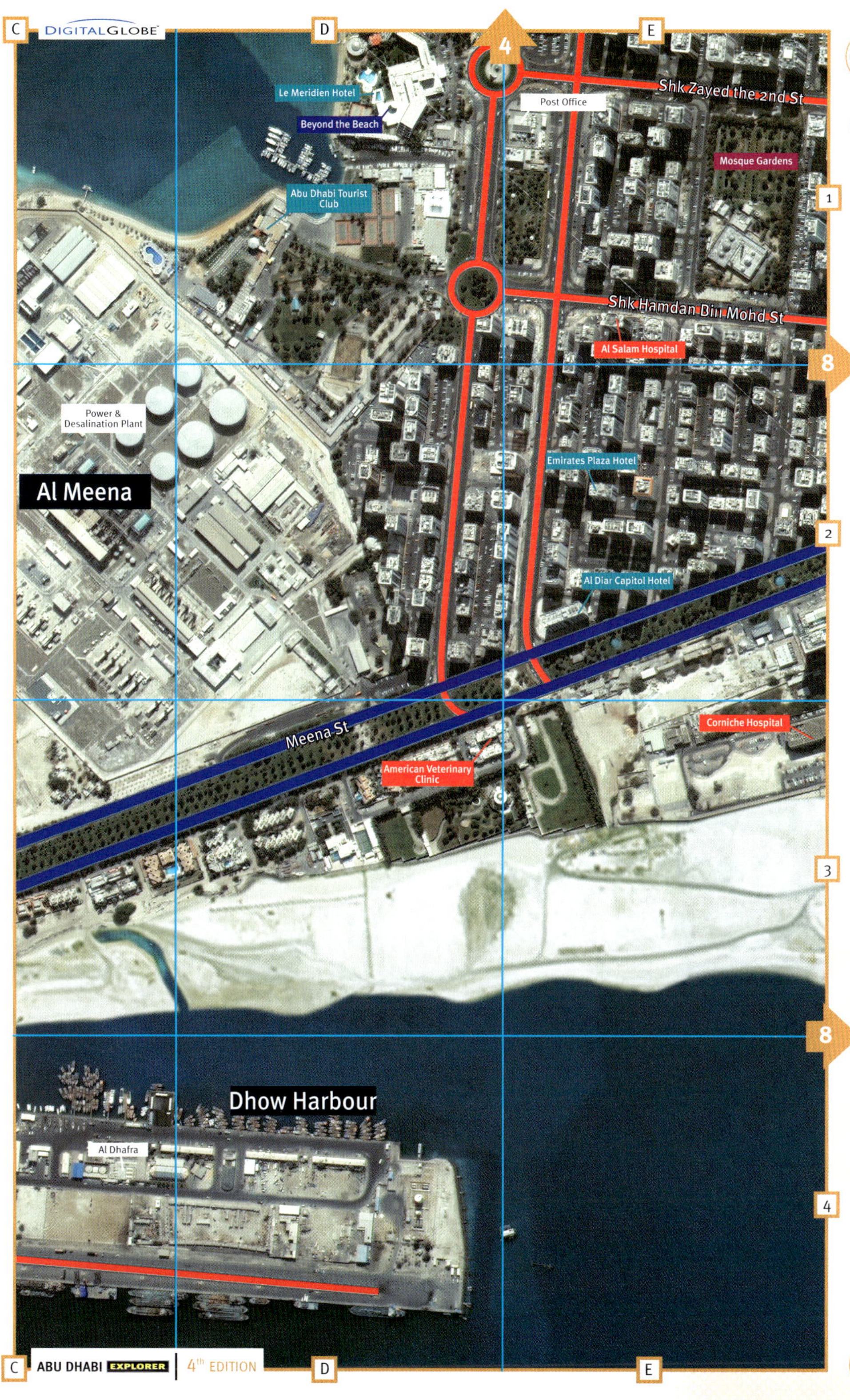

DIGITALGLOBE
Le Meridien Hotel
Beyond the Beach
Abu Dhabi Tourist Club
Post Office
Shk Zayed the 2nd St
Mosque Gardens
Shk Hamdan Bin Mohd St
Al Salam Hospital
Power & Desalination Plant
Al Meena
Emirates Plaza Hotel
Al Diar Capitol Hotel
Meena St
Corniche Hospital
American Veterinary Clinic
Dhow Harbour
Al Dhafra

7

Maps

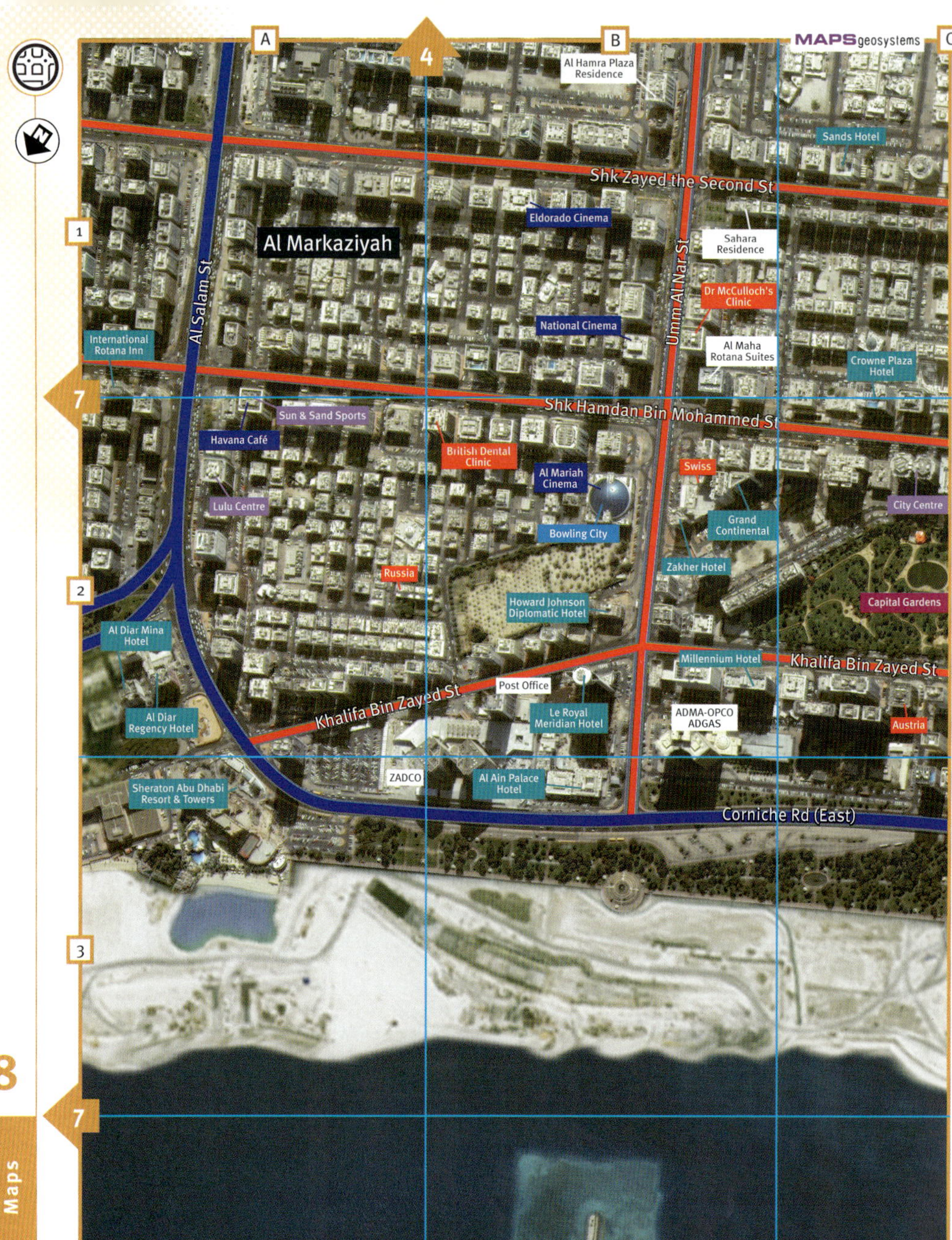
A
B
C
4
MAPSgeosystems
Imagery courtesy of MAPS geosystems – Master Reseller for Digital Globe
Al Hamra Plaza Residence
Sands Hotel
Shk Zayed the Second St
Eldorado Cinema
1
Al Markaziyah
Al Salam St
Umm Al Nar St
Sahara Residence
Dr McCulloch's Clinic
National Cinema
International Rotana Inn
Al Maha Rotana Suites
Crowne Plaza Hotel
7
Shk Hamdan Bin Mohammed St
Sun & Sand Sports
Havana Café
British Dental Clinic
Al Mariah Cinema
Swiss
City Centre
Lulu Centre
Grand Continental
Bowling City
Zakher Hotel
Russia
2
Howard Johnson Diplomatic Hotel
Capital Gardens
Al Diar Mina Hotel
Millennium Hotel
Khalifa Bin Zayed St
Post Office
Khalifa Bin Zayed St
Al Diar Regency Hotel
Le Royal Meridian Hotel
ADMA-OPCO ADGAS
Austria
ZADCO
Al Ain Palace Hotel
Sheraton Abu Dhabi Resort & Towers
Corniche Rd (East)
3
7
4
Lulu Island

DIGITALGLOBE
C
D
E
5
New Medical Centre Hospital
Grand Mosque
Al Sharqi St
Shk Zayed the Second St
Shk Rashid Bin Saeed Al Maktoum St
Etisalat HQ
Cultural Foundation
Al Markaziyah
Marks & Spencer
Bhs
Novotel Centre Hotel
9
Hamdan Centre
Liwa Centre
Gulf Air Building
Dr Firas Dental Clinic
Golden Tulip Dalma Suites
Netherland
Ministry of Planning & Economics
Al Nasr St
Al Markaziyah
Old Souk
Lulu St
Fish Market & Vegetable Souk
Central Souk
Al Noor Hospital
Denmark
Diamond Lease
National Bank of Abu Dhabi HQ
Old Souk
Cannon Square
Khalifa Bin Zayed St
Al Istiqlal St
New Souk
Liwa St
Al Ittihad Square
Corniche Residence (Hilton)
Abu Dhabi Chamber of Commerce
Volcano Fountain
Corniche Rd (East)
Clock Tower
1
2
3
4
9

A
5
B
C
MAPSgeosystems
Imagery courtesy of MAPS geosystems – Master Reseller for Digital Globe
Al Manhal
1
Al Muhairy Centre
Shk Zayed the First St
Sheraton Residence Abu Dhabi
Grand Stores
Platinum Residence
Al Hosn Plaza
Khalidiyah Centre
Old Fort & Qasr Al Husn Palace
Al Hosn
8
Tariq Bin Zayed St
King Khalid Bin Abdel Aziz Saeed St
British Council
India
Abela Superstore
Khalid Bin Waleed St
Al Nasr St
Al Hosn
Al Markaziyah West
2
Al Ghazal Rent A Car
Britain
Bainunah Hilton Tower
Corniche Rd (West)
ADIA
3
8
4
Lulu Island
A
B
C

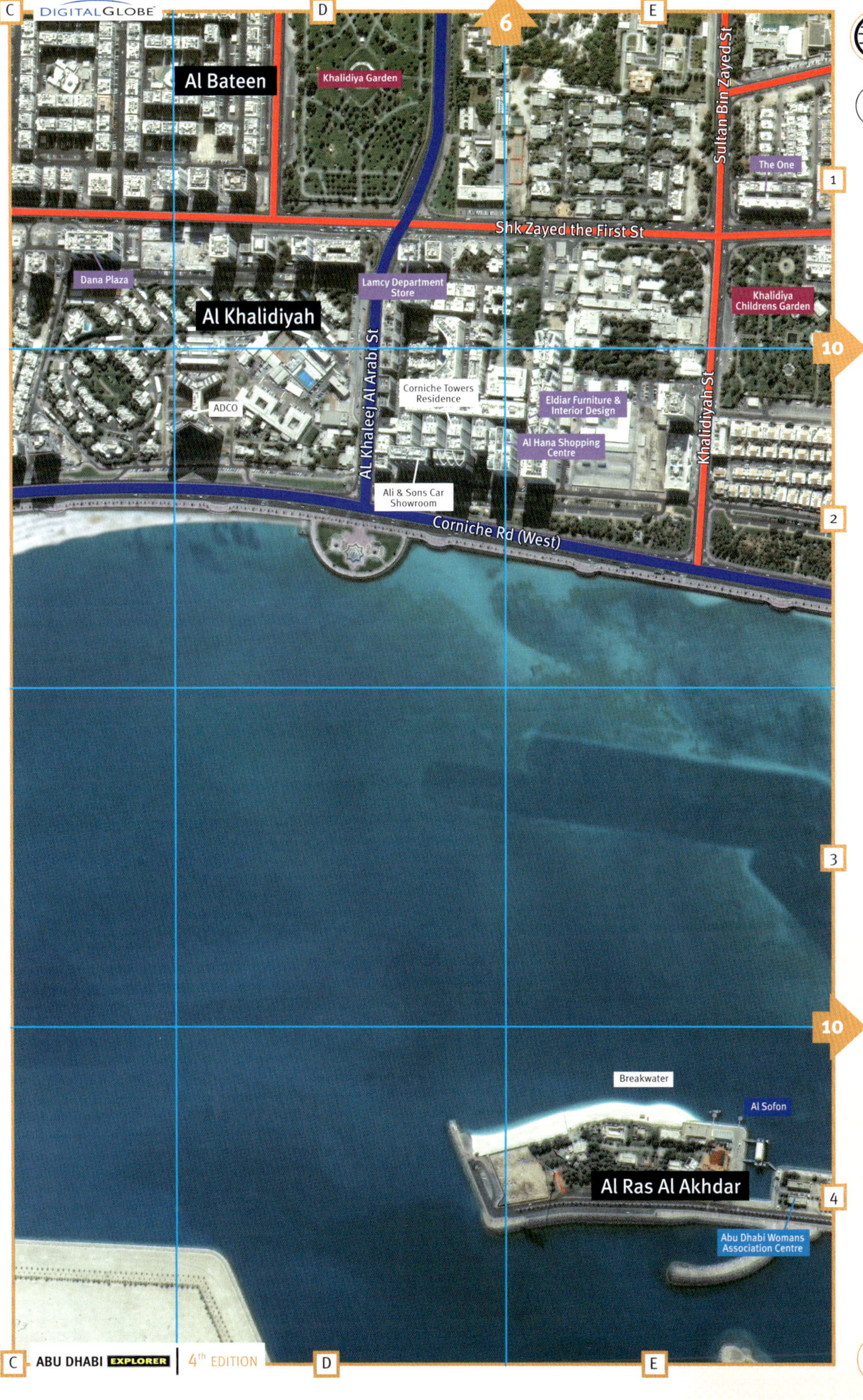

DigitalGlobe
C
D
6
E
Al Bateen
Khalidiya Garden
Sultan Bin Zayed St
The One
1
Shk Zayed the First St
Dana Plaza
Lamcy Department Store
Al Khalidiyah
Khalidiya Childrens Garden
10
AL Khaleej Al Arabi St
Corniche Towers Residence
ADCO
Eldiar Furniture & Interior Design
Al Hana Shopping Centre
Khalidiyah St
Ali & Sons Car Showroom
2
Corniche Rd (West)
3
10
Breakwater
Al Sofon
Al Ras Al Akhdar
4
Abu Dhabi Womans Association Centre
C
D
E

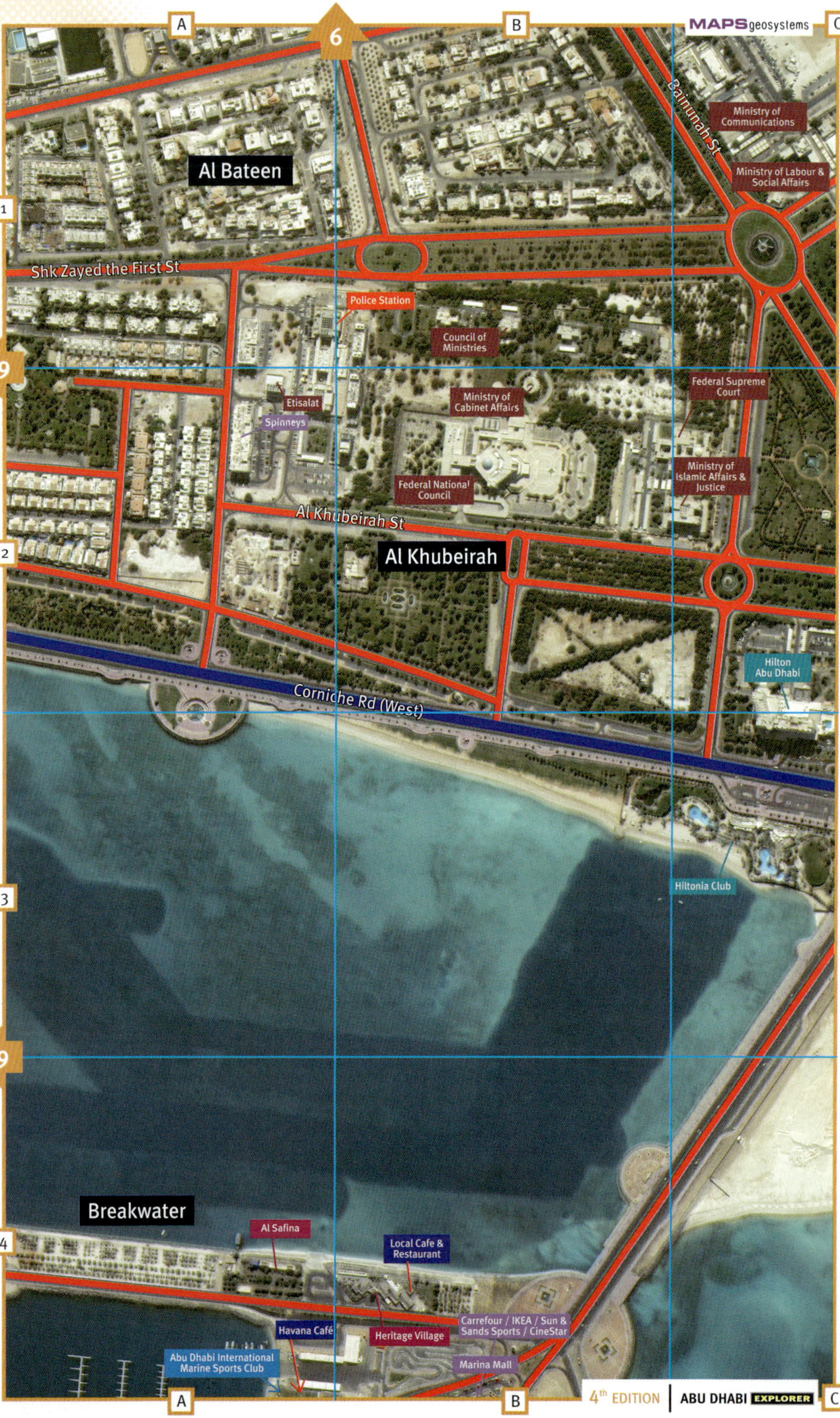

Imagery courtesy of *MAPS geosystems* – Master Reseller for *Digital Globe*

DIGITALGLOBE
C
D
E
1
2
3
4
Ministry of Petroleum & Mineral Resources
Hotel Inter-Continental Abu Dhabi
Bainunah St
Khalidia Palace Hotel
ADNOC
Al Ras Al Akhdar
Emirates Palace Hotel
Abu Dhabi Ladies Club
Cleopatra's Spa
Ladies Beach

10
Maps

Al Ain – Street Index

The following is a list of the main streets and hotel buildings in Al Ain, which are referenced on map pages 1 - 10. Many roads are longer than one grid reference, in which case the main grid references have been given.

Street	Map Ref
Abu Bakr Al Siddiq St	15-B3
Abu Obaida Bin Al Jarrah St	13-A3/B3
Al Ain R/A	14-E4; 17-C1
Al Ain St	15-A2/A4; 17-C1
Al Asar St	see Al Athar St
Al Athar St	13-B1/C1
Al Baladiyya St	12-E4; 14-E1/D3
Al Basra R/A	14-C2
Al Bourj R/A	14-E3
Al Buraimi R/A	15-B2
Al Falah St	13-B3
Al Falaheya St	see Othman Bin Affan St
Al Forousiya St	see Khalifa Bin Zayed St
Al Gaba St	see Abu Bakr Al Siddiq St
Al Ghozlan Garden R/A	11-E4
Al Ghozlan R/A	16-D2
Al Hili R/A	13-A2
Al Hili St	see Mohammed Bin Khalifa St
Al Istraha R/A	15-C3
Al Ja'amah R/A	15-A2
Al Jamia St	see Tawam St
Al Jamia St	14-C4/D3; 16-E1
Al Jimi R/A	14-E1
Al Khabisi R/A	12-C4; 14-C1
Al Khaleej Al Arabi St	11-B2/E2
Al Kharis R/A	15-A1
Al Khatem R/A	15-D4
Al Khatem St	see Khata Al Shinkle St
Al Mahad R/A	14-D3/E3
Al Markahniya St	see Shakhboot Bin Sultan St
Al Mashatel R/A	15-C2
Al Masoudi R/A	12-E3
Al Mira St	see Al Salam St
Al Muraba R/A	15-B3
Al Muttarath R/A	14-D4
Al Nadi R/A	15-A4
Al Nakheel St	12-E3; 13-A4
Al Salam St	15-C4/D4
Al Salama R/A	15-B3
Al Thakteet St	see Al Ain St
Al Thakteet St	17-C1
Ali Bin Abi Taleb St	15-A2/B2
Arah Al Jaw St	13-C1/C2
Bani Yas St	12-E3; 13-B2
Clock Tower R/A	15-A3
Eighth St	see Al Salam St (Eastern Corniche Rd)
Fourth St	see East Rd (New Airport Rd)
Hamdan Bin Mohammed St	14-B1/D1
Hamdan Bin Zayed Al Awwal St	14-C1
Hazah St	see Khalid Bin Sultan St
Hazzaa Bin Sultan St	11-E3; 17-A3
Hazzaa R/A	17-A1
Hilton R/A	15-C4
Hospital R/A	14-E2
Khalid Bin Al Waleed St	12-E4
Khalid Bin Sultan St	14-D4; 15-B4
Khalid St	see Sultan Bin Zayed Al Awwal St
Khalifa Bin Zayed Al Awwal St	14-E3/E4
Khalifa Bin Zayed St	16-D1
Khalifa Bin Zayed St	14-B3; 16-B1/E1
Khata Al Shikle St	15-D4/E4
Lotus R/A	13-B1
Lulu St (North)	see East Rd (New Airport Rd)
Mohammed Bin Khalifa St	13-A4/B1; 15-A1
Mubarak St	see Hamdan Bin Zayed Al Awwal St
Municipality R/A	14-E1
Municipality St	see Al Baladiyya St
Nahyan Al Awwal St	17-B2
Najda St	see Bani Yas Rd (Najda Rd) (East)
Old Airport Rd	see Maidan Al Ittihad St (North)
Omar Bin Al Khattab St	15-C3
Othman Bin Affan St	15-C3
Oudh Alttoba St	see Ali Bin Abi Taleb St
Saeed Bin Tahnoon Al Awwal St	14-D3/D4
Salahuddeen Al Ayyubi St	15-B3
Salana St	see Salahuddeen Al Ayyubi St
Second St	see Airport Rd (South)
Second St	see Maidan Al Ittihad St (North)
Selmi St	see Hamdan Bin Mohammed St
Shakboot Bin Sultan St	11-D4; 14-A3/E3; 15-A2/C2; 16-B1
Shk Zayed Bin Khalifa St	see Shakhboot Bin Sultan St
Silmi R/A	15-A1
Sixth St	see Bani Yas Rd (Najda Rd) (East)
Sultan Bin Zayed Al Awwal St	15-A4
Tahnoon Bin Zayed Al Alawal St	14-A1/B2
Tahnoon St	see Nahyan Al Awwal St
Tawam R/A	16-D1
Tawam St	see Khalifa Bin Zayed St
Tawam St	16-E2
Thirtieth St	see Al Khaleej Al Arabi St (West)
Thirty Fourth St	see Bainona St (West)
Tourist Club Area	see Al Salam St (Corniche Rd)
Twenty Eighth St	seeKhalifa Bin Shakbout St (West)
Twenty Fourth St	see Al Karamah St (West)
Twenty Second St	see Khalid Bin Al Waleed St (West)
Zakher R/A	17-A2
Zayed Al Awwal St	12-B2; 14-C3; 17-B1
Zayed Bin Sultan St	14-D3/E3; 15-B3; 17-E2
Zoo R/A	17-B1

DIGITALGLOBE

MAPSgeosystems

Dubai

Oman

Oman

13

15

17

12

14

11

16

Abu Dhabi

A
B
C
MAPSgeosystems
Imagery courtesy of MAPS geosystems – Master Reseller for Digital Globe
1
2
3
4
Salamat
16
A
B
C

DIGITALGLOBE
Al Ain International Airport
Wadi Tawia
Al Khaleej Al Arabi St
Shahkboot Bin Sultan St
12
14
16
C
D
E
1
2
3
4
11
Maps

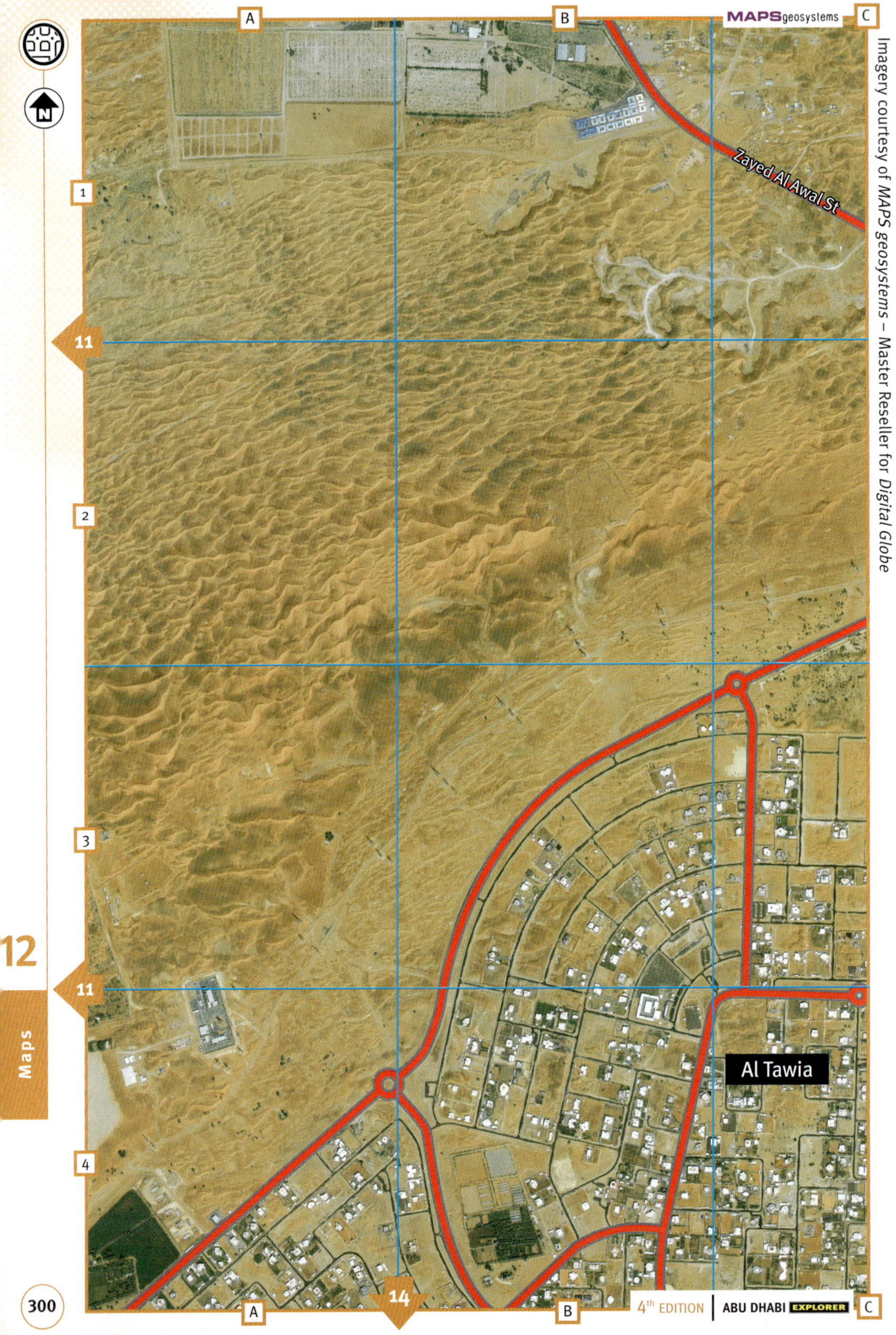

Imagery courtesy of *MAPS geosystems* – Master Reseller for *Digital Globe*

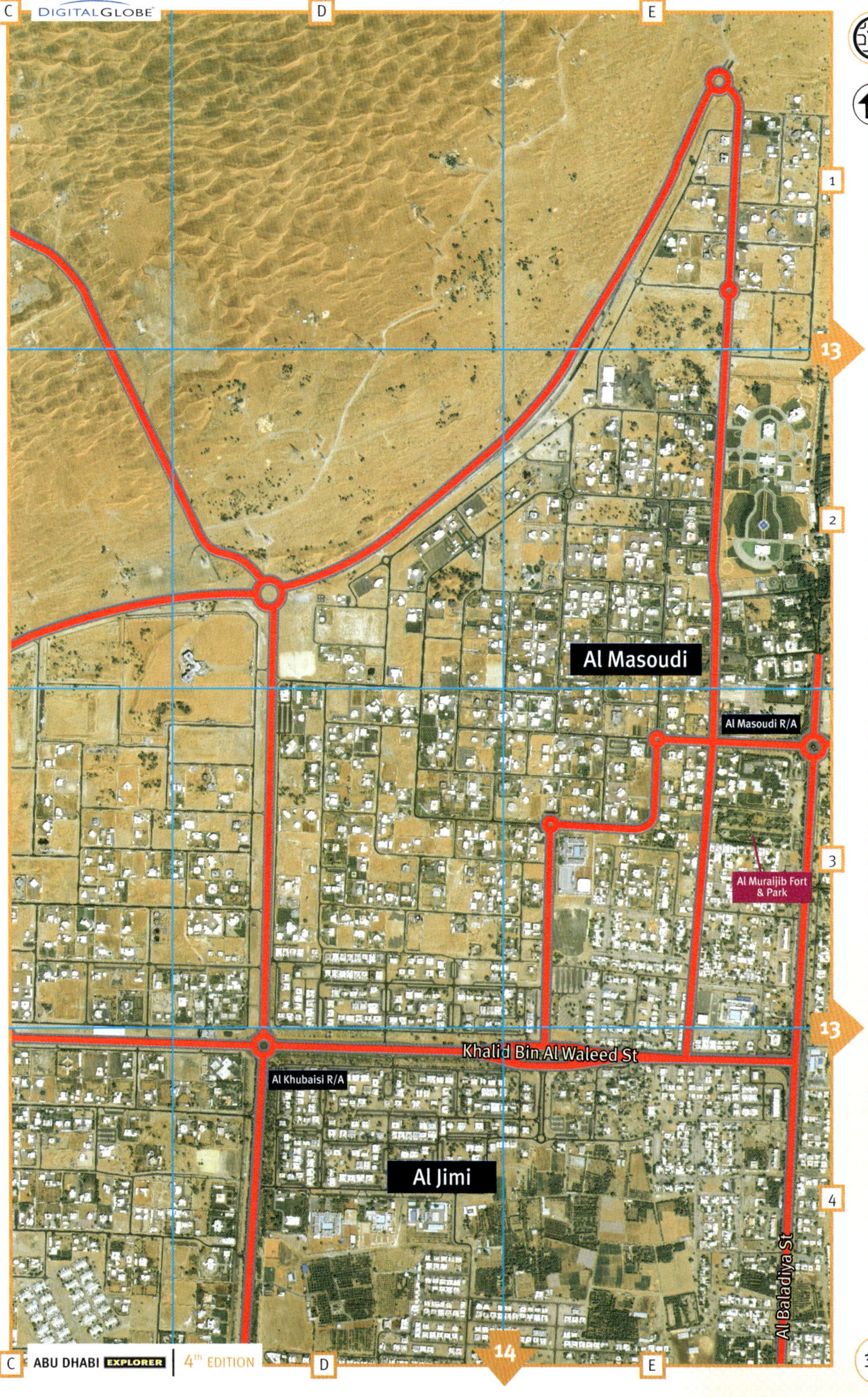

C
D
E
DIGITALGLOBE
1
2
3
4
13
13
14
Al Masoudi
Al Masoudi R/A
Al Muraijib Fort & Park
Khalid Bin Al Waleed St
Al Khubaisi R/A
Al Jimi
Al Baladiya St

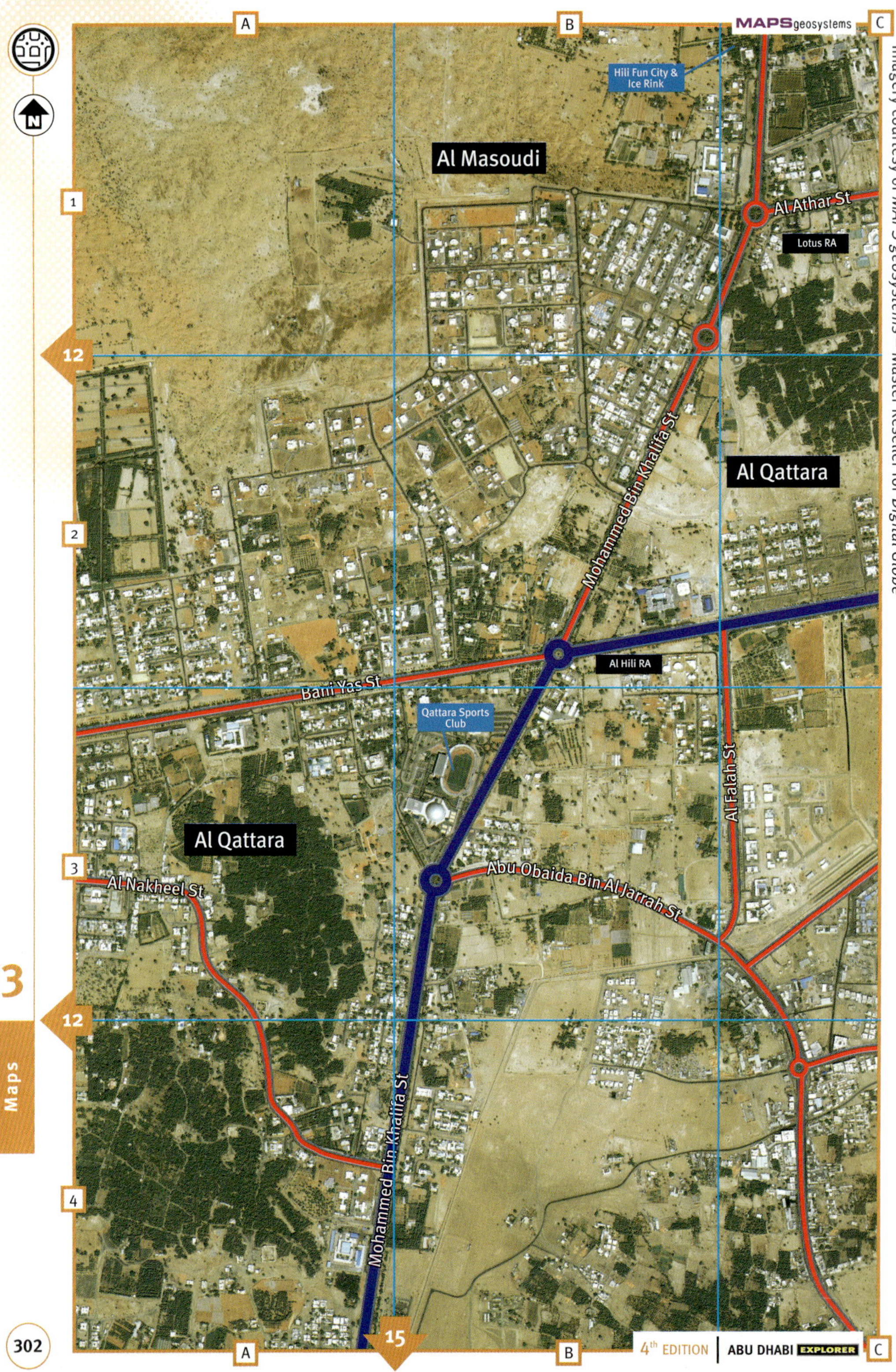
A
B
C
MAPSgeosystems
Hili Fun City & Ice Rink
Al Masoudi
Al Athar St
Lotus RA
1
12
Al Qattara
Mohammed Bin Khalifa St
2
Al Hili RA
Bani Yas St
Qattara Sports Club
Al Qattara
Al Falah St
Abu Obaida Bin Al Jarrah St
3
Al Nakheel St
12
Mohammed Bin Khalifa St
4
15
Imagery courtesy of MAPS geosystems – Master Reseller for Digital Globe

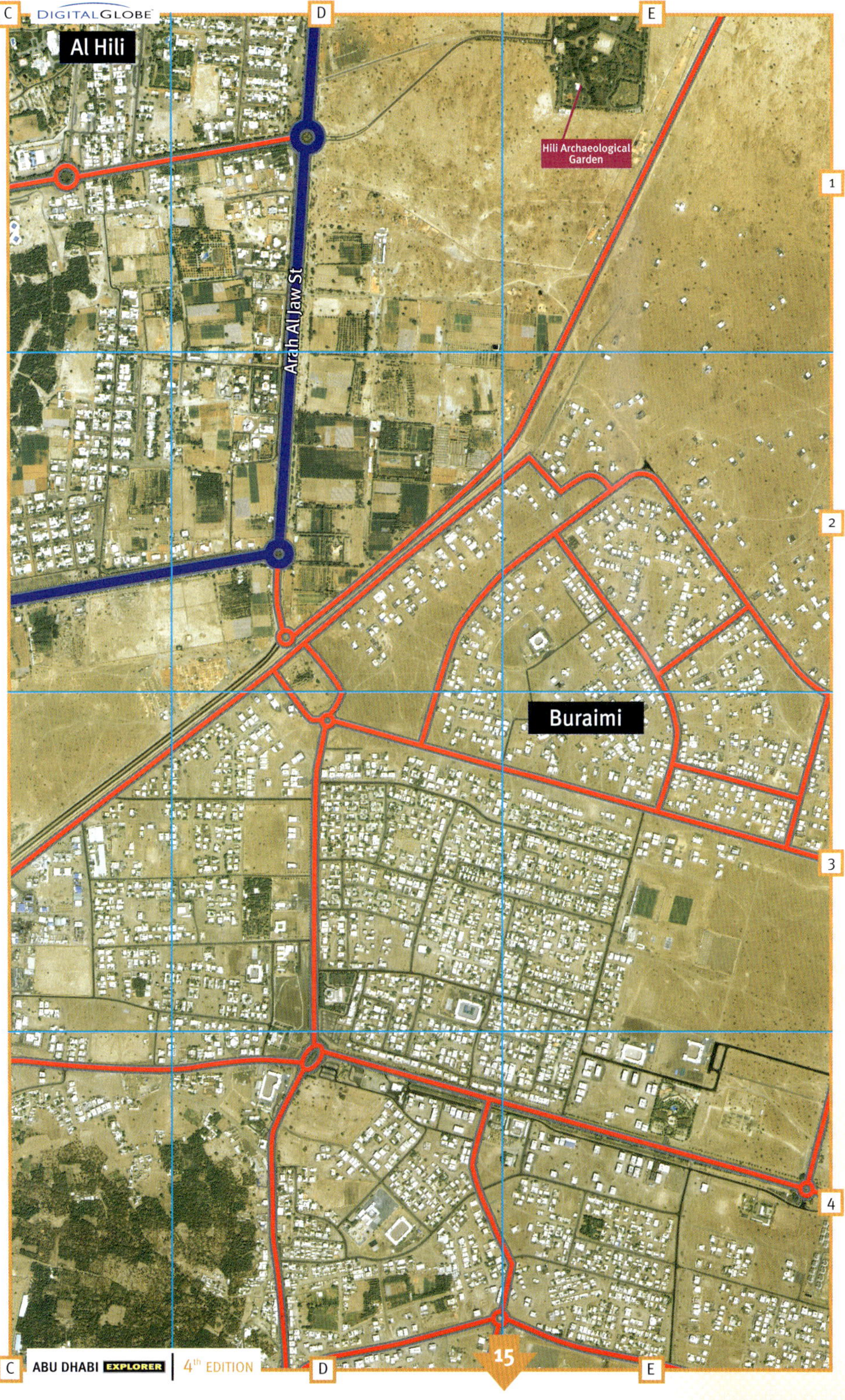
DIGITALGLOBE
Al Hili
Hili Archaeological Garden
Arah Al Jaw St
Buraimi
C
D
E
1
2
3
4
15

13

Maps

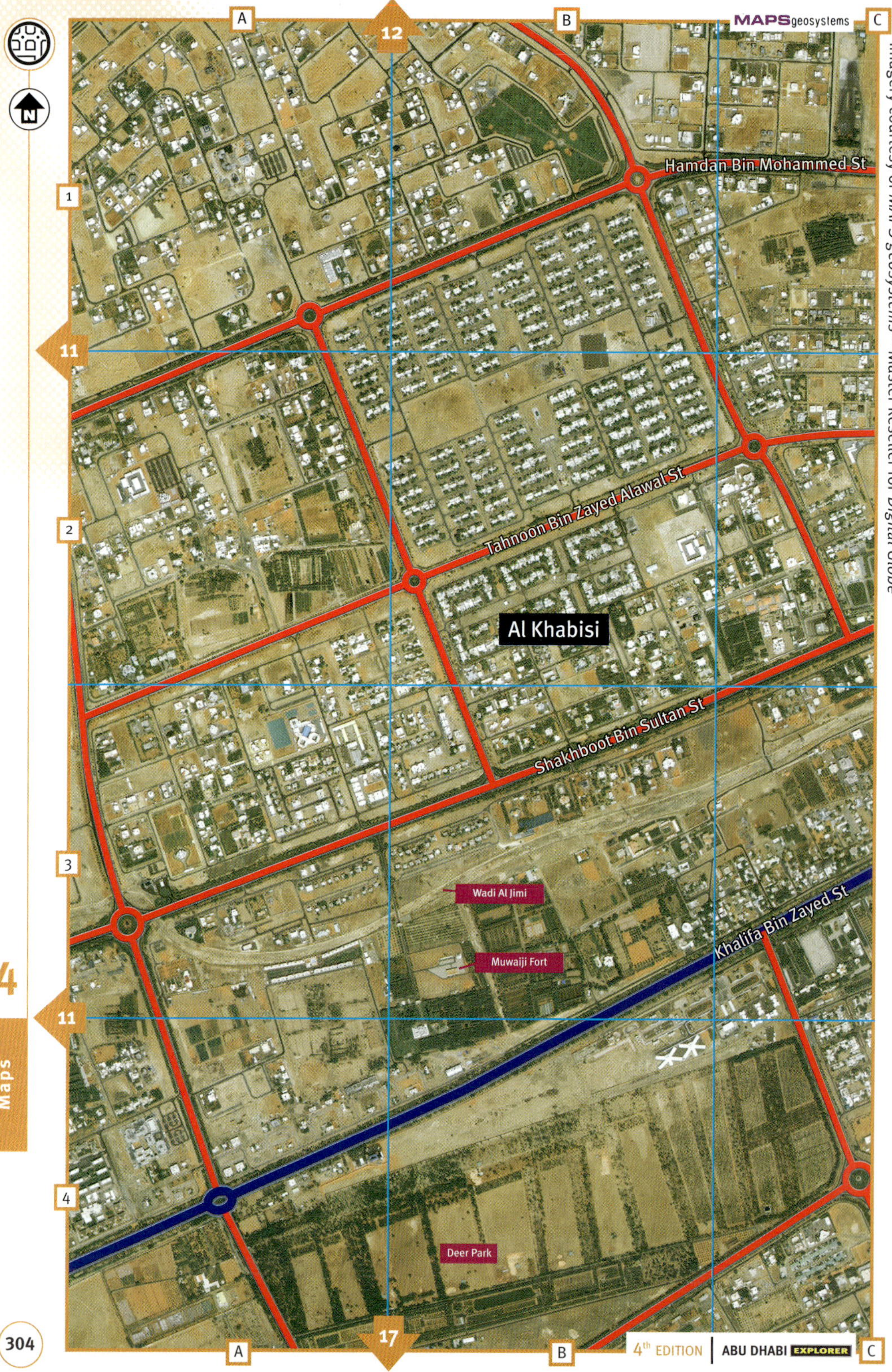

MAPSgeosystems
Imagery courtesy of MAPS geosystems – Master Reseller for Digital Globe
A
B
C
12
1
2
3
4
11
11
17
Hamdan Bin Mohammed St
Tahnoon Bin Zayed Alawal St
Al Khabisi
Shakhboot Bin Sultan St
Wadi Al Jimi
Muwaiji Fort
Khalifa Bin Zayed St
Deer Park

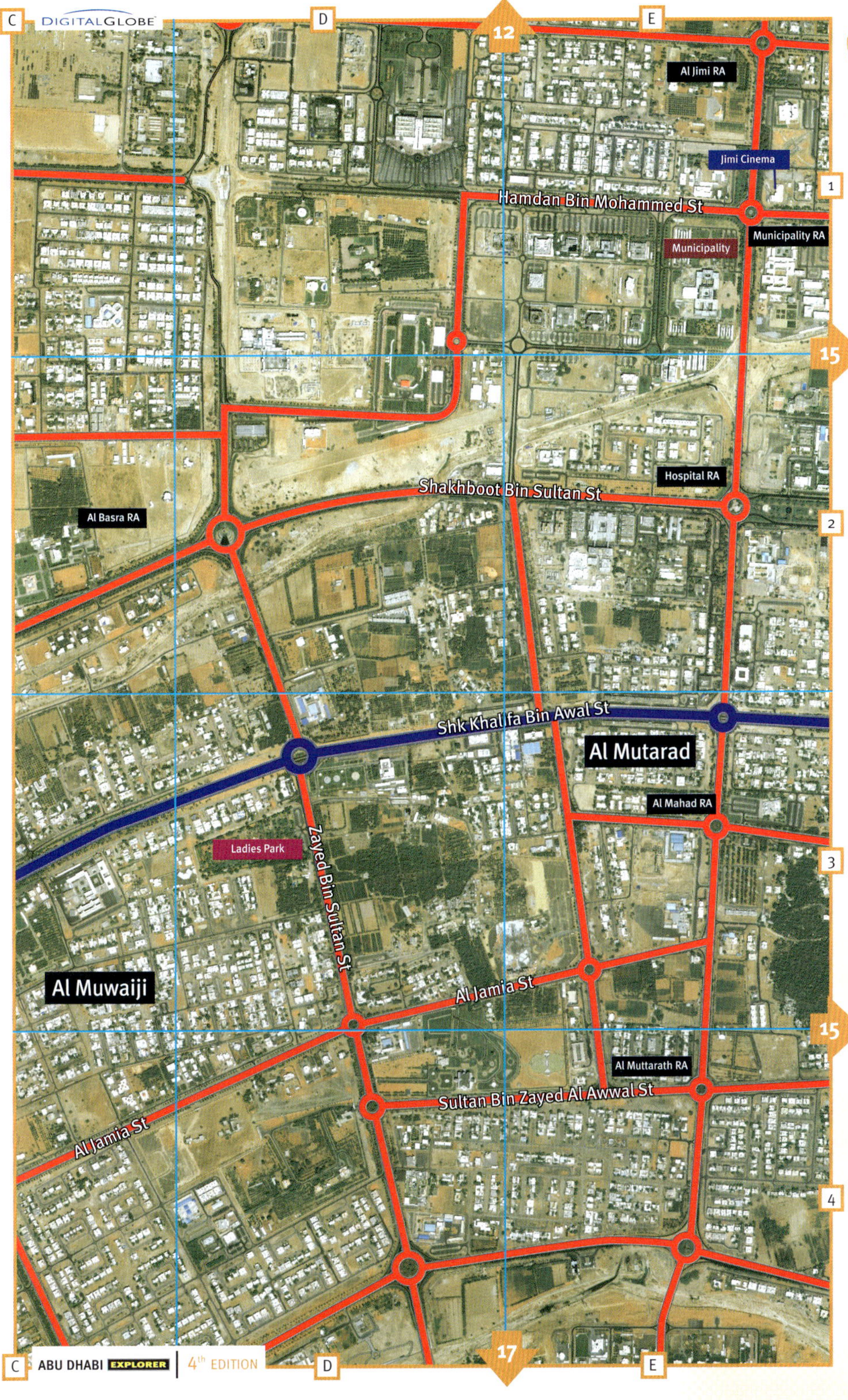
DIGITALGLOBE
C
D
E
12
Al Jimi RA
Jimi Cinema
1
Hamdan Bin Mohammed St
Municipality RA
Municipality
15
Hospital RA
Shakhboot Bin Sultan St
Al Basra RA
2
Shk Khalifa Bin Awal St
Al Mutarad
Al Mahad RA
Ladies Park
Zayed Bin Sultan St
3
Al Muwaiji
Al Jamia St
15
Al Muttarath RA
Sultan Bin Zayed Al Awwal St
Al Jamia St
4
17
C
D
E

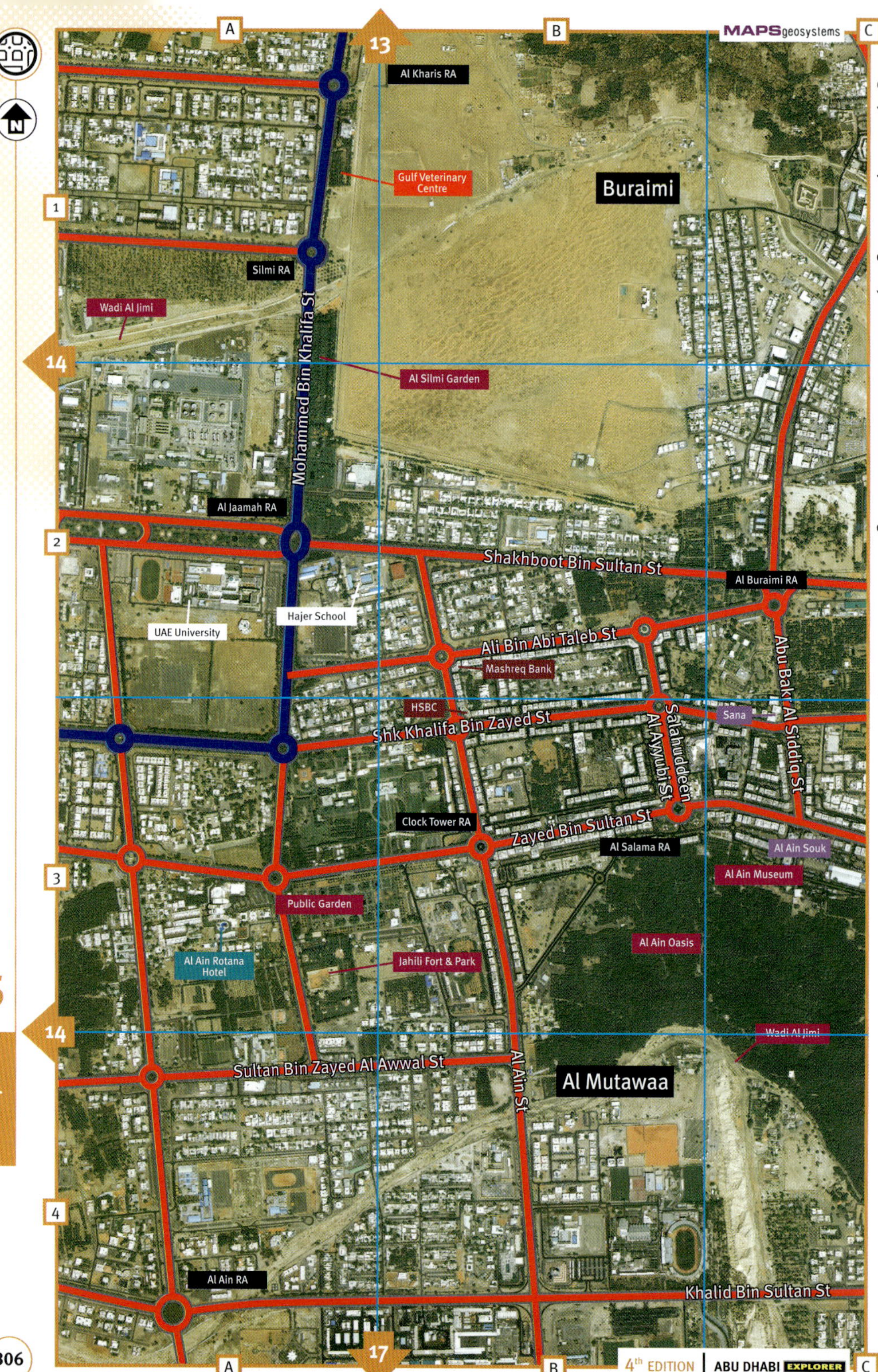
A
B
C
13
MAPSgeosystems
Al Kharis RA
Gulf Veterinary Centre
Buraimi
1
Silmi RA
Wadi Al Jimi
14
Al Silmi Garden
Mohammed Bin Khalifa St
Al Jaamah RA
2
Shakhboot Bin Sultan St
Al Buraimi RA
Hajer School
UAE University
Ali Bin Abi Taleb St
Mashreq Bank
Abu Bakr Al Siddiq St
HSBC
Shk Khalifa Bin Zayed St
Salahuddeen Al Ayyubi St
Sana
Clock Tower RA
Zayed Bin Sultan St
Al Salama RA
Al Ain Souk
3
Al Ain Museum
Public Garden
Al Ain Oasis
Al Ain Rotana Hotel
Jahili Fort & Park
14
Wadi Al Jimi
Sultan Bin Zayed Al Awwal St
Al Ain St
Al Mutawaa
4
Al Ain RA
Khalid Bin Sultan St
17
A
B
C
Imagery courtesy of MAPS geosystems – Master Reseller for Digital Globe

5
Maps

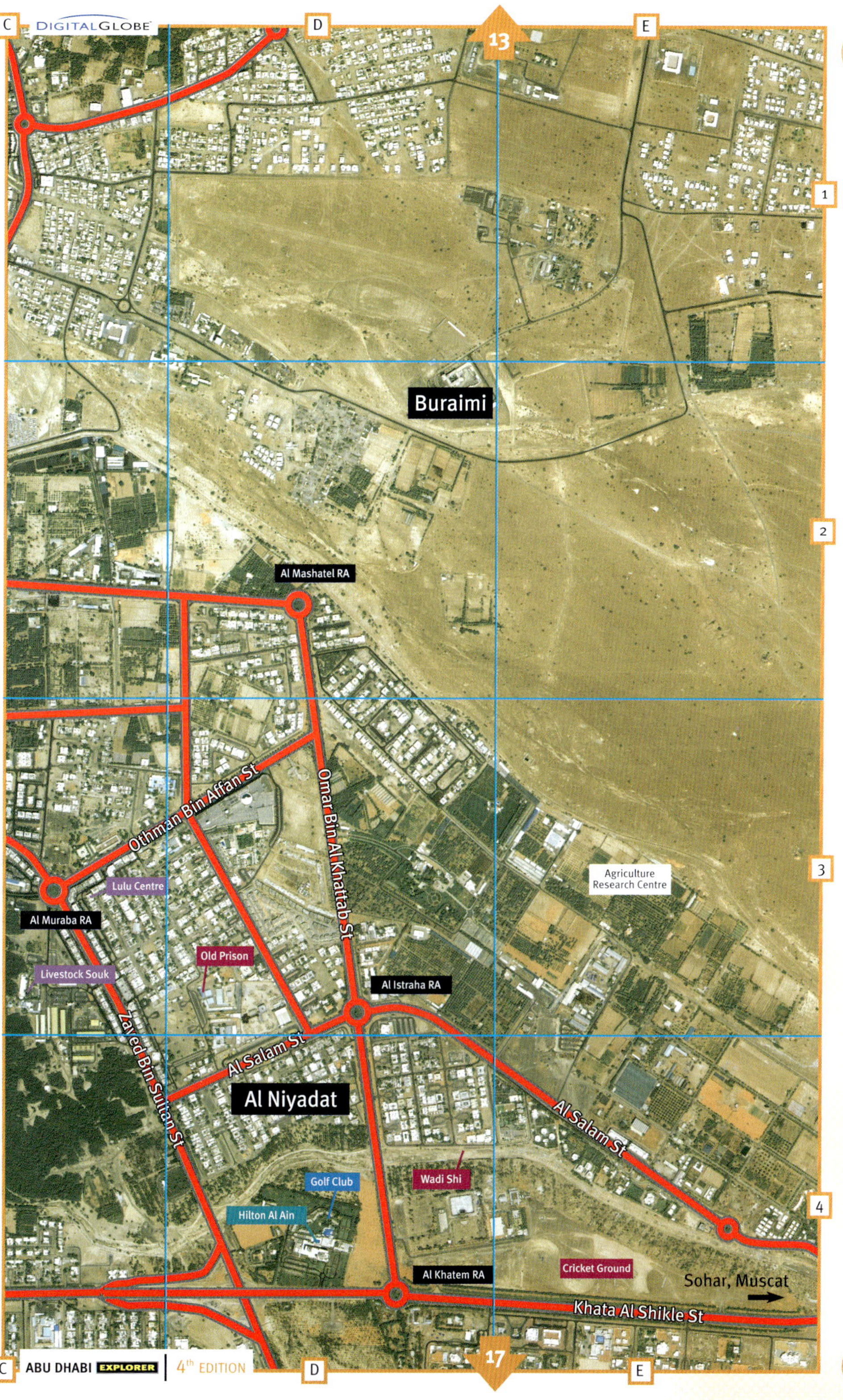
DigitalGlobe
Buraimi
Al Mashatel RA
Omar Bin Al Khattab St
Othman Bin Affan St
Agriculture Research Centre
Lulu Centre
Al Muraba RA
Old Prison
Livestock Souk
Al Istraha RA
Al Salam St
Zayed Bin Sultan St
Al Niyadat
Al Salam St
Wadi Shi
Golf Club
Hilton Al Ain
Cricket Ground
Al Khatem RA
Sohar, Muscat
Khata Al Shikle St
1
2
3
4
15
Maps

A
B
C
11
1
2
3
4
Abu Dhabi
Al Bateen
Shakhboot Bin Sultan St
Ghrebah
Abu Dhabi
MAPSgeosystems
Imagery courtesy of *MAPS geosystems* – Master Reseller for *Digital Globe*

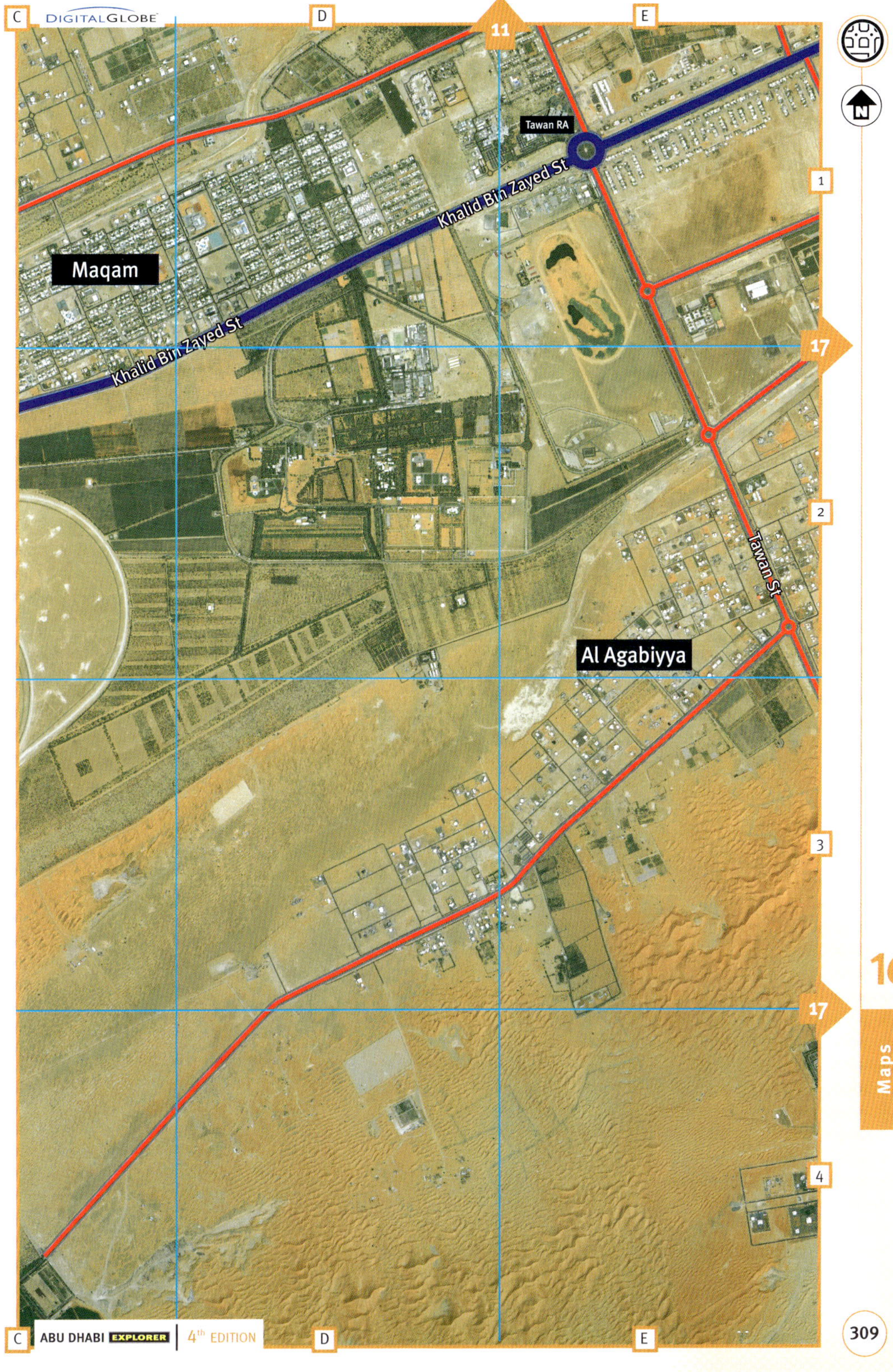
DIGITALGLOBE
C
D
E
11
Tawan RA
Khalid Bin Zayed St
Maqam
Khalid Bin Zayed St
17
Tawan St
Al Agabiyya
17
1
2
3
4
16
Maps

A
B
C
14
16
1
2
3
4
MAPSgeosystems
Imagery courtesy of MAPS geosystems – Master Reseller for Digital Globe
Hazzaa St
Zayed Al Awwal St
Al Ghozlan RA
Hazzaa RA
Falaj Hazzaa
Zoo RA
Nahyan Al Awwal St
Zakher RA
Zoo District
Hazzaa Bin Sultan St
Al Ain Fayda
Jebel Hafeet
17
Maps

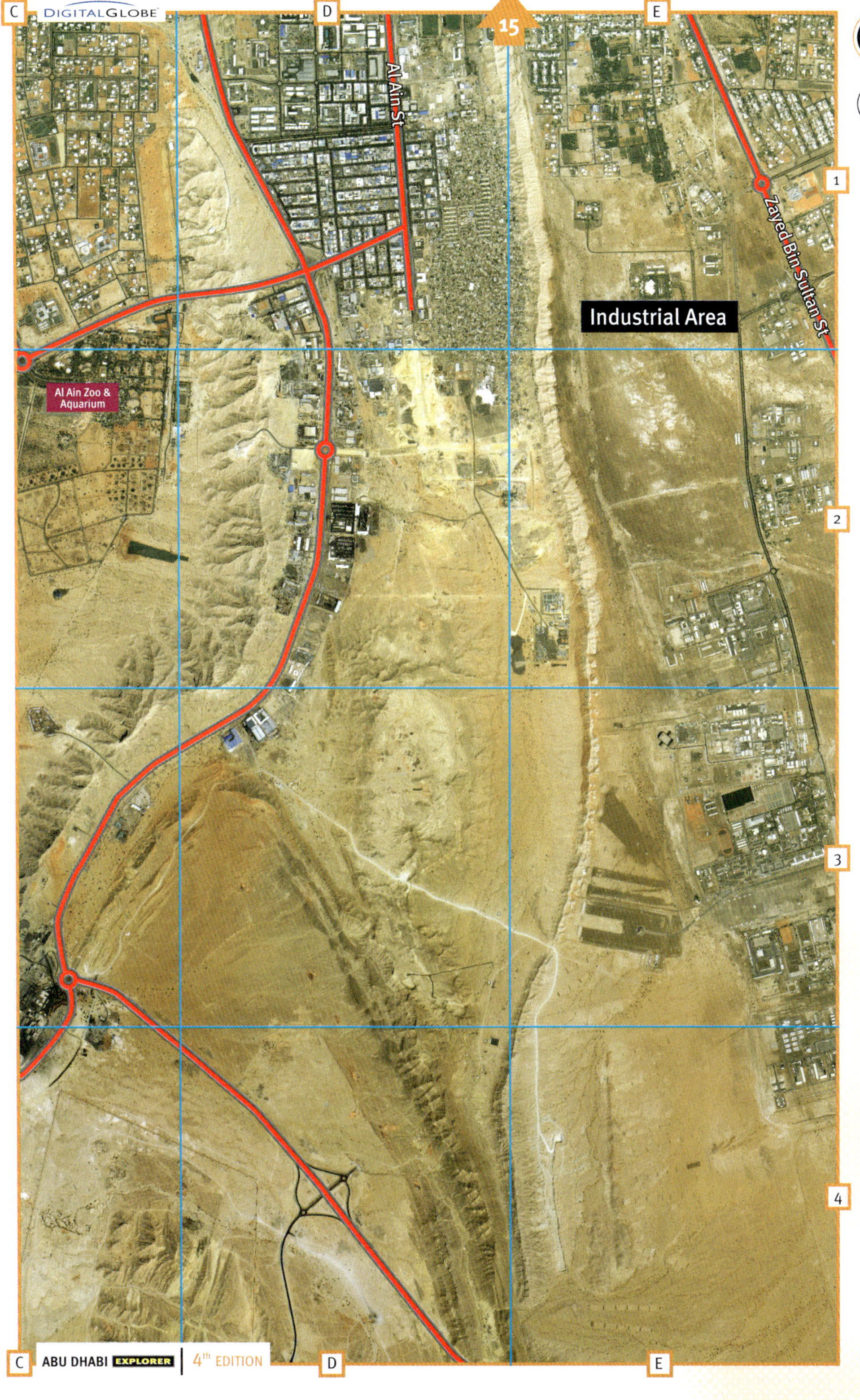
DIGITALGLOBE
C
D
E
15
1
2
3
4
Al Ain St
Zayed Bin Sultan St
Industrial Area
Al Ain Zoo & Aquarium
17
Maps

8

Index

EXPLORER

# #

A

B

G

H

I

J

K

L

Index

M

N

O

P

Q

R

S

T

U

V

W

Y

Z

Notes

Notes

Notes